I0137923

# BAḤĀRISTĀN-I-GHAYBĪ

A history of the Mughal Wars in Assam, Cooch Behar, Bengal, Bihar and Orissa during the reigns of Jahāngīr and Shāhjahān, by Mīrzā Nathan

*Translated from the original Persian by*

DR. M. I. BORAH, M.A., B.L. (DAC.), PH.D. (LONDON).
*Head of the Department of Persian and Urdu in the University of Dacca.*

---

**VOLUME II**

---

PUBLISHED BY THE
GOVERNMENT OF ASSAM IN THE
DEPARTMENT OF HISTORICAL AND ANTIQUARIAN STUDIES,
NARAYANI HANDIQUI HISTORICAL INSTITUTE,
GAUHATI, ASSAM.

1936

DEDICATED

TO

HIS EXCELLENCY SIR MICHAEL KEANE,

K.C.S.I., C.I.E., I.C.S.,

GOVERNOR OF ASSAM,

AN ILLUSTRIOUS PATRON OF

HISTORICAL RESEARCH,

AS A TOKEN OF AUTHOR'S GRATITUDE.

## CONTENTS

### VOLUME II.

#### BOOK III



#### BOOK IV



#### APPENDICES

## BOOK III

*(The first two folios of this book (ff. 206-7) contain a preface in high-flown language in praise of God, the Prophet and the author's spiritual guide. Left out.)*

### INTRODUCTION.

In the name of God, the Beneficent, the Merciful.

Although the solution of difficulties and the attainment of desires derive their splendour from the secret stock of Divine favour, it is incumbent upon the intelligent and prudent men to rely upon the favour of the True Lord, and to put into writing whatever happens and, by the aid of Divine Will, to inscribe on the pages of time the course of the vicissitudes of time, so that the events ordained by the Eternal Will which take place according to Eternal Orders, as well as the different phases of the fortunes of the ancients may become known. These events, which form the caravan that time bears along, are expected to serve as (so many) land marks to the (passing) ships of days and nights. It has occurred to the mind of this most insignificant Ghaybī commonly known as Shitāb Khān *alias* 'Alāu'd-Dīn, well-known as Nathan, and sank deeply down to the bottom of the ocean of his imagination that he should embellish the third volume of the Bahāristān with the ornaments of the pearls of speech, and that whatever had taken place during the rule of the Khān Fath-jang known as Ibrāhīm Khān should be put into writing for the benefit of the readers, so that they might derive pleasure by going through its contents, and by this means this insignificant man might perhaps be remembered in their offerings of benedictory prayers. (480)

## CHAPTER I

*Arrival of Ibrāhīm Khān Fatḥ-jang at Jahāngīrnagar* alias *Dhāka after the overthrow of the fort which Qāsim Khān had raised at Jatrapūr through his foolishness to oppose the imperial officers and Ibrāhīm Khān. (Detailed account of the affairs on Kūch frontier)..*

**Ibrāhīm Khān reaches Dhāka.** When the Khān Fatḥ-jang became free from the affairs of punishing Qāsim Khān. he proceeded to Jahāngīrnagar and reached there within a few days. He then engaged himself in the management of affairs and began to put every place in order. (481)

**Nathan takes the leadership in Kāmrūp.** I shall now give a short account of the affairs of the frontier of the Kūch territory and the rebellion of Ibrāhīm Karorī after the departure of 'Abdu'l-Bāqī from Hājo, and the conducting of the military operations by the imperial officers under the command of Mīrzā Nathan son of Ihtimām Khān, as was (also) described at the end of the second volume of the Bahāristān. I proceed to give the record its final form. The substance of this lengthy affair is as follows: When the period of Qāsim Khān's Ṣūbahdārship came to an end 'Abdu'l-Bāqī proceeded to join Qāsim Khān and on his way he became a captive in the hands of the men of the Khān Fatḥ-jang. All people of the Kūch territory, high and low, excepting Shaykh Ibrāhīm Karorī who had created great mischief in that land, had taken the oath of allegiance to Mīrzā Nathan for the welfare of the affairs of the master and the Qibla. They considered the execution of the work of the master and the Qibla as greater than devotion to God, and at the advice of the Mīrzā, they considered it to be the source of happiness in both the worlds. The Mīrzā, with full authority, girded up his loins of service like a broomstick with a sincere heart and became very warm and enthusiastic in his work, and he strengthened the Thānas in different places. (482)

**Rebellion of Ibrāhīm Karorī.** Shaykh Ibrāhīm, who had served as the *Karorī* for a long period, had misappropriated Rs. 700,000 of the imperial revenues and made a great waste. Being deceived by the wind of madness, he led astray an army of more than three thousand men with him; and being highly afraid of investigation into the account of the money he had misappropriated, he sent men to the Rāja of Assam (i.e. the Ahom King) with the following message:—"As the great imperial army had been annihilated in your country the only course left open (to the imperialists) to achieve the purpose of extirpating you root and branch, is to send, in near future, a big army against you from Delhi. Under the circumstances, if you help me with men and money and make me the king of Kūch I will exert my utmost valour to my last breath, and I will be devoted to you and will never allow the armies of Delhi to proceed against you as long as I live." The aforesaid Rāja welcomed this proposal and he repeatedly wrote to the Shaykh:—"Until you first lead the war against the imperial army in this country and send to me one or two of their men alive or dead, I cannot in my farsightedness believe you all on a sudden. Under the circumstances, if you are firm in this proposal you should utilise this opportunity and put it into execution. The country of Kāmrūp, nay even (the country of) Mānchabāt will be given to you. I will give you even my daughter; and I will give you from my treasury, elephant-stable, artillery and the fleet in such large quantities the like of which you have never seen even in your dreams, not to speak of the hours of your wakefulness." (483)

**Rebel's attack on Dhamdhama.** Accordingly, the aforesaid Shaykh instigated a force of Kūch regiment to proceed to the Thāna of Dhamdhama against Mīrzā Ṣāliḥ Arghūn and he wrote to Sanātan to help and aid this regiment by accepting its leadership and to attack the fort of Dhamdhama by every possible way and to massacre the garrison. When the regiment and the letter of Ibrāhīm reached Sanātan, he started during the day and marching throughout the night he fell upon the fort when two *gharīs* of the night still remained. Mīrzā Ṣāliḥ, due to his good relations with the Zamīndārs of that place, always kept himself informed of the neighbouring places and used to pass the nights in vigilance. The Zamīndārs informed him (about this move beforehand) and (thus) he too was ready for action. So, no sooner did the enemy arrive than he began to fight. Although the enemy with full forces entered the fort on two occasions after heavy fighting, God the Great through His unparalleled mercy came to the aid of the besieged garrison and rendered help by infusing boldness into the Muslims, so that on both these two occasions the inmates turned the perverted enemy out of the fort and gave them a heavy blow with their dreadful swords. *Maṡnavī* (left out). (484)

**Reinforcements sent to Dhamdhama.** Mīrzā Ṣāliḥ, by the first *pahar* of the day, wrote the following details of the situation to Mīrzā Nathan and the imperial officers:—" If no immediate reinforcements come to my aid then the Thāna as well as the imperial territory will go out of hands and we the servants shall also have to give up our lives in the cause of the master and the Qibla. But what is the gain ? Let every one of us be of some use and let the Thāna and the imperial domain not go out of our hands." Then Mīrzā Nathan summoned Mīr Ghiyāṣu'd-Dīn Maḥmūd, Mīr 'Abdu'r-Razzāq Shīrāzī and all the imperial officers to a council of consultation and asked their opinion. Every one showed a way according to his judgment. At last all of them agreed upon the plan which was first suggested by the Mīrzā that Mīr 'Abdu'r-Razzāq should proceed to the help of Mīrzā Ṣāliḥ with a force of junior Manṣabdārs, some of the Afghāns of 'Uṣmān, artillery and some elephants and should stay there to allay the trouble in that region with the aid of the old and the new regiments. In addition to the men and the imperial officers and picked-troops who were staying at

Pāndū, Mīrzā Yūsuf was ordered to proceed to Pāndū to take the chief command and stay there with ease by making necessary arrangements for the security of the fort on land and the fleet on the water. Thus these measures were taken for the safety of the imperialists. In short, the force that accompanied the Mīr was of this order:—the Mīr with his own soldiers; Mīrzā Giw *alias* Mīrzā Bābū, son of Mīrzā Mūmin Marvī; Mīrzā Sultān Murād, son of Muḥammad Murād Uzbeg; Zāhid Beg Maydānī; Muḥammad Mūqīm, son of Qabūl Khān Tulkhānī; some of the junior Manṣabdārs of the 'Uṣmānī Afghāns; three hundred expert matchlockmen, eight male and female elephants, cannon, gunpowder, lead and bullets were also despatched in their company. Mīrzā Yūsuf was despatched to take the chief command of the army at the Thāna of Pāndū. (485)

**The rebels block the passage at Jharighāt.** The idea occurred to his (Nathan's) far-seeing mind that the raid of the enemy was due to the activities of Shaykh Ibrāhīm; so Mīr 'Abdu'r-Razzāq was instructed to keep watch over the movements of the Shaykh and to proceed with caution till he would reach the Thāna of Dhamdhama. But the Mīr, due to his great friendship for the Shaykh, did not like this idea at all; he rather thought that the Shaykh would help him. It did not occur to him that when he would proceed, deception and disgrace would reach him from the Shaykh through this channel (of friendship). Thus in addition to the regiment which was sent with Sanātan against Mīrzā Ṣāliḥ, a large force was despatched by him (Shaykh Ibrāhīm) with instructions to block the passage of the Mīr at Jharighāt[1] so that he might not cross the river and come to the help of Mīrzā Ṣāliḥ. In short, this army reached there before the arrival of the Mīr and fortified the Ghāt. As soon as the Mīr arrived, they offered battle and overpowered the Mīr and not even a bird was allowed to cross. Sanātan's attack on the Thāna of Dhamdhama in season and out of season put the people of the Thāna to a great strait. (486)

**Nathan frustrates the design of the rebels.** When the Mīr saw that many of the followers of the Shaykh under disguise as enemy's men were opposing his way he recognised them, and then he believed and understood to be true what the Mīrzā had said about the part played by the Shaykh. From that place (Jharighāt) he despatched (to Mīrzā Nathan) only the following message :—" Whoever does not love his own people and becomes arrogant after allying himself with a foreign race, will receive his retribution. In short, I saw what I heard. Now you do whatever you think best." Mīrzā Nathan, therefore, sent at night gunpowder, lead and other equipments of war to Mīrzā Ṣāliḥ by a secret route which was not known to them (the enemies) and not even a fly could get scent of it. He wrote to Ṣāliḥ,—" The army which is with you will in fact be able to defend the fort. For a few days you are to keep a watchful eye on adjoining places till this arrogant Hindustānī is punished for his improper conduct." And he also wrote something to the Mīr saying,—" Immediately on the receipt of this letter you are to return to Hājo. The time of your (intended) arrival should be communicated (to me) before your (actual) return in such a way that when your men start from that side, the accursed Shaykh may not come to obstruct your passage across the river Barlia. You are to march from that side and I shall advance up to the bank of the Barlia river from this side by boats along with all the imperial officers ; and thus the army and the equipments will be safely transported." It so happened that the Mīr immediately on the receipt of the letter, started at midnight with the zeal of a bay-horse and arrived there in the first *pahar* of the day. Mīrzā Nathan, with the imperial officers, said his morning prayer on the bank of the river Barlia, and arrived at that place with a large reinforcement and brought the Mīr to Hājo transporting him safely, along with the imperial army. Although the Shaykh (Ibrāhīm) became mortified, he could do nothing. The veil was removed from his activities and his treason became known to every body, high and low. (487)

**Chishtī Khān deputed to punish the rebels.** Mīrzā Nathan reported the state of affairs to Ibrāhīm Khān Fatḥ-jang. The Khān, the governor of the province, sent a representation to the Court of the protector of the world and the reports of Mīrzā Nathan as well as those of the imperial officers of the Kūch frontier, were enclosed with it. As the Khān was already aware of this situation from the regular reports of the Mīrzā and the imperial officers, he apprehended that Mīrzā Nathan and the imperial officers of that region would not be able to suppress the mischievous activities of that knave; so he despatched Mūsā Muḥammad Khān, Muṣtafa Khān, Shajā'at Khān Dakhinī, Sarḥad Khān *alias* 'Abdu'l-Wāḥid, and many other junior Manṣabdārs with a fleet and a large artillery under the chief command of Chishtī Khān and the generalship of Shaykh Kamāl Islām Khānī in order to punish the foolish Shaykh. (488)

**The Emperor orders the capture of Shaykh Ibrāhīm.** When the representation of the Khān along with the report of Mīrzā Nathan reached the imperial Court, a peremptory Farmān was issued through I'timādu'd-Dawla :—" If Shaykh Ibrāhīm has really created such a trouble, then it should be dealt with in such a manner that he may be sent alive to the imperial Court." The aforesaid Khān sent a copy of the peremptory Farmān with a letter of his own to Mīrzā Nathan and the imperial officers of Hājo with Kāẓim Beg, brother of 'Abādu'llah, the *Karorī* of Chatgāon. He wrote thus:— " Proceed cautiously. Until the arrival of Chishtī Khān, and particularly Shaykh Kamāl and the army despatched to that place, do not cut off your acquaintance with Shaykh Ibrāhīm and do not fight with him. Capture him through some stratagem, if you can, and send him alive to the imperial Court. Its reward from the Emperor, the Defender of the Faith, will be greater than that of subduing him by war." (489)

**The Ṣūbahdār adopts conciliatory method.** He (Ibrāhīm Khān Fatḥ-jang) also sent a few encouraging words with his calligraphist Mīrzā Muḥammad and Hājī 'Alī, the

Superintendent of *Mash'al-khāna* (Light-house) to Shaykh Ibrāhīm along with a robe of honour confirming him in the post of the *Karorī* and wrote that on the receipt of the Khān's letter he should immediately proceed to his court leaving his brothers in charge of his work, and thus have an interview with the governor at the earliest opportunity. He would be given leave to return after furnishing some information about the state of affairs in that frontier. Thus these messengers arrived one after the other. The Mīrzā learnt of this design of the Khān and devoted himself towards the realisation of the object. (490)

**The Shaykh evades capture.** The Shaykh put on the robe of honour and kept the aforesaid Mīrzā Muḥammad for a few days on the plea that he would soon start (for Dhāka). When at last the aforesaid person came to know that he had no intention to go, he did not communicate the details of the state of affairs to the Khān Fatḥ-jang as he has been bribed by the Shaykh. But time and often he would come to the Mīrzā and the imperial officers and would give indirect hints. The Mīrzā was always sending messengers to the Shaykh with valuable counsels in the desire that the imprudent fellow should go to the Ṣūbahdār giving up all his vain ideas and thus make himself free from these scandals. As they failed to produce any result, he (i.e. the Mīrzā) thought of renewing his friendship through frequent meetings with him so that he might capture him. Thus, the messengers of the Shaykh also used to come (to the Mīrzā) But occasionally they used to express some unhappy remarks One day his messengers said that the Shaykh had said thus:—"My enemies are carrying on a propaganda against my good name to serve their own interests. Now unless they relieve my mind of apprehensions, I am afraid to go (to the Ṣūbahdār) in this way. I have no other course left open to me but to go direct to the prosperous prince Sultan Parvīz at Patna without seeing the Khān Fatḥ-jang. The Mīrzā thereupon agreed to both these alternatives and sent this message with his (the Shaykh's) messengers:—"If he likes to go to the Prince, (surely) we will not bar his way. We would rather see that he does so." The messengers inquired:—"What do you mean by saying that he does so?" He (the Mīrzā) replied,—"He will march from his place and pitch his camp at the next stage, where there will be the camp of the imperial officers who will escort him up to the boundary of Ghoraghāt and then turn back, so that he may not go to any other direction. If he so desires, we can assure him on oaths and pledges about the (smooth) management of his functions so that he may go with ease to the governor of the province, leaving his brothers in charge of the collection of revenues; or if he wants to remain (where he is), he is welcome to stay with the imperial officers and discharge his duties. (But) he must give up these braggings. He should not be the cause of the death of so many thousands of lives. Let him not court infamy." The messengers went and returned with a reply that the Shaykh was agreeable to the following proposal:—"First, I should be given an assurance (of safety) and be kept near you in the service of this region. And then you should write about my terms to the Ṣūbahdār and secure a Manṣab for me and thus remove my apprehensions that I shall be punished. Then I can venture to go to Jahāngīrnagar." The Mīrzā along with the imperial officers took an oath in the name of the Lord of lords in the presence of the messenger of the Shaykh:—"If the Shaykh gives up his improper ways and renders loyal services and do not go beyond the counsel of the imperial officers, we will labour hard for the arrangement of the affairs of the Shaykh. We will not break our words. The degree of our future success will depend solely on his luck." After this he (the Mīrzā) sent his own messengers with them in order to administer the following oath to the Shaykh: "I had no evil design in the past against the State, nor do I possess any at present. If I do anything against the welfare of the State, it shall amount to a rebellion against God and the Qur'ān." The messengers went and administered the oath to the Shaykh. But they did not observe any purity in his mind. As there was not the slightest sincerity in him, he launched on his improper ways again within a short time. Thus the first act was that when Barkhurdār Kaṃbū, son of Karamu'llah, brother of Shāhbāz Khān, was going with his family from the Thāna to Jahāngīrnagar, he (the Shaykh), under the impression that he was carrying a large property with him brought him in chains and subsequently set him free. (491)

**Nathan's attempt to win him over by friendly gestures.** The Shaykh used to come to the Mīrzā now and then but the latter found no opportunity (to capture him). One day, after mid-day, he (the Mīrzā) was staying in his (own) house with a peaceful mind, and was unprepared for any commotion. He only knew that in the morning two messengers of the Shaykh named Hitam Khān and Shaykh Ḥabīb had come to him. They had represented thus:—" Although the Shaykh has nothing in his mind, yet, as the people are holding him guilty for looting the belongings of Barkhurdār Kaṃbū, he has not the boldness to come. If you send your uncle to take the Shaykh by the hand and thus invite him, he would be relieved of his apprehensions." With this end in view, the Mīrzā sent his uncle Mīr Madārī with the messengers to entreat the Shaykh by holding his hand and thus persuade him to come. But they went by one route and the Shaykh, with all his men, more than one thousand in number arrived at the gate of the mansion of the Mīrzā (by another route). The eunuchs, who were, at the door of the house of the Mīrzā, got frightened and informed him that the Shaykh was standing at the gate with a large and menacing army. What was to be done (under the circumstances ?). The Mīrzā asked the chief of his servants and his boon companions named Sa'ādat Khān and many others as to what should be done. A group of cowards who had no knowledge of things said, " The devoted servants should be called first of all to form a full force and then the Shaykh should be called in." The Mīrzā replied:—" If his object is sincere, then this will have no other result than annoying him and he will go back on the simple plea that he was not called in and kept standing for a (long) while. If he is for battle and strife, he would not have allowed us to gather our men ? He would have immediately forced his way in. Under the circumstances the following is the better course than the former. Unless we call him, he will not come in and let himself (ultimately) be confined in the company of a few of the women of the harem. Then let him be summoned and let us two sit together by ourselves in one place. If we find him false then through the grace of God I shall make him follow me and we shall not have to deal with his soldiers and servants." Having said this, he personally went to the gate and began to beat the gate-keepers who were crowding in the gate. He shook hands with the Shaykh and brought him in. As the Shaykh began to strike the crowd with a whip on account of their hypocritical behaviour and prohibited their entry inside, he (the Mīrzā) snatched away the whip from the hand of the Shaykh and allowed all of them to come in. He then came and sat on the *chārjāl* (?) of the Dīwān Khāna. The Mīrzā encouraged and consoled him in various ways and after a little while ordered his turban and sword to be brought up. He girded up his loins and holding the hand of the Shaykh sent for an elephant. He rode with the Shaykh in the howdah of the same elephant and went to the house of Mīr Ghiyāṣu'd-Dīn Maḥmūd, the Dīwān and Bakhshī. He thought thus within himself :—" First, if the Shaykh has any vain desire it is better to leave the assembly for a ride on the elephant. I shall ride in the front seat and put one of my officers on the rump in the seat of the servant and the third man will be the elephant driver. The second reason is that the Rāja of Assam is in no haste to send his reinforcements to the Shaykh, always apprehending that the people of Delhi might be conspiring against him ; so when the envoys of the Assam Rāja, who are present here, will see us both riding on the same elephant, their confidence in the Shaykh will be shaken." In short, they reached the house of the aforesaid Mīr talking with one another and alighted there. One of the servants was sent to the Mīr informing him about the arrival of the Shaykh and asking him to send the Shaykh back soon with many words of encouragement The Mīr offered much encouragement to the Shaykh and said:—"Although we are men of the pen, yet we are following the Mīrzā. We all agree to the pledges given by the Mīrzā. It is advisable that you too should not break your promise and be firm in your loyalty." In short, the Shaykh returned to his home and Mīr Ghiyāṣu'd-Dīn Maḥmūd remained in his own house. (492)

**Baldev attacks the fort of Pāndū.** On that very night the following letter came from Mīrzā Yūsuf Barlās from the Thāna and the fort of Pāndū where he was staying with the high officials of Mīrzā Nathan:—"Towards the end of this day, Baldev, the brother of Rāja Parıkshit, came with a force of eighteen thousand hill-men and attacked the fort under cover of chariots (*gardūnhā*). We defended the fort to the best of our abilities. Many people were killed on both sides. As long as the gunpowder and lead lasted the matchlock-men did splendid service. Now the enemy, has grown bolder and has advanced their *garduns* up to the bank of the ditch of the fort and are fighting under their cover. If no substantial reinforcement comes (to our aid), it will not be possible to defend the fort with this regiment, and we shall all perish with our men." (493)

**Reinforcements sent to Pāndū.** In order to arrange for the despatch of reinforcements, the Mīrzā went to the house of Mīr Ghiyāṣu'd-Dīn Maḥmūd and summoned all the imperial officers, high and low. Although owing to the mis-management of 'Abdu'l-Bāqī there was no gold with the imperial treasurer, he demanded Rs. 1,000 from his own account and ordered it to be paid to admiral Islām Qulī, the slave of Bāz Bahādur Qalmāq, to enable him to make his own arrangements and to proceed with the fleet to the aid of Mīrzā Yūsuf. Islām Qulī and some others who from the time of the Ṣūbahdārship of Qāsim Khān and the administration of 'Abdu'l-Bāqī had been indulging in unbridled tongue and were in league with Mīr 'Abdu'r-Razzāq, began to play tricks. From the trend of his words it appeared that he would never go to serve under the command of Mīrzā Yūsuf. The Mīrzā was furious and thought within himself: "If I am unable to command this slave to execute the work of the master and the Qibla, to-morrow none of the nobles would act according to my orders." So, with a view to have the work done, and with an eye to the welfare of the master he shouted (orders) to his own officers. They taught the slave a good lesson and brought him to his house as a prisoner by binding his hands and neck. He was immediately sent to Pāndū to Mīrzā Yūsuf with two hundred matchlock-men and a sum of Rs. 500 out of the thousand. A letter was written to Yūsuf Barlās that further reinforcements were being sent in quick succession. In short, many of the imperial officers interceded and stood as security saying that Islām Qulī would no longer make any objection to any work to which he would be appointed. He was then pardoned without hesitation and was given a robe of honour, a horse and Rs. 1,000 from the Mīrzā's own purse as a grant for expenses. Mas'ūd Qāsim Khān was appointed as Sazāwal to escort Islām Qulī to Mīrzā Yūsuf and to bring news as an eye-witness about the condition of the imperial army and the weakness of the infidels, and he was asked to return in a day. After reaching Islām Qulī there Mas'ūd returned and described the condition of the enemy in the following words:—"During the time I was there, they (the enemy) made two successive assaults with a large number of foot-soldiers, cannon, ballistas and rockets of similar nature, and also a large number of *garduns*. They fought hard and though ultimately repulsed, they are still persisting in their opposition and are waiting to watch its effect." (494)

**Nathan's plan to capture the Shaykh.** The Mīrzā thereupon summoned Mīr Ghiyāṣu'd-Dīn Maḥmūd, Mīr 'Abdu'r-Razzāq and Rāja Satrajit and said:—"To-morrow I shall hold a dinner-party to which I shall invite every body, high and low, including the Shaykh. I shall instruct one of my men to come at the time when we shall be all sitting together with the Shaykh, and to say that he was coming from Mīrzā Yūsuf Barlās from the fort of Pāndū. When we ask him about news, he will say that we should listen to him in a private room. Accordingly, with this pretext we, namely you three, myself, the Shaykh and Kāẓim Āqā, will get up and go inside the house along with the messenger. He will begin to say that if any reinforcement reaches Pāndū by this evening, it is well and good; otherwise Rāja Baldev will be triumphant and will wrest the fort from the imperial officers. After this, in consultation with one another we shall place a *pān-dān* (a tray for keeping *pān* or betel leaf) before you Rāja Satrajit, and taking five pieces of *pān* you will offer a benedictory prayer for the victory. After the benedictory prayer, you will leave the place, and as soon as you reach the private-chamber, you will give a signal to your *pāiks* (footmen) to cut off the legs of the horse of the Shaykh and those of the horses of his soldiers all at once. During this interval there will be a confusion and at the cutting off of the legs of the horses, these soldiers will all on a sudden run out. At this interval we six men including the Shaykh will remain within the house. Five of us will fall upon the Shaykh and by the favour of the True Lord, we shall bind him by the hands and neck. At the door of the house each of us will keep two servants. There will thus be five masters and ten servants. We shall also instruct the elephant-keepers to keep the elephants ready for a review. During the course of that tumult they will drive the elephants from four sides towards my buildings and enter with the elephants by breaking the walls down and will besiege the house in which we will be staying with the Shaykh. Most likely at the capture of the leader, the coward flock will disperse themselves. Failing this if the situation is carried to the extreme, then we shall immediately cut off the head of the Shaykh and throw it out so that by the grace of the Lord of Honour, a great disorder might prevail in the ranks of these foolish mutineers." In short, according to this plan, next morning when the sun arose, a great banquet was held and invitations were issued to all, high and low. But Mīr 'Abdu'r-Razzāq due to his lack of courage and weak faith in the True Lord thought in his mind that during the course of the struggle with the Shaykh, the Shaykh might kill some one. So for the execution of this plan, it would be safer for him if he would put on a steel coat under his dress. With this object in view, he put on a steel coat, and through his lack of wisdom he also wrapped a silken rope round his waist thinking that it would be of use at the time of binding the hands and feet of the Shaykh. But he never thought of the saying :—

*Verse :*

"As far as you can, never reveal your secret to your friend,
Your friend has a friend, think of the friend of your friend."

In short, though no outsider could get an inkling of the plot, his steward of the ward-robe and the keeper of the armoury came to know of it. One of the servants of the Mīr who was friendly to a servant of the Shaykh got the information and warned the Shaykh against coming to the banquet. The Shaykh, after one *pahar* of the day, sent messengers to offer his excuses for his inability to come due to illness. But the Mīrzā, having understood from the behaviour of the messengers, showed an indifferent attitude and did not speak anything before them. He ordered the Mutaṣaddīs to take the portion of the Shaykh along with the *degs* (pans) in which the food had been cooked, to the house of the Shaykh, thus showing him due regard. It was accordingly done. The comrades too, after the dinner and the distribution of the otto of roses, returned to their homes. The plan could not be executed. (495)

**The new officers pressed to expedite their arrival.** After two days it was decided to send Kāẓim Āqā to the Khān Fatḥ-jang and to write letters to every one of the auxiliary officers insisting on their early arrival. The departure of Kāẓim Āqā would serve to remove the suspicions of the Shaykh, and secondly, it would make the Khāns, who were coming up at a slow pace reach as early as possible. In the meantime any other plan that could be devised would be quite welcome. For these reasons Kāẓim Āqā was given farewell by all the imperial officers and their representations were entrusted to him. They sent some of their own men in his company so that Kāẓim Āqā might put pressure upon the Khāns in their presence and speed them up under the escort of Sazāwals. They would then be able to forward their reports to Mīrzā Nathan also, with the messengers of the imperial officers. As they travelled with the current, at Rangamātī they, after a short journey, met Shaykh Kamāl, who was coming with the boats unaccompanied by the army and the horses. They delivered the letters of the imperial officers and Mīrzā Nathan and urged upon his early arrival. The Shaykh replied to Mīrzā Nathan and the imperial officers in the same tone in which the Ṣūbahdār had written. He said :—" Many days have already passed; only a few days remain. You have already accomplished whatever there was for you to do. So please wait till my arrival. I am arriving soon. The arrival of the land-force and the horses may be delayed a little. If my army comes up, then by the grace of God, I shall reach you soon without caring whether the other Khāns come up or lag behind." The letter was given to the messengers of Mīrzā Nathan and they were sent back. Kāẓim Āqā reached the Khān (Fatḥ-jang) four days after leaving Rangamātī. He reported the state of affairs and requested the Mīr-Ṣūbah to appoint Sazāwals to make the departing officers, particularly Qulīj Khān *alias* Bāltū Qulīj who had been sent from the imperial Court to hold the post of the Jāgīrdār of Kūch, to travel within the shortest time. The Khān Fatḥ-jang also, who was now free from the quarrels with Qāsim Khān wanted to make him (Qulīj Khān) reach as early as possible by physically compelling him to proceed (literally, by gripping him by the loin-cloth). The Khān also wrote the following significant letter to Qulīj Khān :—" Proceeding so languidly, that even by this time you have not been able to reach (Hājo), shows as if you are riding on a wooden horse. Or, is your slow progress due to your fear of the large army of the *Karorī* reported to you by your personal assistant Rāy Kāsīdās ? " (496)

**Another plan to capture the Shaykh.** Now I shall give a short account of the Mīrzā and the Khāns of the frontier and what they did after the departure of Kāẓim Āqā and the receipt of the reply from Shaykh Kamāl. Mīr Ghiyāṣu'd-Dīn Bakhshī said to Mīrzā Nathan :—" His Majesty the Emperor, I'timādu'd-Dawla, the Khān Fatḥ-jang and Mukhliṣ Khān are all of opinion that the *Karorī* should be sent alive to the imperial Court, by all possible means. Under these circumstances, however hard we try (to capture him alive, if we accidentally kill him) they would think that we had killed him through our personal grudge and greed. Nothing will thus be gained by our exertions. Therefore, if you can devise some plan, it will be rewarded and will also remove the suspicions of the master as well as of the intelligent people and put an end to this mutiny. The stick of aggression always strikes at both ends. It will be better if by the grace of God we can suppress the mutiny by the other method." The Mīrzā replied :—" All your arguments are based on proper reasonings. If we have really to fight against him, the actual facts of the case will never become known to the master and the intelligent people and through the cowardice of our men, all the blame would be laid at my door. Therefore, I have a plan in my mind about which nobody else should know except us two. If you consider it reasonable and yet do not keep it to yourself and go and give it out on streets and markets as Mīr 'Abdu'r-Razzāq did, then there is no help." Mīr Ghiyāṣu'd-Dīn Maḥmūd swore many oaths, and then the Mīrzā explained the plan thus :—" It is known to us all that Shaykh Ibrāhīm in inciting this rebellion is entertaining vain ideas, and he is puffed up with pride and madness. The smallest grain which comes to him is partaken by him in the company of all his followers. To invite him alone to my house amounts to frightening him away. Therefore, one day I shall again extend an invitation to all, high and low, to a dinner consisting of bread, *kushkka* (a kind of thick pottage made of wheaten flour to which meat is added) and *khirsa* (thickened milk). In the morning when the people will come, I shall feed the loyal persons in my own house and I shall send the share of the Shaykh consisting of five big *degs* (pans) of *kushkka* and *khirsa* and five hundred breads cooked with *ghee* and water. A man will go and show excuses and deliver this message :—'Had we invited you, the interested people, who take money from you for their own use, would have again made false allegations against us. As we are of one mind, there can not be any separation. We are therefore sending your portion to your place.' In short, he (the Shaykh) will call together all his men, high and low, and will then fall to repast. I shall give instructions to mix *dhutura* (a kind of poisonous drug) in that food in such a quantity that one morsel of it will be sufficient for all the fish of a river, what to speak of the life of a single man. After this when all people, high and low, along with their leader, will begin to lose their senses, I shall bring them all bound hand and neck by the grace of the Lord of Honour." Mīr Ghiyāṣu'd-Dīn Maḥmūd continued saying, "Most excellent, most excellent!" for a period to two *gharīs*, and finished by saying :—"If this remedy takes effect, then it will be an episode to be recorded in the histories of the age." The Mīrzā returned to his own home and Mīr Ghiyāṣu'd-Dīn Maḥmūd remained in his. At night the Mīr, under the influence of the intoxication of opium, divulged this plan to his personal attendant Ḥājī Lang and it thus reached the ears of the Shaykh. Next morning, before one *pahar* of the day had passed, the Shaykh sent a clear message saying, —"I am not doing anything wrong. Why then are you intriguing in this way and trying to injure me?" The Mīrzā replied,—"Although we have stopped going to each other's place, yet the tongue of the back-biters have not ceased maligning us. After this I undertake not to send anything to you. Whatever you send to me, I will eat immediately in the presence of your messengers, so that henceforth the words of the self-interested people may not be believed." Although the Shaykh was put to shame, the presentation of things ceased from both the sides. (497)

**Flight of Baldev.** Now I shall give a short account of Mīrzā Yūsuf and of the people at the Thāna of Pāndū. When the siege led by Rāja Baldev dragged on, Mīrzā Nathan and the imperial officers sent reinforcements after reinforcements to Mīrzā Yūsuf and to the devoted warriors of the fort of Pāndū. One day in the evening when Rāja Baldev along with the Eighteen Hill-Rājas rushed forward placing their *gardūns* in their front on the bank of the ditch of the fort of Pāndū and pressed hard with his large infantry, the garrison was put to great straits. Mīrzā Yūsuf, Islām Qulī, Sūnā Ghāzī, Zamīndār of Sarāil, 'Ādil Khān, and other admirals of Mūsā Khān, the Zamīndār and many others took a vow binding their wrappers with one another that they would fight and follow one another. They opened the gate of the fort and rushed out. Many of them, through their great courage, jumped down from the towers and walls of the fort before the gate was opened and attacked the enemy from all sides. Within a short time many of the enemy's men were put to the blood-thirsty sword and were sent to hell. Baldev with his brothers took to the lane of safety in flight throwing the dust of disgrace on his head. The announcement of victory was made and the trumpet of conquest was sounded. The report of this victory was sent to the imperial officers. The Mīrzā took this as a good omen for his victory over the accursed Shaykh. (498)

**Nathan wins over two messengers of the Shaykh.** On that very day of the arrival of the news of the victory, Mīr Ghiyāṣu'd-Dīn Maḥmūd struck up an idea and said thus to the Mīrzā :—" It is quite certain that the Shaykh would not have been able to get all these informations, without winning over some of our men. Therefore, it is better that I should also win over some of the men of the Shaykh in the same way in order to know the source of his informations, and who this person is who gives out the secrets of the imperial officers and particularly of myself.

In the meantime Hātim Khān Afghān and Shaykh Ḥabīb, the messengers of the Shaykh, came to discuss certain propositions. The Mīrzā after replying to the question of the Shaykh, held the hands of both of them and took them to a corner with the plea of sending some confidential message to the Shaykh and said,—" The Shaykh has left his own family at Sambhal, but he has alienated the sympathy of the whole world and has lost all his prestige. Under these circumstances you, who have your families at Ghoraghāt and Chūnakhālī, do you like to ally yourselves to the Shaykh at the risk of losing your own honour ?" They replied to the Mīrzā,—"We know that our honour also has been lost and will (continue to) be lost ; but what can we do ? We are under the obligation of his salt." The Mīrzā said,—" But Sultan Khān, the chief of the officers of the Shaykh, Shaykh 'Abdu'r-Rahīm and other Shaykh Zādas left the Shaykh saying these words, —' our companionship and our loyalty to you should be in the proportion of your loyalty to the Emperor. When you have turned away from the shadow of God and cast your faith to the wind of destruction, how can we follow you ?' " They replied,—" The Shaykh still says that he is not a traitor; he is detaining Mīrzā Muḥammad, the calligraphist, in order to go with him to the Khān Fatḥ-jang. So we are in fear and hope alternately, and what troubles us is that, in future, our friends will say,—'you will deal with us in the same way as you behaved with Ibrāhīm.' " The Mīrzā encouraged both the messengers of the Shaykh with oaths, promises and words and promised to them,—" I shall secure for you imperial Manṣabs through the Khān Fatḥ-jang and very good Jāgīrs too. Do remain with the Shaykh but supply us every moment all informations beneficial to the interests of the Emperor. Be at ease and surely we shall never say to you that you will behave with us in the same way as you did with him." In short, when both sides were assured, the Mīrzā asked them about the person who supplied informations to the Shaykh from this side. They replied,—"The news of the plan for his capture was given by the steward of the ward-robe of Mīr 'Abdu'r-Razzāq, and the news of the mixing of *dhutura* was supplied personally by the Ḥājī of the Bakhshī but in the language of the Bakhshī. News from you are supplied by twenty-five of your horsemen who like all other imperial officers excepting yourself, had been bribed by the Shaykh. These twenty-five men of yours accepted money from the Shaykh and supply news about you every moment. They have also promised that on the day of battle, they will throw you down from your horse and will give your head to the Shaykh." The Mīrzā took down in writing the names of every one of these ungrateful men which will be given in course of these episodes. Then he gave *pān* to the messengers of the Shaykh and wrote to the Khān Fatḥ-jang in their presence the true state of affairs about the loyalty of the Shaykh, and after describing many of the incidents he requested him to send a conciliatory letter to the Shaykh. It was then despatched by a very swift boat to Jahāngīrnagar to the Ṣūbahdār and then he granted leave to the aforesaid messengers to return. (499)

**The Shaykh prepares for a surprise attack.** One day, after the Mīrzā's discovery of the sources of the Shaykh's informations, the Shaykh proposed to make a surprise attack upon the Mīrzā and the imperial officers. He armed himself and began to cross the river Barlia. Then the messengers of the Shaykh sent a secret message to Mīrzā Nathan through a slave-boy and gave him the alarm. The Mīrzā thought,—"If I summon the imperial officers to inform them (about this affair) they will desire to go home to arm themselves and after being armed they will ride on their horses. It means much delay. So it is better that I should myself ride to the house of the Bakhshī, bring him with me and arm ourselves in the field." With this object in view he rode on a canopied elephant and went to the house of Mīr Ghiyāṣu'd-Dīn Maḥmūd.

Without alighting, he awakened the Mīr from his sleep, put him on his elephant and came to the field. He then ordered the heralds to bring the imperial Manṣabdārs and the officers of his own estate fully armed along with the elephants. In short, when this news reached the Shaykh that the Mīrzā and Mīr Ghiyāṣu'd-Dīn Maḥmūd, along with the imperial officers, were standing on the field fully equipped for war with elephants in their front, he received a great shock in his far-sighted mind. He consulted his advisers and decided that by all means the battle should be postponed for fifteen days till the arrival of reinforcements from the Rāja of Assam, and he would fight after that. Under these circumstances, as he had awakened the imperial officers, and particularly Mīrzā Nathan, who was sleeping like a tiger, without any provocation so he feared lest they would fall upon him roaring like a youthful lion awakened from its sleep, and scatter his troops to all directions. He therefore thought it better for himself to raise a fort for his protection and to remain in security till the arrival of the Assam regiment. Therefore, he ordered all his men and particularly the Kūch *pāiks* to begin the construction of a fort. This news reached the Mīrzā and the imperial officers and made their joyous hearts pensive. Inspite of this, the Mīrzā remained ready with horses suspecting some designs and tricks. The Shaykh had completed the construction of a high fort with deep ditches beginning the work from the last part of the day and carrying it on till the first *pahar* of the next day. But he did not consider how he would defend the fort with his small force when it will be necessary for him to go out of the fort to fight in some other direction. (500)

**Nathan remains ready for battle.** Next morning the Mīrzā returned to the city to his home along with all the imperial officers. In the evening he ordered Mīr Ghiyāṣu'd-Dīn Maḥmūd to keep watch outside (the city), fully armed, along with all the imperial officers, high and low, as was done on the previous night. As the Mīrzā was unwell, he could not go personally and remained in his home. Mīr

Ghiyāṣu'd-Dīn Maḥmūd made some excuses expressing his inability to join the watch, but ultimately the dominating power of the Mīrzā prevailed and the Mīr was forthwith induced to come to his duties. That night also passed safely. From the third night the Mīrzā again began to stay outside the city fully equipped along with the imperial officers. After the third night when the people began to manifest negligence at night, he ordered that a stockade should be constructed and the nights passed in vigilance, so that if by chance any elephant or horse happened to get loose at night it might not stray out of the fort and be soon caught; and also, if at any time, the enemy made a surprise attack, the soldiers might be able to form into lines and meet them. He summoned the captains of the fleet and the Zamīndārs and ordered them to complete a high stockade by the end of the day, four hundred yards in extent and provided with a deep ditch. The arduous and hardworking workers completed a lofty stockade with a deep ditch at the end of two *gharīs* after evening. The Mīrzā stayed there with all the imperial officers, elephants and artillery. But the heated elephants were ordered to be kept tied beyond the deep ditches of the fort at a distance, and four hundred armed horsemen were kept as guards round the fort. When he left the fort, he divided the entire army into three *chawkīs* or groups of watch-parties,—one under the command of Mīr 'Abdu'r-Razzāq, the second under Rāja Satrajit and the third under Mīr Madārī, the uncle of Mīrzā Nathan. In short, every day the people of one *chawkī* remained alert in the fort, fully armed and ready to defend it, so that during his (Nathans) retirement to the city, the Shaykh might not be able to occupy the fort by an assault. Some days passed in this way and during all this time the Mīrzā used to pass the nights with the imperial officers outside the city in the fort. When fighting was finally resolved upon, the Mīrzā thought it prudent to abandon the Thāna of Pāndū and recalled Mīrzā Yūsuf with all his men of the Thāna, with the idea that Pāndū might be re-occupied after the attainment of this victory. (501)

**Yār Muḥammad raids the suburbs of Hājo.** The brother-in-law of the Shaykh named Yār Muḥammad used to come very often with a company of loafers, raid the suburbs of Hājo and carry away the cattle that happened to fall into their hands. This state of affairs became unbearable to the Mīrzā. Therefore, he sent messengers to the Shaykh saying :—"All this remissness on our part is due to our oath taken in the name of God. But you do not care even for God. You shall have to repent for it ultimately." Then the following verses were sent to him.

*Maṣnavī :*

The messengers said, "O, ye malevolent man,
You deserve many an admonition and punishment.
Thus sayeth the commander Mīrzā Nathan,
O, ye Shaykh, a triator and violator of oath;
God is the witness of the oath between you and us,
When you broke that oath, you are an enemy of God."

The Shaykh also referred to the oath. Although he had not the slightest sincerity in it, he replied in a hypocritical way.

*Maṣnavī :*

When the Shaykh heard, he became much grieved,
And trembled like the leaves of trees.
By his life and head he re-affirmed the oath,
He swore by his sword,
"That I never ordered for the war
Nor do I approve of him who commits such acts.
I will hang him by his legs with his two hands bound and hanging down.
And will order his head to be placed in a mortar.
I will bind the two hands of my brother-in-law as well
And send him to the Mīr, the lover of God."

It has already been mentioned that the Shaykh had not the slightest sincerity in his protestations. Inspite of all these excuses, therefore, the mean persons of the army did not cease their depredations and began to play the tricks of a wolf. Thus compelled, he (Nathan) sent a few words of admonition reprimanding the Shaykh, which was more effective in poignancy than the thrust from a sharp sword. It was delivered in the form of a verse to the purport that to-morrow, by the favour of God, the result would appear.

*Verse* :

Thus sayeth the commander of the army to the Shaykh,—
"By the fortune of the Emperor I will put you on the cross."

As the desire of the Shaykh was not to give up his braggings till the arrival of the reinforcement from Assam, so he used to send his army now and then to carry on raids as a proof of his rebellious intention and to facilitate his negotiations through the envoys of the Rāja of Assam. He satisfied the envoys with many flatteries. (502)

**An ultimatum is sent to the Shaykh.** In the meantime a letter came to the Mīrzā from Shaykh Kamāl to the following effect :—"As the arrival of my army is being delayed so I have decided to go personally to you and join the war by taking a few horses from each of you." Then the Mīrzā thought in his far-sighted mind and spoke thus to all the imperial officers, high and low :—"First, either to-day or to-morrow Assam (i.e., the Ahoms) will lead its attack and will heap difficulties upon difficulties. Secondly, Shaykh Kamāl will come and will not only demand horses from us, but will make us do the hazardous part of the work and will take away the credit of carrying on the war and the attainment of the victory. As up till now no reinforcement has reached Shaykh Ibrāhīm, and our attempts and endeavours have not yet been contaminated by partnership with others, it is better for us to fight now whatever battle is to be fought, with the aid of the Lord of Honour." With this decision he sent Rāy Kedār Mahājan along with two men of the imperial Manṣabdārs, two of the Afghāns of 'Uṣmān named Jalāl Khān Shīrwānī and Bāzū-i-Jhilam on behalf of the Emperor, Badridās, his Hindu Bakhshī, on his own behalf, Ḥājī Lang the personal assistant of Mīr Ghiyāṣu'd-Dīn Maḥmūd on his behalf, Muḥammad Sharīf on behalf of Mīr 'Abdu'r-Razzāq and Ramanāth, uncle of Rāja Satrajit, on behalf of the Rāja, to Shaykh Ibrāhīm with this message:—"If you proceed to the Khān Fatḥ-jang, then you must go to Jahāngīrnagar in the company of Mīrzā Muḥammad, the calligraphist; otherwise you should let him depart and cut off all connection with the imperial officers, so that we may devise some means for dealing with you." On the first day, the Shaykh personally replied to the messengers and also quieted Mīrzā Muḥammad, saying that he would go. On the next day, he constructed a strong bridge on the river Barlia and in order to protect the bridge from the raid of the imperialists, he raised two stockades on this side of the Barlia and posted the Kūch infantry to defend those small forts. The messengers were again sent to him with the following message from imperial officers:—"If you desire your own welfare, dismantle two of the towers of your fort and fall back. Then make the necessary arrangements and proceed with Mīrzā Muḥammad within a week. Know otherwise for certain that you run the risk of bringing into disgrace so many thousands of men." Verse (Left out) .... Then the Shaykh, expressly cut off all connection (with the imperialists) and sent Mīrzā Muḥammad to Khān Fatḥ-jang with the following petition in reply:—"As at present I am in distress for lack of funds, I am unable to come to Your Excellency. After some time when my distracted heart will be pacified, I will present myself most respectfully before you." He again paid a good sum to Mīrzā Muḥammad in addition to the previous bribe and sent him with a happy heart. And he sent the following message (to the Imperial officers):—"You have sent a message to me asking me to dismantle the towers; why don't you first dismantle the towers of your own fort?" *Maṣnavī* (Left out). To this the messengers replied then and there, saying:—"They are all imperial officers. Now they hold the offices of the Fawjdār and the commander of this frontier. If they march and build forts, they do the right thing. But why do not the officers who are dismissed and recalled to the Court, go back out of their own accord if they are loyal ? When they have to go, it is a hundred times more incumbent upon them to dismantle their towers in order to remove the scandal and to save their lives. If they defended their rebellious conduct in the past or want to defend it now, they will bring either to-day or to-morrow the disgrace of both the worlds upon themselves by suffering for the results of their own actions." The Shaykh became very much enraged, but he had no remedy. The messengers returned and when they explained the situation, the Mīrzā sent a message again :—" Repent of your big talk. To-morrow, God the Great will dismantle the towers of whomsoever He pleases."

*Verse :*

" When the morrow will be made bright and hot by the sun,
I shall flash up in the contest with thee like the sun in the sky.
With the aid of the Lord and the fortune of the Emperor,
With the help of the sun and the sky and the army,
At last I will triumph over thee,
Defeating every man who broke his oath.
Thou wilt see, O, ye faithless and heretic Shaykh,
A battle the like of which thou never sawest in any strife.
Such strokes of the mace and the sword will reach thee
That blood will spring out of you like the rain from the cloud."
(503)

**Nathan marches to the field of battle.** In short these verses were written in reply to the Shaykh and then he (the Mīrzā) prepared himself for the battle, and drew up his regiments in battle order. Thus, relying on the aid of the Lord, the centre of the army was kept under the command of himself, Mīr Ghiyāṣu'd-Dīn Maḥmūd and some others whose names will be mentioned below. The vanguard was placed under the command of Mīr 'Abdu'r-Razzāq with all the Afghān Manṣabdārs of 'Uṣmān ; Mīr Saiyid Mas'ud and many other heroes like Islām Qulī, the *Mīr Baḥr,* along with his men were attached to the Mīr and made him very enthusiastic. The command of the right wing was given to Mīrzā Yūsuf ; and in order to satisfy the imperial officers who might say that they were made to follow him because of their low Manṣab, he attached to Mīrzā Yūsuf forty-five of his own horsemen, namely Āmānu'llah and his other brothers, Ṭāhir Beg along with his kinsmen, Ṣafī Bahādur, Chaqān, Bāqī Beg Qalmāq, and others, who being his personal officers, were in intrigue with the Shaykh to injure the Mīrzā. They were thus separated from him in such a tactful manner that nobody could know anything of it. He (Mīrzā Nathan) also kept Mīrzā Yūsuf under obligation by saying :—"As none of the imperial officers was willing to follow you so I had to try hard to give you a commandership and I did it by placing you over my own regiment." Sūnā Ghāzī was also attached to him. The command of the left-wing was given to Rāja Satrajit with his entire army. There was one admiral attached to each regiment. Some inhabitant of the city, the boatmen of the officers and the personal servants of the admirals were attached to the centre and the admirals were ordered thus :—"Ask your own boatmen to remain behind the regiment, each ready with a bundle of green grass on his head, so that the army may look vast in size. If the enemy do not come out on the field considering the time to be inauspicious, a small fort should be raised on the bank of the river and leaving the artillery under its protection, we propose to remain ready on horseback for the whole night. The battle would be fought next day, provided the enemy comes out of their fort; otherwise our own fort should be made bigger. First of all, the control of the river should be secured by firing the artillery and then attempts should be made to cross the river and to enter the fort in which he (the Shaykh) is staying. At the time of occupying the fort the bundles of green grass would be of use." As sixty *shīr-dahan* cannon were transported on the shoulders of the footmen, arrangements were made so that the *gulāndāz* (cannoniers) might be able to fire the cannon satisfactorily from horseback. A force of five hundred matchlock-men and famous elephants were posted in front of the regiment of the vanguard as sentinels. Two or three experienced elephants were attached to every regiment and the army marched to the field of battle depending on the favour of God and the benign influence of the master and the Qibla. *Verse* (left out). (504)

**The Shaykh retreats to his fort.** When the regiments of the imperial officers stopped after marching a short distance, it was rumoured that the enemy intended to defend the fort without coming out of it. Therefore, Mīrzā Nathan summoned Islām Qulī from the vanguard, Sūnā Ghāzī from the right-wing and Rāja Satrajit from the left-wing. The Rāja was in command of his own regiment. He was asked to leave the command with his chief officer Ādam Khān so that he might come and join in the construction of a fort. From the Mīrzā's own regiment of the centre, he summoned a band of boatmen of the officers and some common people of the city who were in their company. When all these people came, he laid the foundation of a stockade, which enclosed an area of 250 yards, the length being greater than the breadth. He shouted to the workers to begin the work in such a way that they might complete by sunset a lofty fort with a deep ditch. As the hard-working men had the bundles of green grass with them, they raised the fort up to the height of the waist of a man in the twinkling of an eye and completed half the ditch. Then again a tumult arose that the doomed enemy, undismayed by the thought of inevitable Divine wrath, had opened the gates of his fort and had come out to fight. The Mīrzā sent Sūnā Ghāzī, Islām Qulī and Rāja Satrajit to their respective regiments. He himself advanced with the regiment of the centre so that he might come to the help of the regiment of the vanguard. In the meantime Nūru'd-Dīn, the commander of the right-wing of the Shaykh, advanced with Kamāl Khān a slave of the Shaykh. Before his followers could come to his aid, both the commanders fell upon the regiment of the left-wing of the imperialists. Before the Rāja could come up to oppose them and to take the command, a number of footmen of the front, unable to resist, broke and fled and Nūru'd-Dīn himself fell upon Ādam Khān Afghān, the chief officer of the Rāja. *Maṣnavī* (Left out). In short, Kamāl Khān, the slave of the Shaykh, turned his rein and instead of joining his own regiment, he joined the regiment of the Shaykh. Nūru'd-Dīn, advanced to attack and struck Ādam Khān with his sword. Ādam Khān, had no time to ward off the blow with his shield, and placed his left hand before his face. His hand was protected by gauntlet which the sword cut and his hand was wounded. But then, with the help of the Lord of Honour, Ādam Khān finished Nūru'd-Dīn by a blow from his javelin. He was a Mughal and a Muslim, but as he was supporting the cause of the rebels and mutineers, so he went to hell. The Rāja (by this time) joined his own regiment. The Shaykh advanced with great audacity with a large army. His army was scattered first, by the discharge of shots from the powerful cannon which had been carried on elephants and on the shoulders of the boatmen and were placed in front of the vanguard, and then also by tne firing of expert matchlock-men. The Shaykh then advanced with more than a hundred brave fighters of his vanguard. As soon as he rushed forward, a gun-shot from a place of vantage reached the chin of the shaykh and grazed his skin. It made no difference to the Shaykh. He advanced forward, fell upon the imperial vanguard and gave a battle like Rustam. But as the fortune favoured the imperial officers, a disorder arose among the dissolute followers of the Shaykh within a short time and they took to flight. At this juncture Ādam Khān, the chief of the servants of the Shaykh, caught hold of the Shaykh's horse by its rein and signalled his brothers to run to it and take it out of the field of battle. They reached the head of the bridge in a state of confusion and attempted to cross over it. The soldiers of their left-wing who were in front of Mīrzā Yūsuf had taken to flight and were crowding on the bridge. Thus the Shaykh crossed with a few men in safety, and the rest in the bustle of the transit were unable to discriminate between high and low lands and jumped right and left from the bridge into the river and became the food of the crocodiles of calamity. Many of them were trodden to death by one another during this commotion. Mīr 'Abdu'r-Razzāq with the soldiers of the imperial vanguard followed them. When he crossed the bridge in this disorder and a number of his followers had yet to cross, the bridge gave way all on a sudden. For this reason the crossing was delayed. The Mīrzā came to take the command of his force posted after the Mīr and the regiment of the vanguard. He dismounted from his horse and rode on an elephant and took with him some of his picked-men on elephants. He then followed the imperial officers in pursuit of the fleeing Shaykh, with Balabhadra Dās his personal assistant and some other warriors in his company, and wanted to repair the bridge quickly so that the regiments might cross over one after the other as soon as possible. (505)

**Sad end of the Shaykh.** Now I shall give a short account of the flight of the Shaykh and of the imperial officers of the advance army (who pursued him) and the events that took place before the arrival of Mīrzā Nathan. When the Shaykh, after crossing the bridge reached his fort, and entered into it, his army became scattered and his following did not number more than thirty to forty men within the fort. Immediately after his entry into the fort, he dismounted from his horse and closed its gate with his own hand. When Mīr 'Abdu'r-Razzāq and the Afghāns of the vanguard reached there in pursuit of him, the Shaykh began to shoot arrows with the aid of that very regiment and repelled the elephants that were driven by the keepers against the gate of the fort, by showers of arrows. The elephants fell back. Among the elephants, there was one named Baḥrī Bachcha driven by La'l Khān, a slave of the Mīrzā. At the repulse of the elephants, the Mīrzā ordered the elephant-keeper to drive Baḥrī Bachcha against the gate of the fort. Then its keeper made three assaults on the gate, and on all these occasions, the elephant was unable to make a stand and had to fall back. The warriors guessed the reason (of this repulse), stopped advancing and every one made a halt. During this period, an elephant named Shāh 'Ināyat, presented to the Mīrzā by the Emperor, was in a state of heat. Though it was very strong and possessed a mountain-like body, it would never move its foot without the order of the keeper. Fatā, the Fawjdār advanced with it. When he reached the gate, he swerved to one side and made the elephant rush upon the tower of the fort. The elephant, through its strength of youth and the heat of rut, crossed that deep ditch with a jump like the impact of a dark cloud inspite of his heavy body and fell over the tower (and got inside the fort). The aforesaid Fawjdār, who was the chief of the elephant-keepers, drove the elephant towards the gate of the fort from inside and attacked the Shaykh and the crowd at the gate. This group of followers left the company of the Shaykh and attempted to ride on horses with the intention to make a stand and obstruct the progress of the elephant, provided they could find some one bold enough to lead them ; otherwise they would fly for safety like others. Accordingly, when the Shaykh also was attempting to ride on a horse, the elephant came upon him and broke the stirrup of his horse, as he was going to ride and the Shaykh had to fall back on his feet. The Fawjdār of the elephant shouted :—" Shaykh, do run away and save your life, because many lives are bound together with yours." But the Shaykh, owing to his audacity and mortification at his retreat from the field of battle, failed to understand that his retirement to the eternal kingdom was going to take place in this (frontier) land. Then the elephant at the signal of the keeper swayed its trunk (to attack). The Shaykh gave a blow with his sword on the left hind-leg of the elephant and it took such effect that it pierced through the flesh and went about four finger-breadth deep into the bone. The elephant, raised the (wounded) foot and gave a loud shriek. Yet again, at the signal of the keeper, it pressed the Shaykh under its tusks inspite of his fatal wound and sat on its knees. But as the tusks of the elephant were very wide, the Shaykh fell between the tusks and only received a good thrashing. After this the elephant at the order of Fatā, the Fawjdār, put his trunk round the waist of the Shaykh and threw him over the wall of the fort, which, with the towers, was twenty-one cubits high, with such force that the Shaykh fell into the middle of the ditch on the side of the imperialists. One footman named Mas'ūd and another Dakhinī Hindu of Mīr Ghiyāṣu'd-Dīn named Kahurām, who were standing on the side of the ditch as spectators, jumped into the ditch, and caught hold of the Shaykh without recognising him and brought him out in a state of unconsciousness. (506)

**'Abdu'r-Razzāq cuts off his head.** Although the Mīr ('Abdu'r-Razzāq) had previously bound himself to the Shaykh with the oath of brotherhood by swearing by the Qur'ān, yet remembering the audacity displayed by the Shaykh during Razzāq's march to Dhamdhama, he immediately ordered his men to kill the Shaykh lest the Mīrzā would come and protect his life. Mīr Saiyid Mas'ūd, and the Afghān Manṣabdārs of his company, particularly Khwāja La'l and Khwāja Mīrzā, requested him not to do so. They said:—"It is proper to keep him alive till the arrival of Mīrzā Nathan, because the imperial Farmāns and the orders of the Mīr Ṣūbah were to capture this imprudent man alive and to send him to the Court." 'Abdu'r-Razzāq did not listen to their advice. Thinking that the Mīrzā would soon arrive, he despatched him to the secret house of non-existence. He cut off his head and hanging it below the howdah of the elephant on which he was riding, he entered the fort. When the other imperial officers who were assisting him saw this incident, they left the company of the Mīr. The Mīr came to the road of the bazar of the fort and his men also engaged in loot, left his company and scattered themselves on all sides. One of the soldiers of the Mīr named Muḥammad Laṭīf who had deserted the Mīr to join the Shaykh promised thus on the day of battle:—"The man who will meet Mīrzā Nathan and the Mīr in the fight shall be myself." He received a gun-shot in the field on the other side of the river and two arrow-shots at the gate of the fort. When the Shaykh was overpowered by the elephant, he, therefore, deserted him, came to the street of the bazar, lost his consciousness and fell off from his horse. The Mīr arrived at that place and his followers recognised the man. An order was issued to separate his head of evil brain from his ungrateful body. The followers of the Mīr struck him with arrows and swords and before his fatigued head was separated Mīrzā Nathan arrived there and said to the Mīr, "What means this halt? Why don't you hunt down that accursed foe (the Shaykh)?" The Mīr cried aloud and said, "I myself have (already) killed him." The Mīrzā thought that the Mīr was joking with him; so he laughed and said, "Mīr, is this the time to indulge in jokes?" The Mīr then pointed out his hand towards the separated head of the Shaykh which was hanging at the howdah of the elephant; he shook it and showed it to Mīrzā Nathan. As the Mīrzā was not aware of the actual state of affairs, he verily believed that this work had been accomplished through the favour of God and by the efforts of the Mīr. He praised him and said, "What is the use of standing inside the fort?" He then came out with the Mīr and ordered a play of the trumpet of victory and the drum of glad tidings, and posted himself in the field at the gate of the fort. At this moment, Rāja Satrajit came to congratulate him. The Mīrzā took the Rāja on the howdah of his elephant. After that when Mīr Ghiyāṣu'd-Dīn Maḥmūd, the Dīwān and Bakhshī arrived there, he asked Mīr 'Abdu'r-Razzāq to take the Mīr on the howdah of his elephant, with the following excuse:— "As there is insufficient room (in my howdah) and two of the descendants of the Prophet of the last cycle of time are present, it is better that they should ride together." Inspite of this Mīr Ghiyāṣu'd-Dīn Maḥmūd did not get up on the elephant and stood by. Mīrzā Nathan, immediately sent for a tuskless elephant of his own estate and gave it as a reward to Mīr 'Abdu'r-Razzāq. The Mīr wanted to observe customary rites of salutation (to Mīrzā Nathan, in acknowledgment of the reward) but the Mīrzā, through his great love for God and for the protection of the prestige of the family of the Prophet, did not allow him to do so. After this the Mīr ordered Muḥammad Sharīf to do so. Muḥammad Sharīf thereupon performed the customary rites of salutation. The head of the Shaykh was ordered to be put on a lance. The Rāja, in order to please the Bakhshī, alighted (from the elephant) and went to the Mīr, the Bakhshī, riding on a horse. (507)

**The Dīwān takes charge of the property of the Shaykh.** After this, the Mīrzā started with happiness and pleasure for his own residence and sent the following message to Mīr Ghiyāṣu'd-Dīn Maḥmūd:—"Our work was to fight. We have defeated the foe of the Emperor by the favour of God. The property for which he gave up his life is in the fort and the fort is placed under your charge." The Hindu officer who was carrying this message to Mīr Ghiyāṣu'd-Dīn Maḥmūd was further instructed thus:—"If the Mīr asks, with which regiment he is to protect it, tell him to get together Rāja Satrajit, Sūnā Ghāzī, 'Ādil Khān and other admirals of Mūsā Khān so that their regiments and followers cannot abscond or desert. In addition, those who possess unreliable following gathered together from a hundred places, should also be made to guard it." In short, although Mīr Ghiyāṣu'd-Dīn Maḥmūd became very much annoyed, he had no alternative (but to obey). He left there Ḥājī Lang, his personal assistant, with the men of the Zamīndārs and then returned to his own residence. The Mīrzā, Mīr 'Abdu'r-Razzāq and the imperial officers, high and low, distributed a large sum of money to the poor in the name of God and returned to the city to their homes in a very grand and pompous style with joy and happiness. He (Mīrzā Nathan) gave leave to Mīr 'Abdu'r-Razzāq and all the imperial officers one by one to return to their own houses, and then he himself entered his own house in safety. (508)

**The Shaykh's head sent to the Sūbahdār.** The head of the Shaykh was ordered to be boiled in *ghee*—(*raghan-i-zard*) and then, stuffed with straw, it was sent to the Khān Fatḥ-jang along with his representation describing all the details and particularly the report of the victory, with Mīr Saiyid Mas'ūd to Jahāngīrnagar in a very swift boat. The workers executed the work very carefully during the night and Mīr Saiyid Mas'ūd started. (509)

**Celebration of the victory.** Three days after the victory, Mīrzā Nathan held a big banquet and extended his invitation to all people, small and great. Shaykh 'Abdu'r-Raḥīm and many of the chief officers of the Shaykh (Ibrāhīm) including Hātim Khān and Shaykh Ḥabīb, the messengers, who had promised to the Mīrzā on a previous occasion that they would be loyal to the Emperor, fled from the field and kept themselves hidden in the jungles and forests apprehending some unpleasantness that might appear in the heat of anger and wrath. Through the mediation of Mīr 'Abdu'r-Razzāq, they came to see the Mīrzā, and they obtained their safety through the Mīrzā's bold, God-fearing and generous mind. The worship of God and the love of the just Lord were put into practice; the tiny market of boldness and courage was displayed fully and the pardon of criminals and the forgiveness of faults were carried to the highest limit. It became a subject of gossip for many years. After the dinner and the distribution of the otto of roses when the whole day was passed in the enjoyment of the music of the melodious singers and in listening to the *Hāfizes* of sweet voice, the Mīrzā presented one horse to each of the men named below from his own stable. The names, of those who received horses are :— Mīr Ghiyāṣu'd-Dīn Maḥmūd, Rāja Satrajit, Mīrzā Yūsuf and Sūnā Ghāzī. At last he turned his face towards Mīr Ghiyāṣu'd-Dīn Maḥmūd and said :—" To-morrow, how are we two going to answer charges ? The high and the low would say that the properties left by the *Karorī* at the time of his death were within the fort, and the fort had fallen into our hands. What then, (they would ask) happened to those properties ? Under these circumstances, a remedy for the safety of all suggests itself to me. I shall take an oath first of all. There is nothing to be ashamed of it nor is there any room for complaint." With this proposal, the Qur'ān for the Muslims and the *Shāl-grām* (fossil ammonite, worshipped by the Hindus as a symbol of Visnu) for the Hindus were brought to the assembly.

First of all the Mīrzā thus took the oath placing his hand on the Qur'ān :—" If any of the imperial properties beginning from a thread up to a sum of one hundred thousand is misappropriated by me or I agree to its misappropriation by others within my knowledge, then it will amount to my turning against God and the Qur'ān." Then he invited all and said that every Muslim should place his hand on the Qur'ān and every Hindu on the *Shālgrām* and return everything seized by them. It was accordingly done. Two hundred and ninety-two horses of different breeds,—'Irāqī, Arabian, cross breeds, Turkish, Yābū or draught-horse, Jangla, Tāzī, Kacchī and Tangan ; and 23½ *Aṣār*[2] gold, one maund and fourteen *Aṣār* of silver, rupees ten thousand and a few hundred in cash, many valuable and rare cloths, various kinds of animals, and different types of articles, large number of maids and slaves along with many well-bred women who had fallen into the hands of some people, including the wives of the Shaykh procured by him at Kāmrūp through his officers, who had fallen into the hands of a sweeper were produced. It became evident that he had tested the salt of his own action. One day the Mīrzā sent a message to the Shaykh admonishing him that he was inviting outrage to the reputation of a number of respectable people of the world from the hands of the ordinary sweepers. In short, the star being favourable, the honour of the Shaykh alone fell into the hands of the sweepers. The total amount of money obtained, including the price of the horses was Rs. 50,000 and a few hundreds. A list was prepared with the seal of the Mīrzā and the imperial officers and it was signed and sealed by Mīr Ghiyāṣu'd-Dīn Maḥmūd, the Dīwān. (510)

**Reward of the officers.** Now I shall give a short account of the arrival of the report of victory of this war before the Khān Fatḥ-jang and the details of its contents. Mīr Saiyid Mas'ūd reached Jahāngīrnagar within four days and presented the letters of Mīrzā Nathan and the imperial officers along with the head of the Shaykh (to the Ṣūbahdār). The Khān Fatḥ-jang and Mukhliṣ Khān praised and thanked Mīrzā

Nathan and all the imperial officers. At the recommendation of Mīrzā Nathan, Mīr Saiyid Mas'ūd, an officer of Qāsim Khān, was given the Manṣab of 150 personal and 60 horse, and was included in the circle of the imperial officers. The Manṣab of Islām Qulī, at the recommendation of Mīrzā Nathan, was increased to 150 horse and he was made an imperial officer. It was decided to increase the rank of Mīrzā Nathan to 600 with 300 horse including the original and the increase. Mīr 'Abdu'r-Razzāq's Manṣab was increased by 50. Many encouraging words were sent to all of them; but neither Mīrzā Nathan nor Mīr 'Abdu'r-Razzāq was satisfied at the promotion of their ranks. He (Nathan) sent the following representation :—" My prestige itself is my promotion in rank. This is sufficient for me that I could show my firmness in my service for the welfare of the master and Qibla and bring this affair to an end, and that on my recommendation two officers of the Ṣūbahdār were promoted to the imperial cadre." In short, all the officers appointed to this frontier, particularly Mīrzā Nathan, were in great anxieties because the rumour of the arrival of the reinforcements from the Rāja of Assam was still in the air. They did not desire to go to Jahāngīrnagar and they remained at their Thānas in that state. (511)

## CHAPTER II.

*Raid of the Assamese. Strong resistance of Mīrzā Nathan. Mīr 'Abdu'r-Razzāq Shīrāzī starts for Dhāka in a state of excitement and goes to Khān Fatḥ-jang.*

**The Assam Rāja censures his officers.** The sum and substance of this long account is as follows: When the death of Shaykh Ibrāhīm received publicity, and was heard by the Rāja of Assam, he became displeased with his Sardārs and wrote to them.—" The destruction of the Shaykh is due to your treacherous conduct. Now if you do not compensate for it, you will feel its consequences." Therefore, this news was reported to Mīrzā Nathan. The Mīrzā reported the state of affairs to the Ṣūbahdār and the imperial officers at Dhāka and busied himself in his own duties. (512)

**'Abdu'r-Razzāq leaves for Jahāngīrnagar.** Mīrzā Nathan, without knowing the true state of facts that Shaykh Ibrāhīm had been killed by his own state-elephant, had presented Mīr 'Abdu'r-Razzāq with a *chakna* or tuskless elephant of his own as a reward for his hard fighting, and had thus made the Mīr famous for his bravery among the people of the world. But the Mīr became very proud of himself and started for Jahāngīrnagar without obtaining leave from the Mīrzā. Within a short time he presented himself before the Khān Fatḥ-jang. For some time he continued to be under the displeasure of the Khān; at last he presented the elephant given to him by the Mīrzā to the minister Mukhliṣ Khān and thus saved himself from disgrace and repentance. But the Khān Fatḥ-jang entertained some grudge in his mind against the Mīrzā and the Mīr because of the presentation of the aforesaid elephant by the Mīrzā to the Mīr and also because of its transfer by the Mīr to Mukhliṣ Khān. He began to make enquiries about it, as will be narrated in the course of this episode. (513)

**Mirzā Yūsuf sent to recapture Pāndū.** Mīrzā Yūsuf along with the force of Pāndū was again ordered to proceed to reconquer Pāndū which had been captured by Rāja Baldev without any battle after its evacuation and to occupy it by the favour of God. Mīrzā Yūsuf and others proceeded and pitched their camp in a *char* or island situated between Hājo and Pāndū. As Baldev had previously received the report of the despatch of this regiment and their arrival, he wrote to Budha Gosāin (i.e., Burha Gohāin),[1] Hāndī Būda (Hātī Barua), Rāj Khawā, Khār Ghūka (Khargharia Phukan), Shumāruyed Kāyeth[2] and the other chiefs of the Rāja of Assam. These people reached the mouth of the river Kalang with a large force and innumerable elephants and boats. When they received the letter, they marched from that place and encamped at the village of Budhadunagar (Bardadhigaon ?).[3] (514)

**Reinforcements sent under Satrajit.** Mīrzā Yūsuf and his regiment, surveying the strength of the enemy, wrote to Mīrzā Nathan and Mīr Ghiyāṣu'd-Dīn Maḥmūd about it and asked for reinforcements. The Mīrzā despatched Rāja Satrajit with his Hindu officer Badridās, the Dīwān, as Sazāwal, to the aid of Mīrzā Yūsuf and the regiments already despatched. They reached that place and reported themselves to Mīrzā Yūsuf and Sūnā Ghāzī Sarāilia. (515)

**Qulīj Khān arrives at Barnagar.** At this time news was received to the effect that Qulīj Khān who had been appointed from the imperial Court to the post of the Jāgīrdār and the chief of the Kūch affairs, had arrived at Barnagar. In short, although he did not immediately require any help or aid, the news of the gradual advance of the enemy was noised about and the aforesaid Khān also could not advance to Hājo without the support of his own auxiliaries and he had to remain at Barnagar. He left one of his trustworthy men named Dūst Muḥammad at the city of Gilahnay and made up his mind to take possession of some portion of this district and, after appointing another batch of officers, to proceed to Hājo with large equipments when necessary. (516)

**Measures adopted by Nathan.** In short, the letter of Mīrzā Yūsuf came at night, and next morning, the Mīrzā along with all the imperial officers went to the aforesaid station (the island in the Brahamputtra). After inspection it was decided that they should construct two strong forts on either side of the river where its course was comparatively narrow and that they should not proceed any further. If inspite of this the enemy would become too bold, then they should not stay at Hājo but should move up to this island. In short, Mīrzā Yūsuf and the party particularly Rāja Satrajit were with great difficulty persuaded to stay there, and the Mīrzā returned with the imperial officers to Hājo to his home. (517)

**Illness of Nathan.** Next morning the Mīrzā suffered from an attack of flatulence. It was so painful that he was almost collapsing. It increased to such an extent that by candle light he could not take even a drop of water and the drugs he took were not assimilated. He was brought down from his bed (*chahārpā*) and every one gave up all hope of recovery.[4] *Verse*. (Left out). At last with great difficulty the drug was assimilated. (518)

**Cowardice of Satrajit.** At this juncture, the Rāja (Satrajit), through his cowardice, fell back from the fighting line and returned to Hājo. When he left, none of the other people had the courage to confront the army of Assam. One followed the other on the plea of the former's abandonment of the out-post and ultimately all of them left. But as the Mīrzā was extremely weak, none of his attendants had the courage to report this to him. They observed complete silence and in their confusion they could think of no means to get out of the situation. Two hours after the medicine had taken effect, the Mīrzā regained his consciousness and inquired if any news had come from Mīrzā Yūsuf and the comrades of the forefront. Balabhadra Dās and Badridās, the personal assistants of the Mīrzā brought those comrades and said:— " Unable to resist the enemy, they evacuated the Thāna and all of them returned one after the other two *gharīs* before evening. They are waiting at the gate for an interview".

The Mīrzā was highly displeased and did not allow any of them to come and see him. He censured both of his personal assistants and said:—"As long as you are my personal assistants you have ample powers to censure and send these foolish and cowardly people back to their posts; or if through their cowardice, they had not courage enough to proceed, you yourselves ought to have striven for the welfare of the Emperor and left me for dead. With these powers in your hands, you ought to have ordered them about. When they could not be successful in the war, they should have fortified Hājo, the seat of the governor, within the night instead of running about and dashing their heads against walls and stones. One of you also ought to have gone to Barnagar to Qulīj Khān, the lover of pomp, to bring him here whether he wished it or not." (519)

**Qulīj Khān asked to hasten to Hājo.**—In short, after many rebukes and censures, Balabhadra Dās on his own behalf and Hājī Lang on behalf of Mīr Ghiyāṣu'd-Dīn were sent during the night to Qulīj Khān. The following letter, accompanied by imprecations and oaths, was despatched to him:—"I desire that you should not lose your fame and prestige only because I am keen about the welfare of the master and the Qibla. The Jāgīrdārship and the commandership of this territory has been assigned to you by the imperial Court. God forbid, if there is a setback, you will also be taken to task. The rebellion of Ibrāhīm came in a little while ago. He wasted his own money and misappropriated the imperial revenues. We saved the (imperial) territories (in this crisis). It was, therefore, incumbent upon you to come to Hājo, as soon as you heard of this incident. That is past. Now when the Rāja of Assam is advancing in triumph, is it worthy of you to sit idle and listen to the report listlessly? In the name of the Emperor and as it concerns also your own welfare,—I have instructed the bearers of this loyal letter that if the officers do not put their feet in the stirrup immediately after going through the letter, they should be gripped by the loin-cloth and compelled to proceed. You should not take offence at this importunity and should start before any unpleasant step is taken by these messengers. In short, I close it with a blessing. Peace (be on you)." They were sent with instructions that if the Khān hesitated to start, they should be stopped by no consideration whatever from forcing him to proceed. (520)

**Messengers sent to Shaykh Kamāl.** Badridās was appointed over Rāja Satrajit and all the Zamīndārs in order to strengthen the defence of the fort of Hājo during the night. A swift boat was despatched to inform and bring Shaykh Kamāl and the imperial officers who had been deputed to punish Ibrāhīm but who had not yet arrived. One of the eloquent and experienced servants was sent for this work. He (Nathan) kept himself busy for the whole night till morning in making preparations for the war. Balabhadra Dās and Hājī Lang rowed for the whole night and reached Barnagar near the august Khān at the first *pahar* of the day by traversing forty-seven *kos* during five *pahars* and delivered the letters. Immediately after their arrival, the Khān sent a letter to his officer Dūst Beg who was staying at Jahāngīrābād *alias* Gilahnay with four or five chiefs and a big army and who was preparing to start for this region even before the receipt of the summons from the Khān. He was asked to make a forced march without any delay from the place where the letter reached him and to join him. (521)

**Qulīj Khān reaches Hājo.** After a long discussion, the Khān was made to begin a forced march on that very day six *gharīs* before evening. After marching for the whole night and two *pahars* of the next day he arrived at the suburbs of Hājo. The Mīrzā, was informed that the Khān had arrived, without the imperial officers. He rode out with a few men and met the Khān with a sincere heart in the suburbs of the city outside the fort, and brought him to his home. After a while in an auspicious moment, the Khān was taken to the house which was arranged for him by the Mīrzā. The Khān entered the house. The portion of the food which was kept ready in a tray for the Khān was decided to be sent to the house of the Khān. The Khān ordered Qulīju'llah, Mīrzā Sayfu'd-Dawla and all his brothers to stay at Mīrzā Nathan's house and he also promised to come to Mīrzā's place in the evening. It happened as arranged. There were various kinds of music and songs by beautiful and sweet-voiced musicians, and the sound of music and song made the birds of the sky stop their wings, and even the wise lost their senses and began to dance. The varieties of sweet scents produced ebullition in the brains. The enjoyment was transferred from the private assembly to the public. After the repast of dainty food and various kinds of sweet fruits, otto of roses was sprinkled. The Khān also came and expressed his satisfaction. After this they went to their resting places. (522)

**Nathan continues to act as the Chief.** Next day, the Mīrzā went to the house of the Khān and without giving up his superior airs he began to speak thus to the Khān :—" Up till to-day whatever was to be done has been done and you should not find fault with its shortcomings.* Now when you are here, I have become your officer. In accordance with the regulations of Jahāngīr, it is obligatory that the administration of affairs should be discharged according to your advice. From to-day you act according to what you think prudent and best." The Khān replied : —" Although I have been appointed to this office by the imperial government, now when the Khān Fatḥ-jang has given the chief command to Chishtī Khān and the generalship to Shaykh Kamāl and has sent them to this region after sending a representation to the imperial Court, how can I take upon myself the management of these affairs ? Who will support me ? " The Mīrzā replied : —" To-day, myself is the chief of

* The sentence is defective : probably some words have been left out by the scribe and no sense can be made out of what remains. From the sequence, however, it would appear that something like what has been rendered in the translation was meant.

this region; as long as I take my stand (before you) with folded hands to serve the welfare of the master and the Qibla, who else is there in this frontier who can venture to disobey your orders? If they withdraw their support for other reasons, they are at liberty to do so. But how are the affairs then going to be managed? Because, with your arrival, I have ceased to hold all powers over the affairs which I so long enjoyed, and there is breach in the continuity of my authority." The Khān said:—"If you mean that any of my brothers will not abide by your advice and will not obey your orders, then you are mistaken. When I accept your leadership by placing my hand on my breast and stand on my feet for the service of the master and the Qibla, which one of my brothers will have the courage to withdraw their support from the imperial cause?" Mīrzā Nathan replied with respect and humility:—"I myself can not do anything against the orders of the honourable Khān (*Khān jiew*).[5] As you, in consideration of the welfare of the temporal Qibla and the Ka'ba, have paid this compliment with sincerity and have assigned this work to me, so it will be my look-out to seek your approval in the execution of the work of my Qibla, and I will work with your advice like a personal assistant of yours. I will not raise any objection." According to the aforesaid agreement a benedictory prayer was offered and they dispersed. Thus, after the arrival of Qulīj Khān also, the charge of the administration of imperial affairs concerning the province and the army continued to remain with Mīrzā Nathan. (523)

**Shaykh Kamāl reaches Hājo.** When the enemy, on the arrival of Qulīj Khān, heard about the proposed assemblage of the imperial officers, they halted at the station of Budhadunagar in order to get the real news and wrote to their Rāja about this matter; there was also a rumour of their retreat. Mīrzā Nathan passed his time with the imperial officers in vigilance and care. When the successive letters of Mīrzā Nathan and Mīr Ghiyāṣu'd-Dīn Maḥmūd reached Shaykh Kamāl and two more letters reached him after the arrival of Qulīj Khān and when his equipments and army joined him, he arrived at Hājo. The imperial officers went to receive him and brought him to Hājo with great honour. On the day of his arrival, Mīrzā Nathan extended a befitting hospitality and offered him a mansion which was decorated with carpets. But as the Shaykh entertained some grudge against the Mīrzā from the beginning of the regime of the late Islām Khān, so he was not sincere at heart. Therefore, he sent some insincere words to the effect that every thing that he owned was due to the Mīrzā's influence and also made other remarks of a similar nature, but did not agree to come to the aforesaid house. Neither did he come to the fort of Hājo but alighted outside the city on the side of the temple of Mādhava,[6] a great idol of the Hindus at Hājo, which is greatly revered by the people of Kāmrūp. He ordered his Zamīndār and other followers who were at Hājo to fix up their quarters on that very spot by erecting a fort. (524)

**The imperialists erect a fort at Talia.** After a week, all the imperial officers were ordered to proceed forward. Although Qulīj Khān did not personally go and stayed behind at Hājo, all his brothers were sent in the company. All the other imperial officers of the company marched with the Shaykh. When they reached a village of Kāmrūp named Talia,[7] the Zāmīndārs were asked to order their boatmen to lay the foundation of a fort of the circumference of one thousand yards and to obtain rushes from the jungles and plant them on the wall of the fort, so that the surroundings of the fort might be cleared of undergrowths and the fort might also be completed soon. The Zamīndārs issued strict orders to their admirals. Towards the close of the day, half of the fort became complete. The Shaykh with the imperial officers returned again to Hājo. (525)

**Assam army ordered to attack Hājo.** As the chiefs of the enemy wrote to their Rāja about the arrival of Qulīj Khān and then again of the arrival of Shaykh Kamāl, and also informed him that the armies of Delhi were marching on and would reach one after the other, so a letter to the following effect was addressed to them by their Rāja :—" As the armies of Delhi have not yet begun their attack and as you have already reached near them with a large army, it is proper for you to begin the battle without further delay, according to the maxim—' He never loses who strikes first ' and watch its results." (526)

**The Ahom system of taking augury.** It is the custom of the Assamese that whenever they engage in a war, they perform some sorceries a day previous to the battle in this way :—They send some magic object floating down the river towards the enemy's side. If it floats down towards the enemy's side, they take it as a good omen. If it travels upstream out of its own accord, they take it as foreboding something against them and consider it as a sign of their defeat and they do not go out to battle. In short, according to that custom, they built one raft of plantain trees which is a well-known fruit of India, and performed *puja*, i.e., worship of the devils, on it, in the following manner. They sacrificed a black man, a dog, a cat, a pig, an ass, a monkey, a he-goat, and a pigeon, all black. Their heads were collected together and placed on the raft along with many ripe bananas, *pān*, betel-nut, *chuwa* (acanthophyllum squarrosum), various kinds of scents, rice paste coloured red, yellow and green, cotton seeds, mustard seeds, mustard oil (*raughan-i-talkh*), *ghee* (*raughan-i-zard*) and *sindūr* (vermillion), and then the raft was pushed adrift. Though they tried to make it float down the stream, it did not go and every time it returned towards them. Their augury proved to be inauspicious, and it was therefore, inadvisable on their part to come to the battle But as the death of so many thousands of men was ordained, they were compelled to fight, as will be narrated below in course of this episode. (527)

**The disposition of Assam forces.** On that very night, the chiefs of the Rāja of Assam came to fight arranging their armies in this order:—The Burha Gohāin at the head of one hundred thousand infantry was to move along the hilly and jungly bank of the Brahmaputtra, leaving the hillock of Sultan Ghiyāṣu'd-Dīn Awliya,[8] on account of whom will be given in the course of this episode,—to his right, and the temple of Kedār,[9] the description of which also will follow, to his left, in order to attack Qulīj Khān, Mīrzā Nathan and those who were in the fort of Hājo, and to finish them. Hātī Barua, Rāja Baldev and Shumāruyed Kāyeth with a force of two hundred thousand infantry, one hundred and eighty elephants consisting of *mast* (heated) and *hushiar-mast*, i.e. the elephants who have not yet come to the state of *mast* or heat,—there is a herb found in Assam called *sarfil* which when administered to the elephants, makes them *mast* within eight *pahars*—were to go along with him by the other side of the river in order to fall upon Shaykh Kamāl, to sweep him off and not to allow even a bird to fly out of the cordon by a charge from the rear. The Rajkhawā, and the Kharghuka (Khargharia Phukan) were to take the command of the fleet consisting of four thousand war-boats of the class of *mānd*, *bachārī*, *kūsa* and *kūs*, in order to attack the fleet of the Twelve Bhuyans who were loyally supporting the imperialists,—to seize them and not to allow any of them to escape by the river with his fleet. The Eighteen Hill-Rājas, who sided with the enemy and rebelled against the imperialists, were to take their position with all their hill-men on the bank of the river to the left of their fleet in order to aid it and not to allow any body to escape towards the Dakhinkul. One thousand war-boats were sent to the mouth of the river Rawrowa[10] to the rear of the imperial army in order to block the passage of ration and communication from Jahāngīrnagar *alias* Dhāka during the days of the seige. In short, the imperial army was brought to bay like games in a hunt. (528)

**The massacre at the shrine of Ghiyāṣu'd-Dīn.** At midnight, the Burha Gohāin came by the hilly and jungly tracks to the hillock of Sultan Ghiyāṣu'd-Dīn Awliyā and the first act perpetrated by him was the massacre of the devotees of that holy shrine. One of the devotees saved himself with very great difficulty and came to the foot of the hillock half-dead. Below the hillock was the residence of Mīrzā Qulīju'llah, son of Qulīj Khān, the cousin (uncle's son) of Qulīch Khān *alias* Bāltū Qulīj, and also of his brother-in-law and Mīrzā Sayfu'd-Dawla. He informed them.[11] Both these noble sons thought that the enemies were small in number and rushed upon them without informing Qulīj Khān about it; and with the idea that they were merely a number of bandits, they went up the hillock and fell upon them. After a short skirmish they found that the enemies were very strong. Thus engaged in the battle, they sent news to the Khān. When the Khān was preparing to go to their aid, an army of the enemy came and attacked the stockade of the Khān which was situated on a small hillock. As this side was strongly fortified, he left his Dīwān Rāy Kāsīdās in the aforesaid intrenchment with a division of experienced soldiers and he himself went to the aid of his brothers. Dūst Beg, who arrived at Hājo after four days of the arrival of the Khān and who was staying in a house on the road leading to the temple of Kedār with a contingent of twenty thousand men, went with his associate chiefs to the aid of the Khān and his brothers, and joined the battle. The enemies came from all sides. Every one of them was killed wherever he was found and was not allowed to proceed farther. *Maṡnavī* (left out). (529)

**Attack on Hājo by land and water.** At the appearance of the dawn with the rising of the sun when Shaykh Kamāl was preparing to go to the aid of Qulīj Khān, the Hātī Barua, Rāja Baldev and Shumāruyed Kāyeth appeared in the front with a huge army and innumerable elephants and infantry advancing in awe-inspiring formations. Shaykh Kamāl arrayed his army in collaboration with his brothers, Rāja Satrajit and some imperial Manṣabdārs, and advanced to fight. They began to shoot arrows and fire guns. Mīrzā Nathan, who was in the main fort of Hājo situated in the centre, proposed to come to the battle to the aid of Qulīj Khān fully armed with all the 'Usmānī Afghān Manṣabdārs who along with some other Manṣabdars were staying with him from before. At this juncture the imperial fleet of the Zamīndārs was attacked (by the Assam fleet) with the aid of their land-force posted to its left and to the right of the Burha Gohāin. It was driven to the foot of the fort of the imperialists. It was also reported that a big army with many elephants had fallen upon Shaykh Kamāl and he was put to great straits. Therefore, he (Mīrzā Nathan) took his stand in a position of vantage to serve the purpose of a reserve. A message was sent to Qulīj Khān:—" The enemies have come from all sides and are fighting in every place. The fleet of the enemy has triumphed and has beaten the fleet of the loyal Zamīndārs in such a way that more than half their boats have been driven to the bank. If you think that you are on the point of defeat and if you do not require my services in any quarter, then I would propose to join you. If you think that ultimately you may have the need of sending me to the aid of some other division I would take my stand in the reserve (*ṭarah*) and I would run to support whomsoever I find in distress from the attack of the enemy." Qulīj Khān approved of this idea and said that it was prudent. In short, in the meanwhile, he sent one of his trustworthy men to Sūnā Ghāzī of Sarāil and to Islām Qulī to encourage them with the following messages:—" Be not anxious; at the time of difficulty think that I am present with you. Do not take your boats away from the shore to deep waters. If any necessity arises, our land-force will be able to attack the boats and fight (with the enemy)." (530)

**Defeat of the Assam land-force.** At this juncture, Shaykh Kamāl sent one of his soldiers to Mīrzā Nathan with a message, demanding his presence. The Mīrzā in reply to the Shaykh sent one of his men in his company, saying:—" Qulīj Khān has posted me in the reserve in order to help the regiment which is being overpowered by the enemy. I am watching and I will not let slip any opportunity that comes up." When they departed, the Mīrzā sent for his helmet and cuirass and began to put them on. Before he could put his second hand into the sleeve of the cuirass (*baghtar*), all on a sudden Rāmdās, a Hindu officer of the Shaykh, made his appearance and cried out :—" If aid is delayed by a moment, every thing will be lost." The men on horseback watching from the hills and eminences also cried out : —" Alas ! alas ! the enemy has swept the regiment of the Shaykh." Then the Mīrzā shouted to his fellow-warriors, and spurring his horse, he rushed out like a lion. When he reached near the temple of Mādhava, he saw that an imperial elephant named Bhetdanta, was flying from the troop of the Shaykh. The Mīrzā thought that as he was unable to take his own big elephant as it had a wound, so probably the Shaykh had sent this elephant in advance for his use to engage in battle with this elephant in his front. But when the animal passed through the soldiers and received several arrow-shots, the Mīrzā definitely understood that the Shaykh had been defeated. The cry of *Allah-u-Akbar* (God, the Great) the shout of *Ya-Mu'Yin* (O, the Helper !) were raised and an immediate rush was made by raising the swords like standards. The army of the enemy, which had come out of its position of vantage and was storming the troop of the Shaykh, was attacked by him in its flank. By the aid of the Lord of Honour, they were repelled after a short skirmish. Then he fell upon the army led by Hātī Barua, Rāja Baldev and Shumāruyed Kāyeth and gave such a fight that it became a prototype of the Day of Resurrection and produced nervousness even in the angel of death in his act of seizing the souls, and the remembrance of God was carried to the highest limit. All the (five ?) hundred youths possessing the characteristics of lions and the fury of dragons paralyzed all the vanquished Assamese. They fell upon them like lions which fall upon a flock of sheep and tear them to pieces. The dead lay in heaps upon one another. The generals of Assam fought so hard that all their quivers became empty of arrows, and the *duta-*

*dāns* (bags for keeping short javelins) became empty of *dutas*, i.e. a kind of javelin which they throw with the strength of their arm and which is always used by them in battles. The affair came to such a pass that they began to hurl from elephant's back their naked *hangdāns* i.e. a kind of half-swords, which they carry in their belts. The *dutas* which struck any man or horse used to pierce them through. (Here follows a *Maṣnavī* poem describing this battle, in which it is said that the Assam army was led by the Hātī Barua; it gives no new information).

When fortune favoured the imperial officers, Shaykh Kamāl also, seeing the stand made by the Mīrzā, returned and joined the war, and a great victory which may be considered as one of the foremost military conquests was attained by the favour of God. The Hātī Barua, Rāja Baldev and Shumāruyed Kāyeth, scattering the dust of disgrace on their heads took their way to the jungles as vagrants. The valiant fighters with all their might and ferocity pursued them without making any discrimination between high and low lands. The Mīrzā shouted to his cavalry to put to the dreadful sword every one of the enemy who had raised his hand of audacity. But they made no attempt to capture their elephants, and the enemy were allowed to flee; otherwise none of the elephants could have gone out of hand. (531)

**Plan for the defence of the main fort.** In short, when they advanced a short distance, news came from the rear that although the large land-army of the enemy was beaten, the army on the hill which was fighting with Qulīj Khān in co-operation with their fleet had defeated the imperial fleet and had driven Qulīj Khān to the temple of Mahādev. Qulīj Khān thinking death to be inevitable, did not make a retreat, and he was faced with a great disaster. Therefore, Mīr Ghiyāṣu'd-Dīn Maḥmūd, the Dīwān and Bakhshī and Mīrzā Nathan ran to the aid of the Khān. The Shaykh also followed them. As the news was brought by an officer of Mīrzā Nathan, so he (the Mīrzā) ran to the help of the Khān ahead of all others. The followers of the Khān were busy in the battle in the same way. Mīrzā Nathan said, "Honourable Khān! The enemies have come to the field with a large number of elephants, and their infantry, is keeping in the hills and jungles, and helping their naval attack. We have not yet been able to repel them and the night is approaching. Under these circumstances, it is proper to think out a plan. If by the time of sunset, the enemies do not run away by scattering the dust of disgrace on their heads and take their way to vagrancy, then we should pass the night with vigilance and care". The Khān replied, "When my comrades have come to my aid after setting their affairs in order, then it is impossible that we should make a retreat from the battle with the pretext of strengthening the fort. That will not be discharging our responsibilities (faithfully). Secondly, the attention of all the officers and workmen of the fleet is directed towards you two. You do whatever you think best for the welfare of the master and the Qibla." Mīrzā Nathan said to the Shaykh:—"If you consider my advice reasonable, you may write to all the imperial officers, small and great, at the time when you direct the posting of the fleet of the loyal Zamīndārs,—that it is advisable for them to leave the river bank and come and stay under the protection of the fort you have raised. We shall endeavour to strengthen that fort of yours by raising a wide wall; if you on the other hand, agree to come to this fort then we should strengthen this fort." The Shaykh replied:—"It is not possible either to help the fleet or to defend it without posting the land-force in this fort. But on whom can I shift my responsibility and leave my own fort to come to yours?" Qulīj Khān gave him a note with his own seal to this effect: "As the welfare of the State demands, it was arranged that the Shaykh also should come from his own fort to this fort." When the Shaykh received the document with the seal of the Khān, he replied, "I shall not be satisfied till it is sealed by Mīrzā Nathan and Mīr Ghiyāṣu'd-Dīn, so that it may not be said in future that the Shaykh was unable to defend his fort and so had to come to our fort." Mīrzā Nathan said, "If this humble self is asked to put his seal on this document then he would attest and write in this way:—'As it was found advisable and obligatory to protect the fleet and as the fleet was unable to move to the foot of the fort of the Shaykh, so all the imperial officers agreed upon this that the Shaykh should come to the old fort of Hājo,' so that you also will not be able to say that Qulīj Khān and Mīrzā Nathan could not defend their fort. Therefore, it is necessary that we should go and defend the aforesaid fort." The Shaykh at first did not agree, but at last when he saw that there was no way out, he agreed to it. He took the aforesaid document with the seal of Qulīj Khān and with the signatures and the seals of attestation of Nathan and Mīr Ghiyāṣu'd-Dīn Maḥmūd. After this it was settled that both these great men, after placing their own regiments as well as of all the imperial Manṣabdārs under Qulīj Khān, would leave him to go and strengthen the fort along with some servants and footmen of the Mīr Bakhshī. (532)

**Defeat of the Assam navy.** All these three nobles started accordingly. The Shaykh suggested that they should go round the entire fort from one end to the other and arrangements should be made to extend or reduce it. Mīrzā Nathan replied:—"The area of the fort is nine thousand yards; it will be evening by the time we go round it. It is proper to go to the mansion of the Khān which is situated on the hill. If we go riding on an elephant to that place, the whole of the fort, being below it, will be visible. After that the places which require reduction will be reduced in size whereas those which require extension will be extended otherwise by the time we finish going round the whole of the fort, it will get dark." The Shaykh as well as the Mīr Bakhshī approved of this. The Mīrzā and the Shaykh proceeded by riding on the howdah of an elephant. Although there was sufficient room in the howdah of the elephant, Mīr Ghiyāṣu'd-Dīn Maḥmūd, in consideration of his own convenience, rode on a horse and accompanied them. When they came up the hill they began to reconnoitre. At this juncture, as the Wise Lord had ordained victory (to the imperialists), so the fleet of the enemy was passing by it (the hill), in the belief that the imperial fleet of the Zamīndārs had been worsted. On this hillock, imperial cannon were kept ready in the mansion of the Khān. Mīrzā Nathan shouted to the *gulandāz* (cannoniers) to discharge their cannon on the enemy's boats which were proceeding after defeating the imperial fleet. He pointed out two boats in particular in which the chiefs were coming with audacity and impertinence. Two cannon which were fully loaded were fired by the cannoniers relying on the favour of the Merciful Lord. Though the shots passed over the boats without touching any man or boat and fell into the water, as the Lord had ordained victory to the Muslims, the soldiers and the boatmen of these boats jumped into the river in a panic. The men of all the boats of the enemy, at the sight of the condition of the boats of their chiefs, jumped into water in terror without knowing who was attacking them. They considered death by drowning better than their safety in the boats. Many of their boats were driven to the bank of the river where they disembarked and took to flight and having scattered the dust of disgrace on their heads they began to wander about in the jungles as vagrants. The leaders of the imperial fleet considered this God-given victory as one of their greatest victories and offered thanks to the True Lord with their heart and soul. They fell upon the fleet of the vanquished enemy and seized a very large booty. The imprudent enemy were put to the blood-thirsty swords and were despatched to hell, and those who sought protection in humility were made captives. *Maṣnavī* (Left out). (533)

. **Death of the Burha Gohāin.** When the Burha Gohāin was engaged in the battle on the hill with his contingents of infantry, more than a hundred thousand strong, the fleet of the enemy was engaged in fight depending on the help of this army and this army also similarly depended on the fleet.

At the sight of the defeat of their fleet, they lost heart and a great confusion appeared among them. Their weakness became apparent to the intelligent people. At this moment Shaykh Kamāl and the Mīr Bakhshī said to Mīrzā Nathan, "What can we do, standing here? We should move on and set to our own work." Mīrzā Nathan replied, "At this time when symptoms of enemy's weakness are visible and their fleet had been repelled by the imperial fleet, and the army of Qulīj having come up the hill are engaged in struggle with the expectation that they would drive the enemy off if reinforcements come and would attack the enemy from the rear,—what is the use of going to fortify the garrison at such a time instead of going to the aid of this army?" Mīr Ghiyāṣu'd-Dīn Maḥmūd Bakhshī expressed the opinion that what the Mīrzā had said was quite right. The Shaykh also did not raise any objection. The Mīrzā placed his hand on the back of the elephant-driver and getting the wall of the fort broken by that female elephant, he entered into his fort. Then he took with him a contingent of his companions and camp-followers and came out of the fort through that breach and proceeded towards the enemy to aid the men engaged in the battle. The cry of *Allah-u-Akbar* was raised. The war loving men with all their might fell furiously upon the enemy who were engaged in the battle, and after a short skirmish they were repelled. Thus the Burha Gohāin was unknowingly killed by one of the officers of the Manṣabdārs whose name and position could not be ascertained. The victory was attained and the trumpet of good-tidings and the kettle-drum of conquest were sounded. Qulīj Khān also came up the hill, expressed his satisfaction, and met all the imperial officers, high and low. From there they returned to their homes with a happy heart by playing the trumpet of joy. A report of this victory was sent to the Khān Fatḥ-jang, the Ṣūbahdār, and they passed the night in rest. (534)

**Casualties and booties.** Next morning all the imperial officers, high and low, rode on horses and went to the place from which the enemy had come to fight. They inspected the forts of the enemy and found that nine strong forts had been built by them close to each other in such a way that even heated elephants working without fear of opposition or danger would not be able to make any impression on the wall of the forts which were made entirely of logs of wood, not to speak of having them dismantled or razed to the ground. In short, when a stock was taken, it was found that out of four thousand war-boats of the enemy engaged in the battle, only two hundred boats escaped, and three thousand and eight hundred boats of the class of *kūsa, bachārī* and *mānd* were seized. Besides, these, seven magnificient elephants and a large booty were secured. The enemy lost three thousand and seven hundred men on the field of battle; double of this number died in the adjacent places and more than ten thousand wounded men fled away half-dead. Of the imperial, high and low, two hundred attained martyrdom and double this number were wounded. Therefore the age began to praise it in language appropriate to the occasion, and the people of the age became a thousand times happier. The heads of the dead enemies were cut off and loaded in the *mānds*-boats and were sent to Jahāngīrnagar to the Khān Fatḥ-jang along with the elephants and the different kinds of booties seized from the enemy. (535)

**Dissensions in the Mughal camp.** But when Shaykh Kamāl sent an absolutely false report to the Khān Fatḥ-jang saying that the victory in this war was attained by him and Mīrzā Nathan had done nothing in this battle, Mīrzā Nathan began to burn within himself in rage at this falsehood which was as clear as the sun. Inspite of his devoted and loyal service, the Khān Fatḥ-jang had appointed Chishtī Khān to take the chief command in the Kūch territory. So his anger increased and he wanted to go to the Khān Fatḥ-jang. The Shaykh thought in his mind that when Mīrzā Nathan would go to the Khān Fatḥ-jang, he would prove that the Shaykh was defeated, and he would have nothing to say in reply. So he instigated Qulīj Khān, the Mīr Bakhshī and all the officers, high and low, against Mīrzā Nathan saying that as long as the question of punishing the Rāja of Assam was before them, they should not allow him to go and they should detain him whether he liked it or not. Rāja Satrajit and the Bakhshī were sent to him with this message :—" As you are going away leaving the imperial affairs in a state of disorder, we will not allow you to go and we will detain you by force." It was also proclaimed that as Mīrzā Nathan was going away leaving the imperial affairs in disorder, no charge would be entertained against any imperialist who would beat and kill Mīrzā Nathan and his men. The Mīrzā replied to the Mīr Bakhshī: —" Why do you involve yourself in this affair and risk your life ? Are you so audacious as to oppose me ? Tell the Shaykh that I will depart six *gharīs* before evening. I challenge you to oppose me and I swear that I will deal with you just as I have dealt with the Assamese. Do not think that your forces will be any use to you. Do you think that the imperial officers who were my companions yesterday and all of whom are my protegees will remain standing as spectators ? Qulīj Khān is not a man of the type that will join with you in these braggings of yours. So the question is between you and me. I shall teach you such a lesson that henceforth you will never indulge in such strange plans in your life." The Mīr Bakhshī, Rāja Satrajit and some other junior Manṣabdārs who were in their company went and reported thus to the Shaykh who was waiting at the sandy plain of the river along with all the imperial officers : —" Mīrzā Nathan does not belong to that class of imperial servants who would run off from his place at the stampings of your feet or at our words. After another four *gharīs* he will start. If you are particularly desirous of fighting, you may fight with your own men and Qulīj Khān is not going to stand in his way. When the Khān has withdrawn himself from this affair, I, being the Bakhshī, will also not take part in this battle. When I secede none of the junior Manṣabdārs will obstruct him. After that you and the party of imperial servants will be left alone. When it will come to actual fighting, these servants also will remain as spectators, and the whole burden will fall upon you two (i.e., Kamāl and Satrajit). Under these circumstances, you may maintain your prestige or cast it to the winds, but you can not make us responsible. Now the thread of better sense is in your hands.

*Verse* :

I tell you what the law of eloquence demands,
Whether you accept the admonition or be sorry at my words.

Therefore, Shaykh Kamāl, having scrutinised the daily record of his own condition, gave up this plan in order to save himself from disgrace, and returned to his quarters. But he wrote a letter with his own seal to the naval officers of the Zamīndārs not only to oppose the officers of Mīrzā Nathan and not allow them to take the boats of the enemy which had fallen into the hands of Mīrzā Nathan's officers, but they should also attack and seize his private boats. If in this struggle any man of Mīrzā Nathan were killed, the Shaykh promised to be answerable to the Ṣūbahdār and the Emperor. Therefore, although Satrajit and his naval-force did not agree to this proposal, Sūnā Ghāzī the Zamīndār of Sarāil and Islām Qulī a creature of Mīrzā Nathan who entertained malice in his heart (against the Mīrzā), barred the way of Mīrzā Nathan. (536)

**Nathan leaves for Jahāngīrnagar.** The Mīrzā set out for Jahāngīrnagar at an auspicious moment and his start was announced by beat of drums. He ordered his fleet to proceed cautiously keeping close to the bank of the river and to teach a good lesson to those who would attempt any violence. In short, the men of the Mīrzā proceeded safely to a distance of three stations according to the settled plan with care and vigilance. The fleet sent by the Shaykh used to fire guns and cannon from far and near. The followers of the Mīrzā did not retaliate without the permission of their master. When the Mīrzā saw the violence of the naval officers, he sent this message to them :—" Proceeding for three nights and days under the showers of bullets, we have reached the limit of showing regard to the imperial regulations. Now it is all right if you go back; otherwise you cannot imagine what will be its consequences." He told his own men:—"If this message turns them back, it is well and good; otherwise you launch an attack and then move your boats to the bank. Let them once come to the bank to attack and they will draw on themselves their own punishment." He took his stand in military array and posting the elephants in his front became ready for an assault. Islām Qulī, who was aware of the Mīrzā's nature thought within himself that now the affair would take a different turn and so he became conciliatory. He gave up the attempt and returned to Hājo. The Mīrzā then sent back his Manṣabdār comrades who had come in his company as friends, with many excuses, and he began to proceed onwards from stage to stage. Within a short time he arrived at the *chawkī* of Rangamāṭī. He left his army and the elephants at the aforesaid place, and reached Jahāngīrnagar within a few days. (537)

**Displeasure of the Ṣūbahdār.** In an auspicious moment he met the Khān Fatḥ-jang, the Ṣūbahdār, and Mukhliṣ Khān, the imperial Dīwān. In the first interview the Khān asked him in a furious mood, "What is the object of your coming here by leaving the imperial affairs in a state of chaos?" The Mīrzā replied, "If I would have created chaos I could have done it when Ibrāhīm rose in rebellion and Assam also pressed on its campaigns. In short, to be just, the real fact is this that I have come here after putting a lustre to the affairs of that country." In short, the Khān got up without uttering a word and the Mīrzā returned to his residence and took rest. Next day, he went to the Khān Fatḥ-jang and after an exchange of a few words the Khān Fatḥ-jang said to Mīrzā Nathan, "Whether you like it or not, you must return to Hājo." The Mīrzā replied, "It will never be. I have so long been the chief of that frontier; now it will be a disgrace for me to serve under the orders of another." The Khān Fatḥ-jang said in an angry tone, "How did you serve under the

Shaykhs during the regime of Islām Khān and Qāsim Khān?" Had the Khān said some thing more and gone beyond limit, the Mīrzā would have killed himself as well as the Khān. Thus overpowered with anger he shed tears and said, "At that time I thought that I was like one of the bondmen which the Firingis keep and thus helpless, I had to work for the welfare of the master and the Qibla. This time, I cherished the idea that God the Great has sent a patron who can appreciate merit and has made Bengal again a land of Islām. Now as you are following the same track I am of opinion that the reign of the Firingis and the Mags is still prevailing." Then he put his hand on his dagger and wanted to commit suicide. Thereupon, Mukhliṣ Khān came to his aid and extinguished the fire of the anger of both. He said, "I also, being displeased with Sultan Parvīz, came from the Deccan to the imperial Court. His Majesty, the Shadow of God, (may a thousand lives be sacrificed for him), insisted that I should go back to Parvīz. I was hopeful of my deliverance even when His Majesty swore and ordered that I must go. Then seeing my disappointment and despair, His Majesty took pity on me, he smiled and consoled me by saying that he did not know that I was dissatisfied with Parvīz to such an extent, and then he granted me liberty. Now, at this moment I find the condition of Mīrzā Nathan similar to that of mine." Then the Khān Fath-jang made his apologies, consoled Mīrzā Nathan and granted him leave to go to his house. The Mīrzā went to his home and passed the night in contemplation. (538)

**Mukhlis Khān consoles Nathan.** Next morning Mukhliṣ Khān came to console Mīrzā Nathan as well as to offer a benedictory prayer for the late Ihtimām Khān who was related to him, and for whom he had not previously offered this prayer after his death. After their meeting and the offering of the benedictory prayer, he consoled Mīrzā Nathan. Mīrzā Nathan presented him with nine horses of the class of 'Irāqī, cross breed, coloured Tāngan and Kachhī (of Cutch) along with a hundred *thāns* of rare cloths of Bengal, one maund of high class *agar* (aloe-wood), and Rs. 5,000 in cash with this excuse that the cloth was given for his carpet, the horses and the *agars* as *pēshkash* or present, and the cash for his entertainment. After this trayfuls of sweet scents and *pāns* (betel leafs) were offered to him. Mukhliṣ Khān, in order to please Mīrzā Nathan, accepted the *agar* and one coloured Tāngan horse and the rest of the things and horses were returned to him and then he went back to his home. He then continued his visits to the Khān Fatḥ-jang in usual way. (539)

**Nathan deputed to conquer the Dakhinkul.** When the New Year's Day arrived and the great luminary entered the sign Aries and the dejected mortals were adorned and refreshed like the heavenly bodies, the Ṣūbahdār arranged a happy banquet in presence of Mukhliṣ Khān. Every day varieties of delicious food, different kinds of fruits and sweets were prepared in large quantites and the days of the needy people were made happy. One day there arose another dispute between the Khān and Mīrzā Nathan. Then it was decided that as since the time of the conquest of the Kūch territory the Sarkār of the Dakhinkul was not taken possession of by any one on whom it was settled in lieu of his salary, the Mīrzā should go along with his own regiment and an auxiliary force consisting of more than seven hundred horsemen and matchlock-men, fifty war-boats and ten heated elephants of the State in order to sweep away all the disturbing elements there and after occupying a secure position in that region he should take it as his assignment. (540)

## CHAPTER III.

*Departure of Mīrzā Nathan in order to clear the Dakhinkul and the despatch of Chand Bahādur, the chief officer of Khān Fatḥ-jang with Mūsā Khān, the Zamīndār, and the Twelve Būmia, i.e., the Twelve Zamīndārs of Bengal and Bhātī, against Madhūsudan son of Jisketu (Brishaketu) a nephew of Rāja Lakshmī Narāyan, Rāja of Kūch, who without the consent of the Rāja had attacked Karaibārī the homeland (waṭn) of the sons of Dumria, a relative of Rāja Parikshit and had captured all of them. They were instructed to bring him to the Court and to establish a Thāna at Karaibārī.*

**Promotion of Nathan.** The substance of this account is as follows:—The details of the appointment of Mīrzā Nathan has already been mentioned before. The Mīrzā was given leave to depart in an auspicious moment with the Manṣab of 700 (personal) and 350 horse including the original and the increase. It was settled that Mīrzā Aḥmad Beg would bring in the rear and after arranging the auxiliary forces at Patladah and consigning them to his (Nathan's) charge he (Aḥmad Beg) would proceed to his destination. (541)

**Expedition against Madhūsudan.** Now I shall give a short account of the condition of the people of Kūch. It was reported to the Khān Fatḥ-jang that Madhūsudan,[1] son of Jisketu (Brishaketu) a relation of Rāja Lakshmī Narāyan, had come from his country towards the Dakhinkul and seized Karaibārī, the most central part of the Kūch country, and was trying to fortify it. It was inadvisable to allow him to stay there. Therefore, Mīrzā Aḥmad was appointed to that task. Chand Bahādur, the chief of the officers of the Khān Fatḥ-jang was given the command and was sent against Madhūsudan along with Mūsā Khān, son of 'Īsā Khān, the Zamīndār; and many other Zamīndārs who were kept under surveillance during the regime of Islām Khān and Qāsim Khān, were granted freedom and were sent along with him. They were instructed to bring Madhūsudan to the court by means of their wisdom and sword in co-operation with Chand Bahādur. If he refused to surrender, he would have only to thank himself for his own punishment. Accordingly, by the time Chand Bahādur was granted leave to start for Karaibārī and Mīrzā Nathan for the Dakhinkul, Mūsā Khān and the Zamīndārs reached Karaibārī before their (Chand Bahādur and Mīrzā Nathan's) arrival at Karaibārī, and brought Madhūsudan as a vassal to Khiẓrpūr to the Khān Fatḥ-jang. (542)

**Nathan reaches Rangamātī.** Then the Khān did not send Mīrzā Aḥmad Beg. He wrote to Chand Bahādur that he should stay at Karaibārī and after making necessary arrangements of reinforcements for Mīrzā Nathan, he should be sent off for the conquest of the Dakhinkul. Accordingly, the Mīrzā left his agent with Chand Bahādur to bring the auxiliary forces and he started for Rangamātī taking with him four elephants of the auxiliary force. He reached that place within a short time and halted there. (543)

**Nathan proceeds to Jasīpūr.** At the appearance of the rainy season he (Nathan) wrote to Ibrāhīm Khān that as the rainy season had already commenced and the auxiliary forces had not yet arrived, so he would decide to stay there; and he also requested him to urge upon Chand Bahādur to despatch the auxiliaries before the end of the rainy season. As aloe-woods (*agar*) of Kūch were presented to Mukhliṣ Khān and not to him, so the Khān Fatḥ-jang was displeased with Mīrzā Nathan. So the Khān became indifferent about the despatch of the auxiliaries and wrote the following unpleasant letter to the Mīrzā :—" Why did you advance without waiting to take the auxiliaries ? Because you have halted at Rangamātī do you want to fix up your permanent residence there on that plea ? If you do not proceed to the invasion of the Dakhinkul immediately on the receipt of this letter you will earn disgrace before the imperial court." The Mīrzā without refuting the words of the Khān, started for the Dakhinkul with his regiment, by the river Brahmaputtra immediately after the receipt of the letter. He reached the village of Jasīpūr,[2] an intervening place between the Dakhinkul and the pargana of Mechpara, and halted there. (544)

**The fleet at Chandankūth sent to Nathan.** He (Nathan) wrote to the Khān Fatḥ-jang :—"Please do not consider me to be a man of that class who is unable to undertake this expedition during the rainy season. I am already on the move ; you may or may not send auxiliaries and the success of the war or the disgrace for undertaking this expedition will devolve on you. If at this moment you are unable to send any other reinforcement, then please send the aid of the fleet. The rest of the arrangements and hard labour will depend on our loyalty. Let us see what result comes out of the invisible screen according to the will of the Merciful Lord." The Khān wrote a letter to Mīr Ghiyāṣu'd-Dīn Maḥmūd, the Dīwān and Bakhshī of Kūch to the effect that the fleet which was at the Thāna of Chandankūth with Islām Qulī should, on the receipt of this letter be sent to Mīrzā Nathan who had been sent with the chief command for the conquest of the Dakhinkul and the suppression of the rebels. Islām Qulī should be sent with his fleet to Mīrzā Nathan to serve in whatever place he is ordered to do so. The aforesaid Mīr through the machination and friendship of Mīr 'Abdu'r-Razzāq detained Islām Qulī by some pretext and sent fourteen ill-equipped boats to the Mīrzā. (545)

**Nathan proceeds against Parsurām.** But before the arrival of the boats and the departure of the Mīrzā, a rebel of the Dakhinkul named Parsurām made plundering raids and blocked the passage of transit of rations for the army in Kūch and Assam. In a way, Qulij Khān, Shaykh Kamāl and the inhabitants of Hājo were put to great straits. Salt was sold at Rs. 42 per maund ; and butter could not be obtained even by paying Rs. 1-8-0 per seer. The creatures of God, being very helpless, sent news to Ibrāhīm Khān with very great difficulties. The Khān sent the aforesaid letter to Mīrzā

Nathan and peremptorily ordered him (to proceed against Parsurām). But it was not an easy thing to do. The Mīrzā then recruited a force of one hundred horsemen and five hundred matchlock-men and proceeded for the subjugation of the pargana of Sāmbhūr and particularly Solmārī which was the centre of Parsurām's activities. After seven marches he arrived at Phulbārī, a village of the pargana of Bāghwān[3] and raised a strong fort there. It was settled that he would leave his family and the belongings of his followers in that place and advance against the enemy by the routes of Bānsbārī and Kantabārī dividing his army into two regiments. (546)

**Parsurām advances to Kantabārī.** In the meantime, the accursed Parsurām having received information of this plan, came with a force of fourteen thousand, and became ready for battle by raising strong stockades in the defile of Kantabārī[4] on either side of a hill. As the pargana of Mechpara and Maluapara[5] were in the Jāgīr of Qulīj Khān, so two of the chief officers of Qulīj Khān named Tāj Khān and Taslīm Khān who stayed there with a force of three hundred horsemen and fifteen hundred infantry, came and met the Mīrzā and explained to him the real state of activities of the rebels. The Mīrzā then found it advisable to adopt the following procedure. He took with him a troop of fifty picked horsemen, three hundred infantry and three elephants which could be accommodated in boats and then proceeded to Chandankūth, leaving the rest of his army and Taslīm Khān and other men of Qulīj Khān in that place. He took from Taslīm Khān two officers named Dutiārī and Bāmun with two hundred expert infantry from the pargana of Mechpara and arrived at Sāmbhūr. (547)

**Defeat and flight of Parsurām.** The aforesaid Parsurām, informed of the departure of Mīrzā Nathan, posted ten thousand men in advance and he himself arrived at Sāmbhūr before the arrival of the Mīrzā, marching by the side of the river and the hills with a force of four thousand infantry, and became ready for the battle by raising a fort on the bank of the river. As soon as the fleet of the Mīrzā reached the bank of the river in safety and the soldiers were going to land, the rebels fired from above a volley of guns, cannon and arrows. Then it became evident that the rebels had fortified the bank of the river. Therefore, the Mīrzā also divided his army into three regiments, two of cavalry and elephants and the other of infantry. The enemy in the fort were also divided into two divisions and protected themselves under the cover of the huge walls of the fort and the dense forest. So one regiment was sent under the command of Mīr 'Abdu's-Samad, one of the most valiant and experienced warriors of the Mīrzā, with instructions to keep one division of enemy's army engaged in battle so that by the favour of God the other two regiments of cavalry and infantry might be able to finish the work of the stronger regiment of the enemy. Then the command of the second battalion was given to one of the bravest warriors of the Mīrzā named Mast 'Alī Beg and a heated elephant named Shāh 'Ināyat was attached to his company. It was said to him :—" I will send the battalion of the infantry ahead of you under the command of Nīk Muḥammad. He will go to attack the fort of the enemy and will press them hard. You should post the elephant in your front and take shelter under this hillock with your regiment and taking your position behind the hillock, you should deliver such an attack from a position of vantage depending on the will of God, that the enemy may not get any time to breathe and may become unable to move their hands and feet. With the aid of the Lord, mete out such a punishment to them by sweeping them like a ball with the polo-stick of bravery, that they might become like a cub which tasted its mother's milk only on the day of its birth and was then deprived of its sweet taste for ever. You should finish the work in such a way that it may be talked of in the histories of the age." Therefore, both the divisions of the cavalry, charged as above, proceeded forward. Nīk Muhammad with his infantry advanced ahead of all, attacked the fort and had a battle evenly balanced. Volleys of arrows, guns, cannon, missiles, and ballistas were showered from the fort. The besiegers from outside began to discharge cannon, cross-bows, rockets and other fire-arms of this type which are the aggressive firearms of India. The inmates of the fort were thus put to great straits. In short, as the Solver of difficulties had ordained the causes of victory, so the enemy at the rush and pressure of the besiegers thought that the entire army was engaged in attacking the fort from that particular side. Therefore, they were quite careless about their rear. From the beginning, the rear of the fort was unprotected and in the heat of engagement, they could make no arrangements for guarding it. So Mast 'Alī Beg got the jungles cleared with great difficulty by his elephants and all on a sudden fell upon the enemy from the rear when they were fighting briskly and were absolutely unaware of what was happening on their rear. The enemy was not allowed to move and after a short skirmish they were repelled and many of them were made the fuel of the fire of hell. The second division of the enemy's army took to flight without a battle. Parsurām, in a miserable plight, fled half-dead to the jungles with great difficulty and humiliation, and began to throw the dust of disgrace on his head. Playing the trumpet of victory and the kettle-drum of joy, the Mīrzā pitched the imperial camp and halted there. He then ordered an enquiry about the condition of the enemy. It was found that three hundred and thirty five men had been killed in the field and about double this number had perished in the neighbouring places. On the side of the imperial army, twelve men were killed and twenty one wounded. The Mīrzā passed the night in happiness and joy. (548)

**Parsurām opposes Nathan at Kandara.** Next morning he (Mīrzā Nathan) started for Solmārī under the guidance of loyal guides. As the vanquished enemy had escaped like a deer wounded by arrows, he considered whether he would despatch a reigment (against him) from that place or (attempt to) surround him. Ultimately, he thought it prudent not to allow him any time to breathe and thus to give him a good defeat. If by the grace of God he (Parsurām) would fall into his hands, he would then do a really substantial piece of work for his master and the Qibla without engaging the services of a large number of people. In short, depending on the favour of God, he proceeded forward and at mid-day he reached a place named Kandara where the vanquished enemy opposed his advance by raising a strong fort. A battalion of the vanguard which was advancing leisurely and was not aware of this fact, was suddenly attacked by the enemy with the discharge of their cannon, guns and arrows. At that time it became evident that the enemy had taken a firm stand to obstruct their way. Mīrzā Nathan formed the cavalry into a separate regiment and ordered Mast 'Alī Beg to make an attempt to break open the fort posting the entire cavalry in the centre. He himself with the whole infantry would fall upon the fort by breaking through the dense forest and skirting the left of the cavalry. Nīk Muḥammad Beg was posted behind the elephant Shāh 'Ināyat which was in a state of heat, with instructions to advance by the right of the cavalry with the elephant and to break the fort and thus teach them a good lesson. In short, the attack was led from three sides. Before the cavalry and the infantry could come to the ditch (of the fort) the elephant-driver broke the wall of the fort and entered into it. Although the enemies from above showered shots and bullets in defence of the fort, it made no difference to the elephant. Many were trampled to death. Parsurām, being also defeated here, fled to Solmārī with a burning heart and weeping eyes. (549)

**Parsurām flies to Makrī hill.** As the army had pursued Parsurām to that place (Solmārī), so unable to resist any longer, he soon fled to the hill of Makrī Parbat[6] carrying all his belongings on the shoulders of the large infantry he possessed. The Mīrzā arrived there after a short time and set fire to his houses and mansions. Towards the latter part of the day he pitched his camp and halted there. The news of the victory was sent to his men who were left behind and were written to, thus :—" It is quite probable that the vanquished enemy after his defeat at Solmārī has evacuated the fort of Kantabel by throwing the dust of disgrace on his head. So it is better that Taslīm Khān and others should proceed to Kantabel *via* Bānsbārī; otherwise, all of you are to come to Solmārī *via* Bānsbārī." (550)

**Reports sent to Hājo and Jahāngīrnagar.** The news of the victory was also written to Qulīj Khān, and Balabhadra Dās, a Hindu Officer, was sent to him with a request demanding reinforcements for the intervening period before the arrival of their other regiments. He also sent reports to the Khān Fatḥ-jang. The aforesaid (report) reached at a time when the Khān was thinking of recalling Mīrzā Nathan and sending him to the expedition of Kawailagarh. A wise secretary of the age wrote a letter of solicitude to Mīrzā Nathan that the arrival of the report of the conquest of Solmārī at that time had given great pleasure to the aforesaid Khān and the members of the assembly. The idea of recalling him was given up and he (the Khān) thought that now when Parsurām, the rebel, was driven out of his place it was quite probable that by the favour of God he would be captured alive. So there was no need of recalling him. The Ṣūbahdār sent the following reply with many encouraging words,—"The splendid services rendered by you have been very well reported to the imperial Court. Be not anxious about anything and exert yourself in such a way that the rebel may either be killed and sent to hell or captured alive." (551)

## CHAPTER IV

*Departure of an imperial army for the conquest of Kawailagarh (Kailagarh) the territory of the Rāja of Tippera.**

**Expedition to Tippera.** The sum and substance of this narrative is as follows:—When Mīrzā Nathan was retained in his former appointment with an encouraging letter, it was decided to send two land-forces and one fleet against the Rāja of Tippera. One regiment, consisting of more than two thousand and seven hundred cavalry, four thousand matchlock-men, and twenty famous elephants, was sent under the command of Mīrzā Isfandiyār, son of Ḥasan Beg Khān—Shaykh 'Umarī. The second regiment, consisting of more than three thousand cavalry, five thousand matchlock-men and fifty elephants, was despatched under the command of Mīrzā Nūru'd-Dīn and Masnad-ī-'Alā Mūsā Khān the Zamīndār. A fleet of three hundred war-boats with large equipments of war was sent under the command of Admiral Bahādur Khān, an officer of the Khān Fatḥ-jang. These regiments started in an auspicious moment, and after reaching the river Brahmaputtra they began to cross it. (552)

**Capture of the fort of Kantabel.** Now I shall give a short account of the affairs of Mīrzā Nathan and their results. Mīrzā Nathan busied himself day and night in order to capture Parsurām and other rebels. Therefore, the followers of the Mīrzā prepared to join him. Thus they requested Taslīm Khān and other officers of Qulīj Khān to go *via* Bānsbārī through their Jāgīr and to join at Solmārī; and they, owing to their inability to take part in the wars and victories of the Mīrzā, took upon themselves the task of fighting at the fort of Kantabel and proceeded forward. A battle was fought at the mountain pass and many were wounded. But the brave warriors, engrossed with the idea that they had been left be-

*The title of this chapter is misleading. It contains more of Assam Wars than those of Tippera.

hind (by the Mīrzā) as useless men, did not let slip any opportunity, and making no discrimination between hills and dales, conquered the fort with all their might. After thirteen days they reached the Mīrzā with all his followers. But during these thirteen days Mīrzā Nathan did not let slip any opportunity and with his small force, he strengthened the garrison and made plundering raids as well. Within a week, he twice sent half his regiment to the fleet and thus collected all his men together, excepting a small number of men that remained in the fleet.* (553)

**A party of non-combatants attacked by rebels.** It happened that one day about evening, a party of footmen started for the fleet without the knowledge of the Mīrzā, unaccompanied by a regiment, with the idea that they would reach the fleet and bring back some of their necessary things, before the Mīrzā could become aware of the move. In short, when they reached near Makrī-parbat, the enemy, finding them small in number came out of the jungles and forests and pounced upon this group. Seven men were killed and the rest concealed themselves in the forest and came out half-dead. Fatā the Fawjdār of the imperial elephant Shāh 'Ināyat and Ma'rūf, the chief of the *kalāwants* (singers) of the Mīrzā were in this company. Fatā obtained martyrdom but no trace of Ma'rūf could be found. The Mīrzā became very much aggrieved at this news and began to strike his hands in sorrow; but it was of no avail. A company of horsemen which was sent at the beginning of the tumult, reached there at a time when the enemies had finished their job and gone away. In short they brought the dead but Ma'rūf could not be traced. Then the Mīrzā buried Fatā and began to make enquiries about Mā'rūf. (554)

**Sad experiences of Ma'rūf.** Now I shall give a short account of Ma'rūf. When he crept into the jungle he remained there for three days and nights and breaking through the

*The construction of the sentence appears to be defective but the sense is probably, as given above.

jungles he came to the bank of the river. During the nights he used to get on tops of trees, and for a day and a half more, he wandered about on the sandy plains and then reached the fleet. From there, the officers of the fleet sent news of him and the aforesaid Ma'rūf was escorted back by a regiment. When he was asked about his condition he said, "During these four or five days I have not taken anything but water and the root of *kajūr* (zedoary, a chinese root). At nights when I lived on the tops of trees, I had no sleep owing to the fear of elephants and rhinoceros. At last God the Great brought me to the shore of safety." (555)

**Nathan proceeds against Kaltakary.** In short, after-six days of this incident, Shaykh Khwāja Aḥmad and other officers of the Mīrzā who were coming *via* Kantabel arrived with all the retinues, and joined the Mīrzā. The Mīrzā established a Thāna at Solmārī and then marched against Kaltakary and his son Tahana[1] who were the most turbulent of the hill-chiefs and had given protection to Parsurām. In the mean time Dūst Beg, the chief officer of Qulīj Khān came from Hājo with Balabhadra Dās, the Hindu officer of Mīrzā Nathan, along with a reinforcement consisting of two hundred horsemen, one thousand Kūch infantry and one hundred matchlock-men, sent by the Khān. The arrival of this regiment was considered by the Mīrzā as a good omen for victory and conquest and for proceeding without any hesitation. First of all he went to a place named Bālijāna in the Rangdān region,[2] situated up the river Jijrām[3] and halted there. From there he marched next morning and halted at the village of Tashpūr.[4] As this place was centrally situated and surrounded by dense forests of the hilly region, so in order to protect themselves from the enemy's night-attack, he ordered the construction of a stockade covering an area of 500 yards. The Sardārs of the *paiks*, at his orders, completed a lofty fort with deep ditches by the first *pahar* of the night. (556)

**Kaltakary negotiates to submit.** Next morning when the kettle-drum of march was played, then Taslīm Khān and other officers of Qulīj Khān arrived at that station *via* Bānsbāri with three hundred cavalry and three thousand infantry, and joined him. Qulīj Khān had assigned Rangdān as Jagīr to Taslīm Khān and others, and a day previous to this, the envoys of Kaltakary came to Taslīm Khān and Dūst Beg and delivered the following message with great humility :—" It is only an accident that Parsurām arrived here. As it will ruin your Jāgīr, so by all means you save us from this trouble and from the horses of the Mīrzā and take proper accounts of your dues from us." Therefore, both Taslīm Khān and Dūst Beg came weeping and *nolens-volens* put a stop to this march and made the Mīrzā halt there with the following agreement :—" If Kaltakary or Tahana do not surrender to you by the mid-day of to-morrow, we shall be guilty of giving shelter to the protector and supporter of Parsurām." Therefore, the Mīrzā unloaded the tents and chattels and halted there. (557)

**The enemy attacks a party of camp-followers.** The camp-followers and other non-combatants of the army of the Mīrzā and of the two regiments of Qulīj Khān who had marched out at the first sound of the kettle-drum straight, reached the *chawkī* of the rebels without caring to know what was happening behind them, and whether the army had marched or stayed there. In short, as soon as they arrived there, guns, arrows and cannon were discharged from both sides. The enemy, seeing the number of these footmen to be small, came out of their enclosure and offering a hard fight turned them away by inflicting a heavy punishment. This flock of foolish sheep at the sight of the excess of the battle and its looting and beatings, ran away one after the other in defeat. The obstinate enemy began to pursue them. By chance two of the fleeing men came with great humiliation and gave the news. The Mīrzā ordered the kettle-drum to be sounded and his cavalry to proceed to the help of the camp-followers in batches of five and ten one after the other and to fall upon the enemy, and thus to save those persons fallen in distress. The experienced warriors found no time to saddle their horses; some of them threw the saddle-cloth on the backs of horses and some rode on bare backs. When the enemies were busy in killing the camp-followers, they arrived there and saved many of them. They made the enemy helpless and did not allow them to proceed from the mountain pass to this side, and kept them in that place giving a hand to hand fight. The panic-striken people were brought back to the camp and he (the Mīrzā) passed that night in great indignation. (558)

**Nathan sets the region of Rangdān ablaze.** Next morning the army was ordered to march. Sa'ādat Khān, his eunuch was given the command of the vanguard and his experienced warriors along with Dūst Beg and others, two hundred horsemen of Qulīj Khān, five hundred matchlock-men, and four thousand Kūch infantry were assigned to him. Taslīm Khān was given the command of the rear with a hundred horsemen, and one thousand infantry consisting of matchlock-men and Kūch soldiers. By one and a half *pahar* of the day, they reached that dangerous place where the enemy had beaten and repelled the camp-followers. The enemy, emboldened by the previous day's engagements, came out of their enclosure immediately at the sight of the infantry of the vanguard, and began to fight. One regiment of the enemy came by the rear and fell upon Taslīm Khān. The news of the engagements with the vanguard and the rear guard reached the Mīrzā. When the Mīrzā was preparing to go to their aid, two regiments of the enemy appeared on the scene, one from the right and the other from the left and surrounded the imperial army. On the receipt of the first news, the Mīrzā had sent a regiment of his picked-soldiers to the aid of Khwāja Sa'ādat Khān and he was waiting to hear the sound of victory but the enemy made an impetuous rush from the right and the left. When the Mīrzā saw that the enemy was advancing with great audacity from the left, he despatched one of his officers named Muṣāḥib Khān with forty warriors in order to test their strength. Muṣāḥib Khān advanced a short distance and became busy in the discharge of arrows and guns. At the repulse of the vanguard of the enemy, the regiment of their right wing which was near the enclosure, seeing the flight of their Sardārs fled away without any fighting. At this, Muṣāḥib Khān and his party fell upon this regiment and drove them away. Taslīm Khān also, being victorious in the rear, joined the central army. All the four regiments jointly marched up to the hill and set Rangdān ablaze. Many people of the enemy were turned into fuel for the fire of hell and a large number of them fled away half-dead and took shelter in the hills and dense forests. In the mean time a wind blew and the fire that was burning the houses of Rangdān spread all over the region. The heat of the fire began to scorch the imperial soldiers. Therefore, some of them by putting the shields before their faces and some throwing mats over themselves, and others with wet things thrown over their bodies and on their faces descended to the foot of the hill with very great difficulty. On one occasion, some men and horses were scorched as if by the simoom or sultry desert wind. The rest were quite safe and no life was lost.' From that place they again returned to their halting place at the village of Tashpūr and took rest, and passed the night. (559)

**Nathan rewards his officers.** Spies were sent to enquire into the condition of the enemy. On the day after the battle, an assembly of pleasure was held and a horse and a robe of honour were awarded to Dūst Beg and a robe of honour to Taslīm Khān. After this the Mīrzā distributed gifts to thirty men who had rendered splendid services in the war. To four of these people, namely, Sa'ādat Khān, Muṣāḥib Khān, Mast 'Alī Beg and Nīk Muḥammad Beg were given robes of honour with horses, and of the rest, to some he gave a pair of shawls, to some one shawl, and to some robes of honour. Every one was encouraged and pacified according to his devoted services. (560)

**A Thana is established at Bālijāna.** He then thought that as it was necessary for him to stay there (at Tashpūr) for a few days more, it would not be possible to keep open the passage of the movement of the army and the supply of ration unless a force was posted in the rear at Bālijāna. Although he sent a message to Dūst Beg to send

Taslīm Khān to that place and to keep this passage secure Dūst Beg showed cowardice and replied, "If I am sent to any place along with all the men of Qulīj Khān I can discharge my duties with all my life, but separated from the rest of the company, it will not be possible to render any service." Therefore, being helpless, he despatched forty horsemen and two hundred infantry of his own under the command of his Bakhshī Badrīdās. This party went and stayed there for a day. (561).

**Nathan hastens to punish Parsurām.** Next morning, a party of horsemen of Qulīj Khān deputed to serve with Dūst Beg, who had fallen behind and had not been able to join Dūst Beg, were coming from the rear. The vanquished Parsurām, hearing the report of the invasion of Rangdān had again taken his position in the rear. He came to the mountain pass situated in the middle of the way which was a dangerous spot for the passers-by and was also surrounded by a marsh. There he kept ready for the purpose of plundering. He then opposed this party on that very dangerous and marshy land and routed them. One of their footmen went half-dead to Bālijāna to Badrīdās, the Thānadar, and gave him the news. The aforesaid Badrīdās sent the loyal Zamīndārs during the night to Mīrzā Nathan with the news of the blockade of the passage. The Mīrzā, due to his great foresight, sent the following message to Dūst Muḥammad :—"Had there been a strong Thāna at Bālijāna, this incident would not have taken place. At present if you join us, it is advisable that you should proceed from this side and Badrīdās with his army from the other side to the place occupied by the enemy, and drive the enemy by striking a good blow, so that the affairs may be set right according to our desire. If you still continue in your negligence, you will experience worse calamities than what you have hitherto experienced." Dūst Beg, through his cowardice and foolishness, showed his audacity and did not utter a word. His object was rather to release himself from these battles day and night with the trick he had played before. He sent the following reply :—"Qulīj Khān had ordered me not to leave your company even by a hair-breadth, nor to allow any of my men to be separated (from me)." On this Mīrzā, got into a temper and prepared to go personally and said, " I was of opinion that the Jāgīr of the Khān should first of all be cleared of rebels and after that attention might be paid to the rebels of my own Jāgīr. As matters stand now, I make up my mind that as you disdain even to carry out my orders and have become self-conceited, I will never look after your affairs, even if a world is set into conflagration. I shall engage my attention in clearing the pargana of Sāmbhūr, Pāndū and my own Jāgīr." With this decision, the Mīrzā marched on. He personally took the command of the centre. Sa'ādat Khān was given the command of the vanguard with a force of 100 horsemen, 500 infantry consisting of matchlock-men and Rohilla and Dilāzāq archers and Mast 'Alī Beg was appointed to the rear with a force of 100 horsemen and 300 matchlock-men. Many valuable directions were given to him (Mast 'Alī) and he was instructed that as long as Dūst Beg and other men of Qulīj Khān were in the train, he should proceed with caution and skill; he should place every body, high and low, in his front and by the time they reached the camp, it should be seen that not even a bird was left behind and every one carried safe to the destination. He then took his position in the centre and marched by putting his camp-followers and the associates of Dūst Beg in front and behind. When the vanguard arrived at the aforesaid mountain-pass where the men of Qulīj Khān had been killed, all the warriors dismounted from their horses and holding them by the reins, they began to descend with great difficulty from the top of the hill to its foot. When ten men had reached the foot of the hill, the three divisions of the enemy's army, which were lurking in the jungles and the valley of the hills, came out from three sides with the beat of drums and fell upon this party. Khwāja Sa'ādat Khān, due to his foolishness, instead of commanding the army, went down ahead of others and faced death. His followers had no other option but to consign themselves to death; so he decided to offer a strong fight to the enemies and fought with them very fearlessly without previous preparation. The men who were left behind, apprehended that if any thing happened to the aforesaid Khwāja, none of them would survive at the hands of Mīrzā Nathan, and could not decide whether they would leave off their horses and go down from the summit of the hill to join the advance troops. By this time the Mīrzā heard about the assault of the enemy and of Khwāja Sa'ādat Khān's descent to the bottom with a small party. The Mīrzā without caring whether he had a large or a small number of soldiers with him, drove his horse forward (by a short cut through the jungles) as fearlessly as he had done one day in a hunting excursion when he saw the track of a rhinoceros and wild buffaloes in the midst of the jungles. The trumpeteer of the Mīrzā was on a horse in the entrance to that short cut. He struck that man's horse with a whip and sent him forward, himself following him by that track. Before the advance army could turn back, the soldiers of the Mīrzā, who had been left behind, followed the Mīrzā one after the other. When the Mīrzā brought his head out of the jungles and came to the rear of all these regiments of the enemy's army, the enemies were busy in having a hand to hand fight with Sa'ādat Khān. The market of the angel of death was made very brisk and there was nothing but remembrance of God. The enemies were pressing this group hard with all their numerical superiority and this small group also was fighting earnestly, depending on the mercy of God, when all on a sudden God the Great caused the Mīrzā to fall upon the enemy's army like a hawk upon a flock of geese. As soon as the sound of the kettle-drum of victory was sounded and before the Mīrzā could come up to the place of action, the enemy scattered themselves to different directions like the constellation of the Bear. They again took shelter in the jungles and forests and in the valley of the hills. Then the Mīrzā from this side and Sa'ādat Khān from the other side dismounted from their horses along with their followers, entered the jungles and drove the impertinent rebels to the hills. Five horses of the regiment of Qulīj Khān which had been captured by the enemies were recovered. (562)

**The rebels disperse.** When they (the imperialists) were planning to send one of the regiments to the hills, they received news that a regiment of the enemy had fallen upon Dūst Beg and the camp-followers. As the entire regiment of Sa'ādat Khān had already advanced and as the Mīrzā also had sent one of his regiments to help Sa'ādat Khān, so the Mīrzā personally ran to the rear along with a group of brave and experienced warriors, and reached there in the earliest possible time. The enemies had seized the sentinel horses and a large number of bullocks of burden from Dūst Beg and his companions, and entered into the heart of the jungles. Dūst Beg and his party dismounted from their horses, but he was afraid that if he would go to the hills, the enemy might come by another route and plunder all his belongings and leave him helpless. In short, when he was thinking whether he would go or not, then suddenly, by the grace of God, the Mīrzā arrived there from one direction and Mast 'Alī Beg from another. The Mīrzā from his horseback ordered Mast 'Alī Beg and the experienced comrades to dismount from their horses and, depending on the will of God to proceed to the hill through the jungles in order to recover the things plundered by the enemy and to punish them in such a way that after this they might give up these vain ideas and might repent of their going astray and of their plundering raids. This party of battle-lovers exerted their utmost and put many of them to the edge of the dreadful sword. They also recovered the things looted by the enemy along with three other horses which had been previously taken away from the cavalry of Qulīj Khān. The Mīrzā made a quick march from that place and pitched his camp at Bālijāna. Next morning, Dūst Beg with his followers returned to Qulīj Khān without being summoned by him. Taslīm Khān and others returned to their Jāgīrs Mechpara and Mālawpara. The Mīrzā halted there for some time. After a week he despatched a regiment under the command of one of his chief officers in order to carry on plundering raids in the places occupied by the rebels. (563)

**The Emperor orders the reinstatement of the Kūch Rājas to their dominions.** Now I shall give a short account of the affairs of Ibrāhīm Khān Fatḥ-jang. Immediately after his arrival in Bengal, he sent a representation to the sublime Court with a request to confer imperial favours on Rāja Lakshmī Narāyan and Parikshit Narāyan and the sons of Pratāpaditya, Rāja of Jessore, who had been sent to the imperial Court by Islām Khān and Qāsim Khān, and to send them to this Ṣūbah by reinstating them to their territories. This act would very much improve the relationship with Kūch and Jessore, as well as with the Firingi pirates. Therefore, the temporal and spiritual sovereign in consideration of the loyalty shown by Lakshmī Narāyan in including himself in the circle of the loyal Zamindārs and that of both the Kūches shown by their presence in the imperial Court, reinstated Rāja Lakshmī Narāyan to the Rājaship of his dominions with great honour. He was given leave to come to Ibrāhīm Khān with gifts of a robe of honour, an 'Irāqī horse, a magnificient elephant, a bejewelled sword-belt and a bejewelled dagger-belt. As Rāja Parikshit had agreed to a *pēshkash* of Rs. 700,000, he was also ordered to be reinstated to his Rājaship on the payment of the above sum. Then he was sent to Ibrāhīm Khān in the company of Mīr Qawām 'Imādu'd-Dawla in order to be reinstated to the Rājaship of his territories after the realisation of that amount of seven hundred thousand rupees. Therefore, Rāja Lakshmī Narāyan who started from the imperial Court ahead (of others) arrived before the Khān Fatḥ-jang in one of the most auspicious moments and attended upon him for a few days.[5] (564)

**Shaykh Kamāl appointed Sardār in Assam.** Now I shall give a short account of Shaykh Kamāl who was staying at Hājo. On the departure of Mīrzā Nathan, the thread of chiefship broke away from him. Chishtī Khān and the Amīrs appointed to serve in Assam arrived at Hājo, but owing to the return of Mīrzā Nathan they could not proceed further in their work. Shaykh Kamāl, without being summoned, went alone in a boat to the Khān Fatḥ-jang, leaving his army at Hājo. For a few days he incurred the displeasure of the Khān, but at last he offered a *pēshkash* of Rs. 80,000 to the Khān Fatḥ-jang and secured for himself an increase of 200 in his Manṣab and the office of the chief administrator (Sardār) of Assam. He also obtained permission to have Rāja Lakshmī Narāyan as one of his followers, and on behalf of the Rāja he pledged himself to the Khān that the sum of Rs. 100,000 the *pēshkash* of the Rāja would be realised in cash and kind and would be sent to him, and the Khān would cease to have any transaction with Rāja Lakshmī Narāyan. Having settled this he also secured Sāmbhūr and other parganās of the Jāgīr of Mīrzā Nathan in lieu of his increased salaries and he got orders issued to Qulīj Khān, Mīrzā Nathan and other imperial officers, high and low, to follow him. Then he started with absolute authority along with Muṣṭafā Khān, Muqarrab Khān, almost all the Zamīndārs of Jahāngīrnagar, two thousand matchlock-men and all the Zamīndārs of Bengal in his company. Rāja Lakshmī Narāyan also started from Jahāngīrnagar in his company. After traversing the stages and stations he arrived at the village of Bāghwān in the parganā of Mechpara. Mīrzā Nathan and the imperial officers of the Kūch frontier became aware of the arrival of the aforesaid Shaykh. The Shaykh also informed them of his letters-patent, and he informed Mīrzā Nathan in particular that the parganā of Sāmbhūr had been assigned to him as his Jāgīr in lieu of his salaries and that the Mīrzā also had been placed under him. (565)

**Nathan does not accept the leadership of the Shaykh.** The Mīrzā, who was staying at the Thāna of Bālijānā, on the receipt of the letter of the Shaykh, summoned his loyal officers and asked their opinion about the best course of action. A group of inexperienced people said that there was no harm in following the Shaykh. Another group who had some amount of prestige said :—" If the Shaykh had any intention of keeping company with us, he would not have managed to transfer our Jāgīr to his name; he would rather have tried to increase it by a few Maḥals more in lieu of our salaries. We never agreed to follow him; now when he is attempting to wrest our Jāgīr, how can we join him? God forbid, that we should go to war in his company or agree to render service with the risk of our lives." Accordingly, the Mīrzā also agreed to this. They found out and settled amongst themselves a plea in order to keep the Shaykh out of their domain in the following way:—"When the Shaykh will come by this way, there is no other route for his soldiers but to pass through the fort of Bālijāna. With the plea that our families are within the fort we will not allow any of them to pass through it. They will have to pass by striking out a route of their own. When the ryots will know that they had not the power to pass by the straight way, will they be able to collect revenues? In short the ryots will have no sympathy for the Shaykh, they will turn their attention towards you and pay you the revenues. The Shaykh, annoyed at this, will voluntarily go from the Dakhinkul to the Uttarkul (the tract of the country lying on the north of the Brahmaputtra)." Then the Mīrzā went out with the plea of searching Parsurām in the hills and forests and left his Hindu officer Balabhadra-Dās at the fort of Bālijāna with a force of one hundred cavalry, seven hundred infantry, four heated elephants, and a large artillery. The aforesaid Hindu was instructed thus:—"Close the gate against the Shaykh and tell him, this: 'The family of the Mīrzā is within the fort and you know the nature of the Mīrzā. I have not the power to open the gate of the fort and to allow your elephants with the advance-tents and the *Farrāshes* riding on them to pass through it, overlooking the houses of the families. I have not the ability, to be answerable to the Mīrzā.' The Shaykh then will be unable to attack the fort in which the families are located. You must not allow him to pass through. He will then strike his head on stone and will pass through the jungles. This will be an obstacle in his way of collecting the revenues. When the ryots will see that he has no authority over the internal affairs, they will not pay any attention to him." In short, the Mīrzā proceeded to the Makrī Parbat against Parsurām, and Balabhadra Dās remained in the aforesaid fort. After a week, the Shaykh arrived at the aforesaid place *via* Malawpāra. Informed of the Mīrzā's departure in pursuit of the enemy, he pitched his camp at Bālijāna and sent 'Ādil Beg Manṣabdār, Saiyid Khān and Shāhbāz Khān the 'Uṣmānī Manṣabdārs, an envoy of Rāja Lakshmī Narāyan and Hātim Khān Afghān, one of his own officers to Mīrzā Nathan with the following message :—" First, this territory has been given to me as a Jāgīr in lieu of my salaries ; secondly, all the officers have been placed under me for Assam service. Now, the officers are evading me by means of tricks and deception and have posted their Hindu officer to oppose me. Instead of withdrawing their hand from collecting revenues they are obstructing me on the plea that their agriculture should not be destroyed although nothing like it is being done. In short, if you follow me, I shall leave the parganā of Sāmbhūr to you ; do otherwise retire from the country and hand over the administration to me, so that after making satisfactory arrangements in this region, I may proceed to Assam." (566)

**Parsurām eludes capture.** In short by the time the messengers reached the abode of Mīrzā Nathan, the Mīrzā had already gone out in search of Parsurām. After crossing the Makrī Parbat, he came to a *jalah* or marsh. Although no boat was available in the *jalah*, he had one small boat carried to that *jalah* on the shoulders of some men. At last through his foresight he found that by the time he could cross the *jalah* with his men by turns, the enemy might fall upon him in large numbers and then, in the absence of help from any other quarter, he might be put to great difficulties, and no remedy would be left to him but regret. Therefore, with the guidance of his far-sighted intelligence, he followed the bank of the *jalah* and came to a hillock on the other side after a great deal of hardship. When he had passed it, he, without his own knowledge and without any body's guidance, suddenly came upon the abode of the enemy. They also had no knowledge that Mīrzā Nathan was there. At the report of Mīrzā Nathan's arrival on the bank of the *jalah,* Parsurām became busy in collecting his forces together to block the passage of the *jalah* and to prevent them crossing over to the other side, and all his people were engaged in this work. But a party of advance-guard who saw a group of men in the jungle cried out in the Hindi language "*Mār, Mār*" (kill, kill), and the trumpeteer, thinking that they had been attacked by the enemy, blew the trumpet. Then the facts became clear to both the sides, and this saved Parsurām and his sons; otherwise Parsurām with his wife and children would have been captured and none of them could have escaped. In short, 2,700 maunds of Assam *agar* i.e. aloes, 170 maunds of brass vessels consisting of 967 pieces, 45 boats and some other booties fell into the hands of the Mīrzā. He then returned to his camp in joy and happiness. (567)

**The Shaykh proceeds to Hājo.** He (Nathan) met 'Ādil Beg and the messengers and received the messages of the Shaykh. After a long discussion, he replied plainly:—"It is well-known to you, to the Ṣūbahdār and to the people of the world what kind of relationship I have with you. Inspite of this, you have again entertained this queer idea. It was improper on your part to have such a foolish notion in your mind and to have my Jāgīr transferred to your name,—a Jāgīr which I wrested from the hand of the enemy with so much exertions. I preferred to take possession of it in lieu of my salaries instead of taking any other imperial domain. You have probably secured an order to send me to some other expedition and you are thinking that you will take Mīrzā Nathan in your company. You must forthwith give up your vain ideas. The invasion of Assam has been assigned to you; so take yourself off from this side and betake your way to Assam which is in the Uttarkul and go to Hājo to begin the Assam expedition. Leave me where I am. The clearance of the Dakhinkul, the capture of Parsurām, Māmū Govinda,[6]

Rāja Baldev and the Eighteen Hill-Chiefs are my business. Otherwise, know it for certain that I shall consider your officers as Baldev, and I will fall upon those officers. The best course for you is not to trouble me but to take your own way. Decide on one of these two courses; either leave me in my place or fight it out with me. You have a large army with you; my humility and the favours of the Merciful Lord are my companions." In short, the messengers noticed the temper of the Mīrzā and went back and informed the Shaykh. They then decided to give up the idea of strife and go to Hājo and to send a report to Ibrāhīm Khān from that place. The Shaykh marched to Hājo and wrote the following letter to Mīrzā Nathan :—"Shumāruyed Kāyeth has constructed two strong forts in the Dakhinkul at Āmjūnga and Rangjūlī.[7] If you can conquer these two forts, that will amount to the conquest of Assam." The letter reached the Mīrzā. The Shaykh then finding no passage through Bālijāna cleared a road through the jungles and marched forward. He crossed the river Brahmaputtra and arrived at Hājo. (568)

**Nathan proceeds to Āmjūnga.** The Mīrzā then marched from the Makrī Parbat to Solmārī. Balabhadra Dās was ordered to march with his men to Mānikpūr,[8] a village in the parganā of Sāmbhūr. Balabhadra Dās reached his destination one day before him. The Mīrzā left Dūst Muḥammad Beg in charge of the Thāna of Solmārī along with a force of forty horsemen and a hundred infantry and during the night he marched to Mānikpūr and reached there. He summoned his loyal officers and held a council of war. After a discussion it was settled thus :—"The Shaykh has not yet crossed the river and he is talking about the rebels of this region with apprehension. The better course for us would be to depend upon the favour of God and attack and capture the fort of Āmjūnga. More so, because the enemies are ignorant as to whether the attack would be led by the entire combined army or only by the troops of the Shaykh." In short, with this decision, Khwāja Balabhadra Dās, the Dīwān, was left along with the army which was posted to the Thāna of Solmārī in charge of Dūst Muḥammad Beg viz: one hundred and fifty horsemen and one thousand infantry consisting of two hundred match-lock-men and eight hundred Kūch *(paiks)*, in order to extirpate the vanquished Parsurām and the rebels of the parganā of Sāmbhūr. At mid-day the Mīrzā held a review of his whole army and four *gharīs* before evening he began his march by dividing the army into three divisions. At midnight he reached the village of Jakhlī[9] (569)

**Regiments sent against Parsurām and Māmū Govind.** The spies brought news that Māmū Govind and Parsurām had reached that night at a place where their families were staying and they were contemplating to remove their belongings from the way of the imperial army and then to enter the fort of Āmjūnga. The Mīrzā ordered two of his regiments, one under the command of Khwāja Sa'ādat Khān and the other under Mast 'Alī Beg to proceed, with the aid of God, under the guidance of the spies to the place where these two rebels were staying with their families and capture them, and then march from that side to the fort. The Mīrzā would also reach the fort by that time and would lead the assault. This was considered to be the most favourable time to attack the garrison and it was expected that they would surely run away at the report of the arrival of the two regiments. Accordingly, those two regiments, under the direction of loyal spies, arrived at the aforesaid place when six *gharīs* of the night still remained. The members of the family of Māmū Govind with his son were all captured alive but Govind himself fell into the hands of a foot-soldier who could not recognise him and allowed him to escape. Parsurām with his wife and children fled away in safety. (570)

**Nathan captures the fort of Āmjūnga.** Early next morning both these two regiments arrived at the fort (of Āmjūnga) by the shortest cut. A battle took place with the inmates of the fort. In the first assault, many men of those two regiments were killed and wounded. The vanguard of the Mīrzā came up at that time and offered a strong fight but the fort could not be broken into. Mīrzā Nathan, who had fallen behind to say his prayers, arrived there. He found that many of his expert warriors were killed and many were busy in the battle. He thought it prudent to keep those two regiments engaged in the same way in the battle and ordered that a third regiment should also come to their aid and thus make the enemy irresolute. But he selected fifteen men from each regiment, and took these forty five men with him. He then thought of going to the rear of the fort which was a hill, dismount from their horses and attack from the rear in order to see what has been ordained by providence. In short, when he was discussing this, Mast 'Alī Beg and his fellow-combatants who were at the foot of the hill were trying to climb the hill. They secured a commanding position when they got at the top. The enemies, apprehensive for their safety, thought thus:—"If we evacuate the fort before they proceed further to the top of the hill and block the path of our retreat, we can safely escape and offer resistance at the fort of Rangjūlī, otherwise the moment they block our path, our position will be like the deer at bay and it will be impossible to get out of it." Therefore, they fled away in a panic. The Mīrzā sounded the trumpet of victory and the clarion of joy. (571)

**Nathan recruits 4000 Gāroes and attacks Rangjūlī.** From there (Āmjūnga) he (Nathan) marched to the foot of the hill of the Gāroes (*gārūān*)[10] who were hill-people. They eat all sorts of things except iron which is the hardest of all and cannot be chewed with teeth. They eat ass and pigs and make no exception of any other thing. He (the Mīrzā) arrived there and pitched his camp. When all their chiefs came and submitted, he gave robes of honour to three of them. After their pacification they said thus:—"It will be better if you stay here for another day and night, so that we may recruit four thousand *paiks*." Mīrzā Nathan, in order to utilise this opportunity, halted there for another day and night. Taking those four thousand hill-men in his company, he marched from that place and attacked the fort of Rangjūlī dividing the army into four regiments. Shumāruyed Kāyeth, the head (i.e. the brain) and the chief of the garrison, was staying within the fort. He defended the fort and the battle was equally balanced. The besiegers pressed the siege on with all their might and endeavoured to break open the fort. The dead lay upon one another in heaps but it was of no avail. When the sun reached its meridian, the Mīrzā picked up fifteen men from each regiment. He took with him all these sixty men and the elephant Shāh 'Ināyat in his front. He left all the four regiments in their engagements and he led an attack from the fifth side. Such a terrible battle was fought that owing to the heavy showers of arrows from both sides the birds of the air could not fly. Not to speak of mortals, even the angels began to applause, and it reminded the Day of Resurrection. In short, as no side was gaining or losing, the Mīrzā, at the approach of the evening, thought it advisable to pitch his camp and to raise a fort of his own and then to besiege the (enemy's) fort by advancing under the cover of *sības* or artificial barriers to demolish their places of shelter. With this decision he took with him all the regiments that were fighting in different places and came to the open field. Khwāja Sa'ādat Khān was ordered to take his stand with all his soldiers in the field and to watch so that the enemy might not come out of the fort. He personally came and ordered the chiefs of the *paīks* to raise a fort with an area of two thousand yards. The industrious workers began the work of the construction with full zeal and raised a lofty fort with a deep ditch around beginning from the last *pahar* of the previous evening to the first *pahar* of the next day. During the whole night a regiment of armed warriors remained ready at the watch-post, on horses and on foot. (572)

**Raid of the adjacent villages.** Early next morning a force of a hundred horsemen and five hundred infantry was sent under the command of Muṣṭafā Qulī Beg to raid the villages of the hill-men at the outskirts of the hills. Another fort extending over two hundred cubits was raised and the centre of the battle was carried adjacent to the fort of the rebels, at a distance of one cannon-shot. The regiment which was sent for raiding purposes, attacked three villages of the hill-men at the base of the hills. These were burnt and destroyed and about five hundred men were brought as captives. Amongst the captives was a Muslim chief named Jamāl Khān. He took the lead in bringing the hill tribes into subjugation and one of the rebel chief named Jānkara who did not yield was brought alive through him as a captive by the despatch of a regiment. This opened the eyes of many others. (573)

**An unsuccessful night-attack on Rangjūlī.** During the night of the fifth day, the warriors of the company of Mīrzā Nathan held a consultation amongst themselves and decided to storm the fort. The Mīrzā was not in favour of it. But through the instrumentality of Mast 'Alī Beg and Muṣṭafā Qulī Beg, many men were wounded and killed, and the fort also could not be captured. The summary of the details of this incident is this :—One night they formed into two regiments and rushed upon the fort of the enemy one after the other. As the Mīrzā was against this measure, he merely watched on as a spectator and supplied them with every material of war they demanded. But as God had ordained that the conquest of the fort would take place in some particular time, many of them got wounded and twelve men were killed. At last the Mīrzā rebuked and censured all of them and the warriors kept quiet for three or four days. (574)

**Another attempt to capture the fort.** The Mīrzā according to military regulations demonstrated (to them) the manipulation of artificial barriers. Every day the artificial barriers were pushed forward. Four days after that night attack, the comrades of the Mīrzā, in order to wipe off the disgrace they had suffered that night, again rushed forward without the knowledge of the Mīrzā with the idea that when the battle would commence, their master also would come forward to help them without showing any indifference. In short, they rushed forward and attacked the fort forming themselves into two battalions. A great fight took place. The Mīrzā, on the receipt of this news, rode on his horse and personally came to their help and discharged the duties of a commander. The battle was evenly balanced. In the mean time one of the eunuchs of the Mīrzā named Khwājā Bihbūd who advanced with greater boldness than others attained martyrdom. This incident mortified the Mīrzā. These arduous fighters, who brought nothing but loss to their regiment, were recalled from the battle. They were given wise admonitions and it was decided that they should advance under artificial barriers and should carry on plundering raids in the adjoining places. (575)

**Nathan advances under the cover of barriers.** The Mīrzā now for the first time turned his back towards the east and facing the west raised a stockade and closed the path of the supply of rations to the enemy's fort. About the time of sunset it was completed, and a regiment was posted there with instructions to watch that passage and not to allow a single man to enter the fort or come out of it. He himself remained armed with the rest of his men and passed the whole night between the big fort and this small one with the elephants in his front. He ordered the native infantry to cut grasses for three days and nights and to keep them ready in bundles. On the fourth day he advanced about the distance of one arrow-shot from this stockade. As the fort of the enemy was near this intrenchment, he raised another small stockade in that place. Although the enemies were discharging arrows, guns and cannon and the sun was enveloped in darkness, and heaps began to be formed of dead bodies, yet depending on the will of God and the fortune of the master and the Qibla he did not let slip any opportunity. By the end of the day, he completed a fort commanding the fort of the enemy. Cannon were posted on it and the *gulandāz* or cannoniers began to pick off the rebels of the garrison within. The battle was equally balanced till the sun set in the west and brought the night for the repose of men and animals. Then both sides ceased fighting and engaged themselves in eating and drinking. The Mīrzā kept the army standing at that place with full equipments and he alone came to his men posted in the new intrenchment. He encouraged them and returned again to the place where he had left the army. (576)

**700 Rābhas desert Nathan.** In the mean time Dutiārī, Bāmun Lāshkar and Shyām Dās came and said:—"A group of the Rābhas[11] formed a conspiracy amongst themselves and became disloyal and have gone over to the fort of the enemy and joined their rank with seven hundred of their own men. The trumpets and the kettle-drums were sounded at candle-light in honour of their arrival." The Mīrzā asked them what should be done? These people devoid of any intelligence, replied:—"We should this very night advance without the knowledge of the enemy and take our position in the rear. We should first free ourselves from the trouble of these Rābhas by an attack from the rear. Then we should fall upon the enemy." The Mīrzā said:—"All our designs depend on the favour of God. If my reliance was on help from outside, I would not have undertaken this expedition single handed with my own army on this side of the Brahmaputtra and without the aid of the army of the imperial officers (on the other side). Now by the favour of God, I have reached this land and I have not come here relying on the strength and power of the natives of this region. I rely simply on the favours of the Merciful Lord. Consider these people to be dead and to have hastened to hell. They have placed their quivers with the quivers of Rāja Baldev and Shumāruyed Kāyeth. They will be paid in their own coin. But it is against the rules of military profession and able management of affairs to proceed forward from this place. Because, the enemy will no longer give us any respite. They will advance upon our fort and will not allow us to remain in this country. In short my intention is either to be victorious or to die." At last, all of them agreed to this plan and passed the night with ease. (577)

**Balāi Lashkar and Jadū Nāyak attack a raiding party.** Next morning he sent a regiment of a hundred horsemen and five hundred infantry under the command of Nīk Muḥammad Beg in order to raid the adjoining villages. This army was opposed on their way by the enemies and a battle took place. The brave warriors making no discrimination between hills and dales began to pursue the enemy as soon as they repelled their first assault and whoever opposed them was put to death. But on their return, Shumāruyed Kāyeth sent Balāi Lashkar with one thousand brave infantry to oppose their way with this instruction :—" When the regiment will return with captives and booties, divide your army into three divisions. At first the attack will be made by one regiment and then the two regiments will surround them from the left and will rout the men who are carrying the booties. Most likely a disorder will appear among that troop and a hard blow might be inflicted on them." Balāi Lashkar with the aid of Jadū Nāyak[12] blocked the path of this regiment and a great battle was fought. When the sound of the guns and trumpets was heard, Mīrzā Nathan despatched a regiment from this side. They also arrived at that place and joined the battle. Many people were killed and wounded on both sides. But the victory was attained by the imperialists and from these they came to the Mīrzā in a triumphant mood. One of the Afghāns, who had rendered splendid services, was killed in the battle. So Mīrzā Nathan appointed the brother of the Afghān in his place and presented him with a horse. He also gave rewards to all the rest. (578)

**The enemy sets fire to the defensive barriers.** The Mīrzā ordered the *paiks* to cut grasses for three days and to collect the bundles during day time and to plaster them with mud at night in the foremost intrenchment in order to strengthen it. It was accordingly done. On the fourth day the third intrenchment was begun and by piling the bundles of grass one upon the other till mid-day it was raised very high. The inmates of the (enemy's) fort kept defending it from above with courage, but the work was carried on till the sun reached the meridian. When the heat of the sun became unbearable to the bodies, the workers were given a little respite to begin the work afresh. The Mīrzā took rest for a while in the second intrenchment. When the two foremost intrenchments were under construction, the enemy made a tunnel from the interior of their fort to their ditch. They came out through that passage to the ditch. For a while they took their stand in proper order in the ditch. Then all at once some of them rushed forward with burning thatches tied to long bamboo poles with two thousand men in their trail. A musketeer of the intrenchment where the Mīrzā was dozing saw this. He shouted and said to the men who were in the newly built third intrenchment, "Beware! Beware! the enemy has come out to fight." He then fired his musket. But it was of no avail. By the time the soldiers could come out, they set fire to the heaps of grass and before the perplexed water-carriers could think of bringing water, the fire caught on and in the twinkling of an eye all the bundles of grass were burnt to ashes. The barriers raised before these people by the men of the intrenchment were removed in this way and the enemy became triumphant. Thus the Mīrzā, who was in the second intrenchment found himself surrounded by the enemy, and the men of the third intrenchment fell back. Khwāja Sa'ādat Khān, Mast 'Alī Beg, Nīk Muḥammad Beg and some others who had been left in the camp of the first intrenchment as a reserve force with instructions to advance with the elephants in their front and help to meet such emergencies, came out of their position of vantage and attacked the enemies. The enemies who were attacking the men of the intrenchment, with audacity, were swept away, with the favour of God, like leaves of trees in a hurricane and were driven away. They fled throwing the dust of disgrace on their heads, and forthwith they returned to their ditch and entered the fort through the tunnel. The dexterous warriors pursued them up to the bank of the ditch, but owing to the heavy showers of arrows and guns from the fort above they had to stop and fall back. A victory was achieved but the labours of four days were thrown to the wind. (579)

**Nathan's attempt to advance under the cover of gardūns.** Then the people began to complain about the trenches which were built facing the west. It was settled that the intrenchments should be made facing the south with their backs to the north and the artificial barriers should be pushed forward and the defensive positions of the ramparts (*ṣābāt*) of the intrenchment should be built overtopping the enemy's fort so that the garrison might be put to great straits. In short, the whole of that day and two other days were spent in cutting grass and another intrenchment was raised by means of that grass according to the process mentioned above. But the *thatari*, i.e., a big wheel or chariot (*gardūn-i-kalānī*) under the cover of which the elephants can attack the fort, which had been constructed, was delayed in transit. At first he sent his trustworthy servant named Muṣāḥib Khān to bring the *gardūn* quickly to the bank of the ditch. He himself busily went on with the work of finishing the intrenchment. The poor servant went and fetched the *gardūn* to a short distance. But arrows and shots from cannon and guns were showered from the fort above in such profusion that the world became enveloped in darkness and they fell around with great noise like hailstones. The servant persisted in his attempt but the people who were carrying the *gardūn* could not advance a single step. For the second time, the Mīrzā sent in his own place his most intimate friend Khwāja Sa'ādat Khān with strict orders (to bring the *gardūn*). Then Mīrzā Nathan, unable to bear the idea that he (Sa'ādat) should brave the arrows and guns and he himself should remain in a place of safety, himself went in the third instance, and coming under the *gardūn*, he placed his shoulders underneath the machine and attempted to make it move. The pullers of the *gardūn* as well as the soldiers, putting aside their pride of high birth, began to push the *gardūn* together. But with many oaths they took the Mīrzā out from beneath the *gardūn* and led him to the side of some trees, saying:—" Unless you take your stand in that place, we shall not be able to carry the *gardūn*." The Mīrzā replied, " I go with the stipulation that none but

Khwāja Sa'ādat Khān should remain with me. All must remain behind the *gardūn*." In short, the Mīrzā and the aforesaid Khwāja took their stand under the cover of a big tree. The *gardūn* was moved. Then a cannon was fired from the fort which struck the *gardūn* and broke it. The head of one of the *paiks* who were pulling the *gardūn* was blown away. Muṣāḥib Khān was scratched on the skin of his forehead; another man was hit on his arm and his arm was broken; the fourth man was struck on his ankle and thrown down; the fifth man was struck on his turban and had it blown away from his head. The shot of the cannon then struck the ground and went down to a depth of one cubit. The *gardūn* could not be moved any farther. (580)

**Nathan erects a new stockade.** It was decided to raise an intrenchment in the aforesaid place and they began the construction of a stockade. The enemy, with the knowledge that the Mīrzā was standing behind the trees, discharged three cannon-shots from above the fort which struck that tree. When they found that the Mīrzā had evaded those shots, they fired another cannon from a position of vantage aiming at his feet, but by the protection of God, he was not injured. The arduous workers completed the stockade within a short time. As the foremost intrenchment facing the west had been left by the Mīrzā in charge of a regiment, so another regiment was posted in this intrenchment with instructions to plaster it with mud during the night, and to pass their time with vigilance and freedom from anxiety. After this arrangement, a raiding party was sent every day to raid and plunder the villages adjacent to the fort, and the regiment used to return at night and pass the time in vigilance. For four days grasses were cut and on the fifth day another enclosure was raised in front of this enclosure, and stockade after stockade was constructed till these enclosures were carried to the bank of the ditch in order to secure a commanding position over the enemy's fort. (581)

**Satrajit comes to the aid of Nathan.** The details of these affairs were reported every week to the Khān Fatḥ-jang.

Therefore, the Khān wrote to the imperial officer posted at Hājo not to show any negligence in sending reinforcements to the Mīrzā. Accordingly, Rāja Satrajit advanced to help Mīrzā Nathan with a regiment of his own consisting of one hundred horsemen and three hundred brave infantry. When this troop reached the Mīrzā, he wrote to the Ṣūbahdār an account of the sympathy of the aforesaid Rāja. (582)

**Result of the Tippera expedition.** Now I shall give a short account of the doings of the regiments that were sent against the territory of the Rāja of Tippera, and their results. When two land-armies and one naval force traversed the stages and stations and arrived at Kawailagarh, the Rāja of Tippera planned to lead a night-attack against the imperial officers. Therefore, he came out with a force of one thousand cavalry, sixty thousand infantry and two hundred elephants and at midnight fell upon Mīrzā Isfandiyār who had crossed Kawailagarh and reached the vicinity of Udaypūr.[13] A contested battle was fought and many were killed and wounded on both sides. But as the fortune of the Emperor, which is never in its wane, came to the aid of the loyal officers, a fortunate victory was attained by the Muslims. The trumpet of victory was blown in its highest pitch and the Rāja of Tippera, leaving behind many (of his followers) to be killed ran away as a wanderer to the desert, scattering the dust of disgrace on his head. The imperialists captured seventy of his elephants as booties, and they obtained a victory which may be considered as one of the leading victories of an army.

When this vanquished man, defeated at this place by this army, was traversing the way of adversity, he happened to meet on his way the army of Mīrzā Nūru'd-Dīn and Masnad-i-'Alā Mūsā Khān, the Zamīndār. As he found the soldiers to be dozing in the sleep of negligence in a state of carelessness, he fell upon them. He fought here for three *gharīs*, and he again suffered a defeat at this place and ran way. (583)

**Flight of the Rāja of Tippera.** As soon as the Rāja reached Udaypūr he despatched his fleet by the river and an army by land against the imperial fleet, with instructions to block the passage of the imperial fleet by constructing bridges on the river from one end to the other and by the erection of forts on either side. The Sardārs of the Rāja of Tippera acted according to the orders and put forth their greatest efforts. But what can be done by human efforts ? The will of the True Lord always prevails in the matter of accomplishing a work. In short, the men of the (imperial) fleet also, arrived at that place (near Udaypūr) triumphant and victorious. On the arrival of the fleet and the land-army they immediately marched on Udaypūr. The imperialists received an information that the Rāja had fled in the morning with his wife and children. They followed him for three days and nights and proceeded on horseback as far as it was possible to go on horses ; and then dismounting from their horses, the high officials rode on elephants and the common soldiers marched on foot and entered the hills and the jungles in search of the Rāja. (584)

**Siege of Rangjūlī drags on.** Now I shall give a short account of Mīrzā Nathan. When the siege of the fort of Rangjūlī dragged on for a long time, advance was made from one enclosure to another till they (Nathan's men) reached the fifth enclosure. As three of the enclosures were not plastered with mud, he (the Mīrzā) endeavoured not to make any further delay : and the Mīrzā himself completed the fifth barrier, keeping awake the whole night. He remained at the enclosure till two *gharīs* before morning. Many of the soldiers represented that they should take rest for a while and then be ready for action. The Mīrzā replied :—"The barrier has been brought close to the ditch of the fort of the enemy. You have witnessed what the enemy did the other day. It is my considered opinion now that such mischief should not recur." In short, the high and the low insisted on it. Then the Mīrzā returned to his place of rest with this agreement that three-fourths of the soldiers present should remain in the enclosure and if the day passes safely, he would not make any further attempt of pushing the enclosure forward at night. First of all he would finish the work of mud plastering of the three enclosures and then he would think of pushing the enclosures further on. In short, within less than two or three *gharīs* of the Mīrzā's departure, the enemy moved again. First of all they sent a regiment against the enclosure facing the west and fought a battle. When the news reached the resting-place of the Mīrzā, his servants informed him of it. While still in bed, he deputed a regiment to go to the aid of the besieged persons of the aforesaid enclosure. Then the enemy sent a regiment out of their fort under the command of the son-in-law of Govind Māmūn i.e. the uncle of Rāja Parikshit, in order to attack the resting place of the Mīrzā from a position of vantage. That strong-headed man came on triumphantly. The Mīrzā sent Mast 'Alī Beg to oppose this regiment and he remained asleep. In the mean time one party of the enemy came upon the big fort where the camp and the camp-followers were stationed under the command of Badridās, the Bakhshī of the Mīrzā. This news also was reported to the Mīrzā. He then sent a regiment under the command of Saiyid 'Abdu's-Samad to the aid of the aforesaid Bakhshī and the people of the fort. This regiment went there and engaged in battle. When the enemy saw that the soldiers and the regiments of the Mīrzā had become scattered they sent a regiment by that underground route as they did previously through the ditch of the fortress. This regiment set fire (to the barriers) in the same way as they had previously done and rushed forward. The comrades of the barriers were watching the battle to the left and other directions, unmindful of the rear, and negligent in their duties. By the time they became aware of the attack on the rear, the piles of grass in the barriers caught fire. In short, by the time the water-carriers ran to bring water to pour over the fire, it blazed out and in the twinkling of an eye the barriers vanished. The battle became very thick. The high and the low fell upon one another, one knowing not the other. The Mīrzā, in that extraordinary tumult, came out (of his tent) all alone. Of the horsemen, no body else except two men of Khwāja Sa'ādat and one man of Ṭāhir Muḥammad were present with him. Of these, the latter was affected with palsy. He was made to ride on the horse with very great difficulty. Of the infantry, there was none with him except four or five of his eunuchs and two or three grooms. But the elephant of the Mīrzā named Shāh 'Ināyat which was in heat was immediately brought to the Mīrzā by the driver fully equipped for war. The Mīrzā definitely decided that if the men of the barriers would fall back then he would himself fall upon the short-sighted ones (enemies) with the elephant in his front. But it was not the desire of the True Lord to cause havoc upon a large number of men; so as soon as Mast 'Alī Beg and this regiment had killed the son-in-law of Govind Māmūn and repelled the opposing forces with great triumph, the enemy lost their position and became scattered from one another like the constellation of the Bear. The victory was attained in the best possible way. The age began to applaud it in significant language, and the people of the world became heartily pleased. The trumpet of victory and the clarion of good-news were blown. But the fort remained in the same state of siege. (585)

**Nathan sends a regiment to raid Bachādharī.** Next morning, the Mīrzā again despatched a regiment of more than two hundred horsemen, two thousand infantry and three elephants to raid and to destroy the distant villages of the rebels. All the ryots of the adjacent villages had gone to those places with their properties and cattle and owing to their numerical superiority they were grouping in different places assuming an attitude of arrogance and were supplying rations to the enemy's fort. So long, the regiment that went out for raid used to return to the camp at night. Now they were permitted to stay out for two to three nights and to render effective service depending on the favour of God. Accordingly, the aforesaid one made a forced-march for two days and a night and raided Bachādharī the chief village of the parganā of Bāohantī.[14] It was the order of the Mīrzā not to leave any of these rebellious persons but to bring every one of them alive as captive; and the cattle which would fall into their hands, if found difficult to be brought over, were directed to be ham-strung. Therefore, about three thousand cows were ham-strung and seventeen hundred rebels, big and small, were brought as prisoners. After five days they returned to Mīrzā Nathan and became the recipients of many favours. Whoever was recommended (for reward) received his share in full. After giving rest to the horses for four days, Khwāja Sa'ādat Khān and others were again despatched according to the previous way. On this occasion, the aforesaid one having rendered splendid services returned after three days. As the enemy had blocked the path of food-supply, the food of the men and animals in the company of the aforesaid Khwāja consisted of the meat of cows which had been ham-strung on the former occasion. (586)

**Nathan erects wooden barriers.** Attempts were made to carry the barriers close to the wall of the fort in order to obtain a commanding position over the enemy's garrison. It had always been their desire to do so, but when the work had neared completion, the enemy had twice defeated this purpose in the way (described above). Mīrzā Nathan ordered the native *paīks*, who were engaged in raising the barriers, to bring logs of small and big wood along with green wooden binding material (i.e. creepers) instead of grass. With these, the Mīrzā arranged the construction of barriers in proper order and moved forward by making barrier after barrier. (587)

**Baldev sends a strong force to Shumāruyed.** Therefore, Shumāruyed Kāyeth, the commander of the enemy's force, wrote to this suzerain Rāja Baldev about the mobilization of the army of Islām. Accordingly, his Rāja with (the aid of) the Assamese, sent a reinforcement to Shumāruyed consisting of about ten thousand brave men recruited from the men of the Eighteen Hill Rājas, from the Assamese and from his own men, under the command of the Rājkhawa. The Rājkhawa came from Rāja Baldev to Shumāruyed Kāyeth to the fort of Rangjūlī. (588)

**Nathan recruits 1000 soldiers from Hājo.** When, on the arrival of the Rājkhawa, a commotion arose among the army that the Assamese have come to the help of Shumāruyed Kāyeth, the Mīrzā sent one of his eunuchs named Khwāja 'Aẓmat and his Hindu officer Banwārī Dās with Rs. 10,000 to Hājo to recruit a large number of experienced horsemen, infantry, musketeers and archers. In short, they arrived at Hājo and within a short time recruited one thousand men and brought these picked-warriors to the Mīrzā. Among these there was a unique matchlock-man named Ṣādiq Bahādur. He came without fixing his salary in that place with the idea that he would fix his salary in the presence of the Mīrzā in accordance with his worth. The very day he arrived, he said,—" Please construct a *gargaj*, (i.e. a covered outpost, made of big logs of wood posted on the ground and fixed with beams and scaffolding with a seat on it) for me which should command the view of the enemy's fort." In short, the Mīrzā immediately constructed a *gargaj* during the night and that man took shelter in it. In the last part of the night of the second day of his arrival, Ṣādiq Bahādur rode on his *gargaj* and ordered a musketeer to pick the enemies within the fort one by one with shots from gun. Under the direction of this able man endowed with divine favours and courage, a few shots of gun were fired in such a way that a tumult arose on both sides and the people of the garrison in particular had to acknowledge the excellent quality of the firing and praise his feats. On that day, seven men were killed by the shots from his gun; and this commotion by the will of God became warm. Therefore, the enemies also began to gather logs of wood and although they remained in terror during the day, at night they took measures to protect themselves from the firing from the *gargaj*. The logs of wood, brought by the *paīks* during the day, were used by the Mīrzā at night in constructing new small barriers to the right and the left of that *gargaj*. In the last part of the night the aforesaid Bahādur climbed on the *gargaj* and dismantled the protective barriers which the enemies had raised during the previous day, labouring up to the evening. The firing of guns was directed upon the enemy from another quarter. They had no opportunity to move about during the day and had to take shelter under the walls. Inspite of this precaution, not a single day passed without four or five of them being sent to hell through fire from muskets. In this way, the Day of Resurrection prevailed among the people of the fort for fifteen days in succession. (589)

**Sa'ādat Khān sent again to raid the villagers.** The Mīrzā again suggested to Sa'ādat Khān and others that a fresh raid should be carried on. The aforesaid Khwāja and his companions said :—"No village or place has been left unraided within an area of twelve *kos* from the fort. Now nothing effective can be done unless some one goes further and proceeds on and on for the purpose of raiding." The Mīrzā said:—"Go to Bachādharī this time depending on the favour of God and stay there by making a fort. Then, from that place proceed on your raids farther on." In short, with this decision he was sent with a force of two hundred horsemen, fifteen hundred infantry consisting of expert matchlock-men and archers and three elephants along with all other equipments necessary for the expedition. (590)

**Feats of musket firing by Ṣādiq Bahādur.** He (the Mīrzā) kept himself busy in the same way in manoeuvring the artificial barriers. Ṣādiq Bahādur was ordered to climb the *gargaj* and to fire. The aforesaid Bahādur performed splendid services by the discharge of his gun. He created a great panic among the soldiers of the garrison. One night four *gharīs* before morning, after the Mīrzā had spent the whole of that night in making a new barrier and a new *gargaj*, he left Bahādur on it with Khwāja 'Aẓmat to watch his musket-firing and he went to his bed-chamber for a rest. By chance Ṣādiq Bahādur picked up a conversation with the inmates of the fort. Bahādur claimed thus and called out to them :—"I can strike at any target you point out." On the first occasion, these rebels brought a lance and placed it between two towers of the fort and asked him to hit that target.

Bahādur shattered it to pieces with his first shot. Then one of the inmates desired to deceive Bahādur by talking with him and at the same time he asked his musketeer to fire at him. While Bahādur was engaged in the conversation, that musketeer raised his gun through a louvre-window and looked through it. This immediately caught the eye of Bahādur. He said, "Come out like a man; let us see whether you hit me first or I hit your gun before you hit me." Immediately after saying this he drew the cock of his gun and fired straight at the muzzle of that man's gun and blew away nine inches from it. He saw a *zambūrak* (swivel) posted between the two towers. He shouted out and said, "Look at this third performance of mine," and he directly fired at the barrel of the *zambūrak* in such a way that the bullets of the musket which were almost equal in size to the bullets of the *zambūrak* went straight into its mouth and lodged in its chamber and the *zambūrak* was absolutely shattered. At this sight not only the besiegers but even the besieged applauded and began to shout "Bravo! Bravo!", without any hesitation. Bahādur in a smiling countenance sat on the *gargaj* facing his own people and with his back towards the enemy and began to file his gun. During the course of filing he kept talking with Khwāja 'Aẓmat. In the mean time, a bullet of destiny finished his affair. The details of this sad and instructive event is this :—one of the musketeers of the enemy fired a musket without any aim. This unlucky bullet passed through the chink between two wooden posts of the barrier in front of the *gargaj* and hit him just below his head. He thus gave back his life to its Creator and retired to the Kingdom of Heaven. As Khwāja 'Aẓmat had twice come to the Mīrzā to inform him about his (Bahādur's) ability in shooting so when he ('Aẓmat) came for the third time and shook the feet of the sleeping Mīrzā, the latter thought that he had again brought the news of the shooting down of some person (by Bahādur) and replied indifferently to the Khwāja with closed eyes, "There is no doubt about his marksmanship. When I wake up you will tell me everything in detail." The Khwāja slowly conveyed the news of the aforesaid event to the Mīrzā's ears. The Mīrzā became bewildered and without making any further enquiry he came to that barrier and found the conditions to be quite different.

(Here follows a *marṣiya* or elegy on the death of Bahādur written by Mawlānā Mubārak. Left out). (591)

**Death of Ṣādiq Bahādur kept concealed.** The Mīrzā then ordered that no one from within the barrier should go out nor any body from outside should come into the barrier. The dead body of Bahādur was ordered to be kept concealed on the *gargaj* so that the enemy might not be aware of this incident. The aforesaid Bahādur had a slave who was brought up as his son. He was occasionally made to discharge his (Bahādur's) big gun and he also had acquired remarkable skill in shooting. The Mīrzā asked him to keep on firing now and then in the same way as Bahādur did. In short, when the world-illuminating sun set in the west and the darkness of night caused men and animals to retire to bed, the Mīrzā ordered the corpse of Bahādur to be brought down on the ground, tied to strong ropes. After this he was buried in that very enclosure. To the heirs of Bahādur provisions were made in the following way :—His brother-in-law was to receive an annual allowance of Rs. 250 ; his wife was to receive Rs. 150 per annum ; Rs. 100 were given to his mother-in-law and Rs. 120 to his slave who had been adopted by him as a son. This dispensation became a source of encouragement to others. The sons of Bahādur were given Rs. 300 for their water and soup i.e. for entertainment. A banquet was held in his presence in honour of Bahādur and thus he satisfactorily settled this matter. Then after the fourth day the inmates of the enemy's fort understood the truth and shouted aloud,—" Most probably we have keeled your *pahlawān* (hero). If he is not dead, he has left your service." The men from this side said, " With the gun of the *pahlawān* bodily present before you, how can you guess like that ? " They replied, " Had his gun not have been active we would have known for certain that he had left his job. At present, his musket is kept firing on; but previously, if he missed one, he would make four other dead hits. Now out of four, sometimes two to three shots miss their mark and one or two become effective. For this reason we are led to believe that he is gone." As it was necessary to keep the secret, so the men of this side did not make any admission. The soldiers of the army became more terrified than before. The Mīrzā went to each of them and said, "Think within yourself that you saw Ṣādiq Bahādur only in dream in the battle field. Invoke the blessings of the Prophet to help you in this difficulty. Why should you be perturbed?" In short, in this way the uneasiness in the hearts of the soldiers was laid at rest. (592)

**Sa'ādat Khān routs the force of Baldev.** Now I shall give a short account of the affairs of Sa'ādat Khān and other men of the raiding party and what had happened after their departure. When he (Sa'ādat) marched from this place and reached Bachādharī, he erected a fort. On the second day, he decided to carry on the raid. Then the chief of the village of Bachādharī named Govind came to him and said:—"Whom are you going to attack? Rāja Baldev has sent against you Govind Lashkar and Sunābaria with a force of two thousand picked-men of his own and another two thousand picked-men from the fort of Rangjūlī. They will march throughout the whole of this night, halt at Panchgīrī[15] and will stay there for the whole of to-morrow. In the last *pahar* of the day they will march from there and reaching here by sunset they will attack your fort. They have planned to keep on firing for the whole night. If you evacuate the fort and run away during the night, it is well and good for them; otherwise they will bring the *thataris* or *gardūns* next day and will make an attempt to conquer the fort with these (machines) in their front." The comrades therefore decided amongst themselves to proceed against the enemy before they could come up and attack them. In short, they left a regiment in the fort, marched in the last *pahar* of the night, and arrived there (before the enemy) in the first *pahar* of the day. The enemies, made the river their protective barrier and posted two hundred men to defend it; the rest engaged themselves in taking food and rest. Immediately after their reaching the river, those two hundred men advanced and attacked them. Sultan Khān Panī and a party of brave warriors (*bahādurān*), left all the other soldiers, behind and engaged in the battle falling upon them from a position of vantage with an elephant in their front. They crossed the river through some device and took the fighting foes by surprise. The enemies, unable to stand any longer, took to flight. Then the high and the low of this army crossed the river and fell upon the entire force of the enemy. As the enemies were absolutely unprepared for it, they were defeated and began to run away. Unable to resist, they became wanderers in forests. Whoever made any resistance was turned into fuel for the fire of hell. In short, they took with them the heads of forty-two men of the enemies who had fallen in battle and forty-two men were captured alive. Then the trumpet of victory was played and they joyfully returned from that place to their fort. (593)

**Govind Sardār joins the imperialists.** First of all they hanged the heads (of the enemies) from the tower of the fort and then the forty captives were ordered to be beheaded in presence of Govind Sardār. When fifteen were executed, Govind, in fear for his own life said :—" If you promise safety to my own life and to that of my son-in-law, then I promise that, by the favour of God, I will do whichever of the following two things you desire. First, I may lead you to Rāja Baldev who is staying at the fort of Bāohantī with a force of five hundred infantry and one hundred cavalry along with his family and elephants. It is at a distance of six days journey from here but I can lead you to that place by a route which will take only six *pahars* to reach there. You can capture him along with his properties, family and elephants. Secondly, you may take me to the Mīrzā so that by the favour of God I can make you conquer the fort of Rangjūlī within one *pahar*. I will lead the army to such a vulnerable point that the fort will be conquered immediately after your arrival." Therefore, Khwāja Sa'ādat Khān thought of returning with all and not to proceed against Rāja Baldev. He wrote to the Mīrzā the details of the victory and the aforesaid promises of Govind. The Mīrzā arranged during the night fifty horsemen and three hundred infantry and all necessary foodstuffs and sent them under the command of his Bakhshī Badrīdās. He wrote the following letter to Khwāja Sa'ādat Khān and his comrades:—" As the impediment on the way of your proceeding against Baldev was due to the want of a *Naqāra* elephant (the elephant on which the kettle-drum is carried), take with you one hundred and fifty picked horsemen from among the entire cavalry and twelve hundred infantry from your own company, the very day you receive this letter and as two elephants will accompany you, you, leave the female *Naqāra*, elephant with the rest of the cavalry and infantry in the fort and proceed against Rāja Baldev. This force would serve as an intermediary guide to supply rations from us to you." We shall forward rations to them and they, by the favour of God, will forward the same to you. In short, Badridās and this party started in the last *pahar* of the night and during the first *pahar* of the day he met two groups of men on this side of the fort of Sa'ādat Khān who were marching back (to Mīrzā Nathan). Badrīdās showed him (Sa'ādat Khān) the letter and explained to him that if his object was to get rations, they had been sufficiently provided; but it was of no avail. They had already left their original base far behind and the leader had lost control over the cavalry and the infantry. They proceeded on their way and reached Mīrzā Nathan one after the other. (594)

**Nathan blocks the path of enemy's food supply.** The Mīrzā, displeased at this act, came forward to meet these people and said, " What is the object of your coming back?" All the Sardārs replied, " We have brought Govind with us. God willing, we shall conquer the fort of Rangjūlī within one *pahar* and after this we shall think of others." The Mīrzā bcame highly displeased and said in reply, " There is still one and a half *pahar* of the day. Let me see how you conquer the fort?" These people, out of shame wanted to go (forward and attack the fort). But as the work must be properly executed, so at last he brought them all to the trenches with encouraging and flattering words and kept quiet. When the night advanced, the loyal officers of the State were summoned. Govind was brought to the assembly and they asked him about the prudent course of action. Govind said :—" For the welfare of the State, I have told you every thing I had to say. Now it is your choice. I take upon myself the responsibility of leading you, according to your orders. As you have granted the safety of my life, it will be *harām* (unlawful) on my part to take a full meal as long as I do not repay you for it." The Mīrzā, in order to encourage him, took an oath in the name of the Lord and affirmed :—" If you can render such a service then I am not the son of my father if I cannot make you the Rāja over the *Hizdah* Rājas (i.e. the Eighteen Hill-Chiefs) in place of Baldev." Then he was given suitable robes of honour. Early next morning, after being assured of the fortification of the trenches, he (the Mīrzā) rode on a horse and went to the rear of the enemy's fort under the guidance of Govind and he came to the head of the road through which rations were supplied to the fort. Govind suggested the erection of a fort in that place and the posting of a regiment, blocking the path of ingress and egress of the garrison within. The Mīrzā laid the foundation of a stockade and gave strict orders to the workers to work hard in its construction and fortification. He then ordered one hundred horsemen to go ahead to a distance of one *kos* and to take their position on either side (of the road). When the rations would reach there they should seize the food-stuffs and the suppliers should be taught a good lesson. This party took their stand there. The suppliers of rations arrived at that place by mid-day. The soldiers came out of their ambush and gave them a heavy blow. Many of them were put to the dreadful swords and a large booty was seized. The path of the supply of rations from this side was closed. But although it was not the rainy season, it began to rain towards the close of the day, in such a way that (God forbid!) the part of the stockade which was raised came down and all attempts made to preserve it went for nothing. The Mīrzā ordered a palisade to be raised all round the place where the wall of the stockade was to be constructed in such a way that the wall might be raised under its cover; and, if necessity arose, the musketeers would also be able to render services through the favour of God, under the cover of the palisade. In short, when this device was made, the fortification of that stockade was completed in three days. The Mīrzā posted in that stockade one hundred cavalry and three hundred expert matchlock-men under the command of Sultan Khān Panī; and Ratikanta, son of Sarbā Gosāin, the paternal uncle of Rāja Lakshmī Narāyan, was appointed with all the soldiers of the Rāja to help Sa'ādat Khān. Then he asked the aforesaid Govind, "What should be done now?" He replied, "One route of their supply of rations was from the side where you have first raised a stockade with its back to the west; and the other important route was this which has been lately blocked. Now there is a short route between these two stockades by which also rations may be supplied. This should also be blocked. The garrison will then have nothing else to subsist upon except dust." Therefore, he (the Mīrzā) went to that place and ordered the building of a fort. Here also it began to rain for three days and nights and the fort was constructed by raising a palisade in the same way (as mentioned before). A force of eighty cavalry and two hundred and fifty matchlock-men was posted there under the command of Muṣṭafā Qulī Beg; and Bhawānī Rāy, an officer of Rāja Satrajit, was attached to the aforesaid (Muṣṭafā) with auxiliaries to help this army. Thus assured of the safety of this place he (the Mīrzā) again asked Govind as to what other steps should be taken. He said, "I believe that as soon as we occupy the most advanced outpost, the enemy will leave the fort without any delay and will take to flight." But it was surprising that inspite of the siege of that place the enemy did not leave the fort and they remained within it scattering the dust of dejection on their condition. Then it became apparent that it was the will of the True Lord that all of them should be captured alive. Therefore, they willingly put themselves into the *Qamargāh* (hunting-ring). (595)

**Nathan occupies a commanding position.** When the situation came to this extremity, the Mīrzā sent two of his intelligent and skilful warriors named Mast 'Alī Beg and Sayf Khān with Govind to inspect a very high place which was situated there. If a fort could be raised in that place, the enemies could be captured alive. They went and inspected the place. They found the place so high that it commanded a full view of the fort including even the legs of men and animals that were moving about within it. In short, when they finished their inspection and returned, the inmates of the fort became panic-striken. They thought within themselves that if a fort was raised by the Mīrzā in that place, there would be no way left for their escape. So they immediately attempted to get out of the fort by making a breach in its wall on the side of the deep ditch and by constructing a bridge over the flowing water of the ditch where boats could easily ply. When those two men returned and explained the details to the Mīrzā, he at first appointed a party of men to construct a fort in that place within the night, and he himself moved to that place. But at last at the advice of the aforsaid Mast 'Alī Beg and Sayf Khān, the construction of the fort was postponed till the next day. The reason was that the surroundings of that eminence were filled with rain water and there was no other place excepting that eminence where the soldiers could alight; and further, the workmen owing to the water-logged character of the place and their hard labour for days and nights, might show sluggishness in the work during the night. It was also probable that the enemies might evacuate the fort within the night. It would be very good, if that happened; Otherwise, he (the Mīrzā) would personally go early next morning and after finishing the fortification of that place by the close of the day, would come back, leaving the place under the command of some other officer. (596)

**Occupation of Rangjūlī.** Mīrzā Nathan passed the aforesaid night in rest in the trench from which he previously used to move artificial barriers towards the (enemy's) fort. But he issued strict orders to the men of all the trenches to pass the time in vigilance and not to allow any man to be negligent of his duties. Accordingly, though every thing was in proper order, the Mīrzā kept himself engaged in devotion to God at midnight, seated on his bed *(pālong)* and kept his ears open. Then suddenly he heard a noise. It appeared to his mind that this noise must be due to two things, viz: either the enemies were attacking one of the trenches or they were flying away with the dust of disgrace scattered on their heads. Therefore, he woke up Khwāja Sa'ādat Khān who was sleeping by his bed and took him in his company. The torch-bearer (*mash'alchī*) who was guarding at the door and who silently approached the bedstead, was also taken with him. Then he went out of his bed-chamber and came to the barriers. He stood there for a while, and understanding the situation he said to Khwāja Sa'ādat Khān, "If the enemy would have attacked any of our trenches, surely fire would have been lighted. But it appears to me certain that the enemies have evacuated their fort throwing the dust of adversity on their head." From there he went to his own enclosure and informed the guards. Before this party could advance, the Mīrzā went to the bank of the ditch of the enemy's fort along with Khwāja Sa'ādat Khān and his own torch-bearer and without any hesitation he jumped into the ditch. Then he ordered Khwāja Sa'ādat Khān to take the torch from the torch-bearer and the latter was ordered to climb up to the top of the fort by cutting some steps on its wall with his dagger and to see whether the enemies were within the fort or had left it. The torch-bearer immediately cut a few steps on the wall and scaled to the top. In the mean time the soldiers from the barriers rushed forward. But the torch-bearer reached the top of the wall before any body else. After this, he took the torch from Khwāja Sa'ādat Khān and saw that not even a single bird was within the fort, which was quite empty. Then holding the torch in the same way with his left hand, he lifted the aforesaid Khwāja with his right hand and the Mīrzā was pulled up to the top of the fort after him When a tumult arose, soldiers from all the trenches rushed into the fort and trumpet of victory and the clarion of good-news were blown. The Mīrzā inspected the entire fort during that night and returned to his place of rest at the sixth *gharī* of the last part of the night. (597)

**Nathan proceeds in pursuit of Shumāruyed.** The soldiers thought that as the fort was conquered on the forty third night after a siege of forty-two days, they should retire from this place to some inhabited place to spend a few months (in rest). During this period (of siege) there was practically no supply of provision since the seventeenth day. Whoever had something in his store used to eat a little and give to others if he was prompted with generous feelings. Otherwise, he who had nothing used to suffer privations for two or three days together. Some of the horses remained without food for eight to nine days; even the state horses of the Mīrzā had to go without any grain for four days. But Mīrza Nathan was bent upon not allowing any breathing time to the enemy who had fled away severely punished by a siege of forty-two days and had escaped from his hands like wounded deer. He thought that before they could collect their dispersed forces they should either be driven away or brought as captives by the favour of God. With this decision he ordered his Bakhshī to despatch a force of two hundred cavalry, two thousand infantry and five elephants under Khwāja Sa'ādat Khān as vanguard. And he himself was to follow after staying there for three days and making satisfactory arrangements for the safety of Balabhadra Dās and others who were left in the rear in pursuit of Parsurām. In short, next morning when the sun arose the Mīrzā personally went to despatch Sa'ādat Khān and the vanguard. First of all Sultan Khān and his brothers devised some excuses for not proceeding; then Mast 'Alī Beg and other leaders did not agree to advance.

The Mīrzā became very much displeased at this and returned to his camp. After midnight he sent one of his devoted servants named Khwāja Aḥmad, brother of Shaykh Amānu'llah, with a force of seventy horsemen, five hundred infantry and the elephant named Shāh 'Ināyat which was in heat, in order to help Khwāja Balabhadra Dās who held the command at Solmārī to extirpate the accursed Parsurām. Early next morning the kettle-drum of his march was played. In the mean time Ratikanta, son of Sarbā Gosāin, the paternal uncle of Rāja Lakshmī Narāyan, expressed his determination not to proceed. The Mīrzā sent some of his confidential officers to advise him. Thus one *pahar* was wasted. When the affair had passed beyond that stage and he (Ratikanta) rode on his horse with his baggage to go away, Khwaja Sa'ādat Khān was sent with a hundred horsemen with the following instructions:—"If he returns to the right path, it is well and good; otherwise, bring his head. As he is behaving improperly to-day in imperial matters, I shall consider him as another Baldev and inflict capital punishment on him, and am prepared to answer the charge of an (imperial) enquiry." Sa'ādat Khān and this party went to him and when they advanced in search of him, he saw no way out and agreed to come in their company. Inspite of the fact that there was only one and a half *pahar* of the day left, he marched through the dense forest around the fort of Rangjūlī and pitched his camp in a field. The report of the conquest of the fort which was made with full triumph was sent to the Khān Fatḥ-jang. The Khān was greatly relieved from the worries of this problem. (598)

**Capture of the Rāja of Tippera.** Now I shall give a short account of the affairs of Mīrzā Nūru'd-Dīn and the imperial officers who pursued the Rāja of Tippera and how these ended. For three days and nights they pursued him on horse back as far as the road permitted them to do so and then they rode on elephants. When he (the Rāja) came near the hills, he left off the elephants, as it was not possible to cross the hills on elephants and also with a view to mislead the (imperial) army which was pursuing him. Therefore, the imperial officers also left their elephants and pursued him on foot through the hills and jungles. By chance one of the slaves of Mīrzā Nūru'd-Dīn followed by a Mughal of Mīrzā Isfandiyār arrived at the top of a hill. They saw a few women walking one after another. This slave ran after one of these women and wanted to catch her. She shrieked. The Rāja, was hiding under a tree and saw both of them. He came out and fell upon the slave. He struck on the head of the aforesaid slave a blow with his sword. Although it was effective, the slave also struck the Rāja with his sword; and when he (the slave) raised his hand to give another blow, the Rāja cried aloud,—" I am the Rāja of Tippera." Then the slave held back his sword and caught hold of the waist of the Rāja. But as the Rāja was of strong build and as the salve was profusely bleeding, the former ran away and the latter fell senseless, shouting to the Mughal :—" I have finished his job. Do not let him go." The Mughal ran up to the Rāja, seized him by the waist and threw him on the ground. When he was going to bind him up, Mīrzā Nūru'd-Dīn, Mīrzā Isfandiyār and Mūsā Khān arrived there one after the other and made the Rāja a captive. The wives of the Rāja who were hiding themselves in that jungle were captured along with the jewels, the jewelled-weapons and a big treasure. They stayed there for five days and seized all the elephants of the Rāja which had been let loose. From there they returned to Udaypūr in triumph and joy, and a detailed report was sent to the Khān Fatḥ-jang. The Khān sent messengers with strict orders to Mīrzā Nūru'd-Dīn, Mīrzā Isfandiyār and Masnad-i-'Alā Mūsā Khān that they should leave the entire army in that place and should proceed to Jahāngīrnagar along with the Rāja of Tippera and his family and belongings. They acted according to the orders of the Khān and took the Rāja to the Khān along with his elephants, family and all the belongings. Every one of them was highly honoured with great favours according to his loyal services. The news of this victory was then reported by the Khān Fatḥ-jang to the sublime Court. (599)

**Sufferings of Nathan and his army.** Now I shall revert to the previous theme as to what happened after Mīrzā Nathan's march from Rangjūlī through the jungles outside the fort and his encampment there at nightfall. Next morning he (Nathan) marched from that place and continued his march till a quarter of the day was left, and halted at Bakū[16] on the bank of the river Bakū. But as all the soldiers were starving, some of them for four days, some for three days and others for two days, so the Mīrzā himself in sympathy with the starving condition of his men did not take anything for two days. In short, most of them were affected with nausea and nobody had the will to inquire after the condition of any body else,—so much so, that even the Mīrzā began to vomit and feel irritation in his stomach from next morning. The drugs which he took were not assimilated into his system up to four *gharīs* of the night. Then the Mīrzā had a sound sleep. (600)

**Encounter with Shumāruyed.** In the mean time Chatsa Rāja[17] and Rūpābar, brother of Akra Rāja, who were sent to bring news of the enemy after his (Mīrzā's) halt, came and reported that Shumāruyed Kāyeth had come at night to a passage between two hills and had begun the construction of a fort in that mountain pass; and that if the army hurried to that place that day, it would be possible to cross over; otherwise when that stupid man would finish fortifying the pass, no other means would be left to the army but to take a roundabout route covering a journey of six days. Khwāja Sa'ādat Khān, Mast 'Alī Beg and Sultan came and awoke the Mīrzā by pulling his leg and explained the situation to him. The Mīrzā said, " Ask them the time I shall take to reach the place, if I start from here." They said, " You may easily reach there within one and a half *pahar* of the day." The Mīrzā said, "Take me on a *sukhpāl* (palanquin) and let us march. By the time we reach there, I shall regain my strength and I shall be able to ride on horse." It was accordingly done. A company was left behind under the command of Ya'qūb Khān the Mīr Sāmān (Superintendent of the household) of the Mīrzā in order to follow (the army) along with the camp-followers with their goods and chattels. They then made a vigorous march and reached the vicinity of that pass after one and a half *pahar* of the day. Then they (the officers) informed the Mīrzā. The Mīrzā also, fully armed and equipped, rode on a horse and advanced by dividing the army into three regiments. As soon as Sa'ādat Khān arrived with the van at the foot of the hill, Shumāruyed and his followers began to fire guns and cannon. They dismounted from their horses and rushed upon the fort of the pass putting the shields before their faces. The enemy continued their fight fearlessly. The infuriated heroes, having put their utmost exertions, did not allow any defection to creep into their ranks and fell upon the enemy with one mind and one will. The elephant-drivers, inspite of the thickness of the battle, drove the elephants to the wall of the fort. Shumāruyed, unable to resist any longer, became a wanderer in the desert and fled away by a secret track to his left. The heroes of the vanguard, making no distinction between hills and dales, began to pursue the fleeing enemies by dividing themselves into two parties. (601)

**Flight of Baldev to the hills.** It so happened that when the army of the Mīrzā reached near (the mountain pass), Shumāruyed sent messengers to Rāja Baldev with the following message :—" The fort is incomplete, and the Mīrzā is coming with full force. The elephant-force of the Mīrzā is remarkably strong. It will be well and good if you send your heated elephant in order to oppose the elephants from within our fort." Accordingly, Rāja Baldev sent some horsemen along with the elephant named Chandi-Prasad. These horsemen arrived there with the elephant at the time when Mast 'Alī Beg and some other warriors had reached there before the arrival of the vanguard and were standing in the front as sentinels. They met one another, and as soon as they led an assault, the men of Baldev suffered a defeat after a very short skirmish and fled away with the elephant. This party pursued them. When Khwāja Sa'ādat Khān reached this place from the rear, he made no enquiries about these people, but went by the left and all on a sudden, he arrived before the fort of Rāja Baldev. As the fort of the Rāja had not been properly stengthened, he had not the power to offer a resistance unaided and as soon as this regiment reached there he forthwith ran away. He carried his family on elephant's back, took his cash and jewelleries with him and proceeded to the hills with the intention of taking shelter with the hill-Rājas. Sa'ādat Khān entered into the fort of the enemy and played the trumpet of victory. The Mīrzā, who arrived after him, hearing the report about the enemy's cavalry and the elephant and of the pursuit of the enemy by Mast 'Alī Beg and other heroes, followed them. When he was passing by a river which ran by the side of Baldev's fort, he came to a path through which his (the Mīrzā's) soldiers were pursuing the enemies. But at this place he received the news that Khwāja Sa'ādat Khān had gone against the enemy's fort by another route to the left. Therefore, he thought thus in his mind:—" That army has fled away and my soldiers are pursuing them. But when Khwāja Sa'ādat Khān has gone to the fort of the Sardār, the battle may be equally balanced and he may be put to a difficult situation unless he is aided from the rear." So he despatched seventy horsemen under the command of one of his personal attendants named Muṣāḥib Khān, and said :—" Let me see what help you can render to Mast 'Alī Beg and others in the battle." He then personally proceeded to the fort with all his soldiers. But this place had already been conquered. So when he saw that none of his three desires, was realised, namely, neither Baldev was captured, nor his family nor his elephants, he became very sad. He left that place, crossed over to the other side of the river and began to search for the elephants in the jungles, and ordered his camp to be pitched in a field. (602)

**Surrender of Akra Rāja.** In the mean time Akra Rāja came and expressed his loyalty and he became one of the loyal Zamīndārs. As the wardrobe of the Mīrzā had not yet reached there, so, inorder to honour Akra Rāja, he took off his own special turban from his head and presented it to Akra Rāja and made the following convenant:—" If you remain firm in your loyalty and do not step out of its bounds, then, in consideration of the fact that you have submitted before any other Rāja, I will make you the Sardār (chief) over all the Eighteen (hill) Rājas, and place you in the position of Baldev when he is captured. But your first duty is to seize the properties of Baldev who, before the arrival of the army had managed to send all his belongings on boats to the territory of Umed Rāja who is your *Upaṙiya* Rāja (i.e. Rāja of the upper hill regions)." He (Akra Rāja) said, " As at present Umed Rāja strengthened by his league with Rāja Baldev has withdrawn his hand (of friendship) from me, I shall be able to fulfil my obligations if I receive help from you." The Mīrzā gave him *pān* (betel leaf) and granted him leave to return to his home. (603)

**Nathan proceeds to Barduwār.** The Mīrzā then summoned Govind and asked him what should be done next. Govind said:—" When the army was scattered I did not offer any suggestion. Now when all the regiments from different places have arrived and assembled together we can proceed from this camp to the territory of the Rāja of Barduwār[18] which is a journey of four *gharīs*. Baldev, who has entered the hilly region, shall have to pass by that Duwār (gate or pass). So, if we go ahead and remain ready in that place, he will have to surrender himself into captivity, along with his family and elephants in his attempt to pass through the Duwār." Accordingly, the Mīrzā summoned the Bakhshī (Pay-master) of the army and said:—" As the men and animals are starving for four to five days and the horses for nearly ten days, so enquire of the officers, high and low, who are bold enough to accompany me, and are prepared to enlist voluntarily. Take their names and let me know how many of the cavalry and the infantry are prepared to gird up their loins of courage. Then it will be time to think of marching forward." In short, after going round the whole army it was found that only twenty one horsemen, whose names will be mentioned below, had volunteered to accompany him. Five men of the Mīrzā who owned state horses were compelled to go; so it came to twenty-seven horsemen including the Mīrzā himself. Further, there were twenty-six infantry consisting of six musketeer, two Afghān foot-soldiers, two grooms, one standard-bearer, six *kahārs* (palanquin-bearers) of the Mīrzā's *Sarkār,* and nine sentries who agreed to follow. Of all the elephants of the Mīrzā, one imperial elephant named Ganesha, whose driver 'Abdu'r-Raḥīm had the boldness to accompany him, was taken with him. As the Mīrzā was suffering from fever so the *kahārs* showed their loyalty by carrying him in a *sukhpāl* (palanquin). The Mīrzā encouraged his companions and said, "It is a journey of four *gharīs* only. After that I shall ride on a horse and go to fight." Accordingly, they accompanied him. He started one *gharī* before the close of the day and asked Badridās, the Bakhshī of the army to order half the army to keep their horse saddled and the other half to remain ready for the next half of the night (for guard duty). The Bakhshī was also ordered to remain fully equipped and pass the whole night in vigilance. From there he (the Mīrzā) proceeded with a determination to give fight. The following are the names of persons who accompanied him in this expedition by girding up their loins of courage after a period of starvation of five days for men and ten days for horses:—Khwāja Sa'ādat Khān, Mast 'Alī Beg Badakhshī, Sultan Khān Panī with his five brothers, Mīrān Saiyid 'Abdu's-Samad, Shīr Khān Kārgar, Shaykh Ruknu'd-Dīn, Niẓāmu'd-Dīn, Muṣṭafā Qulī Beg, Sayf Khān Lūdi, Shaykh Amānu'llah, Shaykh Isma'īl, Mīrān Shāh, Shaykh Mida, Bulaqi the musketeer, Khwāja Iqbāl, Jānkara Khān, Bhawānī Rāy and five other men of Rāja Satrajit, Dariya Karrānaychī (the beater of kettle-drum) and Ma'rūf Kalāwant. These twenty-six horsemen started and reached the aforesaid Duwār six *gharīs* after evening. (604)

**Ingenious plan of Govind Lashkar.** As Govind Lashkar accompanied them riding on a horse, he was asked, " Now we have reached this place ; what else should be done ? " He replied, " You must excuse me if I use any unbecoming language in order to get a clue and gain my object." The Mīrzā said, " You are at liberty to say whatever you like." Govind shouted in the language of the Kūch, " Is there any body here ? " No one replied. He again shouted. Then two men began to talk in a low voice between themselves, " Ātā, i.e., Bābā (father) Govind, who was captured by the Bangāl (the soldiers of the imperial army were termed by the Kūches as Bangāl), is shouting." The other man said, " Keep silent and listen." Govind again shouted and said, " Why don't you respond ? " Then one of them replied, " Ātā, i.e., father ! You were a captive of the Bangāl ; how did you escape ? " Govind immediately began to abuse the army of the Mīrzā and said, " I was a prisoner, but I obtainad my release by bribing the guard with the sum of Rs. 4 which I had in my belt. When I came to Mahārāj (Baldev) and was talking with him, the Bangāls came again all on a sudden and attacked the fort. The Mahārāj with his wives rode on elephants and retired to the hills. He told me to follow him with the cavalry. Therefore I have come here with the cavalry and I want to know which way the Mahārāj is gone, so that I may take the cavalry there." " In short, after this conversation the man came out. The moment he saw the regiment of the Mīrzā he became surprised and asked, Ātā (father !) who are these people ? " Then Govind said, " You contemptible man ! If you utter a word, Mīrzā Nathan will cut off your head immediately. Tell me which way is he gone ? " That distracted fellow spoke out the truth, " Four *gharīs* to evening, he (Baldev) had gone to the country of Bāmun Rāja." The Mīrzā asked him, " How far is the country of Bāmun Rāja ? " Govind replied, " The distance will be almost the same as you have already traversed." **(605)**

**Nathan proceeds to the territory of Bāmun Rāja.** The Mīrzā then consulted with Khwāja Sa'ādat Khān, Mast 'Alī

Beg and Sultan Khān. All the three agreed with the Mīrzā and decided that when they had already come so far from their camp, they should proceed farther. They took with them the man who gave them the information and made a swift march. The Mīrzā rode on a state horse and proceeded. Jānkara Khān, one of the horsemen was appointed to be the supervisor over the *kahārs* with instructions to make them march with earnestness and to carry the *sukhpāl*. He (the Mīrzā) himself marched with exertions and reached the territory of Bāmun Rāja two *gharīs* after evening. As he (Bāmun Rāja) had no fort and as he lived in an open field, so the following message was sent to him:—"If you desire your welfare, then hand over Rāja Baldev, the (proclaimed) thief of the Emperor (*duzd-i-Bādshāh*), whom I have driven to your country with his wives and children." He sent a reply, "I have neither any jungle nor forest to keep the elephants concealed therein. I can tell you that although he is a relation of mine and I tried hard to detain him, he did not stay. He has gone to the territory and the abode of Rāja Kanwal (Kamal?) who is also a relation of his.[10] (606)

**Duplicity of Kanwal Rāja.** In short, as there was truth in what he said so the Mīrzā left that place and asked Govind, "How far is the country of Kanwal?" He replied that the journey may be covered by midnight. The Mīrzā then ordered (his followers) to proceed forward and a swift march was made from that place. After having traversed a portion of the road, he (the Mīrzā) came to a jungle and found a short route leading to the bank of the ditch of the fort of Rāja Kanwal. In short, when after a continuous march they reached a place at a distance of one *kos* from the fort and the abode of the aforesaid Rāja, the Mīrzā ordered an enquiry about his men, so that none might be left behind. When an inspection was made it was found that Jānkara Khān with the *kahārs* and the *sukhpāl* had fallen behind. Therefore, they halted at that place. A horseman was sent to enquire about them, and after a while another was sent. For the third time the Mīrzā said to Mast 'Alī Beg, "I shall have no peace of mind until you personally go to enquire about them." Mast 'Alī Beg rode very fast. When no news of the *sukhpāl* came even after the departure of Mast 'Alī Beg, then the Mīrzā thought in his mind, " I am carrying on the fight with the aim of seizing the elephants and for attaining fame. God forbid, if I cannot capture the elephants and go back losing the *sukhpāl*, nowhere shall I be able to show my face." Then he returned along with every body, high and low, by the same route by which he came. When he brought out his head from the jungles and forests and entered the plain field, Mast 'Alī Beg reached from the opposite side and said, " I went to a distance of two or three *kos* from the village which is visible from here and found Jānkara with the *sukhpāl* and I have brought them up to this village with very great difficulty. But after reaching the village the *kahārs* fell down (on the ground). Two of them disappeared in the village, four others did not get up and said that they would not be able to move even if their heads were cut off." He (the Mīrzā) again sent Sa'ādat Khān to bring them by all possible means and swearings. Khwāja Sa'ādat Khān after saying much " Allah " and Billah " (swearing in the name of God) brought five *kahārs* with the *sukhpāl*. The Mīrzā slept there for a short time and at the advice of Govind Lashkar he sent two men to Rāja Kanwal with this message :—" We have pursued the proclaimed thief of the Emperor with his family and elephants and driven him to your fort. Hand over the rebel to us as a prisoner, if you desire your welfare. Otherwise you will have to repent for your action." When the messengers delivered this news, Rāja Kanwal came with humility and said most respectfully, " It is known to you that Rāja Baldev has entered my fort with a large army of cavalry, elephants and infantry with full strength. Under these circumstances I have not the power to hand him over to you in fetters. But if you agree to post your army on his way, I will turn him out of my fort. Then you may surround him from that side and I will render my loyal services from this side." The Mīrzā agreed to this proposal and proceeded. But as there was no sincerity in him (Kanwal Rāja), so as soon as the messengers returned after delivering the reply, he informed Rāja Baldev and sent him with his family out of the fort and after that he (Kanwal) made the Mīrza's army take its stand on the path of his (Baldev's) escape. When it became morning, four horsemen and six foot-soldiers were seen on the side of the fort of Kanwal Rāja. The cavalry of the Mīrzā made a rush and surrounded them. On examination it was found that among them were two wives of Rāja Baldev,—the daughters of this Rāja Kanwal and Bāmun Rāja who had been left behind (by Baldev). When they were captured, it was given out that Rāja Baldev had fled away six *gharīs* before morning. (607)

**Capture of the family of Baldev.** The Mīrzā grew very wild and he held a council of war with his loyal officers. Some of the inexperienced men said, "Let us attack this fort of Rāja Kanwal and punish him." Some said, "Let us go back and come with an army against Rāja Kanwal and deal out such a heavy blow to him that nobody in this *Chakla* (district) would dare give shelter to Baldev again. Some suggested, "Let us stay here and summon the army and find out some plan to punish this rebel." Mast 'Alī Beg, who possessed courage and wisdom, said, "The distance which we covered at night in one *pahar* can be covered now in the day within two *gharīs*. The day is bright and clear and even the flying animals can be seen to a distance of four *kos*, not to speak of elephants and armies. Let us take the trouble of search for another *pahar*. If this rebel falls into our hands it is well and good; otherwise, we shall take our way to our own camp and will do whatever is thought best." Accordingly, the Mīrzā also approved of this opinion. He thanked him (Mast 'Alī) and advanced forward and trotted on like a wolf. Before they travelled a distance of one *kos*, Rāja Baldev appeared in front of them with his army of elephants and cavalry. Although the Mīrzā rode very fast, yet seven of his heroes, who were in the van, whose names will be mentioned below (were even quicker and) fell upon Rāja Baldev.

The Mīrzā shouted to the *Karrānaychī* (the beater of the trumpet) to beat the trumpet in order to terrify the enemies who were coming on with sinister motives. The *Karrānaychī* sounded the trumpet in its highest pitch. The Mīrzā, who followed those seven men (of the van) with a company of six horsemen without stopping anywhere, raised the cry of "*Allah-u-Akbar*" (God is Great) and fell upon them by drawing out his sword. No sooner did the Muslims fall upon the pagans than the Muslims attained a victory (over the pagans) with the influence of the world-conquering fortune of the Emperor. *Verse.* (Left out.) In the mean time, out of the seven men of the van, Sa'ādat Khān, Sultan Khān and Muṣṭafā Qulī Beg rendered splendid services by shooting their arrows. As soon as the Mīrzā reached that place, after a short skirmish, Rāja Baldev, unable to resist any longer, dismounted from his elephant in the rear of his army, ran to a high hill and began to climb on it. When his followers saw him fleeing, they became separated from one another like the constellation of the Bear. The desired victory was attained and the standard of conquest was unfurled. Nine big elephants along with eighty four horses were seized as booties in that victory, and all the belongings of Rāja Baldev including his wives and children were captured. As the number of the Mīrzā's followers was small it was not possible to remove all the booties. They took with them three elephants and about fifty horses. Out of more than a thousand cannon and guns which were lying in the field, they loaded on elephants as many big cannon as they could. From that place they resumed their march in proper order to their camp at Bāohantī. (608)

**Second encounter with Shumāruyed.** When they proceeded a short distance, Shumāruyed Kāyeth, the knave, appeared before them with a force of one thousand brave infantry. He (Shumāruyed) was under the impression that the Rāja (Baldev) was coming on elephants with his wives and children. The Mīrzā presumed that it must be mischievous Shumāruyed, the head of the rebels in Kūch and the chief officer of Rāja Baldev, and so he proceeded slowly. The moment when he (the Mīrzā) saw that the enemy had approached a distance from which friends and foes might be discriminated, he rushed upon him (Shumāruyed) with naked swords and Shumāruyed Kāyeth, the knave, ran to hell sustaining a heavy defeat. Thus victories were attained one after the other. In the latter part of the day they reached their destination. The men of the camp came to congratulate them and they become happy. But immediately after their arrival at the camp the Mīrzā was attacked with fever and he began to vomit and he could not digest any drug or water he took to stop it. (609)

**Surrender of Bāmun and Kanwal Rāja.** Next day he (the Mīrzā) marched from that camp and wrote to the hill-Rājas who are known as *Hizdah* Rājas :—" If you desire your own welfare, you must surrender to me by tying the thread of obedience on your own necks ; otherwise, you shall have to repent like Rāja Baldev." Bāmun Rāja and Kanwal Rāja, who had suffered sufficient loss came to the Mīrzā on that very day when he had traversed half the way from his camp. Every one of them received a horse and a robe of honour and returned immediately to their own homes so that other hill tribes might not be frightened and might come to submit in the earliest opportunity. From there he made a swift march and pitched his camp at a central place. (610)

**Nathan congratulated.** Next day, he marched and halted on the bank of the Brahmaputtra. Mīr Ghiyāṣu'd-Dīn Maḥmūd, the Bakhshī, Rāja Satrajit and all the Bengal Zamīndārs who were posted at the Thāna of Hājo of the Ṣūbah of Kūch, came to meet Mīrzā Nathan and began to praise him. After the display of the elephants seized in the victory they returned to Hājo. The Mīrzā halted there for three days and nights. (611)

**Rāja Bhū Singh and Mān Singh submit.** When he found that the Rānī, mother of Rāja Bhū Singh, Rāja Bhū Singh himself and his brother Mān Singh had not come personally to pay their homage and had sent Gopāl Dalai the maternal uncle of Rāja Bhū Singh to pay homage (on their behalf), he became very angry and proceeded to conquer his (Bhū Singh's) territory without giving him any respite. Rāja Bhū Singh, unable to resist, came out to a distance of four *kos* from his abode, and having put the thread of obedience on his neck, he paid his homage. The Mīrzā presented him a horse and a robe of honour. He halted in that place and ordered Govind Lashkar to raise a fort, fifteen hundred yards in length and breadth. Govind Lashkar assigned the work of half the portion of the fort to four thousand *paīks* of the country of Lāmdānī[20] who were in his train and the other half to the followers of the Eighteen Rājas (*Hizdah* Rājas). These hard-working men constructed a lofty fort with a ditch around it within two days and nights. The Mīrzā began to stay here with a contented heart. God, the Great, had granted him a glorious expedition and a speedy recovery of health. (612)

**Nathan rewards his officers.** The Mīrzā then ordered his Bakhshī Khwāja Badrīdās to present these seven men, namely, Khwāja Sa'ādat Khān, Mast 'Alī Beg, Sultan Khān, Saiyid 'Abdu's-Samad, Muṣṭafā Qulī Beg, Sayf Khān Lūdī and Jalāl Khān Kākar who had been posted in the van in the battle against Rāja Baldev, with seven horses along with robes of honour, and seven swords with gold and silver hilts and belts and bands. Accordingly, the Bakhshī and the Mīr Sāmān brought these things together and honoured them with the presents of horses and robes of honour. It gave a great impetus and encouragement to the devoted service of others. (613)

**Māmūn Govind captured by Hasta Rāja.** Hasta Rāja brought the news,—"Māmūn Govind with his son has been captured by my soldiers and I will do whatever you order." The Mīrzā ought to have sent one of his trustworthy officers to bring Māmūn Govind from his (Hasta's) men, but Hasta Rāja *alias* Kandana who was brought up under the fostering care of the Mīrzā and enjoyed his (the Mīrzā's) highest confidence was ordered to arrange for sending Māmūn Govind. But as there was no sincerity in the mind of Hasta Rāja, he failed to render this service properly. As soon as Māmūn Govind promised him to give his daughter in marriage, he let loose Govind from his bondage and allowed him to abscond. He then brought this information,—" Before I reached there he got out of my men's control through some device." Although he (Hasta) deserved punishment, yet the Mīrzā, remembering the fostering care with which he had brought him up, pardoned him, and waited patiently relying on God. (614)

**Capture of Parsurām.** After a few days news came from Balabhadra Dās that the vanquished Parsurām had been captured by him with his family. The details of this episode are as follows:—It has been mentioned before that when the Mīrzā proceeded to the expedition of Āmjūnga and Rangjūlī, Balabhadra Dās was left in the pargana of Sāmbhūr in order to finish the job of Parsurām the accursed. After the conquest of Āmjūnga and the fort of Rangjūlī, a force of cavalry and infantry along with the elephant Shāh 'Ināyat was sent under the command of Amānu'llah and Khwāja Aḥmad in order to help Balabhadra Dās. The aforesaid one (Balabhadra) proceeded against Parsurām five days after the arrival of the reinforcement. Although Parsurām could not be captured that day, his eldest son along with two young sons and one of his wives were made captives; but of this he (Balabhadra) did not send any report that day. This reduced the rebel to helplessness. He sent some mediators and proposed with great humiliation to obtain the release of his sons and wife by paying money. While he was thinking whether he would submit or not, Balabhadra Dās despatched Ḥabīb Khān with a party of Afghān infantry to the hill. Ḥabīb Khān with his whole regiment followed him by the skirt of the hill. As God the Great had willed to make him (Ḥabīb Khān) famous, he captured Parsurām alive with the help of the Afghāns and the report of his capture was sent (to the Mīrzā). The

Mīrzā, on account of his confidence in Sa'ādat Khān, sent him by a boat to fetch Parsurām. Sa'ādat Khān reached there by making an expeditious journey and brought the rebel with him. When the news of the capture of Parsurām reached Qulīj Khān, he, smarting under the disgrace of his failure to capture Parsurām, sent a regiment to seize Parsurām at any cost from the hands of Mīrzā's men. Although Qulīj Khān sent a large army, Sa'ādat Khān sent Parsurām to the Mīrzā ahead of him by throwing dust on the eyes of that regiment and he himself proceeded to Hājo. Qulīj Khān thought of picking up a quarrel with him but Mīr Ghiyāṣu'd-Dīn came to the rescue and sent Sa'ādat Khān to Mīrzā Nathan and extinguished this fire of dissension. After some time Ḥabib Khān and others arrived with Parsurām and his family and Sa'ādat Khān arrived next day in a happy mood and presented himself before the Mīrzā to the joy of the people of the age. The Mīrzā in order to honour Balabhadra Dās and his men and to encourage others sent a horse and a robe of honour to Balabhadra Dās and his salary was doubled. Ḥabīb Khān and others who had rendered this service were given an increase of salary by ten or fifteen (rupees) and every one of them was presented with a robe of honour according to his rank. (615)

**Rāja Kūk and Rāja Sanjoy submit.** One day a force of three hundred cavalry, three thousand infantry and ten elephants were despatched under the command of Sa'ādat Khān against the country of Hangrabārī[21] and Kūk Rāja. As soon as they went, Rāja Kūk and Rāja Sanjoy came forward and made submission, and Hangrabārī had to be raided. (616)

**Expedition against Rāja Umed and Akra.** It has been mentioned before that Akra Rāja was deputed by the Mīrza to seize the belongings of Rāja Baldev which were in deposit with Rāja Umed. Akra Rāja, with the view of saving himself from accusation, sent *petārās* (boxes) of useless things secured from Umed Rāja in charge of his younger brother Rūpābar. The Mīrzā become enraged at this. Therefore, he sent a regiment of two hundred cavalry, five hundred matchlock-men and three thousand native *paīks* under the command of his Bakhshī Badrīdās against Akra Rāja and Rāja Umed with the following instructions :—" If immediately on your arrival the deposits of Rāja Baldev are handed over to you, it is well and good ; or otherwise, you are to raid the Lāmdānī (hills of the lower regions) and the Uppara (hills of the upper regions) territories of the Rājas, capture both of them and send them in chains to me." Govind Lashkar also was attached to his company. As these two Rājas were not favoured by Divine grace, Umed Rāja fled away, and Akra Rāja and his brother were brought in chains. This incident, ultimately produced a consternation among all the hill-Rājas. Then all the small and great Rājas, *Dal-Dalpati*, *Takris*, *Lashkars*, and the *Dakuhs*,[22] came and submitted. (617)

**Desertion of the hill-chiefs.** One afternoon Mīrzā Nathan came out and took his seat and all the officers, high and low, presented themselves. Sultan Khān, Mast 'Alī Beg, Saiyid 'Abdu's-Samad, Sayf Khān, and Mīrān Khwāja Aḥmad in consultation with Khwāja Sa'ādat Khān said to the Mīrzā, " It is reported that the hill-Rājas are proposing to become *harām-khwūr* (disloyal). Now is the best opportunity to imprison all these big and petty (chiefs) who are present here, and then let us go to Garal and stay there, free of the troubles of this territory." The Mīrzā replied, " I have pledged myself to God ; under no circumstance can I break my promise. Please excuse my inability to do so." In short, when Sa'ādat Khān began to speak, all of them insisted upon the Mīrzā (doing so.). When the Mīrzā saw that he was unable to get out of it and they were insisting upon this proposal, he ordered all the small and great Zamīndārs who were sitting there to go back to their respective houses and he himself returned to his own house. He thus left the council in disagreement relying on the favour of God. A week after this all on a sudden there arose a tumult after one *pahar* of the night and the Rājas and Zamīndārs fled away. The Mīrzā came out of his house and sent some men to enquire . They found that all of them except the Rāja of Barduwār and the son of Bāmun Rāja had fled away. These two were brought to the Mīrzā. Mīrzā Nathan said, " Why did these unlucky people throw the dust of repentance on their heads ? " Both of them replied, " Had we been associates of their conspiracies, we would have run away before them. We know nothing about them." Mīrzā Nathan said, " If you also desire to be *harām-khwūr* (disloyal), I give you a *pān* (betel leaf) and you also may depart, if you so desire ; or, if you like to stay, you may stay on." They said, " At first we proposed to go and then we decided to remain loyal till our death as long as we live. But when in future these ill-fated people will come to fight in some place and will cry aloud saying, ' why do you believe these men ? are not these men our companions ? ' then what will happen to us ? " The Mīrzā gave them *pān* to pacify them and said,—" If you go, I give you farewell with these *pāns*. If you stay then these *pāns* are your guarantees that I will never believe whatever is said by others against you." They were given leave to go to their beds and he also took rest. After two or three days they also fled away. (618)

**Rebellion of the hill-Rājas.** After their flight, the big and the petty hill-Rājas joined together and raised a fort at Rānīhāt. The Mīrzā despatched a cavalry regiment, which attacked the aforesaid fort as soon as it reached there and levelled it to the ground. But thrice they raised such forts and on all these three occasions they were demolished. But in the second battle Hasta Rāja, who was loyal among all the Zamīndārs, openly went over to the enemies. The Mīrza became depressed and in the evening he returned to his fort and place of rest. Next morning, the Mīrzā sent some men to bring the women (*maḥal*) of the Mīrzā to that fort. The family of the Mīrzā which was at Chandan Kuth was brought over in great haste. Most of the officers who had wives or maid servants also brought them there. (619)

**Siege of Rānīhāt.** The enemies i.e. the hill Rājas thus appealed to the Rāja of Assam :—" If you help us, we shall bar Mīrzā Nathan's progress towards the kingdom of Assam ; otherwise, if this year he becomes victorious over us, nothing will prevent him from destroying Assam next year." The Rāja of Assam sent Hātī Barua, the chief of his Sardārs with a force of eighty thousand men to the aid of the hill-Rājas, and the Rājkhawa and the Khārghuka (Khārgharia Phukan) were attached to his company. Rāja Baldev and Shumāruyed Kāyeth, who had suffered defeat after defeat at the hands of the Mīrzā and had gone to seek help from the Rāja of Assam before this incident losing all their elephants and artillery and leaving their wives and children as captives, were also sent in their company. Strict orders were issued (by the Assam Rāja) that they should fight in such a way as to capture alive this entire regiment, specially Mīrzā Nathan with some of his officers who had the hardihood to attack an army of thousands without flinching; and also he (the Mīrzā) should be sent with his family by boats to him (the Assam Rāja). Hātī Barua and all others reached Rānīhāt. He did not not raise any fort in that place.[1] He went to a hill to the right of the fort of the Mīrzā and constructed a fort close to the hill and fully strengthened it within the night. From that place he began the construction of a series of forts in order to bring the Mīrzā and his army to bay like the deer in the Qamargah (ring-hunt). The Mīrzā, out of his foresight, remained on horseback for the whole of the day and appointed one thousand *paīks* under his eunuch Khwāja La'l Beg in order to cut down the jungles and to clear the surroundings of his fort. (620)

**Death of Govind Lashkar.** Govind Lashkar, who was brought up under the fostering care of the Mīrzā, came and said, "The enemy is intending to attack and destroy my home land Kamārgāon.[23] Therefore if you permit me to go with all the *paīks* to raise a fort, it will not only give security to myself but will also stop the descent of the hill-men from the Lāmdānī region." Accordingly, the Mīrzā gave him all the *paīks* and the Sardārs to raise a fort at Kamārgaon. He (Govind) took leave and left in his place Naraharī Zunnārdār (holder of the sacred thread i.e. a brahmin) with the Mīrzā as the Barkāyeth i.e. the *Mushrif* or head of the *paīks*.

He went and fortified the place. The enemies made two night-attacks upon him but they were defeated on both the occasions. During the third attack, when the number of enemies was very large, the Mīrzā himself ran to the aid of Govind, after having made satisfactory arrangements for the big fort. When he reached a place one *kos* off from Kamārgāon he saw that the fort was burning. Therefore, he rode very swiftly. The enemies by that time retired to the hills. The details of this episode are as follows:—When the enemies came, Govind thrice came out of his fort and routed the enemies. Then he entered the fort. In the mean time, Jadū Nāyak, one of the Sardārs of his *paīks,* who had some grudge against him for the death of his father, broke the wall of the fort from this side and joined the enemies. The enemies entered the fort through that breach. Govind, suffered a defeat and sought the way of safety. At this time a Mech (*Mechua*) named Sanātān, whose father was killed by Govind, stabbed Govind with a dagger. The enemies, who with Jadū Nāyak were pursuing him, appeared on the scene, cut off the head of Govind Lashkar and fled to the hills with it (the head). The Mīrzā was greatly mortified, but it was of no avail. He returned to the fort, consoled the *pāiks* and engaged them in their work. (621)

**The enemy attacks the jungle-clearing force.** Every day the work of jungle-clearance was carried on. The morning after the jungles had been cleared up to the proximity of the enemy's fort, the Mīrzā himself took his position on horseback along with the whole army in the open field and ordered his men to carry on the work of jungle-clearance. When two *pahars* of the day had passed, some letters came from Jahāngīrnagar *alias* Dhāka from the Khān Fatḥ-jang. The Mīrzā went to his fort in order to write a reply to the aforesaid Khān, and Sa'ādat Khān was left with the entire army to help in jungle-clearance. The spies of the enemies informed them about it; they came through the jungle and appeared all on a sudden before the army and began the battle by a discharge of arrows. The large number of arrows reminded one of a heavy hailstorm. The Mīrzā was informed about it. He also came out of the fort playing on the kettle-drum. But by that time Khwāja Sa'ādat Khān, who was commanding the army, was wounded by an arrow on his knee. The foot-soldiers seized his rein and brought him out of the field of battle. The Mīrzā arrived there and offered a stiff fight. He said to the expert matchlock-men, "Every one who kills an enemy to-day and vindicates the wound of Sa'ādat Khān will be rewarded with a pair of golden bracelet." The powerful musketeers, particularly one named Būlāqī, said, "Depute a trustworthy man with me in order to count and report to you the number of enemies I kill with musket-balls." Accordingly, the Mīrzā sent one attendant named Ibrāhīm in his company. This expert soldier killed seven men within three *gharīs* in such a way that all these seven men deposited their lives through his musket balls to the keepers of hell. The Mīrzā presented to Būlāqī in that battle-field a bracelet of gold weighing twenty *tolas* which he had in his hand. A wonderful battle took place, and at the close of the day, both the parties retired to their forts. (622)

**The enemies change their plan.** Next morning, the Mīrzā through his foresight, raised a wooden stockade blocking the way of these people (i.e. enemies). The regiment of Rāja Satrajit, Rāja of Bhusna,[24] who came to help the Mīrzā, was posted at this wooden stockade with an additional force of expert musketeers as their auxiliaries, and thus secured from the attack of the enemies, he (the Mīrzā) passed his time with ease. When the Assamese saw that this stockade stood on their way of advance they changed their plan. They turned towards the right and adopting the same procedure they proposed to raise a series of forts up to the ditch of the fort of the Mīrzā in order to secure a commanding position from their fort over that of the Mīrzā and thus to harass the garrison within and put the besieged into a position of difficulty. The Mīrzā raised a barrier of wood and mud in front of his main fort where his own family and those of his officers were staying, so that the women might be protected from the arrows and cannon. In short, inspite of this, the enemy, under the cover of a series of forts, reached a distance of one arrow-shot from the barrier of the Mīrzā. So long they used to erect their fort at night but now when they approached near the fort of the Mīrzā, they attempted to raise a fort during the day time. It was reported to the Mīrzā that the enemies were showing their audacity by raising a fort during the day time. The Mīrzā ordered the Sardārs of his infantry to proceed with a hundred men to the wooden barrier and to stop the enemies from raising the fort by the discharge of their artillery. The soldiers went and did justice to their marksmanship. Thus many of the enemies were wounded, and a large number, who became the targets of arrows and guns, surrendered their lives to the keepers of hell. Therefore, unable to stand the fire, they gave up the work. When one *pahar* of the night had passed, they renewed the work of raising the fort. During the day time they began the work of the fort from the right side of this fort but at night they began the work from the left and expeditiously accomplished the work which was left incomplete during the day. The matchlock-men remained busy for the whole night in firing on the same side on the right of the enemies which was situated to the left of the imperialists' fort. The enemies clung to the left side and towards the last part of the night, they almost completed the construction of the fort except in that portion of the locality which was within the range of the shots of guns and cannon. The wall of this fort was joined with the wall of their foremost fort. When four *gharīs* of the night still remained, the Mīrzā came to the place where the musketeers were firing their muskets. For a short interval some of them fell to dozing and some stopped fire and loitered out in the open field. He (the Mīrzā) made an inspection and found that the gunpowder and the bullets that had been spent during the night had made no effect, and the enemy had raised the wall of the fort and joined it with their fort, excepting in that portion of the field which was within the range of cannon.

Now they were trying to complete the fort before the rising of the world-illuminating sun. (623)

**Seven forts of the enemy demolished.** The Mīrzā therefore cried out, "To-day our project is to conquer the fort and the house of Rānī," and he ordered the imperial soldiers to arm and equip themselves. When the regiments were arrayed for the battle, he said that they should come out of the fort through the western gate. He himself took his position at that gate. When the high and the low assembled at the gate, all on a sudden the door was opened and he ordered them to rush upon that new fort of the enemy placing the shield before their faces. As the fort of the enemies was incomplete, it was expected that they would fly for shelter immediately after the assault and the discharge of one round of ammunition. And (then) without allowing them (enemies) to rally, he (the Mīrzā) would get into the second fort by some means and the smart warriors would also follow him. God the Great granted the successful working of this plan. This strong fort of the enemies fell on the first assault. But a wooden passage, built by the enemy in the manner of a bridge leading out from the wall of the fort gave way in this *melee* with the enemies through the heavy weight of the valiant heroes of the Mīrzā, put upon it. Thirteen men of the Mīrzā who were fighting with the enemies entered their strong fort. When this bridge gave way it stood on the way of these heroes like a rampart (*ṣābāt*). The enemies, who were fleeing for refuge scattering the dust of disgrace on their heads, seeing the small number of men who had entered that fort, returned and gave battle. By the time the Mīrzā could break the wall of the fort with the help of the *bīldārs* (miners and sappers), and could enter with his elephants and horses, the enemies had thrice driven these imperial soldiers who had entered within, to the wall of the fort occupied by the imperialists. On all these three occasions, these heroes had to strive hard with foams on their lips and with the intoxication of bravery, they fell upon the distracted enemies and drove them back to the wall of the fort which was under the possession of the enemy. When first of all the driver of the elephant named Nayansukh brought the aforesaid elephant into the fort, Mast 'Alī Beg and Nīk Muḥammad, who were engaged in the battle, rushed forward with the elephant in their front. On this occasion the enemies were repelled in such a way that they were not allowed to turn back and were driven to their third fort. When the enemies entered the fort in a state of confusion, the tiger-like heroes also entered into it. By the time the sun had reached its meridian, seven forts were captured by fighting in this way, and the battle was pushed to the eighth fort. At this place many men were killed and wounded on both sides. As this fort was situated amidst dense bamboo groves close to a hill, the battle was equally balanced; and the war-loving fighters of both the sides withdrew their hands from the battle. An Afghān named Ḥabīb Khān, who was the commander of a regiment, sent words to Mīrzā Nathan,—"Unless you personally come to this battle, it will not probably be possible to gain a victory". Therefore, although the other Sardārs dissuaded him from going and said that they themselves would be able to finish the work and that the Mīrzā should discharge the duties of a Commander-in-chief remaining on his horse, the Mīrzā, through his keen sense of honour, joined the regiment of Nīk Muḥammad Beg by placing the shield before his face. He advanced forward immediately after his arrival. The Afghāns, who desired to have the Sardār in the battle, could not render necessary help in the battle. In all, two regiments, one in which the Mīrzā joined, and another regiment of the left wing, carried on the fight up to the bank of the ditch. Nīk Muḥammad Beg, being wounded, fell on the wicket of the gate of the fort. The enemy, being bold, came out and tried to take the head of Nīk Muḥammad. But then such a battle took place that it reminded one of the Day of Resurrection, and Nīk Muḥammad was saved with great difficulty. The clarion of victory was played. Then he (the Mīrzā) said that as all these seven forts conquered from the enemies were made of wood, so for every piece of log that would be carried to (his) fort, a reward of Re. 1 to Rs. 5 would be paid according to its size. By candle light, all the logs numbering more than 20,000 pieces were removed. The walls were levelled to the ground by elephants. Thus the work done by the enemy with the labour of thirty to forty days was absolutely undone within a *pahar* and a half. From there he (the Mīrzā) returned to his camp and sent a report of this great victory to the Khān Fāth-jang. (624)

**The enemies attempt to stop water supply.** For a period of fifteen days, the enemies, gave up the idea of raising forts, and began to harass the elephants and cows that went to graze in the field; but nothing substantial was done. Then, as the fort of the enemy was situated on the summit of a hill and as the elephants and the horses used to pass by the side of the gate of the fort for drinking water, they used to fire cannon from above. The men and animals were unable to drink water according to their desire, and many were killed at the time of fetching water. Therefore, the Mīrzā ordered the construction of a stockade in such a way as to cover half the portion of the river on this side and half of the other side, with the stream running between them. He also ordered the construction of two bridges on the water on either end of the fort, and of a fortified post over those bridges on the river. The hard-working and industrious men constructed a very strong fort as was desired with deep ditch around it. The people of the camp used to come at all times to this fort from the main one and carry water, and the elephants, the horses, the cows and the asses also could drink water with ease. The washermen used to wash the clothes within this fort, and the people had their baths in it. Although the enemies tried to bring it within the range of their cannon they could not become successful. Thus, if they fired cannon and guns, they could strike only at the base of the fort, and if they aimed at the top the shots used to pass above the top without hitting any man or animal. (625)

**The enemy tries to block the paths of food supply.** Hātī Barua deputed Māmūn Govind, the uncle of Rāja Baldev, with a brave army of four thousand men to obstruct the supply of rations to the imperial army. Govind, in order to accomplish this task, came and began to make plundering raids. Mīrzā Nathan also set up a fort on his (Govind's) way at Hāligāon,[25] a village in the pargana of Pāndū, and posted there a force of one hundred cavalry and three hundred matchlock-men and archers under the command of Darwīsh Bahādur. Thus securing the path of the supply of rations, he raised another fort on the bank of the river (Brahmaputtra) at Garāl and posted there his Mīr Baḥrs (admirals) with their fleet and a force of forty horsemen and one hundred musketeers. It was arranged that the men of the fleet in co-operation with this (land) army would forward rations to Halīgāon and the people there would send them on to the fort of the Mīrzā (at Rānīhāt). For a long time rations were supplied in this way. Māmūn Govind's desultory attacks on the suppliers of rations could not do anything. When the heavy rains overflooded the land, the fort of Garāl on the bank of the river was washed away. Therefore, the boats of the fleet were taken into the water of the *jheel* (marsh) and a fort was raised at the village of the Kacharis. Rations were carried from there to the fort of Hālīgāon and thence to the fort of the Mīrzā (at Rānīhāt). When the flood blocked all the ways of transport by bullocks, the Mīrzā, was constrained to send a herd of ten elephants to bring the rations. In this way rations were carried from the fleet to the main fort. (626)

**Capture of Panchkala Jhūlia.** When the spies reported that Panchkala Jhūlia of* Rāja Parikshit was staying in one of the villages of the pargana of Chumria,[26] the Mīrzā sent a fleet of five fully equipped war-boats under the command of his eunuch Khwāja La'l Beg (to

*No mention of relationship in the text.

seize him). The aforesaid Khwāja proceeded with great zeal, reached that place and brought Jhūlīa and his family as prisoners to the Mīrzā. He (La'l Beg) was sent back as the Sardār of the Afghāns who were posted to that Thāna, and the Mīrzā began to pass his time in joy and happiness. (627)

**Enemy's futile attempt to cut off communication.** When the Assamese saw that the rainy season had come and nothing substantial could be done by them, they despatched Māmūn Govind with a force of ten thousand men with these instructions:—"It is well and good if you can raid the fort of Hālīgāon; failing that you should block the way of food supply and of the fleet by raising a fort at a distance of half a *kos* (from their fort), so that the men of the garrison at Hālīgāon faced with a difficult situation may not send rations to the main fort. If we have to join this expedition, these people (the imperialists) will find out that the (defences of the) fort have been weakened and they will attack this fort." Accordingly, Māmūn Govind with his appointed army started (for Hālīgāon). He reached there four *gharīs* after day-break and began to raise a fort. The report of his arrival reached the Mīrzā by mid-day. The Mīrzā summoned Sa'ādat Khān, Mīrān Khwāja Aḥmad and Mast 'Alī Beg and said to them:—"I am going with a force of one hundred cavalry, five hundred infantry and eight elephants in order to punish the rebels who had blocked the path (of communication). I leave you here with these instructions that if the enemies, informed of my departure, attack the fort you are to form yourselves into three regiments. Mīrān Khwāja Aḥmad with the regiment under his command is to take his position in the centre of all the three forts and should be on the alert, so that the enemies may not enter into any of your forts by any stratagem. If perchance, they come, Mīrān Khwaja Aḥmad should attack that army from that position of vantage. The other two regiments,—one under the command of Sa'ādat Khan and the other under Mast 'Alī Beg should come out and fight, depending on the favour of God, whether the enemies appear with one regiment or two." In short, the comrades remained ready. The Mīrzā started fully equipped with the forces mentioned above and arrived at the fort of the rebels one *pahar* before evening. The soldiers of the fort of Hālīgāon also came out and joined the Mīrzā. At the advice of the Mīrzā, the forces were divided into two regiments and the fort of those short-sighted rebels was attacked from two sides. When at first the regiment of the Mīrzā reached there, a few of the horsemen and infantry rushed forward with the elephant named Nayana in their front. Thus two men, one Turkish slave named Khurshīd and another officer of the cavalry named Rurba rendered splendid services. In that field of battle, God the Great showed a great favour to Mīrzā Nathan such as was never shown to any mortal. An arrow discharged from the side of the enemies veered round towards the enemics themselves from a distance of ten steps (from the Mīrzā). The notched part of the arrow fell on the breast-plate (*baghtar*) of the Mīrzā. The sight of this Divine favour did not produce any effect on the fools but the wise offered thousands of thanks to the Lord. In the meantime, the second regiment led an attack against the gate of the fort from the other side with the elephant named Panchamī Sambhat in its front. Arrows were showered like hailstones from within the fort. The elephant received more than fifty arrow-shots and many of the warriors were wounded. From the other side the Mīrzā, with his feet on the stirrups of the saddle, looked towards the left and saw that the fort of the enemy was not protected on that side. He then shouted to Nīk Muḥammad Beg, Shīr Khān Kākar and some other heroes, saying :—" Comrades ! The enemy has not fortified the side to your left. Why are you allowing your men and horses to be wounded there ? Why don't you attack from that side ? " And he himself, having turned his rein, spurred his horse and galloped. As soon as the enemies heard the Mīrzā shouting to his comrades and asking them why they were not attacking that side (ie.

the unprotected side of the fort), they took to flight for safety; and scattering the dust of adversity on themselves, they became wanderers in the desert of wretchedness. The dexterous heroes riding on their horses despatched one hundred and twenty men to hell by cutting off their heads. A large number of enemies were wounded and fled away half-dead. The age began to applaud the victory with significant language and the people of the age expressed their satisfaction from thousands of hearts. The trumpet of victory was played and the clarion of good news was sounded. The Mīrzā ordered the elephants to be brought up and said:—"As the wounded rebels are lying hidden in this forest in a state of confusion, they should be trampled under the feet of the elephants just as the corns are trodden under the feet of bullocks in order to separate them from the stalks, (an operation) which is termed *dā'īn* in the Hindi language." (628)

**Nathan returns from Hālīgāon to Rānīhāt.** At this time, suddenly a footman came from the main fort and reported thus:—"One and a half *pahar* before the close of the day the enemies came out of their fort in three divisions. The men of the *Sarkār* have also formed three regiments according to the previous plan. Mīrān Khwāja Aḥmad and others were keeping watch in their posts in the centre of the three forts as ordered. Khwāja Sa'ādat Khān and Mast 'Alī Beg formed two regiments and went out to fight. They have sent me to inform you." Therefore, the Mīrzā abandoned the search for refugees in the forest and ordered the wounded men to return slowly with the elephants. Darwīsh Bahādur and others were left at the fort of Hālīgāon according to the previous arrangement, and he himself proceeded to the main fort with the swiftest possible speed. After making a journey of two *pahars* within six *gharīs*, he arrived there four *gharīs* after evening. By that time these people (the imperialists) had overpowered the enemies and had driven them to their fort. The soldiers of the enemy, in spite of their defeat, began to question the followers of the Mīrzā in a loud voice, "Where did you go? How did you fare with Māmūn Govind?" Some people replied, shouting, "We attacked your fort and have returned after levelling it to the ground." They again asked, "How many of our men have you killed in all?" A group of clever men in order to terrify the enemies invented an expedient falsehood and said, "About five hundred men of yours were put to the blood-thirsty sword." One of them laughed and said, "I believe, our Assam Rāja will take his food twice to-day." One of the soldiers of the Mīrzā asked, "What do you mean by this?" He replied, "It is the custom of our Rāja not to take his food unless rightly or wrongly he kills two or three hundred men." Mīrzā Nathan was overpowered with laughter and he said, "My comrades! we are dealing with such enemies that when we have killed five hundred of their men, they think that their Rāja will have two good meals." In short, when this conversation seemed to be hard and unpleasant to some of the chicken-hearted people, the Mīrzā in order to encourage them, said, "Although it is beyond our imagination, yet God the Great, who is powerful over all, made a gnat overpower Nimrūd and humiliate him. Though we are extremely insignificant beings, our Merciful God is strong, as it is said, 'Have a high ambition. Because your honour before men and God is in proportion to your ambition.'" Every one approved of it and then they went to their camp, took rest, and offered many thanks to God. But as many men of Mīrzā Nathan were killed and wounded during these day and night warfares of the last four months, he sent messengers to the imperial officers at Hājo asking for help and insisted on their sending equipments of war. (629)

**Parsurām attempts to regain his freedom.** Parsurām, who remained in captivity for sometime, realised that he would not be able to regain his freedom unless he pays some money. He informed Mīrzā Nathan,—"I am prepared to pay Rs. 10,000 provided myself and my family are released. But as I have nothing with me and I have buried my entire cash in the forest, if you allow me to go there under the escort of your men, I will pay the amount agreed upon." The Mīrzā could not separate himself from Sa'ādat Khān, but as it was an affair of trust, so in spite of the heavy flood, he sent the aforesaid Parsurām in charge of Ḥabīb Khān Lūdī and Sayf Khān Lūdī along with their brothers and expert matchlock-men on fourteen boats. Balabhadra Dās and his followers were directed by a letter to maintain complete peace and concord with the aforesaid Khān. Khwāja Sa'ādat Khān came to meet Parsurām most ceremoniously and consoled him by saying, "When you fulfil your promise I hold myself responsible for the safety of your life and immediate release." But as he was not sincere, so he planned to take them to the biggest forest either to fall upon them at night when they would be tired and worn out, or to get rid of them by some other stratagem. Accordingly, he reached Solmārī and finding no opportunity, returned from that place bringing with him about 150 *tolas* of gold by digging in his deserted houses. The Mīrzā became annoyed at this behaviour and punished him. This *harām-zāda* (villain) took Sa'ādat Khān for the second time with him and did not manifest any malicious intention. But as he was ordained by fate to remain again in captivity, he came back bringing about 50 *tolas* of gold and 300 *tolas* of silver. It became apparent that first, his attempts were directed to his flight, and secondly, he was afraid of disclosing the place where his buried treasure lay containing all his cash, lest all the money would be seized. Every time he would take men with him and come back (without the money). Henceforth he was never believed and he was put in strict confinement. (630)

**Duplicity of Shaykh Kamāl.** Now I shall give a short account of the departure of the Mīrzā's messengers to Shaykh Kamāl and the imperial officers at Hājo to ask for reinforcement, and of the indifference shown by Shaykh Kamāl. Shaykh Kamāl was the head of the administration at that time and Qulīj Khān *alias* Bāltū Qulīj was removed from the office he held in the territory of Kūch and particularly in that of Kāmrūp. Shaykh Kamāl, who bore grudge against Mīrzā Nathan, showed indifference and did neither send any help nor any clear reply, so that the Mīrzā might raise an army on his own account. An officer of the Mīrzā named Madārī who went to Tandah to purchase arrows, bows, gunpowder and lead arrived at Hājo with a boat-load of these materials. But as the decree of Fate had come to many men and women, the boat went down in the river the very day it started from Hājo, after having traversed a short distance, and not a single thing could be saved. This news reached the enemies. (631)

**The enemies renew their aggression.** A letter came from the Rāja of Assam, severely censuring the Hātī Barua and all the Sardārs, and he sent two hundred *Hangdān Dharas* (Ahom swordmen) with the following orders:—"Whoever falls back this time (from the battle) will be cut into two at the waist by the *Hangdān Dharās.*" Therefore, the Hātī Barua, the Rājhkhawa, Kharghuka (Khargharia Phukan), Rāja Baldev, Shumāruyed Kāyeth, the Eighteen Hill-Rājas, Dangar Dev, son of Dumria Rāja, and Gopāl Dalpatī along with all the *Dals* and *Dalpatīs* consulted with one another (and came to the conclusion) that this time there was no other way but to die. Accordingly, they left their forts in charge of a small garrison and in an auspicious moment all the Sardārs came out with their armies to a place situated on the side of Ganjbaib to the south-west of Rānīhāt at a distance of one big-cannon-shot from the (imperial) fort. There they raised within a night a lofty fort with a deep ditch around and equipped it by posting big cannon on its walls and towers. More than fifty thousand men were engaged in the construction of this fort so close by, but it was not known (to the imperialists) till two men went out for some other work. When towards the last part of the night a regiment came out to the field of battle, the news was received that the enemies had raised a big fort at a distance of one cannon-shot from the fort and they were ready for battle and strife. (632)

**Arrival of reinforcements.** On that day Mīrzā Nathan remained silent and kept himself busy in making preparations for raising a fort. On that very day Lamūdar (Lambudar), son of Rāja Madhūsudan came to the aid of the Mīrzā with a force of one hundred cavalry and four hundred infantry. The Mīrzā received Lamūdar with great respect in his own house and extended his hospitality. It was settled that when the new fort would be completed Lamūdar with his army would be posted to defend it. Accordingly, the Mīrzā also went next morning to help in the construction of the fort and a small fort was raised between the main fort and the fort of the enemies. The scene of battle with them (the enemies) was transferred to this fort and the main fort where women lived was kept beyond the range of enemy's cannon and arrows. Although the enemies were firing cannon and guns and did not allow (the imperialists) any respite and the dead and the wounded lay in heaps upon one another, yet Mīrzā Nathan completed the stockade with towers, by the time when the sun reached its meridian. After this three ditches were completed on three sides before evening. The completion of one of the sides which was within the range of the enemy's guns was put off for night. The Mīrzā posted there fifty Mughal and Afghān infantry in addition to five hundred native *paīks* who had been posted there. When the night had advanced, both sides slackened their activity and Mīrzā Nathan came to his main fort. But the discharge of guns, and cannon and the shooting of arrows continued from both sides. (633)

**Governmental changes in Kāmrūp.** Now I shall give a short account of the doings of the officers at the Thāna of Hājo. As the relation between Khān Fatḥ-jang, the Ṣūbahdār and Qulīj Khān *alias* Bāltū Qulīj was not cordial, so Ibrahim Khān Fatḥ-jang, relying on the report of Qulīj

Khān's habit of incessant drinking, sent a representation to the imperial Court and reported thus :—"Qulīj Khān through his habit of excessive drinking has become useless. So he has been removed from holding the charge of the affairs of the Thāna of Hājo and I have appointed Shaykh Kamāl (in his place)." Therefore, Qulīj Khān went from Hājo to Jahāngīrnagar *alias* Dhāka to the Khān Fatḥ-jang and took leave to go to the imperial Court. Shaykh Kamāl became confirmed in the Sardārship of the aforesaid Thāna. (634)

**Treacherous design of Shaykh Kamāl.** When the agents of Mīrzā Nathan kept demanding reinforcements and arguing with him (Kamāl) and when the arrival of the invading forces of Assam was proved beyond doubt, then Shaykh Kamāl appointed Mīrzā Ṣālih Arghūn and Mīrzā Yūsuf Barlās along with all the junior Manṣabdārs and three hundred matchlock-men (to help Nathan). Although outwardly he gave leave to these people to proceed to the aid of Mīrzā Nathan, but as he entertained malice with his heart and soul against the aforesaid Mīrzā, he sent secret messages to these people, saying :—" As the enemies are leading a grand attack, it is not known whether Mīrzā Nathan will be able to keep his position up to the time you reach there. It is proper that you should proceed after understanding the situation." Accordingly, a group of timid men acted according to the instruction given by the aforesaid (Kamāl). But five Manṣabdārs of 'Uṣmānī Afghāns, namely, Naṣir Khān Panī, Bahādur Khān Kākar, Yatim Khān Shīrwānī, Bāzū-i-Jhilam and Shīr Khān Lūdī, who were very friendly with the Mīrzā and who from a long time past had kept company with the Mīrzā in all imperial affairs, manfully and loyally marched with thirteen of their own warriors and started for the (place of the) aforesaid (Mīrzā). Now I shall revert to my original theme and describe the condition of the Mīrzā. (635)

# CHAPTER V

*War of the Assamese with Mīrzā Nathan. A fatal misfortune overtakes the army of Islām. The second struggle of Mīrzā Nathan with the Assamese. Re-occupation of the whole region of the Dakhinkul. Capture of Shumāruyed Kāyeth along with the Eighteen Hill-Rājas and the death of many of the Sardārs of the Rāja of Assam.*

**A force despatched to Minārī.** Three days after the construction of the stockade by the Mīrzā in front of the big fort of the Assamese, Shumāruyed Kāyeth, the leader of this struggle, on the advice of the Sardārs of the Rāja of Assam, gave currency to the following false rumour :—" I have despatched Māmūn Govind, uncle of Rāja Parikshit, with a force of ten thousand *pāiks* to Hālīgāon where on a previous occasion Govind suffered a defeat at the hands of the Mīrzā with a force of four thousand. He has been instructed to build a fort at a distance of five *kos* from the fort of the Mīrzā and to block the path of supply of rations and communication." Therefore, the Mīrzā sent a force of one hundred cavalry, five hundred infantry and eight experienced elephants under the command of Sa'ādat Khān against Govind with these instructions : —" When the enemies have planned this wise, I myself should have gone and taught them a good lesson. But as I have to take my bath to-day and also have to look after the fortification of this new stockade, I shall remain (here). Go yourself with your army to Hālīgāon and strike a manly blow to these short-sighted fellows." Sa'ādat Khān marched to Hālīgāon with this experienced army with the greatest possible speed. When he reached there, he came to know that the enemies had played a trick and none of their forces had been despatched to that place. So as a precautionary measure, he (Sa'ādat) left half of his army to help Darwīsh Bahādur the Thānadār of Minārī and thus assured of the safety of that region, he returned (to Rānīhāt). In the meantime forty horsemen and three hundred infantry of Rāja Lakshmī Narāyan who were sent as auxiliaries to Mīrzā Nathan after the departure of Lamūdar, son of Rāja Madhūsudan, arrived (at Minārī). Sa'ādat Khān, without the permission of the Mīrzā, under the impression that these men were meant for that place, deputed them to help Darwīsh Bahādur and returned to the Mīrzā with the thought that it would no longer be necessary to send reinforcement (to Minārī) every time from the main fort. During this time the enemies ordered some of their men to drive away to the hills the female elephants and the bullocks of the Mīrzā's camp, which used to graze at some distance from the fort. These men came, drove away the female elephants and the bullocks and went away. The Mīrzā on the receipt of this information ordered his *Mīr Sāmān* Ya'qub Khān to proceed with a regiment of cavalry which was ready on saddles at the watch-post, to the side of the hill and to bait the enemies, and prevent them from indulging in such activities. This regiment, coming out of the fort, ran after the enemies. (636)

**The Rājkhawa attacks the new stockade.** The spies informed Shumāruyed :—" The cavalry which was kept ready on horseback in the fort of the Mīrzā has gone out in two batches one after the other and at present none of the horsemen of the Mīrzā is on saddle (in the fort), and he himself is engaged in his bath." So he (Shumāruyed) sent the Rājkhāwa with a force of twenty thousand Assamese infantry to effect an immediate destruction of the stockade before the Mīrzā and his men could get time to gird up their loins. The Rājkhāwa and his men came to the new fort which was at a short distance from their fort and attacked it. A tumult arose when the enemy attacked the fort. Therefore, the Mīrzā, with the idea that by the time he would summon up his men the enemies might finish their work, did not pour water on his head, and, depending on his sense of honour and the God-given constitutional prowess, he ran with his bare body without any weapon of war with his bathing *lungi* (loin-cloth) twisted in the manner of a belt over his underwear and with a turban over his head. He rode on a sentinal horse which was ready there and came out of the fort. As he was getting out, he snatched off a javelin from the hand of a Hindu officer who was at the gate of the fort and with this weapon he proceeded against the enemies. In the meantime three horsemen of the Mīrzā named Sayf Khān Lūdī, Shāh Mīr Jawān Saiyid Zāda and Shaykh Isma'īl immediately came out of their houses to help the Mīrzā, without even waiting to put on their coats of mail. As soon as the Mīrzā came to the field of battle he saw the enemies like ants and locusts surrounding the ditches of the stockade which was situated at a short distance from his main fort. He addressed Sayf Khān Lūdī and said:—" If we stop here then undoubtedly the men in the stockade will not be able to stand the shots of cannon discharged from the enemy's big fort and the stockade will be demolished. After that no remedy will be left." Then he led the attack crying " Allahu-Akbar " and " Ya Mu'yīn " and all these three men followed him. A party of opponents, who were in front of them, took a firm stand on the bank of the ditch of the stockade and were intending to jump from the ditch into the fort. They discharged one round of arrows, which were ready in their bow-string, upon these lovers of battle. But through the protection of the Protector of life, no harm befell any of them except that the horse of Shāh Mīr was struck on the breast and made unable to move from that place. He (the Mīrzā) fell upon the centre of the enemies without any fear and drove that party from the bank of the ditch and some of them were put to the dreadful sword. The Rājkhawa with his fleeing followers opposed him and carried on his attack on this lion of the thicket of bravery and his two companions, from the sides and corners. When the horses began to sink up to their breast in a pool of water which had collected during the rains in the vicinity of the enemy's fort, he (the Mīrzā) was compelled to turn back. The enemies returned from all sides and again rushed forward to the bank of the ditch of the stockade. The Mīrzā's sense of honour did not permit him to retreat any further. He turned back and again fell upon the enemies with the cry of " Allahu-Akbar." The enemies were thus repelled for the second time. In short, the enemies were thus thrice attacked and were driven up to that pool and then he had to turn his rein as before. By this time all fighters of the army of Islām, high and low, came fully equipped with arms and joined Mīrzā Nathan with elephants in their front. Lamūdar, son of Rāja Madhūsudan also arrived there with his followers. He said to the Mīrzā :—" As you have inflicted such a punishment upon the enemies with three men and as the enemies have failed to occupy the stockade, now, when we have all come armed to the field, the enemies have not the power to overpower us. Please go and take your bath. This time the tide of battle is in my charge. You will see how I deal with the enemies." The Mīrzā was deceived by the big words uttered by him without remembering the powerful Lord ; and being proud of his achievement of such triumph over the enemies and of his killing a large number of them he himself with a few of his attendants returned from the field of battle to his fort, and wanted to take his bath after his return from the battle. Every moment he sent words to Lamūdar and his own men :—" So long, God the Great has preserved our prestige ; but as to-day the Divine influences seem to be against us, you should not take aggressive parts but should keep the field under control and be at the beck and call of the stockade and its men within." (637)

**Shumāruyed Kāyeth attacks the watch-post.** In the meantime Shumāruyed Kāyeth himself came with a force of four thousand brave Assamese infantry and attacked the other stockade which was built by the Mīrzā on either side of the river in front of the main fort in order to have control over the water of the river. During this time, the army of Islām, was occupied with the defence of the watch-post and so could not come to the aid of this stockade ; and the other armies also lay scattered in different places and had not yet arrived. So he (Shumāruyed) made a strong sally. The

Mīrzā, again, without taking his bath, came out through the gate of his main fort with a party of his men and facing the water of the river began to discharge guns and arrows from an advantageous position on the enemies who were attacking the wall of the stockade. At this juncture Ya'qūb Khān and his men, who went to release the female elephants and the bullocks from the enemies hands, came back after securing them and joined the Mīrzā. He (the Mīrzā) posted this regiment in his place and returned to the fort to take his bath. After an hour he finished his bath, put on his clothes and began to read the letters which came from Jahāngīrnagar from Ibrāhīm Khān Fatḥ-jang and his agents and friends. (638)

**Plight of the imperialists.** Then he (the Mīrza) heard the sound of a kettle-drum and was informed that Sa'ādat Khān who went against Māmūn Govind, had returned with his regiment. The Mīrzā, due to his extreme foresight, sent a message (to him) saying :—" Beware ! Do not proceed against the enemies by that way. Come to the fort. No auspicious sign is manifest in our battle to-day." But the regiment of Sa'ādat Khān thus expressed their desire on this occasion :— " As our comrades have already proved their mettle and our master had fought single-handed with credit, let us also show our proper strength to the enemies and then return to the fort." Before the arrival of the Mīrzā's messenger, Khwāja Sa'ādat Khān said to his followers, " Wait here. Let me go to our master and obtain his permission to deal out a defeat to the enemies and then to return to the fort." Saying this he went to the Mīrzā. Mast 'Alī Beg and Nīk Muḥammad Beg, who were the leading warriors of that regiment, said to Mīrān 'Abdu's-Ṣamad and some other companions, " It is quite certain that the master will give permission. Let us fall upon the enemies before the arrival of Sa'ādat Khān." Their companions, high and low, refused to agree. Then these two brave men galloped with their horses, arrived at the place where Lamūdar and other regiments of the Mīrzā were standing against the enemies, and congratulated these men. The men, absolutely ignoring other factors, began to say :—" We always fight the battles but the people at large give the credit of the fight to you. It is better that you should fight as far as you can, while we stand as spectators." These two heroes, through their pride and arrogance of military profession, did not take into consideration the fact that all these people were mere spectators and were enjoying a fun and the master had not given permission to fight. All on a sudden they led the charge into the midst of the enemies without taking even an elephant-driver in their company. Although the enemies were constantly receiving chastisement at their hands they, under the impression that they would be joined by all the followers of the Mīrzā, great and small, allowed these two brave men to advance on and on. But at last when they (the enemies) perceived that none of the men was joining them, they surrounded these two men from four sides and charged them with arrows. In the twinkling of an eye they and their horses were pierced with arrows. These two brave men turned their reins, and the elephant-driver of the famous elephant of the army named Shāh 'Ināyat who went with the elephant to their help also turned back. The enemies created an uproar (and shouted):—"We have repelled the elephant Shāh 'Ināyat along with Mast 'Alī Beg and Nīk Muḥammad Beg." All men on the enemies' side, high and low, who had returned to their fort and were intending to take some rest, rushed out and put the soldiers of the (imperial) regiment into great straits. Before Sa'ādaṭ Khān could meet the Mīrzā and return to take his men back and call them off from fight, the situation had taken quite a different turn. The men in the fort of the Mīrzā, who were watching the situation from the top of their houses, raised a tumult, saying that on the retreat of the regiment and of the men of the stockade, the enemies had entered the stockade and set fire to the houses within it. (639)

**The imperial army demoralised.** The Mīrzā, without going through the contents of the papers which were in his hand, ran out in a state of excitement. With a javelin in his hand he rode on that very wounded horse named Pūr-i-Hīra (the son of Hīra). The horse had already received one gun-shot and seven arrow-shots in the first battle. The Mīrzā had totally forgotten whether the horse was wounded or not. Four caparisoned (*kuha* ?) elephants which were kept ready along with horses in the *chawkī* outside the gate of the Mīrzā's house were placed in his front and he came out by a passage through the western gate. He was followed by about twenty to thirty brave footmen. He saw that his whole army had dispersed and was falling back in a state of confusion, and the stockade had been demolished. He conceived the idea of proceeding against the enemies by the rear, relying on the mercy of God, and thus to infuse courage into his men to make an united attack from that direction and drive the enemies away. At this juncture, a cannon was fired from the enemy's fort the shot of which hit one of the elephants in his front. The elephant shrieked and took to flight. Although the other three elephants were war-hardened animals, the shriek of this elephant made them panicky and they also ran away. At this the foot-soldiers also lost their courage and stood confounded. Mīrzā Nathan, compelled by circumstances, turned the rein of his horse from this side towards the army and joined it in the twinkling of an eye. He encouraged them and tried to prevent the army from falling back, but it was of no avail. (640)

**Sa'ādat Khān wounded.** In the mean time, Sa'ādat Khān, who went to the fort to change his wounded horse, joined the army. Immediately after his arrival he was wounded by a poisoned-dart on his right leg which, had once before been wounded in the first battle, and it went so deep that it did not come out. The Mīrzā, owing to his great love for the aforesaid (Sa'ādat), ordered some men to carry him immediately to the fort and to extract the arrow but Sa'ādat Khān did not like to leave his company. The Mīrzā gave him the following directions :—" You are to go and stay at the gate of the *maḥal* (harem). As soon as you hear that I have attained martyrdom in the field, perform the rites of *jawhar*, with all the inmates of the *maḥal*, big and small, and take your journey to the Kingdom of Heaven with eternal honour." Accordingly, the aforesaid Khwāja was carried to the fort. (641)

**The final struggle.** A great battle took place; in fact no body had the courage to advance with boldness. The Mīrzā stuck to what he had uttered by his tongue; so he could not go back upon it. (Mast) 'Alī Beg and Nīk Muḥammad, each of whom had received four to five wounds took those two horses profusely bleeding to the fort and they came back riding on (two) other horses. Being ashamed of their badly executed business they said, "We are determined to carry on the struggle. Tell us who will accompany us." The Mīrzā swore and said:—"Whoever is a man and is born of man, will not fall behind you." In short, they led the charge, and the Mīrzā alone was true to his words and joined them. The enemies were attacked and repelled so violently that a regiment of their's, which was busy in looting the stockade jumped from it to the bottom of the ditch regardless of consequences and took to flight, and a great tumult arose. But as it was the will of the True Lord to grant victory on that day to the heathens, not a single man followed his master and these two heroes. All of them (imperial soldiers) sought the lane of safety. When the enemies saw from all sides that these three brave men alone were fighting, they pressed from all sides. The horses were severely wounded; so the infantry of the enemy tried to cut the legs of the horses of Nīk Muḥammad and Mast 'Alī Beg which were unable to move. But on every occasion, Mīrzā Nathan with the lance in his hand fell upon (the enemies) crying "*Huy*" and came to the help of these two heroes and did not allow the enemies to cut the legs of the horses. Then the Mīrzā and these two warriors joined their army. The army had fallen back so far that by the time of sunset it had crossed the *nālah* (ditch) which was formed by heavy rains in front of the gate of the fort. Therefore, the Mīrzā, thinking his death to be certain, placed in his front a few of his elephants whose drivers were bold enough to keep his company and took his stand with the *nālah* before him. The enemies thought that the Mīrzā was within the fort with his wife and children and they decided not to fall back till they would find his dead body at the gate of the fort. All people, high and low, decided to perform *jawhar* and to die after killing their wives. These people also took their stand by the side of the *nālah* in great suspense and began to make a stockade according to their custom. When the night advanced, the Mīrzā said to some of his comrades who wanted to be his companions in martyrdom, "If you take a firm stand here, I shall go to encourage the men at those four forts and I shall return to you after having made satisfactory arrangements for communication from one fort to another." These people remained at their posts and took their stand with the elephants in their front, and the Mīrzā went to encourage the besieged people. As soon as he entered the main fort, the men of the stockade, situated adjacent to the watch-post (*chawkī*) on the river, evacuated the stockade and came to the main fort. Thus this stockade was lost without any battle. He then encouraged and consoled the men of the other three forts, i.e. the mainfort, the two stockades, situated on either side of the stream, and another stockade on the way to the foremost fort of the enemies, and came back to his own place. He passed the whole night in vigilance and care. (642)

**The enemy brings the imperialists to bay.** In the last part of the night it was found that the enemies had raised a high fortification with a deep ditch around it, beginning from one end of the hill, and had surrounded all the three forts of Mīrzā Nathan like the prey in a ring-hunt (Qamargāh). The enemies shouted thus:—"Soldiers of the imperial army, be hold, how we have surrounded you. If you want to live, the best course for you is to surrender to our Rāja of Assam, otherwise, we shall not allow even a bird of yours to escape and we shall make a general massacre." The Mīrzā and his comrades who had wrapped their shrouds (*kafan*) on their heads with the desire of attaining martyrdom and who had been compelled to fall back on the previous day against their will, replied thus in a loud voice:—"As we have taken the salt of Jahāngīr, we consider martyrdom to be our blessings for both the worlds. You will see what (feats) we perform before you, till our death." Therefore, the enemies also, inspite of their huge armies, had not the courage to fall upon these (imperialists) all atonce to finish their job. The Mīrzā brought out trays of gold vessels from his *maḥal* and piled them together. He then summoned the Bakhshīs of his army and ordered them to pay the salaries of all the cavalry and the infantry. He made the Musalmāns to take an oath by the Qu'rān and the Hindus according to Hindu custom, to the effect that they should not leave one another's company and should accept martyrdom following one another's footsteps. When the time of mid-day prayer approached, Darwīsh Bahādur and some other people, who stayed in the fort in the centre of the route of the supply of rations and who used to send rations to the main fort, hearing that their Mīrzā was being besieged by the enemies, started from that place and reached near the Mīrzā, true to their salt. When the enemies failed to raise their fourth stockade owing to the firing from the Mīrzā's stockade they constructed another stockade of the length of fifty five cubits and brought the garrison to bay. Darwīsh Bahādur and those people who came from that side and a regiment of the Mīrzā who went to their help were also shut up by the enemies inside the fort like the prey in a ring-hunt. From hour to hour the enemies became more and more aggressive, and gun-powder, bullets and cannon balls of the Mīrzā's army ran short. The spies of the enemies carried this news (to the enemy). (643)

**Nathan evacuates the fort.** The Mīrzā and his men had no other alternative but to accept martyrdom. When the second night arrived, a band of thirteen 'Uṣmānī Afghān Manṣabdārs, who were coming from Hājo, as mentioned before, to help the Mīrzā, reached him by candle light with coffin-cloths wrapped about their heads. Many of the dispirited men of the army of the Mīrzā consisting of the common footmen and camp-followers, went out of the fort to take the path of safety. These deserters met them (i.e. the party of

Afghāns) on the way and told them the unhappy news, but this did not stop them. This group (of the Afghāns) were helped to get inside the fort by the garrison within. The Mīrzā said to them:—"My comrades, this kind of death like the deer of the forest caught inside a ring-hunt with all the offsprings, has been welcomed just to keep the prestige of the imperial army. During these nineteen months we have not shown any negligence in battles and our records are wellknown and clear to the people of the world. Now you see that I am still prepared to offer a manly battle at this gate which has not yet been blocked by the enemies, provided that a Sardār goes out with two to three hundred horsemen and one thousand infantry and plays the kettle-drum in order to make the enemies believe that reinforcements had come to the imperial army. Then, by the favour of God, we can give a manly fight from within the fort and by breaking this strong fortification of the enemies we may finish their job. If we are to act according to this plan, you should signify your approval. Otherwise, as you know all the circumstances, I shall follow, your advice, entrusting my fate to God, if you can point out any other way." The Afghāns explained to him the manner in which Mīrzā Ṣāliḥ Arghūn and Mīrzā Yūsuf had been despatched (to Nathan's aid) and disclosed also the secret messages (sent by Shaykh Kamāl). Then they said:—"We are the only reinforcement, and we have come with loyalty and fidelity welcoming our death. Not even a bird would come to your aid, besides us. This kind of death will be disastrous to imperial affairs and ruinous to the imperial elephants and the artillery; nor will it bring any credit to you. You have neither a son nor a brother of that type who would be able to take vengeance on your internal and external foes. The proper course from the point of view of military profession is to get out of this place and then wrapping the shroud on your head come again with proper reinforcements of your own and punish the enemies and blacken the faces of your internal and external foes. Otherwise, you stand to lose both your temporal and spiritual gains." In short, the Mīrzā, in his helplessness, agreed with these people to come out of the fort. He passed the night with great care and vigilance. When two *gharīs* of night still remained, the evacuation of the fort was begun. But as some of the timid followers left the towers and the walls of the fort during the night and fled with their lives, the enemies, immediately after day-break, rushed from all sides into the fort of the Mīrzā and began to fight within it. The Mīrzā sent away some of his women in the company of two officers on an elephant which he could procure. But as the whole of the imperial artillery was loaded on the other elephants, no elephant was left for the servants (*khidmat-gārān*) of the *maḥal*. He ordered that they should perform *jawhar*. Thus about fifty to eighty persons of the Mīrzā's *maḥal* performed *jawhar*, and many of the men of the army, who thought that they would lose their honour, also performed *jawhar*. Mīrzā Nīk Muḥammad Beg who for four generations, had been confident and a house-born person of his (Mīrzā's) ancestors, was sent with the elephant of the *maḥal* with the following instructions:—"When you see that I have attained martyrdom, finish the affair of these three persons (under your charge): after that display whatever manliness you can and attain eternal happiness." (644)

**The Enemy pursues the Mughals.** The enemies, from all sides, set fire to the fort and the Mīrzā was surrounded by a storm of arrows and bullets. The audacious foot-soldiers of the enemy began to cut the legs of horses and men. The Mīrzā shouted to his own as well as to the imperial auxiliaries and encouraged and cajoled them to return and to take a firm stand against the enemies; but as God, the Giver of strength had taken away the courage of these people, none of them had the boldness to turn back and to take a firm stand according to military profession. There arose a confusion of a strange nature. After this, the Mīrzā thus addressed the 'Uṣmānī Afghāns:

—"You and we are imperial servants. Although this flock of cowards are behaving like timid slaves, it is not proper that we should also lose our heart and fail to rally even once. It seems that your courage was limited to the days of 'Uṣmān." Others did not reply, but Bāzū-i-Jhilam who was an intimate friend of the Mīrzā from a long time said to the Mīrzā in a loud voice:—"Turn back and see, if this crowd of the enemies which is coming towards us may be turned away by the attack of a few of us. Yes, turn back and fight if you have chosen to be a martyr and if you want to make a name. Whoever has any courage in his heart will follow you and attain eternal glory; or, otherwise there is no hope of escape from this field even for a bird. After this when you die, all your people will be slaughtered like dogs in nooks and corners or made captive." The Mīrzā shouted to Bāzū-i-Jhilam and said:—"O, Afghān! you desire to enjoy the spectacle of my making myself a martyr. It is for this reason that you are taunting me in this way. If you are of noble origin, wait for a moment and see what I do." Having said this, he turned the rein of his horse named Hīra, and with the cry of "Allahu-Akbar" he rushed forward. At this time three imperial Manṣabdārs, namely, Bahādur Khān Kākar, Yatim Khān Shīrwānī and Bāzū-i-Jhilam, and Sayf Khān Lūdī, one of the officers of the Mīrzā, had the boldness to accompany him. They turned back and rushed forward. The enemies, who were advancing by cutting off the legs of horses and men, fired, all at once, the shafts that were ready in their bows. Forty thousand arrows passed over their heads like a huge flock of sparrows springing up from a corn-field, and were showered like hailstones upon them. Two of these arrows struck Yatīm Khān Shīrwānī and the horse of Bahādur Khān Kākar. By that time, five of these men plunged into the midst of the enemies and after a short skirmish the enemies were driven back. When the enemies, after retreating a short distance, saw that only these five men were fighting and the others had not turned back, about seven to eight thousand Assamese turned back and began to discharge arrows from the right flank of the Mīrzā from a position of vantage. The Mīrzā said to his officer Sayf Khān Lūdī :—" As we have repelled the soldiers of the front rank, similarly, by the favour of God, we shall disperse the soldiers of the right wing also." As the horse of the Mīrzā though it had received more than fifty wounds including those received in the previous battle, was the bravest and the swiftest of all, the Mīrzā turned its rein and galloped towards the right side against the enemy's force. All those four followers plunged into the midst of the enemies. At this juncture, five other persons, namely, an imperial Manṣabdār named Nāṣir Khān Patanī, and four officers of the Mīrzā named Saiyid 'Abdu's-Ṣamad, Walī Beg, Shīr Khān Kākar, and Shaykh Yūsuf, at the sight of this commotion, turned back and made a rush against the enemies and joined the battle in a critical moment. The enemies were given an effective smashing from two sides and repulsed, thirty to forty of their men being killed. When they reached the village of Mālīkūtī,[1] the enemies with a force of more than ten thousand men took shelter behind bamboo groves with which the place abounds, and began to shoot arrows. For a while they took a firm stand, but when the Mīrzā arrived there from this side with his nine horsemen, and Lamūdar, son of Rāja Madhūsudan, along with his brother and one horseman, and when two other horsemen of the Mīrzā arrived from the rear, the enemies, according to the will of God, left their position and took to vagrancy. The Mīrzā with a group of sixteen horsemen including himself, pursued the enemies. Mast 'Alī Beg was sent by the Mīrzā before the battle was begun to Nīk Muḥammad Malik to instruct him to carry the women and the elephants of the imperial artillery not through dense forests but by field route. He (Mast 'Alī) returned from that place and followed the Mīrzā, shouting, " O, Mughal, look behind your head. Inspite of this decisive victory of yours, all your men instead of turning back are running away. You can not defend your reconquered fort with this following of yours. Then why should we not take the way to safety before the horses are tired out ?" As there was the light of truth in his advice which was given in the spirit of a military man, it secured the approval of all the comrades. The Mīrzā then turned his rein and followed his own flying army. After traversing a short distance, he saw that the enemies were following him again in large numbers like ants and locusts. So he proceeded slowly. Some of the wounded men who were lying on the way but who had the strength to move were picked up on his way. Then he arrived at a *nālah* which was on his way. Every body, high and low, who had arrived there before him, were crowding together to cross it. The enemies also arrived there, and began to discharge their arrows and guns. Although the Mīrzā asked his musketeers to fire some guns in order to check the enemy's advance and to enable his men to cross (the *nālah*), it was of no avail. The musketeers took recourse to tricks and deceptions and crossed over from that place. Mīrzā Nathan offered to one of the musketeers a gold ring from his own finger saying, "Let me see how you fire on this crowd of enemies." Greedy of gold, the musketeer agreed to fire his musket but delayed in firing with the intention of getting the ring first. The Mīrzā threw his ring at him. The musketeer, holding the ring in his mouth, fired an empty gun against the enemies, a gun in which there were no bullets. He then offered an excuse that he did not know whether the gun was loaded or not. The Mīrzā again asked him to fire a fresh gun. The greed (for gold) made him play tricks (and delay), until the Mīrzā threw at him another of his rings. The musketeer then, in the same way, took the ring in his mouth. This time, the Mīrzā stood behind and encouraged him, saying, "Do not be afraid, I am standing behind you." He summoned up courage and fired the musket against the enemies. From the uproar among the enemies, it became apparent that four or five men had been shot through at the same time. But yet the enemies did not fall back. Some of the men, particularly, Ya'qūb Khān, the Mīr Sāmān of the Mīrzā, Khwāja Sandal, a eunuch of Rāja Satrajit, who was the chief of his (Rāja's) regiment and Dariyā Khān, an Afghān officer of the Mīrzā showed their cowardice. Thus Ya'qūb Khān, was overpowered by the heat of his body, but did not know how to relieve himself from that heat by removing his arms. The Mīrzā standing behind him, sympathetically untied his belt and let him cross the *nālah*. With the exception of the following two men, *viz.*, Khwāja Sandal and Darīya Khān Afghān who were in a state of great nervousness, all others had crossed the *nālah*. After this, the Mīrzā asked his companions to try and cross the *nālah*. One of these men found out a way in the midst of the bamboo groves on the bank of the *nālah*. All of them began to cross. In the mean time, Shaykh Khwāja Aḥmad, one of the *pīr-zādas* (sons of spiritual preceptor) of the Mīrzā, fell on the ground with his horse. One musketeer named Būlāqī leaped down from his horse to help Shaykh Khwāja Aḥmad and pulled him out from below the horse and the horse also got up. Shaykh Khwāja Aḥmad rode on his horse, and Būlāqī crossed with them by the passage through the bamboo-groves. The men crossed one after another with great care through that passage. The Mīrzā and Bāzū-i-Jhilam were the last to get through. They started saying to each other :—" You cross first." The Bāzū said, " You cross first." When the Mīrzā showed his foolishness by these importunities, the Bāzū saw that both of them were going to perish. So he drove his horse forward. As the bed of the *nālah* running through the bamboo-groves was dry, the men used to cross the *nālah* through the bamboo-groves dismounting from their horses. The Bāzū dismounted from his horse and came to the *nālah* and Mīrzā Nathan followed him. In the mean time the *patta* or *kalkī* (an aigrette) of the horse of the Mīrzā along with the *sarī* or steel *qashqa* (a kind of armour for a horse's head) slid down on the face of the horse while it was crossing the *nālah* and produced a great obstruction. The enemies even at this sight, did not venture to come forward, fearing that some of these fellows who were always ready (for death) with shrouds wrapped round their heads might be lying in ambush. More so, because the Khwāja and the Afghān were visible with their two horses as well as with some cavalry belonging to the latter. They had dismounted and were sitting on the bank of the *nālah*. But the enemies kept sending showers of arrows. The Mīrzā, immediately, cut the *sari* or *qashqa* of the horse with a knife and took it on his shoulder and at the same time put the *patta* or *kalkī* again on the horse and followed Bāzū-i-Jhilam. But the Bāzū had no knowledge of these happenings. The *qashqa* of the horse remained on the shoulders of the Mīrzā as an indication of the situation he had passed through. Sayf Khān Lūdī and Bahādur Khān Kākar saw it from the other side. Although the enemies kept shooting their arrows, the True Lord brought the Mīrzā to the other side of the *nālah* under His protective care. That eunuch (Khwāja Sandal) and the Afghān (Dariyā Khān), whose death had come, committed suicide. The enemies were detained for some time in looting the properties and horses in that place. The Mīrzā with his followers came to the bank of a channel of the Brahmaputtra and he found that Nīk Muḥammad Beg had crossed this channel by a ford with the women and the elephants of the artillery and had carried them to one of the villages of the Mīrzā named Suālkūchī,[2] the ryots of which were loyal to him. While the other men were crossing, the Mīrzā also came up and taking a boat safely crossed over to the other side of the channel with his companions. After crossing to this side when he was intending to ride on his horse, the enemies arrived at the other bank of the aforesaid channel and began to discharge their guns and arrows. The Mīrzā sank the boat in the channel and started for the Brahmaputtra. Five *gharīs* to evening, he reached the bank of the Brahmaputtra. Hearing the report of the defeat of the imperial army, Rāja Satrajit, who was with the force of the Zamīndārs, sent five boats of his fleet (to that place). The Mīrzā began to cross (the Brahmaputtra) immediately on his arrival. But the boatmen, in order that their boats might not get broken by the rush of the fleeing men, kept the boats at a distance (from the bank) and had the men carried in *gudāras* (ordinary ferry-boats) to the *kūsas*. A great delay was caused (by this procedure). By this time, the enemies, had crossed that channel, and arrived at that crossing station two *gharīs* after evening and began to shower arrows upon these men. Pressing against one another, many of these confused men fell into the river and preferred to be drowned rather than offer resistance to the enemies. The Mīrzā with a party of men took a firm stand, but it was of no avail. These cowards crowded together and the Mīrzā along with these people was driven to the water at each detonation of the cannon (*ẓarb-i-deg*). The Mīrzā took hold of his sword and dispersed the crowd from his side by wounding some of them. Then he came up to the bank and began to shoot arrows. A few of the musketeers, summoned up courage and fired their muskets. Owing to this firing the enemy had not the boldness to capture all these panic-stricken people. Thus, by the end of three *pahars* of the night, he (the Mīrzā) crossed the river Brahmaputtra with all his followers. (645)

**Nathan reaches Suālkuchī.** After reaching this side of the river it was found that the men of Rāja Lakshmī Narāyan had left thirty five horses of theirs on the other side of the river in the Kukrazār forest and they themselves had crossed over to this side on foot. But when the arrow had left the bow, there was no remedy. He showed his great displeasure to these people and then remained silent. Next morning he reached Suālkuchī. (646)

**Nathan resolves to retrieve his prestige.** Shaykh Kamāl, Rāja Madhūsudan, Rāja Satrajit, Mīrzā Ṣāliḥ Arghūn, Mīrzā Yūsuf and all the Manṣabdārs, high and low, came to see the Mīrzā and to offer their excuses. Before their arrival, the Mīrzā removed the black wrappers from the flags and standards of the elephants and having removed the turban from his head, he wrapped one of these pieces on his head and another was torn and put round his neck. In short, although the Shaykh and the Rājas and Manṣabdārs tried to take the Mīrzā to Hājo, it was of no avail. When the Shaykh took an oath and promised that after three days he would be provided with sufficient reinforcements to proceed against the enemies, he (the Mīrzā) agreed to go to the village of Rāmdiya.[3] He swore, "I will go with you to Rāmdiya, but I am not a person to wait patiently. After four days, by the will of God, I shall proceed from Rāmdiya against the enemies, whether you supply reinforcements or not. I shall either lose my head or take this country,—as the proverb goes, "Either I will give my head or wear a crown." Having said this, he ordered his *maḥal* and the women of the soldiers to be carried to Chandankuth where all the families lived. He himself went on a boat to Rāmdiya. (647)

**Nathan recruits a fresh army.** Next morning it became known that Shaykh Kamāl, without supplying any reinforcement, was speaking in the following strain:—"The Dakhinkul has gone out of control, (now) they want that I should loose the Uttarkul as well." The Mīrzā began to recruit his soldiers and on the fourth day, according to his own plan, he marched from Rāmdiya. On the fifth day, he held a review of his army and found that there were five hundred cavalry and one thousand brave infantry, fully equipped and armed. He marched forward stage by stage. (648)

**Re-appointment of Qulīj Khan.** The Ṣūbahdār Khān Fatḥ-jang, hearing the report of the state of affairs, became very much perturbed. Apprehensive that the imperial Court might ascribe this disaster in the Kūch territory to his dismissal of Qulīj Khān from office, he immediately sent in a swift boat the chief of his personal officers named Mīr Shams, orginally a destitute but appointed in the army by the favour of Ibrāhīm Khān and now transformed into a companion of the aforesaid Khān,—with a very conciliatory letter to Qulīj Khān. The Manṣab of Qulīj Khān was also increased by 500 (personal) with 500 horse, and he was recalled. Mīr Shams brought him (Qulīj) back from Jatrapūr to Jahāngīrnagar. The Khān gave much consolation to Qulīj Khān and sent him again to the Thāna of Hājo to hold the office of the Jāgīrdār and the Sardār of the territory of Kūch with these instructions :—" Mīrzā Nathan, the hero, being ashamed of the disgrace, is at present not in good terms with the imperial officers, and at this disgrace and loss of prestige he is thinking of killing himself. The well-being of the Emperor demands that you should go to the aforesaid (Mīrzā) wherever he is staying, as, through shame, he will not come to you. If you consider that the triumphant enemies may be ousted, give him proper aid and drive the enemies by every possible device by inflicting a proper punishment upon them and thus put him (Nathan) under obligation. Failing this, you should pacify him by all means and make him abandon this resolution with brotherly counsel." He also wrote a letter of consolation (to the Mīrzā) : —" You yourself are capable of judging whether any of our fellow members has, during this period, thought it proper to put on a rag on his head (as a sign of penance for a defeat). The military profession sometimes means victory and sometimes a defeat. It is proper, that for the welfare of the Emperor, you should work in consultation with Qulīj Khān so that the affairs of that frontier may not be dislocated." Accordingly, Qulīj Khān proceeded swiftly from stage to stage and within a short time he reached the mohāna of Jogīgoqa (Jogīghopa).[4] (649)

**Nathan raises a loan at Gilahnay.** Mīrzā Nathan ordered his army to cross the river Brahmaputtra opposite Chandankuth, and he made a forced march to Gilahnay in order to raise a loan. He obtained Rs. 30,000 from the relations of Chūbī Chintāman with the promise of repaying within seven months. Then he returned from there to Nagarbera[5] with his camp and army and waited for Qulīj Khān with the expectation that Qulīj Khān, who had reached near his place, would call upon him according to the orders of Ibrāhīm Khān Fatḥ-jang. (650)

**Nathan halts at Jumuria for reinforcements.** But Qulīj Khān, in view of the fact that Mīrzā Nathan had included the parganās of Sāmbhūr and Pāndū within his own Jāgīr in lieu of his salaries, after his (Qulīj Khān's) dismissal, evaded meeting him (the Mīrzā) and proceeded to Hājo through the waterways of a *jalah* (swamp). Then, in order to safeguard himself from blame, he (Qulīj Khān) wrote a letter to Mīrzā Nathan, saying :—" As the current of the water is very strong and dangerous, I have proceeded avoiding it. For the sake of the well-being of imperial affairs I shall supply you with a strong force. It is proper that you should once come to meet me." Accordingly, as Qulīj Khān held out hopes of supplying reinforcements, the Mīrzā went to him immediately. His purpose was also to stop Qulīj Khān from saying in future, that he had (always) wanted to render assistance but it was Mīrzā Nathan who had never come to him but had gone straight against the enemies without taking it, and consequently, it was the Mīrzā who was at fault. When Qulīj Khān was coming out of the *jalah* and was entering the Brahmaputtra, the Mīrzā reached him. Qulīj Khān wanted to take the Mīrzā to Hājo, but he did not agree and said, " If your object is to send reinforcements to me from Hājo, I shall proceed slowly up to the village of Jumuria[ii] and shall wait there for the arrival of the reinforcements. After this, if during this interval no reinforcement comes, then, depending on the favour of God, I will proceed against the enemies and will try to subjugate the country of the Dakhinkul, so that you may not say that Mīrzā Nathan proceeded without waiting (for your help)." They bade adieu to each other in that place and proceeded to their respective Thānas. Thus after six days Qulīj Khān reached Hājo and Mīrzā Nathan arrived at his station within three *pahars*. (651)

**Booties sent to the Sūbahdār.** He (Nathan) halted at Jumuria for a week. Four of the elephants which were seized from Rāja Baldev, brother of Rāja Parikshit, along with many gifts were sent to the Khān Fath-jang and his wife Begum in charge of his (the Mīrzā's) trustworthy officers.

He then slowly proceeded on. The officers of the Mīrzā arrived with the elephants at the Khān's place. The Khān Fatḥ-jang sent the elephants with the presents to the imperial Court, as he had received them. (652)

**Jadū Nāyak opposes Nathan.** When the Mīrzā reached a place of four *kos* to Dhaknabuyi,[7] the spies informed him that Jadū Nāyak had come to Ḍhaknabuyi with a force of four thousand *pāiks* and was engaged in raising a fort. He then held a council of war with his loyal followers. All of them agreed upon this that as the enemy had not yet been able to strengthen his fortification they should go forward and attack the fort. Accordingly, the Mīrzā, who was still riding on his horse, did not dismount but proceeded to the aforesaid fort. The spies had told him that the whole way up to the fort of the enemy was plain, but although he marched by that way he came to a dense forest, and the day also came to its close. He sent some men to his Dīwān, Khwāja Balabhadra Dās, who was in charge of the van, with this message :—" I do not see good signs for to-day's battle. The soldiers still entertain a certain amount of fear for the enemies. It will be better if by the grace of God a victory can be attained in the first assault. Therefore, it is expedient that we should turn back and halt for to-day. It is an undertaking involving the capture of a fort and who knows what will happen at night. To-morrow, with the aid of the Merciful Lord, the fort should be attacked in whatever manner we consider best and God willing, it will be blown out of its foundation." Balabhadra Das, immediately on the arrival of the courier who carried the news, stopped his horse and sent some men to those who had gone ahead of him and brought them back. But by that time Nīk Muḥammad Beg and 'Īsā Khān Astrānī laid wagers against all the rest (and raced for the fort) and as soon as the fort came in sight, they attacked it. Thus 'Īsā Khān was wounded by an arrow and the horse of Nīk Muḥammad also received wounds. Inspite of this, both these men (about ten letters effaced in the Manuscript here) were brought back from the foot of the fort. About the time of sunset they came out of the Kukrazār (thickets of reeds ?). As the whole of that region (about eight letters effaced) was full of jungles and marsh, they pitched their camp on a small (clear) plot of land which was available on a side. From the first part of the night, the enemies, surrounded the camp of the army and kept discharging arrows. But Mīrzā Nathan passed the night with care and vigilance and posted on every side from which the enemies were attacking, brave and experienced regiments to drive them back. Early next morning when the kettle-drum of march was played, the enemies scattered themselves like the constellation of the Bear. A Brahmin named Naraharī Barkāyeth (Purkāyeth ?) who accompanied the army as a loyalist, led the army for crossing the river of Dhaknabuyi (Koolsi ?) to a place where the water came up to the knee of men and horses. The enemies evacuated the fort of Dhaknabuyi without any battle and became vagrants of the world. But as there was no road, Naraharī rode on an elephant in the front followed by all the other elephants in batches of ten and these were employed in clearing the jungles of Kukrazār by trampling upon them three times in succession. He proceeded thus by clearing the way and the army followed him till they came out to the village of Jumna.[8] The men of the village offered a short skirmish, but at last, unable to stand, they fled away. All the corns, properties and cattle of that village came into their possession. They halted there for the night. As during the last few days, the scarcity had made itself felt in the army, so every one took with him as much as one could carry. (653)

**Nathan halts at Dhaknabuyi.** Next morning they proceeded to Dhaknabuyi clearing the jungles in the same way with the elephants in their front. The army was divided in to four divisions and the camp-followers were placed in the middle. The enemies, who also advanced clearing the jungles, blocked their way when they had crossed half the distance. When the van had advanced forward and the regiment of the rear was at a distance they (the enemies) fell upon the camp-followers who being in the middle could not get any aid either from the van or from the rear. They seized all the copper utensils of the kitchen of the Mīrzā and wounded many of the *kahārs* (bearers) and camp-followers. One *pahar* before evening, they pitched their camp at the plain of Dakhnabuyi. The Mīrzā ordered the erection of a stockade of plantain trees,—a fruit tree which grows in India, specially in Bengal. In short, although this fort was of no use after three or four days, still, it was quite strong for these three or four days. Arrows and bullets from guns had no power to pass through this barricade. The stockade was strongly fortified, and Balabhadra Dās, the Dīwān was sent from Jumna to Qulīj Khān in order to ask for reinforcements. He (the Mīrzā) stayed here for twelve days. Every day a regiment was sent to raid the adjacent villages of the hill-Rājas and large booties consisting of cattle and other things were seized. (654)

**Nathan proceeds to Minārī.** When the return of Balabhadra Dās was delayed, he (the Mīrzā) marched from that place to Minārī.[9] The enemies attacked him two or three times on the way but they could not do anything. He reached the plains of Minārī and pitched his camp. As this place was convenient for fortification, he ordered to begin the construction of a fort. The work was done with such expedition that within one *pahar* of the day and four *pahars* of the night the fortification round the camp was completed. (655)

**Encounter with Shumāruyed.** Shumāruyed Kāyeth, the head of the rebellion and mutiny in the country, was staying with Rāja Baldev and the Sardārs of the Rāja of Assam, near the *mohāna* (mouth) of the river Kalang at a place named Hangrabārī. When he heard of the arrival of Mīrzā Nathan (at Minārī), he (Shumāruyed) came to Minārī within the night and raised a big fort adjoining a hill in front of the fort of Mīrzā Nathan. He also cut down the banks of some hill-streams in such a way that within the night the environs of the Mīrzā's fort were submerged in water, and no place except an elevation within the fort was left dry. The depth of the water all around this area came up to the knee or the chest of a horse. Next morning, this disaster became visible and created a panic among many of the dispirited men. But the Mīrzā remained quite cheerful and gay submitting to the will of God and waited for the arrival of Balabhadra Dās. (656)

**Reinforcement sent by Qulīj Khān.** Now I shall give a short account of the affairs of Balabhadra Dās. He started from Jumna and reached Qulīj Khān within three *pahars* proceeding up the river Brahmaputtra. He informed him of the details of the conquest of the fort of Dhaknabuyi and requested him to send his reinforcements, saying, "When a gentleman makes a promise, he fulfils it." Qulīj Khān had no other alternative but to send messages to Rāja Lakshmī Narāyan and Rāja Madhūsudan and it was settled that Rāja Lakshmī Narāyan would send Rām Singh, son of his uncle Sarbā Gosāin, with an adequate force, and Rāja Madhūsudan would send his eldest son Pashupatī. Accordingly, they despatched these men, and Balabhadra Dās, having crossed the river Brahmaputtra, halted at Garāl with the intention of proceeding to join the Mīrzā. Pashupatī, son of Rāja Madhūsudan played false. He (Balabhadra) was delayed for two or three days on his account and he tried to make him realise the situation as far as he could. When he found him to be very stupid, he started with Sarbā Gosāin in his company. The enemies, informed of their impending arrival, sent a regiment to oppose them on the way. A battle took place and the sound of guns reached the ears of the Mīrzā. The Mīrzā through his foresight used to go out riding every day with the view of escorting the reinforcements that would come from Hājo. On this day also he went out and returned (before he heard the reports of guns). So he immediately sent a party of brave heroes running to that place in order to bring news about these sounds. By the time Sayf Khān Lūdī and some others reached that place, the enemies had become triumphant over this party and had seized the kettle-drum and the horse belonging to the son of Sarbā Gosāin which carried the kettle-drum (*āsp-i-naqāra*). When Balabhadra Dās and the son of Sarbā Gosāin were in this plight, these men (sent by the Mīrzā) came to their rescue and brought them to the Mīrzā. It then became known that Pasāi (Pashupatī) son of Rāja Madhūsudan was thinking of bringing the rebels of the Dakhinkul under his control and then he would return to Hājo, and would not join the Mīrzā. (657)

**Pashupati joins Nathan.** The Mīrzā took with him one hundred horsemen, five elephants and five hundred infantry and marched in the night and reached the camp of this foolish man early in the morning. Balabhadra Dās was left in charge of his (Mīrzā's) fort. Pashupatī, at first mistook this regiment to be that of the enemy's and came out to fight; but at last he came and offered his excuses. The first thing the Mīrzā did immediately after his arrival, was to hold him by the hand in a brotherly way and then he said to him :—" We have waited for you for a long time and you should (now) start." At last when he came to know that he (Pashupatī) would not give up his pretensions, he told him plainly : —" You must do one of these three things. First, if Qulīj Khān has sent you to me, you must proceed immediately with me; secondly, if you do not accompany me you must immediately cross the Brahmaputtra and go back to Hājo to Qulīj Khān and your father; if you have any other intention besides these, you must fight us." When Pashupatī saw that the situation had became very tense, he became helpless and agreed to follow the Mīrzā and proceeded on. As the day was coming to its close, the Mīrzā halted at the village of Jumna in order to pacify him and passed the night with ease in that place. Early next morning they started from that place and safely reached the Mīrzā's fort after mid-day. (658)

**Nathan conquers the fort of Minārī.** Next morning without taking any rest, the Mīrzā went on horseback to find out some means to surround the enemy's fort and he went near the fort. Leaving out the army of his officers which was posted in his fort, the rest of the soldiers were divided into three regiments in this way :—Pashupatī with his followers formed one regiment. They were ordered to go into the jungle behind the enemy's fort and to raise a stockade in a place where it was possible to dig a trench opposite the enemy's fort. The second regiment was formed of Sarbā Gosāin and some of his own men. They were posted to his left in a trench between the fort of the Mīrzā (and that of the enemy). They were further assured by the Mīrzā that in spite of this arrangement, he would take his stand by their side. He, himself, being fully equipped, took his stand between these two trenches depending entirely on the favours of God as to what would come out of invisible screen. The enemies also formed one army and came out of their fort and stood in the jungle. As soon as they saw Pashupatī entering the jungle, they planned to attack Pashupatī from the rear and to ruin him and his army. The Mīrzā sent Darwīsh Bahādur and some other with fifty horsemen, two hundred infantry and two elephants with instruction to fall upon this army of the enemy from the rear and to finish the job. Seeing this, that army (of the enemy) returned to the fort by the same way through which it had come out and it failed to do any fighting. In short, Pashupatī went and attacked the fort of the enemy. Darwīsh Bahādur also reached from the rear and attempted the conquest of the fort. From the other side, the soldiers of the Mīrzā and of the son of Sarbā led their attack. And from a central place, the Mīrzā himself followed them dismounting from his horse and rushed upon the fort. From the other side the soldiers of the fort of the Mīrzā waded through the water which went up to their neck and chest and attacked the fort. A wonderful battle took place on every side and the enemies offered a strong defence of their fort. The dead lay in heaps upon one another and gradually the garrison within was reduced to great straits. It was only then that the brave and painstaking warriors in the company of the Mīrzā could cross the ditch of the enemy's fort without any fear for the first time; and, following the Mīrzā who rushed forward with the shield before his face, they entered the fort after a hand to hand struggle. The clarion of victory was played and the kettle-drum of happy announcement was sounded. At this juncture Pashupati also entered the fort from the other side with the men of the Mīrzā. The son of Sarbā Gosāin on account of his previous discomfiture (at the enemy's hand) made a strong sally and the soldiers of the fort of the Mīrzā had to put forth their efforts with double vigour, as they had to fight against water as well as against the fire of the battle. Shumāruyed Kāyeth, Hātī Barua, Rājkhawa and Kharghuka (Khargharīā Phukan) the sardars of the Rāja of Assam and the Eighteen Hill-Rājas,—every one of them,—became wanderers in the desert of vagrancy with the dust of disgrace scattered on their heads. The Mīrzā took his stand within the fort in a very happy and pleasant mood. (659)

**Capture of Shumāruyed.** As the enemies had fled by two routes, so two armies were despatched to (pursue them). Mīrzā Nathan sent his own men with five famous elephants and one thousand infantry under the command of Mast 'Alī Beg to the track on the right side, and the second army was sent to the left under the command of Pashupatī. He himself remained in the fort with the rest of his men to take rest and kept his ears open to listen to the sound of victory after victory. Some one cried aloud that Shumāruyed Kāyeth had been captured by Mast 'Alī Beg and he was being carried on an elephant and would reach here presently. The substance of this long account is this:—When Mast 'Alī Beg and his party started, the Mīrzā instructed every one of them that if by the will of God they happen to meet Shumāruyed they should not hurt him even if he attempted violence, but they should bring him alive as a captive. Accordingly, Mast 'Alī Beg pursued him and seized one of his *pāiks* and wanted to kill him. The *pāik* sought safety for his life with the promise of disclosing the place of concealment of Shumāruyed and with the promise of helping to make him captive. Therefore the *pāik* in the hope of saving his own life, showed the hiding-place of Shumāruyed. In the mean time, Shumāruyed with five or six men, who were in his company, heard the sound of the neighing of the horse and took to flight. He was met by an Afghān named Jawhar Khān, brother of Ḥabīb Khān, who was formerly an officer of Rāja Parikshit and knew Shumāruyed full well. Jawhar Khān said:—"Barkāyeth, I shall secure the safety of your life. Come and surrender to our master." Shumāruyed had an iron stick like a spear in his hand, he threw it at Jawhar Khān and Jawhar Khān was wounded. But in view of the instructions (of the Mīrzā) he did not injure Shumāruyed. He again spoke to Shumāruyed in a friendly and conciliatory way. But he (Shumāruyed) threw another stick on him. When Jawhar Khān saw that he (Shumāruyed) would go out of hand after killing him, he struck him (Shumāruyed) with his sword on his head. Shumāruyed fell senseless (on the ground). Jawhar Khān shouted to Mast 'Alī Beg:—"I am pitched against the man, search for whom is convulsing the whole world. He had wounded me and is running away. Who will come to my aid?" Mast 'Alī Beg arrived there, seized the rebel, bound his hands together and took him on an elephant and thus brought him to the Mīrzā. The Mīrzā offered two genuflexions of prayers of thanks (to God) and waited for the arrival of Mast 'Alī Beg. In the mean time Saiyid 'Abdu'ṣ-Ṣamad and Sayf Khān Lūdī stood up and said:—"The True Lord has fulfilled your desire. The man who was responsible for the defeat of all these armies has been made a captive. It is proper that you should offer thanks to God and put on your turban again." The Mīrzā acted accordingly. From the day of the last defeat upto the day of the aforesaid victory, the Mīrzā, for this period of three months and eighteen days, had been tying a piece of rag round his head, and was waiting for Divine favours for a day when he would regain his fame and realise his objects. (660)

**Humane treatment to Shumāruyed.** Shumāruyed had thought that as soon as he would be brought to the Mīrzā he would be torn to pieces. But immediately after his arrival, his fetters were removed by the Mīrzā with his own hands and the surgeons were ordered to dress his wounds and to heal them. Shumāruyed was accommodated in the same house where the Mīrzā lived by putting up a screen and the Mīrzā tried to heal him. He gave him much consolation, saying :—" God the great has sent this guidance to our community that we should protect friends and foes alike and should recognise the quality of forgiveness to be superior to that of revenge. You people behave in such a way that not to speak of a male enemy, you kill even a woman who happens to fall into your hands. So be at peace. If you submit loyally, I shall show great favour to you." Shumāruyed, put to shame by the generosity of the Mīrzā, decided to summon his five sons with their families to surrender to the Mīrzā. He wrote a letter to his son and summoned all his people. In short, the plant of generosity sprang very high in the garden of humanity and magnanimity and the love of God became apparent and justice was meted out to courage and manliness. Next day, a great banquet was given to his (the Mīrzā's) companions, and the men who had rendered loyal and valiant deeds were honoured with the gifts of horses and robes of honour. The Mīrzā halted there for seven days for treating the wounds of Shumāruyed, and the report of the victory was sent to Hājo and specially to Jahāngīrnagar to the Ṣūbahdār, the Khān Fatḥ-jang. Every day a detachment was sent to raid the territories of the Hill-Rājas. (661)

**Raid of the territory of Kanwal Rāja.** On the eighth day the camp was removed to Haldiya Duwār in the territorry of Kanwal Rāja. In the twinkling of an eye a high fort was raised with deep ditches around, and the walls and towers were mounted with big cannon. The army was ordered to enter the hills and to raze the villages of Kanwal Rāja to the ground, to put every opponent to the edge of the dreadful sword, and to bring the rest as captives. This was accordingly done. Kanwal fled to the region of the upper hills and took shelter with the Rājas of those regions, and he sent envoys saying,—" Unless Bāhtua (Hātua ?),

Rāja of Bar Duwār, the chief of the Eighteen Hill-Rājas, submits, none of us will surrender and we shall struggle against our ruin to the best of our power. If you desire that we the Rājas of the hills must submit, all your attempts should be directed against the Bar Duwār (Rāja)." It was also affirmed by the Zamīndārs of the Dakhinkul region. (662)

**Invasion of Barduwār.** On the fifth day, the Mīrzā marched from that place. One regiment was posted at Haldiya Duwār under the command of Balabhadra Dās and he (the Mīrzā) proceeded to the territory of Bāmun Rāja which was situated between Bar Duwār and Haldiya Duwār. Another regiment was left in this territory under the command of Mast 'Alī Beg. Next morning he (the Mīrzā) marched to Bar Duwār and halted there raising a fort. Immediately after his arrival, the *hāt* (market place) of Bar Duwār was raided and attempts were made to climb the hill of Bar Duwār. Nīk Muḥammad Beg with some of the lovers of battle went up to the aforesaid hill with great difficulty. Some of the very brave and fearless hill-men who were fighting with big knives weighing sixteen Indian *seers*, were killed and their heads were brought. This produced a great panic among the hill-men. The Rāja unable to resist any longer, went to Upra Rāja Khamranga, i.e. the Rāja of the upper hills and took shelter there.

The hill of Khamranga was a place of such security that none of Rāja Parikshit's ancestors up to the seventh generation could ever bring it under subjection. Once Bajādhar Dalai (Gadādhar Dalai ?) a relation of Rāja Raghu Dev went there, but he perished there and could not return. No other man had ever attempted it. The Mīrzā, immediately on the receipt of this news, sent some devoted spies in order to inspect the ways to that hill and to bring news. He (the Mīrzā) himself stayed there (Bar Duwār-hāt) and used to send a regiment to raid the Haldiya Duwār and the territory of Bāmun Rāja every alternate day. It was decided by the Mīrzā to stay in his fort till the arrival of his reinforcements. That army having entered the hill attacked the fort which was raised by Bāmun Rāja and Kanwal Rāja between the hills. The villages within the hills were raided and destroyed. (663)

**Capture of Rāja Khamranga.** The spies went to Khamranga[10] under disguise as fish-mongers and brought the informations. The Mīrzā, leaving a detachment in his camp, proceeded himself and arrived there after one *pahar* and a half of the day. By chance the Rāja of Khamranga with his wife came alone to the *hāt* (weekly market) in order to enjoy the sight of buyers. He became heavily drunk and wandered about in the *hāt* in a state of intoxication. First of all, the Mīrzā reached that strategic position where Bajādhar Dalai was killed. He posted there Pashupatī, son of Rāja Madhūsudan, and the son of Sarbā Gosaīn with a detachment of his famous warriors, and he got into the centre of that place and raided the *hāt* of Khamranga. As it was ordained by the True Lord that the object would be achieved with ease, the Rāja of Khamranga with his wife was captured. Whichever of the hill-men set up an opposition in the *hāt* was put to death. The Mīrzā, keeping in view the rules of military profession, took the Rāja with his wife and other booties and returned to the camp without delay, and reached his destination at the time of sunset. (664)

**Khamranga granted freedom.** After an hour, when Rāja Khamranga regained his senses from the stupor of intoxication and found himself in captivity, he could not see any way for his safety except loyal submission. He promised thus :—" I will hand over to you Hātwa Rāja of Bar Duwār in chains provided you spare my life and grant me liberty along with my wife." The Mīrzā, administering an oath in the name of God, released one of the men of the *hāt* as an expedient measure. He (Rāja Khamranga) sent a message to his nobles saying :—" If you desire me to live and to be released from the hands of the Mīrzā, then immediately find out Hātwa in whichever hill he is staying, and bring him to the Mīrzā bound in ropes." The man reached that place next day and delivered the message. These people brought him bound within three days from the hill where he was hiding. The Mīrzā presented the Khamranga Rāja and his wife with robes of honour and granted them leave to depart with great honour. He was further instructed that the Rāja should communicate to all the Rājas of the upper regions that they must refuse to give shelter to the Rājas of the Lāmdānī i.e. lower hills. They must know it for certain that as there is no better strategic position than that of Khamranga, all of them, small or great, would be captured and imprisoned along with their families. (665)

**Surrender of the Eighteen Hill-Rājas.** When the hill-Rājas lost their strategic places, all the Eighteen Rājas tendered their submission to the Mīrzā within three days, one after another. The Mīrzā placed all the Eighteen (Rājas) under surveillance, and then directed his efforts towards securing the sons and families of Shumāruyed. (666)

**Surrender of Shumāruyed's Family.** In the meantime, an enemy of Shumāruyed conspired with the surgeon who was treating him. He bribed him with some money to practise certain rites of sorcery upon Shumāruyed, so that he might die. Accordingly, he performed such a sorcery that his wounds which had been cured, began to bleed without any stop. Shumāruyed was in the agonies of death. The Mīrzā, being informed of this affair, ordered that surgeon to be trampled under the feet of an elephant. The surgeon confessed and said, "If you do not put me to immediate death, I will apply some remedies." When he was brought out of the elephant's feet, he immediately read some spells on a handkerchief which he had in his hand and turning it over the head of Shumāruyed he threw it behind his own back. As soon as he did this, the blood, which was gushing out like water from a fountain, stopped and from moment to moment the patient changed colour and came to his normal state. At this second favour shown by the Mīrzā through the will of God, for the safety of his life, Shumāruyed wrote a very strict letter to his wife (asking her to surrender). Although the wife of Shumāruyed did not take away her eldest son named Bagla from the company of Raja Baldev, the brother of Rāja Parikshit, still she surrendered to the Mīrzā along with her other four sons at the earliest opportunity. The Mīrzā, immediately after the arrival of Shumāruyed's wife and sons, brought him out and enrolled him in the circle of the loyal Zamīndārs with the gift of a robe of honour. Twenty *Mauẓas* of the Dakhinkul were assigned to him for his maintenance. He was then entrusted to Amānu'llah and his brothers who were the trustworthy officers of the Mīrzā to keep him under surveillance and pacified him with the following promise:—"The day when the *mohāna* of the *Kalang* will be occupied, you will be set at liberty and will be made the Sardār over all the Eighteen Hill-Rājas and all the *Pāiks* of the Dakhinkul will be placed under your command, and you will be given a place in the circle of my personal favourites." (667)

**Nathan proceeds to Rānihat.** From there he (Mīrzā Nathan) marched to Rānīhāt and halted there. At the advice of Shumāruyed, he despatched a force of four hundred cavalry, three thousand and five hundred Kūch *pāiks* and seven hundred expert matchlock-men to Hangrabārī under the command of Ḥabib Khān Lūdī to establish a fortified post. (668)

**Gifts from the Subahdar to Nathan.** At the report of this victory, Ibrāhīm Khān Fatḥ-jang, the Mīr Ṣūbah, sent to the aforesaid Mīrzā with Mīr Mu'izu'd-Dīn, Rāja Raghūnāth and Mīrzā Malik Ḥusayn an imperial robe of honou which had been sent to him about this time from the imperial Court and also a horse and a robe of honour on his own behalf. It was written to Qulīj Khān, Shaykh Kamāl, Rāja Lakshmī Narāyan, Rāja Madhūsudan, Rāja Satrajit, Mīrzā Ṣāliḥ Arghūn, Mīrzā Yūsuf Barlās and all the officers, high and low, that they should not go beyond what Mīrzā Nathan advises. He who would not send his army to Mīrzā

Nathan or would not personally go (to his aid) would be guilty before the Emperor. In short, immediately after the arrival (of the letter) at Hājo, Rāja Satrajit, Rāja Madhūsudan, Mīrzā Yūsuf and all the 'Uṣmānī Afghāns along with their respective armies went to Rānīhāt to the Mīrzā. The Mīrzā came out to receive them and took them with great respect to his fort. Qulīj Khān and Shaykh Kamāl also each sent one hundred cavalry. (669)

**Nathan Receives the gifts at Pāndū.** Mīr Mu'izu'd-Dīn Muḥammad and Rāja Raghūnāth wrote (to the Mīrzā) thus:—" As we are bringing the imperial robes of honour, horse and standard to Pāndū, it is proper that you should come to Pāndū and pay your respects to these imperial gifts. You will also meet Qulīj Khān and Shaykh Kamāl there. After making necessary consultations with them you may proceed in whatever manner you like to seize the *mohāna* of the Kalang from the hands of the enemy." The Mīrzā was not agreeable to this, but at the insistence of Mīr Mu'iz'd-Dīn Maḥmūd, he agreed to go to Pāndū. In the mean time an agent of the Pay-Master-General (*Bakhshi-i-Kul*) of the Ṣūbah of Bengal came to inspect the armies of the Mīrzā. He inspected the muster roll of the soldiers and then intended to go to Hangrabārī to inspect the army which had gone forward. The Mīrzā sent him there and wrote a strict letter to Ḥabīb Khān Lūdī:—" As the distance between you and the enemy is very little, be careful, about fighting in the open field, until I write to you (to do so). Do not come out of the fort to present your army before the agent of the Bakhshī. Keep your soldiers ready within the fort in their respective posts and present them for inspection. The horses also should be presented within the fort." After this he (the Mīrzā) started for Pāndū with a force of fifty cavalry, one hundred infantry and four elephants. Sa'ādat Khān, the eunuch, was left as the Chief Officer over his own men as well as over the imperial officers at his fort. He reached Pāndū within four *gharīs* and received the robes of honour along with the horse with great respect, and became happy. After this he had a friendly interview with Mīr Mu'iz'd-Dīn, Rāja Raghūnāth and Mīrzā Malik Ḥusayn. It was arranged that Qulīj Khān and Shaykh Kamāl would come by boats from Hājo to hold a council of war in the morning. (670)

**Loss of Hangrabārī.** In the mean time Rāja Satrajit, who was friendly with Shaykh Kamāl and inimically disposed towards the Mīrzā, conspired with Shumāruyed. Shumāruyed Kāyeth, inspite of all those favours shown by the Mīrzā to him, wrote thus to his Assamese brethren:—"Mīrzā Nathan has gone to Pāndū; till he returns none of this army will go to the aid of the regiment sent in advance. If you desire your well-being, fall upon this regiment and besiege their fort immediately on the receipt of this letter. Whether they come out (to fight) or not, attack the fort and finish their work. After this, when Mīrzā Nathan will return from Pāndū all the regiments will obey his orders and you will be reduced to great straits." A secret message was sent to the agents of the Bakhshī who went to inspect the advance-regiment to this effect:—"Unless you inspect that army by bringing them out of the fort you will not be able to verify the number of soldiers in that Thāna, as submitted by Mīrzā Nathan." Accordingly, that foolish man insisted on this question and brought that foolish army out of the fort. Ḥabīb Khān through his Afghānī foolishness left the protection of the big fort where this army was staying, arrayed the soldiers and came out with all those forty horsemen and five hundred infantry in order to hold a review of the army. The enemies took it as God-send and came forward to fight. When they (the enemies) saw that these people were coming out without any apprehension, they brought a *jāl*, i.e., a big net with which wolves and wild buffaloes are caught, and set these in front of their own army and offered battle. This army (i.e. imperial army) was unable to make a galloping charge with courage. Thus the enemies, occupying a secure position, began to discharge arrows and guns and *chandrabāns* (rockets ?). They also hurled stones from slings and shot arrows from cross-bows. They ordered ten thousand brave *pāiks* to attack the fort and to attempt its capture. Ḥabīb Khān, who had come out of the fort through his rashness, found no time to rally and only made two or three sallies with the horses against the enemies; but they were of no avail. The net stood on their way. By that time the fort was raided and set on fire. The army outside (the fort) being scattered, lost courage. Inspite of this, the experienced warriors to whom the act of dying together appeared like a solemn feast, offered a stubborn resistance. Thus seven hundred brave men of the cavalry and infantry of the Mīrzā became martyrs in this battle. (671)

**Intrigue of Shaykh Kamāl and Qulīj Khān.** The news of the defeat reached Mīrzā at the time of candle light. The Mīrzā became mortified, wanted to leave Pāndū and proceed to his fort that very night. But Mīr Mu'iz'd-Dīn Muḥammad, Rāja Raghūnath and Mīrzā Malik Ḥusayn detained him for the night at Pāndū by showing their sympathy and offering excuses. As the Mīrzā suffered this reverse due to their invitation to Pāndū so they promised thus :—" As Qulīj Khān, Shaykh Kamāl and Rāja Lakshmī Narāyan have not yet reached here, to-morrow we shall accompany you to your Thāna and we shall return after making all the soldiers of that place obedient and submissive to your command." The Mīrzā passed the night in great care and anxiety like a broken-headed snake. Early next morning he started (for his place) and these comrades also accompanied him. When they had travelled half the way a confidential letter from Shaykh Kamāl reached Mīr Mu'izu'd-Dīn Muḥammad and Mīrzā (Malik Ḥusayn). They, being very friendly with the Shaykh, turned back and Rāja Raghūnāth was also persuaded to come away. The enraged Mīrzā (Nathan), without caring whether they would go or not, proceeded to his own Thāna. As Qulīj Khān and Shaykh Kamāl had written also to Rāja Satrajit and the officers who were already there, all of them desired to go back leaving the Thāna in disorder. Thus Satrajit left at once, and he was followed by the soldiers of Mīrzā Ṣāliḥ, Mīrzā Yūsuf and Qulīj Khān. The cavalry of the Shaykh also, under the plea of the departure of others, went away. But Rāja Madhūsudan, owing to the bold attitude taken by the men of the Mīrzā not to allow him to leave the fort without the Mīrzā's permission, became ashamed (of his own conduct) and remained in the fort with his regiment. In short, all these departing groups met the Mīrzā on their way one after the other and every one of them showing some pretexts went to Hājo. But the officers of Shaykh Kamāl, under instructions from their master, laid the blame on others and returned with the Mīrzā with their army. After mid-day the Mīrzā arrived at his Thāna and fortified it. He presented Rāja Madhūsudan with a good horse. He wrote a letter to Ibrāhīm Khān Fatḥ-jang commending the services of the aforesaid Rāja and describing the obstructive movements of his comrades, and it was immediately despatched. Next morning he proposed to go with that small army to the place where his men became martyrs (i.e. Hangrabārī). Rāja Madhūsudan, with many entreaties, stopped him from executing that plan. He then stayed there for another fifteen days. (672)

**Nathan moves to Hālīgāon.** When it began to rain continously for days and nights, the fort was washed away by the water of the heavy rains. So it became inexpedient to remain there during this season. At the advice of Rāja Madhūsudan, he shifted to a place, about a *kos* distant from the village of Hālīgāon, and raised a fort there. As there was very little water there, the army could not get sufficient supply of (drinking) water. Somehow or other three days were passed. On the fourth day water was brought to the fort by digging a canal from the river which was flowing by Rānīhāt. He stayed there for another month and pacified the whole of the Dakhinkul and realised its revenues. (673)

**Shumāruyed's intrigue with the Assamese.** During this time Shumāruyed Kāyeth sent a letter to the Sardārs of Assam through a *pāik* named Sanātan, saying:—" Some of the hours of the night are spent by the Mīrzā in negligence witnessing the dances of courtezans relying upon my keeping guard at the *chawkī*. If you lead an attack towards the last part of the night, it is quite possible that you will be able to capture the fort of the Mīrzā." But owing to the Mīrzā's many virtues, the True Lord did not desire that such calamities should come upon him one after another. The aforesaid letter fell into the hands of Mīrzā's men. In view of the fact that the Mīrzā had promised asylum to Shumāruyed, he did not say anything to Shumāruyed, in spite of this behaviour on his part. He was again entrusted to Amānu'llah and his brothers to be kept under surveillance. (674)

**Nathan Transfers his camp to Suālkuchī.** When the rainy season was at its height he (the Mīrzā) ordered an army to proceed further and to erect a fort at (Suālkuchī ?) (the letters are blurred), so that the entire army might remain on this side of the river Brahmaputtra. A mansion was ordered to be built on the other side of the river Brahmaputtra opposite the aforesaid fort of Suālkuchī for his own residence with his children. When it was completed he marched from this place and halted at the aforesaid fort. Rāja Madhūsudan was given a robe of honour and was granted leave to depart. Shaykh Kamāl, through necessity, recalled seventy of his horsemen leaving thirty with the Mīrzā. (675)

**A Regiment is sent to Minārī.** When a week passed in this way the Assamese came and began to carry out their plundering campaigns in the villages of the Dakhinkul. Therefore, a force of five hundred and fifty cavalry, seven hundred infantry and Kūch archers and one hundred musketeers was despatched under the command of Darwīsh Bahādur to Minārī, situated in the centre of the region in order to guard the territory. (676)

**Nathan takes the captive chiefs to the Sūbahdār.** As the Khān Fatḥ-jang had repeatedly written expressing his desire that Mīrzā Nathan should go to him along with the hill-Rājas, Shumāruyed and others to stay in his court for a period of twenty-five days and should then come back, so the Mīrzā appointed his Dīwān Balabhadra Dās to be the commander of this fort on the bank of the river and handed over the charge of administration to him. Leaving his children at Suālkuchī he (the Mīrzā) started to meet Ibrāhīm Khān Fatḥ-jang along with the Eighteen Hill-Rājas,—Shumāruyed and his family, the unlucky Parsurām and his son, sons of Rāja Baldev, and the wife and daughter of Māmūn Govind, uncle of Rāja Parikshit, who were his captives. Two of the elephants seized from Rāja Baldev along with many gifts were taken with him on boats for the Khān Fatḥ-jang. He started for Jahāngīrnagar *alias* Dhāka in an auspicious moment. Proceeding very swiftly from stage to stage, he reached the vicinity of Jahāngīrnagar at the ninth stage. There he heard the news that the Khān Fatḥ-jang had left for the country of Tippera on the night of his (Mīrzā's) departure. (677)

**Ibrāhīm Khān takes a pleasure trip to Tippera.** The sum and substance of this long account is this :—It has been mentioned before that Ibrāhīm Khān Fatḥ-jang had despatched some of the imperial officers with three regiments against the Rāja of Tippera. These people after heavy fighting defeated the Rāja successively in two or three battles. They captured his capital city named Udaypūr and pursued the Rāja. The Rāja in course of his flight, when his army became unluckily separated from him, left his elephants in order to mislead the imperial pursuers and entered into a dense forest. The imperialists also entered the hills on foot. First of all a slave of Mīrzā Nūru'd-Dīn came across that impudent Rāja and they fought with each other. This slave was wounded by the Rāja and he also wounded the Rāja. While he was attempting to seize the Rāja, one of the soldiers of Mīrzā Isfandiyār arrived at the spot and joined in the capture. The Rāja was caught with his wives; and the imperialists also seized his elephants after a great search. Then they were sent to Jahāngīrnagar *alias* Dhāka to the Khān Fatḥ-jang in charge of Mūsā Khān Masnad-i-'Alā, son of 'Īsā Khān, the chief of the Zamīndārs of Bengal. The Khān Faṭh-jang, hearing good reports about the climate and beauty of the country of Tippera, intended to take a pleasure trip to that country and to return to Jahāngīrnagar after pacifying that region. (678)

**Nathan presents the captive chiefs to the Sūbahdār.** The Mīrzā passed by Jahāngīrnagar and proceeded in the same way to Tippera with the elephants on *mānd* boats. When he reached the river Pankiya (Meghna ?) he had to leave the elephants in a *char* or island owing to the high waves of the river during the rainy season. After making satisfactory arrangements for their food and ration, he proceeded forward. The waves rose so high that two of the swift boats of Mūsā Khān, who was accompanying the Mīrzā to go to Ibrāhīm Khān, sank in the river. But by the protection of the Protector of fate no damage was done to the boats of the Mīrzā. The Mīrzā reached Udaypūr two days after the illustrious Khān had reached that place. In an auspicious hour, he paid his respects to the aforesaid Khān and presented the hill-Rājas,—Shumāruyed and the other Zamīndārs,— who had been brought to wait upon the Khān, and made them kiss his feet. The Khān paid a high tribute to the Mīrzā's loyalty and devotion and gave him much encouragement. He (the Khān) stayed there for another two days. Udaypur was assigned to Mīrzā Nūru'd-Dīn as his Jāgīr and he was appointed to be the Sardār (Chief officer) of that country. A portion of the territory of Tippera adjacent to the Jāgīrs of Mīrzā Isfandiyār was assigned to the aforesaid Mīrzā in lieu of his salary. Then he started for Jahāngīrnagar and arrived there within three days. The other officers reached Jahāngīrnagar on the fifth day and waited upon the Khān according to their rank. The Khān became very happy. (679)

**Nathan recommended for promotion.** Mīrzā Nathan, at a happy moment, presented before the Khān Fatḥ-jang, the elephants and all the gifts brought by him and had to offer all of them as *pēshkash* to the Khān. Over and above this *pēshkash*, he presented the Khān with one hundred small and big boats. The Khān, highly pleased at this, sent a representation, commending the devoted and loyal services of the Mīrzā to the sublime Court and its officers, and particularly to Her Majesty Nūrjahān Begum, and prayed for the promotion of his rank and title. Therefore, it became incumbent upon the Mīrzā to send also a suitable *pēshkash* to the Court and rare gifts to Her Majesty NūrJahān Begum, Nawab I'timādu'd Dawla and the nobles of the Court of the protector of the people. Accordingly, all the rare presents in his house as well as all the things purchased or obtained by him on credit together with a suitable elephant for His Majesty (may a thousand lives be sacrificed for him!) and a female elephant for the Begum were sent to the Sublime Court in charge of Hātim Khān Afghān and one of his Hindu officers named Gopāl Dās. The total value of the *pēshkash*, rare gifts and elephants amounted to rupees forty-two thousand. (680)

**Mag raids in Bengal.** During this time, the naval forces of the vanquished Rāja of the Mags came from Rakhang to raid the parganās of Bengal. They plundered some of the villages and took the people of those villages as captives. When Ibrāhīm Khān was arranging to send an army to punish those people, news reached at night that the Rāja of the Mags had come to the *char* or island of Baghāchar with seven hundred *ghurābs* (floating batteries) and four thousand *jaliya* boats, and he was contemplating an attack. Therefore, the Khān Fatḥ-jang, through his innate courage, proceeded in the last *pahar* of the night against the Mags with the boats which were ready in the *chawkī* before his gate, without taking the famous officers in his company and without requisitioning the Zamīndārs with their boats. When he reached a place at a distance of three *kos* from the enemy's camp, he found that he had only thirty swift war-boats in his company. Although the far-sighted followers of the Khān anticipated danger and represented it to the Khān, still, the courage and boldness of the Khān was beyond the pale of fear. Having prepared himself for the contest, he halted at the place where he had reached. He proposed to send his nephew (brother's son) Mīrzā Aḥmad Beg for the defence of Jahāngīrnagar. But Aḥmad Beg did not agree to leave the company of the Khān and remained with him. After a day and a night, the great nobles, all the Maṣabdārs and the loyal Zamīndārs arrived one after another in troops and companies with large equipments. The Khān praised those people who arrived foremost and those who came late, were thoroughly censured with casual words of displeasure, a (form of) rebuke which is more effective for men of good lineage than a thousand fatal wounds, and the vinegar of repentance was poured into the cup of their evil brain. Every one was then ordered to hold a review of their troops; and within a short time, more than four to five thousand war-boats were found ready and he (the Khān Fatḥ-jang) thus prepared for the war. The accursed Mag came forward with the idea that Ibrāhīm Khān would not personally lead the attack and so he would be able to go back after inflicting a heavy loss on the imperialists. When the Rāja saw the courage and speedy arrangements of Ibrāhīm Khān and the large number of world-conquering imperial soldiers, he considered it prudent for him to return without any battle and he turned back towards Rakhang. He returned (to Arracan) leaving two thousand *jaliya* boats in the frontier of his kingdom. (681)

**Strengthening of the Thānas at the Mag frontier.** Ibrāhīm Khān proceeded to Bhalwa from a place named Phuldūbī[11] by transporting his land-army of seven to eight thousand cavalry over the river Andal Khān. From Bhalwa he proceeded two *kos* farther and held a council of war with the loyal officers, namely, his nephews Mīrzā Aḥmad Beg and Mīrzā Yūsuf, Mīr Mu'izu'd-Dīn Muḥammad, Mīrzā Hidāyat Beg Dīwān, Mīrzā Ashraf Bakhshī, Mīrzā Nathan, Mūsā Khān Zamīndār, Rāja Raghūnāth and some others. Mīrzā Aḥmad Beg, due to his violent nature, began to say,—" Every thing is ready; the only thing needed is courage." Then the Khān, annoyed at this, asked (the opinion of ) Mīrzā Nathan. Mīrzā Nathan replied :—" Whoever has any doubt about the bravery of the Nawāb, ought to think that if the Nawāb had no courage then he, being the ruler of the Ṣūbah of Bengal where in fact he occupies the place of the master and Qibla, would not have come personally with a few followers without caring for the smallness of his army to fight with the Rāja of the Mags and to give battle with a fleet of thirty boats against the fire-emitting fleet of two to three thousand boats of the Mags. Now, all the necessary preparations for the expedition have been made at the direction of the Nawāb. But as this humble self is not aware of the season of battle in this region so he can not venture to give any opinion. One suggestion which occurs to the mind of this insignificant man is this, that the decision to launch on a war should be arrived at subject to the condition of the weather of this region so that the affairs may be concluded to the satisfaction of the imperialists." Ibrāhīm Khān Fatḥ-jang became highly pleased at this frank talk of Mīrzā Nathan and praised the prudent counsel of the Mīrzā. As there were severe rains and storms, so all the Thānas established against the Mags were strongly fortified. The fleet of the parganā of Phuldūbī was placed in charge of Khān Mīrzā a relation of Nawāb I'timādu'd-Dawla. Then he (Ibrāhīm Khān) returned to Jahāngīrnagar, and all the imperial officers entered the delightful city of Jahāngīrnagar in order of their precedence. (682)

**Punitive expedition against Bahādur Khān.** Bahādur Khān Hijlīwāl, the Zamīndār of Hijlī was summoned to render helpful services to the governor, but he, in intrigue with Mukarram Khān, governor of Orissa, did not come to Ibrāhīm Khān. After a few days, Muḥammad Beg Abākash, brother-in-law (sister's husband) of Aḥmad Beg and Mīrzā Yūsuf, was appointed to the Fawjdārship of Bardwān with the instruction, that if he (Bahādur Khān) with the help of his good fortune would desire to come, then he should be brought to the Fatḥ-jang's court with all kindness and promises (for his safety); and if by the influence of his evil star he would still persist in disobedience, he should be brought to senses from his sleep of negligence by the infliction of a suitable punishment, and his territory plundered. He should either be sent as a captive or his impertinent head should be removed from the burden of his shoulders and sent to the court (of the governor). It was also written to the Jāgīrdārs of that region that all of them should accompany the aforesaid (Muḥammad Beg) and render proper services. Two hundred war-boats of Mūsā Khān and his brothers were sent for his help. (683)

**Rebellion in the Uttarkul.** Mīrzā Nathan was summoned by Ibrāhīm Khān from the Thāna of the Dakhinkul for a period of twenty five days inclusive of his journey and attendance at the court. But eighteen months had already elapsed and rebellions had broken out in many parts of the terriotry of the Uttarkul. So he (Ibrāhim Khān) was compelled to send Mīrzā Nathan back to the Dakhinkul so that no trouble might arise in that region. His (Nathan's) rank was increased by 300 personal, and 150 horse, and he was asked to leave his agents at the (governor's) court in order to receive the assignment of his Jāgīrs from the imperial Dīwāns. (684)

**Expedition to Arracan.** Mīrzā Nūru'llah wrote from Thāna Udaypūr of Tippera that the people of Tippera had volunteered to lead the imperial army to Achrang (Arracan) by the route which was taken by the Rāja of Tippera on his way to the territory of the Rāja of the Mags. So Ibrāhīm Khān, under the guidance of Mīrzā Nūru'llah started for the country of Achrang with a force of two thousand war-boats, forty thousand cavalry and infantry, one thousand elephants and large equipments of war. Having crossed both the rivers of Fenī, he proceeded through a jungly route which was impassable even for an ant. Throughout the way not only others but even the Khān himself cleared jungles with his own hands and he proceeded onward till he arrived at a place where the boats could not ply any farther. A small gondola was carried with the Khān with very great difficulty. The horses also could not be taken farther. The elephants proceeded with very great difficulty. The scarcity of food became so great that a seer of oil (*raughan*) could not be procured for Rs. 15. The price of rice rose to two seers per rupee in the country of Bengal. *Kūknār* (poppy-seed) was not available even for Rs. 40 per maund. The state of all other things may be imagined from this. (685)

**Official changes in Sylhat.** During this time news came that Shaykh Sulaymān, the Thānadār of Sylhat, had died. So Ibrāhīm Khān said to Rāja Raghūnāth and Mīrzā Malik Ḥusayn, a relation of Mīrzā Nathan, to write to Mīrzā Nathan to come back immediately to His Excellency and to take the office of the Sardār of the country of Sylhat by paying an imperial *pēshkash* of Rs. 2,000. The Rāja and Malik Ḥusayn sent a *piyāda* (bailiff) by a boat swift like the wind in order to bring Mīrzā Nathan from the parganā of Sūnābāzū, the Jāgīr of the Mīrzā to which he had proceeded from Jahāngīrnagar. This *piyāda* with the efforts of hardy boatmen arrived there from Achrang within a period of twelve days by traversing a distance against the current of the river which a caravan would take two or three months to cover. The Mīrzā was informed of this at a time when he was preparing to proceed to Hājo after settling the revenue and administrative affairs (of his Jāgīr). Being informed of his recall, he proceeded to meet the Khān Fatḥ-jang and reached Jahāngīrnagar from Sūnābāzū within two days and a half. There he arranged Rs. 12,000 from the Mahājans who had transactions with him, and then he started for the camp of the Khān. Within five days he reached near the Khān on the bank of the river Little Fenī at a time when the Khān, owing to many deaths in his army for want of food, had returned (from his expedition) and had appointed the son of Shaykh Sulaymān to the Sardārship of Sylhat as a deputy for Mīrzā Aḥmad Beg. In short, at the arrival of the Mīrzā, the Khān became very much ashamed. He gave much consolation to the Mīrzā saying,—" I will give you a better land than that." Then he (Ibrāhīm Khān) left for Jahāngīrnagar. As the Mīrzā suffered from some illness due to the strain of the journey, he was permitted (by the Khān) to return to Jahāngīrnagar according to his convenience. He (the Khān), making a forced march, reached Jahāngīrnagar within three days. Mīrzā Nathan entered the city after five days and waited upon the Khān. (686)

**Aḥmad Beg appointed governor of Orissa.** In the mean time, an imperial Farmān obeyed by all the world was received and it was to the following effect:—" As Ibrāhīm Khān does not agree to the transfer of Mukarram Khān. Mīrzā Aḥmad Beg, whom we have honoured with the title of Khān, should be sent to assume the Ṣūbahdārship of Orissa." In short, when through the mediation of Begum, the wife of Ibrāhīm Khān, Jalā'ir Khān was appointed to the governorship of Orissa on a promise of a *pēshkash* of Rs. 300,000 from his income, Mīrzā Aḥmad Beg Khān sent a representation to Her Majesty Nūrjahān Begum and got a fresh Farmān issued to Ibrāhīm Khān to the effect that if that Jalā'ir Khān had gone to Orissa, he should be recalled and Aḥmad Beg Khān should be sent to assume the governorship of Orissa. Ibrāhīm Khān was compelled to send Aḥmad Beg Khān (to Orissa). Jalā'ir Khān, in demanding the return of the money paid, suffered many troubles. He was about to lose his Jāgīr and his original Manṣab, but he retained them with great difficulty. He was reinstated to his old Jāgīrs with (the assignment of) their (arrear) revenues of twenty two and (in some cases) thirty months, in compensation for his loss of the Ṣūbahdārship of Orissa and for his promotion of Manṣab. (687)

**Mukkarram Khān aids Bahādur Khān.** Now I shall give a short account of Mḥammad Beg Abākash who went against Bahādur Khān Hijlīwāl, and the happy end of this affair through the influence of the fortune of the Emperor. The sum and substance of the particulars of that war of Muḥammad Beg is this:—When he started for Hijlī from Bardwān by mustering his troops, Bahādur Khān wrote a letter to Mukkarram Khān. Mukkarram Khān failed to understand that this was an affair concerning the Zamīndārs of Bengal with which Orissa had no connection. He despatched a troop of one thousand cavalry to the aid of Bahādur Khān, and made the commotion of the war very warm. Three battles were fought. Muḥammad Beg, after raiding some of the villages and outposts of Hijlī, communicated the true state of affairs to Ibrāhīm Khān. (688)

**Ibrāhīm Khān proceeds to Jessore.** During this time, news came from Jessore that Suhrāb Khān, son of Asaf Khān. Ja'far, kept drunk day and nighṭ and did not take care of the territories of Jessore. The Firingis were daily carrying on their raids in the territory of Jessore and had taken away fifteen hundred men and women from the villages as captives. Whatever advice was given to Suhrāb Khān by Ḥasan Mashadī, the Dīwan, Bakhshī and Wāqi'-navīs, for the welfare of the administration, was never listened to by him. Owing to the ill-feeling that existed between them, Suhrāb took the counsels offered by Ḥasan very lightly. Therefore, from two considerations viz :—first, to go to Jessore in order to put the affairs of that territory in order, and, secondly, to punish Bahādur Khān Hijlīwāl, he (Ibrāhīm Khān) proceeded to Jessore. After traversing a large part of the straight route, he took the route by the side of the swamps *(āb-i-shur)*, and proceeded under the guidance of experienced Zamīndārs. The Amīrs and all the Manṣabdars followed the Khān Fatḥ-jang one after another. But as there were many streams and *nālahs* (canals) on the way, very few men except the Mags and the Firingis were familiar with that route. Ibrāhīm Khān, himself, for a period of five days wandered from one stream to another and from one *nālah* to another by losing his way and suffered a great trouble. There was neither any inhabited place nor any traffic of merchants. He was put to great distress through dearth of food-stuff. After a great deal of trouble he reached his destination and pitched his camp at a place named Kagraghata, three *kos* off from Jessore towards Hijlī. (689)

**Bahādur Khān surrenders.** Immediately after his arrival, Mīrzā Aḥmad Beg, Mīrzā Yūsuf and Jalā'ir Khān were sent to Hijlī along with his numerous Amīrs, small and great, and with Mūsā Khān and the Twelve Bhuyāns of Bhātī; and he wrote a letter offering many admonitions to Bahādur Khān Hijlīwāl. After a few days, this party reached the vicinity of Hijlī, and advanced from the side of the salty sea (*Dariya-i-shūr*) by raising intrenchments towards the fort of Hijlī which was already besieged by Mīrzā Muḥammad Beg Abākash and the imperiailsts. Bahādur Khān was put to great straits. They sent the letters of the Khān Fatḥ-jang to him and gave much consolation on their behalf for the pacification of his heart. The Amīrs, who left Jahāngīrnagar for Jessore, following the Khān, reached near the Khān after suffering untold miseries. The Khān, inspite of his knowledge of the conditions of the route, censured the officers and did not accept their reasonable excuses. Day and night he put forth his efforts to humiliate Bahādur Khān. Suhrāb Khān, the chief officer of Jessore, was disgraced with rebukes and reproaches. Mīrzā Nathan also arrived there after eight days of the arrival of the Khān. Inspite of the fact that the aforesaid Mīrzā had no army with him and was fatigued with wars in the Kūch frontier and Assam, the Khān said many unpleasant things to the aforesaid Mīrzā. The Mīrzā extinguished the fire of the Khān's wrath by offering reasonable excuses and thus pacified him. The Khān used to get on a boat every morning and after finishing the review of the boats, he used to disembark and engage himself in discharging arrows for a period of four *gharīs* and thus a strange commotion was created. Most of the imperial officers also displayed their excellence in archery. This used to create an uproar among the spectators, and commanded admiration from the wise. Then he would return to his camp and take his food in the company of his friends. Then every one of the comrades was allowed to go to his own camp after offering a *Fātiḥa* (benedictory prayer) for the long life of the Emperor. Some of the people who used to keep constant company with the Khān used to spend their time in playing chess for the remaining part of the day till the comrades reassembled. After the assemblage of the friends he used to engage himself in the discharge of administrative and revenue works and would never keep the business of the people in suspense. Every body in the camp of the Khān Fatḥ-jang, high and low, received satisfaction and used to offer his thanks. Bahādur (Khān), in view of the indifference shown by Mukkarram Khān by withdrawing his help upon the arrival of the Khān Fatḥ-jang, found no other way than to submit to the Khān. In order to save his life and honour he sent some men as mediators. On the promise (of safety) given by Mīrzā Aḥmad Beg and Mīrzā Yūsuf through the mediation of Mūsā Khān, he surrendered to Mīrzā Aḥmad Beg, Mīrzā Muḥammad Abākash, Mīrzā Ṣāliḥ and Mūsā Khān, and then he came to kiss the feet of the Khān. The Amīrs also obtained the honour of kissing the hand of the Khān. The Khān imposed upon Bahādur a fine of Rs. 300,000 for his guilt and allowed him to retain his home and territory in accordance with the old rules. (690)

**Bahādur Khān brought to Dhāka.** Then he (the Khān) thought of returning to Jahāngīrnagar by dismissing Suhrāb Khān and appointing one of these three Sardārs, viz: Jalā'ir Khān, Mīrzā Nathan and Mīrzā Isfandiyār in his place at Jessore. In the mean time Jalā'ir Khān was on the point of death from an attack of a swelling of the stomach. He could not pass excrecent, urine and wind for four days after which he got relief and by the favour of God he obtained a second life. As Mīrzā Aḥmad Beg did not agree to the appointment of Mīrzā Isfandiyār, so the Khān offered the Sardārship of Jessore to Mīrzā Nathan. The Mīrzā represented to the Khān thus:—" May the Nawāb be pleased to pardon Suhrāb Khān this time and retain him in his office and supply him with war-boats, as requisitioned by him, so that people may not say 'when a friend is treated like this, woe betide the strangers.' After this I will be answerable if Suhrāb Khān demands more boats than the previously fixed quota." Sixty fully equipped boats were given (to Suhrāb Khān) and a letter of covenant was taken from him making him responsible for the protection of Jessore. Then it was sent to the imperial Court along with his own representations and he (Ibrāhīm Khān) started for Jahāngīrnagar with Bahādur Khān in his company. The Amīrs started one after another and reached Jahāngīrnagar in order of their rank within a few days. The Khān, began to pass his time as usual at Jahāngīrnagar. (691)

**Rebellion in Khuntaghāt.** Now I shall give a short account of the events of the Kūch territory. When the season for *Kheda* i.e. the capture of wild elephants, came, Qulīj Khān, the Sardār of the Kūch territory, sent a youth named Bāqir in order to catch elephants in the district of Khuntaghāt. A force of three hundred cavalry, five hundred matchlock-men and fourteen elephants was sent with him. Bāqir arrived at the parganā of Khuntaghāt and establishing friendly relationship with the ryots of that place he took with him a party of professional elephant-catchers and went to begin the *Kheda* operation. Shayk Kamāl, without being summoned by the Khān Fatḥ-jang, left Hājo and went to the Khān and waited upon him. Bāqir brought a large number of elephants to the *Pālī* or Qamargāh (Ring). But when he wanted to get the elephants out of the enclosure and make them captive, the elephants went out by breaking one side of the enclosure. This inexperienced officer then put some of the chiefs of the elephant-catchers to prison; one or two of them were killed and the rest were severely scourged. He said to them,— " You must catch the elephants which were in the ring or pay a fine of Rs. 1,000 for each of the elephants." This group of disaffected men roused all the people of the district against him and they made a night-attack. Bāqir was seized alive and he was cut into two at the waist. Every one of his army who opposed them was put to death. The rest were taken as captives, and the imperial elephants were seized by them. They proclaimed one of the Sardārs of the elephant-catchers as their Rāja, rose in open rebellion and created an amazing situation . (692)

**Qulīj Khān appeals for help.** Although Qulīj Khān sent his chief officer Dūst Beg with a force of six to seven hundred cavalry and one thousand matchlock-men over and above the regiment which was at Gilahnay with Mīrzā Qulīju'llah and Sayfu'l-Muluk, he failed to suppress the rebellion. He sent two of his Sardārs Tāj Khān and Taslīm Khān to Gilahnay and made Rāja Satrajit and others report about the conditions of the rebellion, the capture of elephants and the death of Bāqir, and demanded help (from Jahāngīrnagar). (693)

**The Mags raid Dakhin Shāhbāzpūr.** The vanquished Mags came and raided some of the villages of the parganā of Dakhin Shāhbāzpūr[12] and halted with a large fleet in a *char* or island of the river. Immediately on the receipt of this information, the Khān Fatḥ-jang proceeded from Jahāngīrnagar at midnight with a fleet of four to five thousand armed boats which were ready at the *chawkī* on the river. Early in the morning he reached Bikrampūr and the other Khāns joined him one after another with their fleet. Mīrzā Nathan also presented himself. (694)

**Nathan deputed to suppress the rebellion in Khuntaghāt.** The Khān asked Mīrzā Nathan,—" If I send you to the Kūch territory, what force would you require to suppress these rebels and to recapture the elephants ? " The Mīrzā at first replied,—" The strength of the army of that place should be taken into consideration and it should also be considered to what extent these men have failed to accomplish this task and are demanding further reinforcements. The arrangements to be made should depend upon these considerations." The Khān Fatḥ-jang said in reply :—" Had not the vanquished Mags again led an expedition, then it would have been possible to make these considerations. But now as the affairs of that expedition can not be brought to a happy conclusion with the land-force and as the entire fleet has been requisitioned to this expedition, so it has become incumbent, to keep these facts in view. The man who girds up his loins of courage for this service shall be highly rewarded." Mīrzā Nathan, out of his great courage and extreme bravery and dependence on the ever increasing fortune of the Emperor and particularly on the unlimited favours of God, began to say with sincere loyalty and faithfulness :—" By the favour of the Merciful Lord, I shall be able to inflict satisfactory punishment on these foolish people and recapture the elephants, with a fleet of fifty fully equipped boats." The Khān Fatḥ-jang said,— " You ought to give in writing that you will be able to accomplish this task with this force." The Mīrzā replied :—" Up to this time, no body has ever made a promise about warfare, because it is a two headed stick, and victory or defeat depends on the will of God. Inspite of this when, tying the shroud on the head and depending on the Merciful Lord, I am going in pursuit of this object either to attain victory or death, I expect that with the influence of the Emperor's fortune I shall be able to realise this aim, and I will give you the document. But if the rebels transport the elephants over the river Banās (Manās) before my arrival and send them to the Rāja of Assam, the Nawāb should allow me to proceed to Assam with this force and fight them there. I should have these conditions ratified by your own tongue, as the affair concerns the welfare of the Emperor. I accept your offer and I will give you in writing that I will go with this army up to the mouth of the Kalang to fight with Assam." The Khān Fatḥ-jang agreed to have the covenant drawn up in this way :—" If by the time of my arrival the rebels stay at Khuntaghāt with the elephants, then by the favour of the Almighty Lord, I will properly punish them and recapture the elephants from them with the aid of these fifty fully equipped boats and hand them over to the imperial officers." Mīrzā Nathan agreed to it and handed over a document to the Khān Fatḥ-jang with those conditions, and he also proposed to put his seal on it if the Khān so desired. The Khān greatly wondered at this God-given influence of Mīrzā Nathan over the Kūch territory through which he had already given such severe blows to the people of that country and was now agreeing to sign such a covenant. He then ordered the imperial Dīwān and Bakhshī and his Hindu officer named Jawharmal Dās to go through the aforesaid document. After reading this they said, "May Mīrzā Nathan be helped by God in this matter! No one else has the courage to make such a covenant." The Khān laughed and said, "Alright, I shall consider it in the morning and shall get the document sealed by him." (695)

**Burmese invasion of Arracan.** Towards the close of the day, information was received that the Rāja of the Mags had returned to his own country in order to fight against an enemy of his named Barhama (the King of Burma) who had attacked his country from the other side. The Khān appointed his Bakhshī named Mīrzā Bāqī with a fleet of six hundred armed and useful war-boats to guard the big river, and two *gharīs* after evening he started for Jahāngīrnagar and arrived at the city after midnight. The other Khāns followed him in order of precedence and reached there in the first *pahar* of the day. (696)

**Rebels of Khuntaghāt occupy Gilah.** In the last part of that day an assembly was held. As it was the month of Ramaẓān, when the Khān was engaged in breaking his fast, another letter came from Hājo, with the following communication:—"The rebels have marched from Khuntaghāt and have come to Jahāngīrābād *alias* Gilahnay. Dūst Beg and a regiment which was posted there were cut off after a hard fight. Mīrzā Qulīju'llah and others showed their boldness and escaped with their lives. The whole family of Qulīj Khān has been imprisoned and Jahāngīrābād has been raided and occupied by the rebels. The cause which led to this event is that when Balabhadra, the Hindu officer of Mīrzā Nathan went with his fleet to plunder a village of the Dakhinkul, he raided that village and returned leaving there a number of his men with elephants for raiding purposes. This had excited the rebels and they marched upon Jahāngīrābād and created this situation." Accordingly, the Khān summoned Mīrzā Nathan and the Mīrzā came to the dining table. After taking his dinner, the Khān gave the letter to the Mīrzā, saying—"Read it aloud." The Mīrzā began to read, and when the Mīrzā wanted to say something about the aforesaid Hindu, the Khān Fatḥ-jang in fairness began to say:—"A flock of unfair and timid persons are insinuating that the Hindu officer of Mīrzā Nathan raided a village (and that led to the disaster). How did that action make the enemy audacious ? War is not made of *halwa* (a kind of sweet cake or paste made with flour.) If some of them were killed, they should thank their stars that they could give their lives for their master. They fail to protect their Thāna and blame Mīrzā Nathan and expect that he should protect the imperial territory from Jahāngīrnagar." Therefore, the Mīrzā remained silent. In that evening every one made some suggestions till the comrades were granted leave to go to their homes. The Khān retired to bed. (697)

**Nathan refuses to follow Shaykh Kamāl.** Next morning, as soon as the Khān came out with usual splendour and took his seat, he summoned Shaykh Kamāl and asked,—"What should be our plans regarding this affair." The Shaykh took upon himself the responsibilities of suppressing this insurrection and obtained an order to take with him a group of imperial officers. As the Mīrzā was also included in that group, the Khān summoned the Mīrzā. The Chamberlains brought the Mīrzā to the Khān from the bath-room where he had gone to take his bath. When the Mīrzā came and took his seat, he saw that his name was in the list of the followers of the Shaykh. He writhed within himself life a snake. He looked at Jawharmal, the Hindu officer of Ibrāhīm Khān, and said, "Why have you written my name in this group ?" Jawharmal asked, "Are you not going ?" The Mīrzā replied, "You should send some other party as I with my party am engaged in other imperial affairs. The Uttarkul should be defended by the whole of the imperial army, and leave the Dakhinkul alone to my men." Ibrāhīm Khān, having heard this talk, asked Shaykh Kamāl,—"I do not know what kind of relationship you bear with the imperial officers and particularly with this man. At your very name, he wants to get out of the world." The Shaykh with great humility and meakness, as is the custom of the *Shaykh-zādas* (sons of Shaykhs), came forward and began to say,—" I have no other relation with them but sincere friendship. But I am ignorant of the manner in which the stars ordain my fate." Ibrāhīm Khān wanted to bring about a reconciliation between the Shaykh and the Mīrzā who had long-standing quarrels, but it was of no avail. Mīrzā Nathan point-blank refused to agree. Thereupon, the Khān Fatḥ-jang flew into a rage and hastened to his *Maḥal*, and the other Khāns returned to their homes. (698)

**Plan of Shaykh Kamāl.** After an hour, the Khān summoned Shaykh Kamāl to his private chamber and told him,—"Probably, this expedition will have to be undertaken without Mīrzā Nathan." The Shaykh replied,—" Mīrzā Nathan is a great asset for the pacification of that country, and he is indispensable." Then the Khān Fatḥ-jang said,—" He would agree to his death but never agree to follow you. What plan should be made to make him accompany you and to bring the expedition to a satisfactory end ?" Shaykh Kamāl replied,—" It is better to appoint him first as the Sardār of that expedition ; and then when he will be fully busy in fighting the rebels, I may be sent as the Sardār after him. Then he will not be able to turn away and will adhere to the expedition in this way till its end." Ibrāhīm Khān approved of this plan. Next morning Mīrzā Nathan was called in preference to all others and he was invested with the insignia of the Sardārship for the suppression of the Kūch insurrection. Then he was despatched at an auspicious moment with a force of one hundred and twenty Manṣabdārs, one hundred and forty Firingis, eight hundred matchlock-men, fifty fully equipped war-boats and large equipments of war. Owing to the heavy rains of the season it was not possible for men and beasts to traverse the way except by boats. So he prayed for some more boats, saying,—" The warriors of the fifty boats are accommodated in those boats. This humble self will some how manage to go with his own followers. But the other two to three thousand men will require boats of their own. If it is not possible to provide boats from the State, please order me to procure these boats from the *Bepāris* (traders) either on hire or purchase or by force for the execution of imperial affairs. I will pay the money from my own purse and will also manage to secure boatmen for these boats." Ibrāhīm Khān agreed to this and ordered him to procure (the boats) from whomsoever he could. The Mīrzā returned to his residence and appointed some of his trustworthy officers to accomplish this work. The merchant-princes of Jahāngīr-nagar who were inclined to transact business with him advanced Rs. 100,000 to him against deeds of loan (*tamassukāt*). His officers brought the boats of the *Bepāris*. Those who agreed to give the boats on hire sent their own boatmen and gave security for their presence. The rate of hire was fixed and they were paid. Price was immediately paid to those who agreed to sell. Seven hundred boatmen were appointed and they were given two months' salaries in advance. (699)

**Nathan kills a rhinoceros.** Eleven days after the permission to leave, he left the Khān Fatḥ-jang and started (for Kūch). His first halt was made at Bhāgalpūr and the second halt at Sahād.* At the latter place a rhinoceros came to the house of a Darwīsh and took its stand at the door of the house. The brethren of the Darwīsh came and narrated the incident to the Mīrzā. The Mīrzā decided to take an augury from it: if he could kill this rhinoceros without difficulty, he would gain an easy victory over the rebels. He went there and reached the place where the rhinoceros was standing thereby

* A journey of about 6 *pahars* or 18 hours from this place took the Mīrzā to Patladhah. The place was therefore in the present Mymensing district by the bank of the Brahmaputtra. Mr. Sachse notes the presence of rhinoceros in this part of Mymensing (Gazetteer, Ed. 1917. p. 11.) and we are pleased to note that this was a feature of this region even in the early part of the 17th Century of the Christian Era.

confining the Darwish within the house. The rhinoceros was surrounded from four sides and an attempt was made to drive it from land to the *jheel,* i.e., a pool of water collected during the rains, in order to kill it with ease. But it was of no avail. When, by sunset Mīrzā Nathan could not drive the rhinoceros to the water even after an attempt of one *pahar,* he thought that he would not be able to bring it to the water in the darkness of the night. At this time the rhinoceros came to the water out of its own accord and began to swim. He followed it firing from his gondola and killed it in no time. It sank in the water. Howevermuch he searched for it he could not find any trace of the animal. He said to the boatmen that whoever succeeded in finding out the rhinoceros would be rewarded with a sum of Rs. 5 and then returned to his camp. Some of the fishermen who could dive in deep waters remained behind, and three or four *gharīs* after evening, they found the rhinoceros and reported to the Mīrzā. The Mīrzā sent his men with two State boats in order to bring the rhinoceros within the night. They went there and within two *pahars* and four *gharīs* of the night, they brought the rhinoceros to the Mīrzā from the deep waters, dragging it over water by tying ropes to its legs. The Mīrzā gave Rs. 5 to the man who found it out and Rs. 20 to the men of these two boats who went to bring it. Next morning he waited there for four *gharīs* in order to please the boatmen who wanted to take the flesh of the animal. Then he started. After proceeding for two-and-a-half *pahar* of the day, rest was taken for a short while to enable the boatmen to take their food. Six *gharīs* before evening, the boats sailed again and the journey was resumed. After proceeding for two-and-a-half *pahar* of the night, the boats were tied to the *Hijal* trees which had grown in the water of the *jheel,* in order to give some rest to the boatmen and the Mīrzā also took some rest. Two *gharīs* after morning, the journey was resumed. In this way the way was traversed for four days and nights, resting during the last part of the night according to the usual practice. At this time one special boat of Ibrāhīm

Khān was sent by Khwāja Idrāk the chief officer (*Madāru'l-Mahāmm*) of the Khān Fatḥ-jang, to inquire about the distance traversed by Mīrzā Nathan. The Mīrzā was saying his night-prayers sitting on a boat. He himself shouted,—" O, *Kūsāwalla* (boatman)! Whom do you want ? " He replied,—" I am coming from the Khān Fatḥ-jang. I want the Mīrzā." The Mīrzā called him and became aware of the facts. He immediately took the pen and made a representation to the Khān Fatḥ-jang communicating to him the incident of the rhinoceros and wrote,—" By the favour of the Almighty Lord, I am hopeful that the rebels would be killed and captured by this insignificant person." Then he gave the servant of the Khān a sum of Rs. 50 as a mark of hospitality and a pair of fine shawl which he was himself wearing at the time of prayers, and he was sent back with the letter. He orally explained to the servant the nature of his journey and said,—" By the favour of the Merciful Lord, I hope to reach Patladah after two *pahars* of the (next) day." (700)

**Nathan halts at Patladah.** He (Nathan) proceeded from that place and reached Patladah after two *pahars* and two *gharīs* of the day, and halted there. But as of the swift boats which could frighten the rebels, only seventeen had come with the Mīrzā, so he waited there for nine days till the arrival of the Amīrs with their fleet, one after another. The fleet of Sūnā Ghāzī, Zamīndār of Sarāil, which was proceeding to Hājo and the fleet of Bahādur Ghāzi, Zamīndār of Chawra which had delayed on the way, were taken with him and he proceeded forward. (701)

**Nathan occupies Jamra.** The spies brought information that the rebels had fortified Jamra. Then he despatched his admiral Muḥammad Sharīf to Jamra along with one of his chief warriors named Mast 'Alī Beg with a fleet of thirty boats. This army attacked the impudent rebels at midnight, defeated them and brought Jamra under the possession of the imperial officers. Eighteen small and big boats and four cannon were seized from the rebels. Mīrzā Nathan sent a report of this battle to the Khān Fatḥ-jang giving the credit of the victory to the Admiral Muḥammad Sharīf who was an officer of the Khān Fatḥ-jang, and then he advanced forward from that place. (702)

**An army sent to the relief of Shaykh Afẓal.** At this time, the brother of Shaykh Afẓal, a relation of Shaykh Kamāl, who was besieged by the rebels, sent the following request to Mīrzā Nathan :—"Up to this time, my brother is defending the fort of Bāghwān by every possible means. Many people have been killed, and no horse is left alive, all having been killed and eaten for want of food. The rebels are pressing in such a way that it is beyond description. It is quite well and good if you can come to his rescue or otherwise he will perish." Mīrzā Nathan sent a force of one hundred experienced fighters under the command of his trustworthy officer, Mast 'Alī Beg, along with the whole fleet of Admiral Shams Khān, an officer of the Fatḥ-jang, under the command of one of his relations named Muḥammad Sharīf to his aid. Besides the matchlock-men of the fleet another regiment of expert matchlock-men was attached to it so that with the help of the ever-increasing fortune of the Emperor, they might punish the rebels who were besieging Shaykh Afẓal and bring them to their senses by relieving the aforesaid Shaykh from this dangerous situation. He (the Mīrzā) himself followed them with the greatest speed. As soon as Mast 'Alī Beg and these men reached a place named Baliyā (Boalia ?)[13] on the bank of the Brahmaputtra, they raised a fort and halted there. They planned to advance against the rebels by raising fort after fort. The short-sighted rebels, informed about the arrival of the large reinforcement, took the road of safety within the night, leaving the fort of Shaykh Afẓal. Next morning, when Mast 'Alī Beg and Muḥammad Sharīf were going to write the news of victory to Mīrzā Nathan, the Mīrzā himself arrived there with his whole army with which he had made a forced march. (703)

**Shaykh Kamāl succeeds in his plan of superseding Nathan.** At this time letters from Mīrzā Nathan's agents at Jahāngīrnagar came to him with these contents :—" After your departure, on the day when your letter with the horn of the rhinoceros reached the Khān, the Khān personally came to the houses of Sarḥad Khān *alias* Shaykh Abdu'l-Wāḥid and Shaykh Kamāl. He gave a white gold embroidered shawl to Sarḥad Khān and a red gold embroidered shawl to Shaykh Kamāl on behalf of the Emperor, and one horse to each of them on his own behalf, and at the advice of Shaykh Kamāl he has given the chief command of the suppression of Kūch insurrection to Sarḥad Khān and the office of the General to Shaykh Kamāl. He has despatched them after you with their relations Mīrzā Khān, Shajā'at Khān and Muqarrab Khān Dakhinī along with a force of two thousand matchlock-men." Though this news was disquieting to the superficial observers and the friends of the Mīrzā, Mīrzā Nathan himself began to say very cheerfully:—"By the favour of God and the influence of the Emperor's fortune, I shall bring the rebels down to the dust of disgrace and repel them before the arrival of these two Shaykhs. After that I shall make both these Shaykhs taste *halwa* (sweets) to such an extent that they will never again aspire to the offices of the Commander-in-chief and General and after this they will never behave in this way." (704)

**Nathan reaches the Khānpūr.** In short Shaykh Afẓal came to meet Mīrzā Nathan from Bāghwān which was situated at a distance of four *kos* from the Brahmaputtra. After his interview he requested permission to proceed with his army in the company of the Mīrzā. The Mīrzā, finding that all his words were fully tinged with insincerity, left him in that region in his Jāgīr. He then proceeded to Khuntaghāt and reached the mouth of the river Khānpūr with his fleet. (705)

**Regiments sent against the rebels.** The spies brought news that the rebels in order to carry on their operations in Khuntaghāt had built two stockades at Bangāon and Mādhabpur on either side of the river Khānpūr in front of Ghalwāpāra.[14] Now hearing the report of the world-conquering army, they were strengthening the aforesaid forts. Accordingly, the Mīrzā proceeded to the river Khānpūr and reaching there he raised two lofty forts with deep ditches around with the intention of conquering those forts. In the night he sent Muṣṭafā Khān Dakhinī to Qulīj Khān with this message :— " Owing to your disunion, the affair has reached such a pass and your whole family has been imprisoned. Your Jāgīr has been transferred to Shaykh Kamāl and the prestige of the Mughals has been thrown to the winds. If you think deeply over it even now and regard the prestige of the Mughals to be one and the same, and join (me) with a sincere heart, and if you instruct Mīrzā Qulīju'llah, Mīrzā Sayfu'd-Dawla and others to act according to my advice, then by the favour of God, even if I can not have your Jāgīrs reinstated, I hope to be able to get your revenues of this season realised through your collectors." Next morning he (Nathan) divided his army into four regiments. One regiment was placed under Mast 'Alī Beg and Nīk Muḥammad Beg ; the second regiment was placed under the command of the son of Muṣṭafā Khān and the third under Muḥammad Sharīf, a relation of Hāshim Khān. These were sent against the enemy's fort at Ghalwāpāra. He himself remained with the fourth regiment to protect his own forts. (706)

**Occupation of the forts of the rebels.** Besides the river Khānpūr, there was a stream around the forts of the enemies. When these regiments were crossing this stream by means of fishing boats brought by the boatmen on their shoulders, the rebels came out of their fort and opposed the imperialists on the bank of the stream and they began to shoot arrows. These bands of devoted soldiers, inspite of many casualties in their rank, crossed the stream with the help of the gondolas and rushed upon the rebels and their fort under the cover of *thathāries* or *gardūns*. They repelled the rebel forces and drove them towards their fort. Without allowing them any respite (and opportunity) to take a firm stand, they entered the fort of the rebels by offering a hand to hand fight. The rebels, unable to stand, took to flight. Whoever, was audacious and offered any resistance, was put to the dreadful sword. A happy victory was attained and the trumpet of conquest was blown. Besides other booties they seized five *Tāngan* horses of high breed. (707)

**Rāja Raghūnāth and Mīrzā Bāqī meet Nathan.** At this time, Mīrzā Bāqi, the Bakhshī of Ibrāhīm Khān Fatḥ-jang and Rāja Raghūnath arrived there with a fleet of one hundred fully equipped war-boats of Ibrāhīm Khān. They were sent by the Khān Fatḥ-jang with the object that they should first escort the troops of Shaykh Kamāl and Sarḥad Khān which had been left behind and then they should go to Mīrzā Nathan in order to console and pacify him and to make him follow Sarḥad Khān and Shaykh Kamāl. After this they were to go to Hājo to help their own fleet, to meet Qulīj Khān and the army appointed to fight the Rāja of Assam, and to bring Qulīj Khān to his senses from his sleep of negligence by verbal censures. They were further instructed to stay there for a few days, and, if necessary, to help the imperialists; and then, after settling the affairs of the locality on that locality itself, they were to return to him (Ibrāhīm Khān). In short, they met Mīrzā Nathan. Mīrzā Nathan extended a great hospitality to Mīrzā Bāqī Beg, the Bakhshī, and offered to Rāja Raghūnāth various kinds of rice along with fine *khassis* (castrated goats) as a mark of hospitality. Otto of roses was profusely sprinkled. (708)

**Nathan refuses to serve under Shaykh Kamāl.** After this, Mīrzā Bāqī and Rāja Raghūnāth came with Mīrzā Nathan from the assembly to a private chamber and delivered the oral messages of the Khān Fatḥ-jang, and asked the aforesaid Mīrzā to agree to follow Shaykh Kamāl. The Mīrzā became furious and began to say:—" When the Khān himself proposed this, I did not agree. Inspite of this, to make such a proposal in my face merely shows your lack of wisdom. If your object is to defeat the rebels then I have already dealt the first stroke of defeat to them. After having dealt a heavy defeat to the rebels, by the will of the Almighty, I will not allow others to interfere." Mīrzā Bāqī, and Rāja Raghūnāth also became furious and began to say:—" Which of the rebels have you defeated except a band of fishermen who raised a stockade at Ghalwāpāra ?" The Mīrzā also, being annoyed, said thus:—"In fact Masnad-i-'Alā 'Īsā Khān, king of the whole of Bang (Bengal) and his son Mūsā Khān who were your enemies, were well-known as fish-catchers (*Machwagīrī*) or fishermen (*Māhīgirī*). Where shall I find a Dāwūd, son of Sulaymān Karrānī to fight with, in order to please you? However, your master has sent me to release the territory of Kūch from the clutches of these enemies, whether they are *Machwas* or Mughals or Afghāns. Let me know whose defeat you consider to be equivalent to overpowering the enemies? I shall withdraw my hand from the *Machwas* and show you how the enemies should be defeated and punished, and relieve myself from these unreasonable accusations." Both of them said,—"The man who can recover these two places, Rangamātī and Jahāngīrābād *alias* Gilahnay, will be considered as doing splendid services and he may be given the credit of the conquest of the whole of the Kūch territory." Mīrzā Nathan said,—"Give me a few words in writing that the man who will be able to conquer these places shall be credited with the conquest of the Kūch territory. I know how to accomplish it." Accordingly, Mīrzā Bāqī and Rāja Raghūnāth gave it in writing to Mīrzā Nathan and they started for Hājo to meet Qulīj Khān. (709)

**Qulīj Khān's officers join Nathan**. Next morning, Mīrzā Nathan proceeded from that place and coming out of the river Khānpūr he halted in one of the islands of the Brahmaputtra. He sent some men in great haste to his Hindu officer, Rāy Balabhadra Dās in order to bring from him the special cavalry of the Mīrzā along with a hundred horsemen of the Thānadārs of Jamra and all the regiments of the Thānas of Jakhali and Bhujmala[15] by means of *mānd* boats. In short, after six days these regiments arrived with the horses. Muṣṭafā Khān went to Qulīj Khān and brought him to his senses. The Khān (Qulīj) wrote strict letters with his own hand to Mīrzā Qulīju'llah, Mīrzā Sayfu'd-Dawla and his brothers, and Yār Beg and also Aqā Taqī the Sardār of the second land-regiment with instructions to proceed to Mīrzā Nathan by land and water and to act according to his orders. Accordingly, Mīrzā Qulīju'llah, Mīrzā Sayfu'd-Dawla, brothers of Qulīj Khān, Yār Beg and other Sardārs, who were proceeding with their fleet to recover Jahāngīrābād *alias* Gilahnay, went straight to Mīrzā Nathan and alighted at the island, and had a friendly meeting with him. (710)

**Shaykh Kamāl's attempt to win over Nathan.** At this time, Sarḥad Khān and Shaykh Kamāl along with the imperial officers, who came from the Khān Fatḥ-jang, reached (a place) opposite Rangamātī, and encamped at one of the islands of the Brahmaputtra. The *paiks* in the party of Shaykh Kamāl were ordered to clear the jungles on the bank of the Brahmaputtra and to raise a fort there. He (the Shaykh) sent a flattering letter to Mīrzā Nathan by the hand of an experienced man to persuade Mīrzā Nathan by means of flattering words to join the campaign as a follower of Shaykh Kamāl. The Mīrzā replied in a friendly way the contents of which were as follows:—"The heart of this sincere man always desired to have this unity. Thank God, that in near future, he will have the honour of meeting you and will be able to compensate for what had happened in the past." In short, the messenger of the Shaykh was sent back with great honour, and the Mīrzā sent one of his own men, a very trustworthy officer named Khwāja Sa'ādat Khān, the Chief of his eunuchs, with instructions to make a personal inspection of the bank of the Brahmaputtra without caring for the bullets of the rebels; and to see whether Shaykh Kamāl had raised his fort in front of the fort of Rangamātī at the mouth of the river Gajādhar which passes through the city of Jahāngīrābād *alias* Gilahnay, and also to ascertain whether the fort was built on the right or the left bank of that river. After ascertaining these facts, the Mīrzā would proceed and encamp there according to his convenience. Khwāja Sa'ādat Khān went there inspite of the enemy's guns and carried his boat to the bank of the river. He disembarked from the boat and saw that the fort of the Shaykh was built on the right side of the mouth of the river Gajādhar. He then returned from that place by his boat and reported the matter to Mīrzā Nathan. Mīrzā Nathan looked at Mīrzā Quliju'llah and Mīrzā Sayfu'd-Dawla and asked them to recite a *Fātiḥa* (benedictory prayer) and said,—" God the Great has ordained victory to the Mughals." (711)

**Nathan arrives at the mouth of the Gajādhar.** He (Nathan) proceeded in the last quarter of the night and four *gharīs* after morning, he crossed the camps of Sarḥad Khān and Shaykh Kamāl and alighted on the left bank of the mouth of the Gajādhar river, and ordered his camp to be pitched by clearing the jungles. Shaykh Kamāl sent a messenger, saying,—" We kept the dinner ready and waited from evening for your arrival. It is strange that you did not come." The Mīrzā said in reply:—" The desire of this loyal servant was to meet you early in the morning, a very auspicious moment. But my boat ran aground in the sand of a *char* or island and I was delayed. Therefore, as the auspicious hour had passed away and the moon had begun to enter the Sign of Scorpion, I have come here and encamped in front of your august camp. After the disappearance of the moon from the Sign of Scorpion I shall have the honour of meeting you in an auspicious hour for the welfare of the Emperor as well as of ourselves, who had not seen each other for a long period. Therefore, please overlook my shortcomings and do not think otherwise. At present when I have joined your army you should think of our sincerity and unity. Our share of the food which was cooked for us and over which you waited for us, may be sent to us so that we may dine in the company of our friends." The messengers of the Shaykh went and came back to insist on the Mīrzā's going to the Shaykh. The Mīrzā again showed the same excuse of the moon being in the Sign of Scorpion and did not go. On the third occasion, the Shaykh, was compelled to send the food. The Mīrzā said to his comrades and Manṣabdārs,—" I am not so cordial with this man that I can take his food. If his intention was not to force me to follow him, he would have personally come to take me. When he is playing false with me, by the favour of God and the fortune of the Emperor, he will see what a punishment I mete out to him, so that he will never again aspire to become a Sardār after this day." The food sent by him was given to all the imperial officers. He made an excuse to the messengers of the Shaykh that as he was unwell and feeling a burning sensation, he was observing abstinence from food. So he should be excused. (712)

**Nathan proceeds to Bainābua.** In short, when the messengers of the Shaykh returned to him, the Mīrzā sent Sultan Murād, son of Muḥammad Murād Uzbeg with his own officer Mast 'Alī Beg with two very swift boats to go up the river Gajādhar to a place named Bainābua situated at a distance of four *kos* in order to bring news about the movements of the rebels and whether any fort had been raised by them. They went in great haste and brought news that no trace of the rebels could be found. The Mīrzā immediately started for Bainābua by the river Gajādhar and reached there two *gharīs* before evening. He encamped there and ordered the erection of a lofty fort with deep ditches around. The expert boat-men completed the fort by midnight. (713)

**Shaykh Kamāl's plan to delude Nathan.** When the Shaykh was informed of the departure of Mīrzā Nathan, he sent his trustworthy messengers with some messages in which admonitions, censures, and the haughtiness of a Sardār were mixed up. Ultimately he was reduced to say:—"I will not go beyond your advice and I agree to follow you. It is better that you should return from the place and finish this work in accordance with our joint deliberations." The Mīrzā replied,—" If you want to give advice, (you should know) that the entire sphere of the affairs of this humblest of creatures has been consigned to the mercy of God. He is beyond how and why ? Your censures are like this:

*Verse*:

'On the day of battle when you strike with your sword,
The might of the arm of 'Alī, the lion, will be known.'

As to the pride of Sardārship, the Mīrzā does not care even for the Sardārship of the Mīr Ṣūbah; what does he care for you? You want to deceive me by offering the Sardārship. I am not to be deceived. This talk is devoid of any truth. Then being a great man and a Sardār, how does it befit you to adopt falsehood? If you are really serious in making me the Sardār, then it is incumbent upon you to act according to the orders of the Sardār. I consider it expedient that you should come to this place and begin to follow me from this place." In short, three *pahars* of the night were passed in this discussion. There is a saying:

*Verse*:

"Your intelligence has been the cause of my misfortune."

Even so, the messengers of the Shaykh failed to meet the arguments of the Mīrzā. The intention of the Mīrzā, however, was to continue these talks till the end of the night, lest the Shaykh would personally come over and become an obstacle in his way, after the delivery of this reply by his messengers. The Mīrzā detained the messengers by talking to them many topics connected with the Shaykh and also by diverting them with nice words and stories. At last the messengers realised that nothing could be done unless the Shaykh personally came. Very little of the night was left and the Mīrzā would proceed forward in the morning. Thus detained there against their inclination, they (ultimately) returned to the Shaykh. As the distance was long, so they reached the Shaykh when one *gharī* of the night still remained, and communicated to him the aforesaid facts. The Shaykh started for meeting Mīrzā Nathan two or three *gharīs* after morning by very swift boats and reached the fort of the Mīrzā after one *pahar* of the day. The Mīrzā however, had left that place in the morning and had proceeded forward. (714)

**Defeat and flight of Bhaba Singh.** He (the Mīrzā) employed two thousand boatmen in the van and began to proceed by clearing the thick jungles, and making a way, fifty yards wide, for the easy passage of the army. The Manṣabdārs and Aḥadīs, whose horses had not yet arrived from Jahāngīrnagar *alias* Dhāka, were provided with horses from his special stable and with *sukhpāls* (palanquins). The small and big cannon were carried on the shoulders of the boatmen. In short, the way was traversed in this way for three days. The camp was pitched during the last quarter of the days and guarded by barriers around and the nights were passed with care and vigilance. On the fourth day, the march was made under the guidance of his (the Mīrzā's) penetrating judgment and they came in sight of the fort of Jagat-Bīda, (protecting the city) of Gilahnay, situated in the midst of dense forest. A commotion arose among the the Kūches and they shouted,—"Enemy, Enemy," Bhabachan (Bhaba Singh)[16] who had proclaimed himself king and was in possession of Gilahnay, had a fort on the other side of the river Gajādhar. He, with his followers, prepared for battle. The Mīrzā arrived at a fordable place. He found a broken gondola, half of which was under water and the other half was broken. He ordered his men to cross the river with that gondola. When a batch of cavalry and infantry began to cross, the Mīrzā posted one thousand expert Firingis and Indian matchlockmen, on either side of the soldiers who were crossing the river, with instructions to fire on the rebels as soon as they would show their faces, and to deal out such a blow to them that they might never again dare obstruct their passage. Accordingly, fully equipped, they took their stand. When about thirty to forty horsemen and two hundred infantry had crossed the river, Bhabachan rushed forward with a force of ten to twelve thousand *pāiks* with the imperial elephants seized by him, in his front. The (imperial) regiment, which had crossed over to the other side, got frightened and retreated to the river. The rebels came up with all their might and were about to kill a large number of them, when all on a sudden the matchlock-men discharged their guns and repelled the impudent rebels. The elephant-drivers, unable to stand the shots from guns, turned the elephants back and took shelter under the trees in the gardens. Mīrzā Nathan shouted to the transporting officers to transport the men from three points. Thus in the twinkling of an eye, the followers of the Manṣabdārs, the brothers of Qulīj Khān and the men of the Mīrzā were sent to the other side from three different places. It was then decided to divide the army into two regiments. One regiment, consisting of half the strength of all the battalions of the Manṣabdārs, the Mīrzā and the officers of Qulīj Khān, was appointed to attack the rebels under the command of the Mīrzā's officers Mast 'Alī Beg, Sa'ādat Khān and Nik Muḥammad Beg. The soldiers of the other regiment, which was formed in the same way, were to follow in the rear slowly and skilfully in order to prevent the rebels from attacking the former regiment from other sides. Thus, the second army was to serve the purpose of a reserve and be useful from the rear. In short, as soon as the first regiment fell upon the rebels, they after a short skirmish, sought safety in flight, leaving the elephants behind. The imperialists began to seize the elephants and secured five of these including the chief elephant named Hīra Bajra. The trumpet of victory was blown and the Mīrzā encamped at Atharakuth. (715)

**The rebels evacuate Rangamātī.** All the imperial officers came to congratulate him and they received their rewards of horses and robes of honour in order of their meritorious services. On that very night, the rebels evacuated the fort of Rangamātī without any battle. It was decided to send the report of the victory to the Khān Fatḥ-jang with Mīrzā Sultan Murād and the Mīr* brother of 'Abu'l-Ma'ālī, and it was accordingly done. (716)

**Shaykh Kamāl proceeds to Gilah.** When they (the messengers) met Shaykh Kamāl on an island they saw that the Shaykh had removed his tent and was preparing to go to Jahāngīrnagar *alias* Dhāka to the Khān Fatḥ-jang. They

* There is a little blank space after the word Mīr here, but no proper name is recorded.

asked him what he was doing. The Shaykh replied that he was going to the Mīr Ṣūbah on a certain urgent business. Both these men said in reply,—" As we are your comrades, it is necessary for us to speak to you what we consider to be fair and good for you. We shall advise you in terms which may not be considered respectful. The final decision rests with you. How do the officers returning to the Ṣūbahdār propose to show their faces to him ? It was your foremost duty to follow Mīrzā Nathan straight against the enemies. In that case to-day, the laurels of victory would have come to you and all people would have said that the victory was attained solely through the aid rendered by the Shaykh from the rear. Now when the victory has been attained, the prudent course for you is to proceed to Gilah and thence march forward." The Shaykh agreed to this, and sent the things of his wardrobe, which had been already packed, to Gilahnay, and he kept waiting to hear the report of further developments. The Farrāshes (stewards) of the Shaykh with the Mīr Manzil (Superintendent of the household) reached that place and pitched the camp of the Shaykh at the Sān-Ghāt. This was reported to Mīrzā Nathan. The Mīrzā said to Sayfu'd-Dawla, brother of Qulīj Khān,—" My work was to give a defeat to the perverted rebels. By the favour of God and the influence of the fortune of the Emperor I have done it. Now as Gilahnay is your Jāgīr, it is advisable for you to go to your Jāgīr, pull down the tent of the Shaykh and throw it into the river Gajādhar, so that, thus slighted before the ryots, no one may recognise him either as a Sardār or a Jāgīrdār. By the time the reports reach the Khān Fatḥ-jang and a reply comes, you would be able to realise more than half the revenues of the Jāgīr." Mīrzā Sayfu'd-Dawla went there, beat the Farrāshes of the Shaykh, broke the ropes of the canvas enclosures and threw the tent into the river. It was then proclaimed that Jāgīr was still owned by its original possessors. This news reached the Shaykh during the stay of Sultan Murād and the Mīr*, brother of Abu'l Ma'ālī with him.

* Blank space again after the word Mīr.

The Shaykh became greatly mortified and again proposed to recall his advance-tent (*pīshkhāna*) from Gilahnay and to return to Jahāngīrnagar. These two men again explained to him and said, "If Mīrzā Nathan and the brothers of Qulīj Khān behave with your men even worse than this, you should put up with even such kind of treatment. By every possible means, you should join the war and must not ruin yourself, as your return to the Khān Fatḥ-jang is equivalent to your own ruin." Accordingly, the Shaykh proceeded forward and alighted at the Sān-Ghāt. At this time Mīrzā Bāqī Bakhshī and Rāja Raghūnāth also arrived from Hājo from Qulīj Khān, and met the Shaykh. They went to Mīrzā Nathan and congratulated him on the achievement of the victory. (717)

**Shaykh Kamāl joins Nathan.** After this, as the Shaykh offered to pay some money to them they (Mīrzā Bāqī and Raghūnāth) insisted that if even now united action was taken, Bhabachan might be soon captured along with the rest of the elephants. The Shaykh also promised thus:—"If Mīrzā Nathan goes with me with this army by the Kamakhyā Duwār, I will bring Bhabachan alive as a captive within fifteen days." Mīrzā Nathan said in reply to the Shaykh, Mīrzā Bāqī and Rāja Raghūnāth:—"As the object was and is to seize Rāja Bhabachan alone with the elephants, I agree to do my own part. Besides this, I agree to proceed by the Kāmrūp Duwār and bring him as a captive to the imperial officers within seven days." Although it was a day of festivity, he (the Mīrzā) rebuked them (Bāqī and Raghūnāth), saying,—"This is the second time that you have imposed this intolerable trouble upon me. I realised it only after it was an accomplished fact. If it recurs for the third time I shall be rude and you do not know what is likely to come out of me." Mīrzā Bāqī and Rāja Raghūnāth, unable to make the Mīrzā reasonable, returned to Jahāngīrnagar. (718)

**Pursuit of Bhaba Singh.** Next morning, the Mīrzā proceeded against the enemy by the Kāmrūp Duwār, and Shaykh Kamāl, Sarḥad Khān and others by the Kamakhyā Duwār. But Mīrzā Nathan, after marching for three *pahars,* pitched his camp in the fourth *pahar* and halted for the night with care and vigilance by raising an enclosure. The Shaykh, after halting for a day, sent a regiment in advance and raised a stockade. On the second day he resumed his march. Āqā Taqī had been sent from Hājo by Qulīj Khān with a land-force but owing to the opposition of the rebels he could not cross the river Banās and was detained at Barnagar. On the recapture of the city of Gilahnay, when the rebels became scattered like the constellation of the Bear and left the passage free, he crossed the river Banās and joined the army of Mīrzā Nathan in the third stage of his march. Then Mīrzā Sayfu'd-Dawla, proud of having been joined by his own army, blew the trumpet of march ahead of all. The Mīrzā, very much annoyed at this, sent a message to Āqā Taqī,—"The Mīrzās (sons of Qulīj) were like lame ass of Khwāja Ḥasan stuck in the mud, and Qulīj Khān himself, also lost his Jāgīr to his confusion.. Thank God that once again He has granted the recovery of their lost prestige through the mediation of this insignificant friend of theirs. Now I shall proceed to the Dakhinkul. You are to take care of your own affairs and the enemy. Now as I have ousted him from three or four places and driven him to the hill, you should go there and bring him either as a captive or drive him away from that place." He (the Mīrzā) then marched in the evening and proceeded to the Dakhinkul, and all his auxiliary officers were sent back. Then Āqā Taqī, in a state of confusion, ran after him; and as the Mīrzā was proceeding on a *sukhpāl*, he stood on foot in his front and began to entreat and solicit him (to return). After midnight, he brought him back to the camp. (719)

**Capture of Takunia.** Next morning the march was made to Dahīpūr and in the evening they reached that place and encamped there. But as two days were wasted in that unpleasant incident, Shaykh Kamāl reached the enemy's fort at Takunia[17] two days ahead of the Mīrzā, and he captured it from the rebels. Sixty five Tāngan horses were seized. Bhabachan thought that the imperial officers would not give up pursuing him as long as the elephants were with him. So he let the remaining elephants loose in the hills and jungles. (720)

**The rebels driven out of their hill-fort.** Mīrzā Nathan sent his spies to bring news of the rebels. Accordingly, the spies brought news that the rebels were staying in a stronghold among three hills. But as it was not possible to go to that place with horses, so Mīrzā Nathan despatched a force of his one hundred and fifty picked soldiers along with four thousand Kūch musketeers under the comand of his officers Sayf Khān and Ḥabīb Khān Lūdī. This band of devoted soldiers started during the first *pahar* of the night and arrived there next mid-day. They formed into four regiments and attacked the fort of the rebels. The rebels defended their fort. As a result of the attack of the brave heroes, the dead lay in heaps upon one another and it reminded one of the Day of Resurrection and a heavy fighting took place. When the fourth regiment, under the command of Sayf Khān, occupied a position on the hill commanding the view of the fort, the rebels in their helplessness, took to flight, and sought the way of safety by scattering the dust of disgrace on their heads. It was found that more than three hundred rebels had been killed and converted to the fuel of the fire of hell. Double this number had been wounded and had crept into the jungles adjacent to the fort, and the rest had run away half-dead. On the side of the imperialists thirty men became martyrs and about sixty were wounded. The age began to praise the deed in significant language and the people of the age became pleased in their thousands of hearts. They then returned to the camp blowing the trumpet of victory and the clarion of happy news. Defeated this time, the rebels did not gird up their loins again. (721)

**Nathan goes to the Dakhinkul.** After four days the Shaykh came to see Mīrzā Nathan. Mīrzā Nathan *nolens volens* left a troop of the Manṣabdārs with the Shaykh and started for the Dakhinkul with the rest of the imperial officers and his own soldiers. (722)

**Bhaba Singh releases his captives.** Now I shall give a short account of Shaykh Kamāl. When Mīrzā Nathan started for the Dakhinkul, leaving his auxiliary force with Shaykh Kamāl, the Shaykh wrote to Bhabachan who was taking shelter in the hilly region,—" If you desire your own wellbeing, you must release all the members of the family of Qulīj Khān who are your captives and you must give up your improper ways, otherwise you will be followed by the imperial army to whichever hill you go and will be driven from that place." Bhabachan looking at his own records, released the family of Qulīj Khān from the hills. The Shaykh gave the Khuntaghāt region, on lease, to Gopāl Jhūlia (a Kūch chief). Then he proceeded to Hājo and engaged himself in his own affairs. (723)

**Expedition against Jadū Nāyak.** The Mīrzā, in seven marches, reached the Jāgīr of Bagrībārī[18] where he had a *Maḥal* (a revenue division of a parganā) of his own. He stayed there for fifteen days and then started for Suālkuchī. It was decided to stop for a few days at Bhujmala and to send a regiment against Jadū Nāyak in order to put an end to his activities. Accordingly, he crossed the river Brahmaputtra and encamped on the sandy plain of Nagarbera. He despatched a force consisting of more than two hundred cavalry and five hundred infantry of matchlock-men and kūch *pāiks*, with full equipments of war, under the command of Muṣṭafā Qulī Beg, *via* Rangjūlī and Āmjūnga. A letter was written to Ḥabīb Khān Lūdī, the Thānadār of Jumria asking him to form two regiments of his men and he was directed to proceed with one regiment against the rebel *via* Rangjūlī; and the second regiment was to be sent under the command of Sayf Khān Lūdī who was going there with some men, so that he might proceed to Bakū against the rebel *via* Jumria. These regiments marched by the routes by which they were ordered to proceed. (724).

**Qulīj Khān returns to Jahāngīrnagar.** Now I shall give a short account of Qulīj Khān. When Mīrzā Nathan left the expedition handing over its affairs to Shaykh Kamāl, the ryots came to learn that Qulīj Khān had been dismissed from office and they refused to pay him revenues. Therefore, Qulīj Khān recalled his brothers and Āqā Taqī to Hājo. When he (Qulīj Khān) knew that he was to go away he wanted to take the account of the revenues from Āqā Taqī who was his chief officer. But as Āqā Taqī had misappropriated all the money of Qulīj Khān, he pretended to be ill of dysentry in order to save his skin. Qulīj Khān imprisoned his clerks and took his accounts and then he proceeded to Jahāngīrnagar taking his (Taqī's) family as hostage and arrived at the camp of Mīrzā Nathan. The Mīrzā extended a befitting hospitality to him and presented him with a high-bred horse. Qulīj Khān, who had received so many services from Mīrzā Nathan in the preservation of his prestige, ought to have come to him with many presents; but owing to his unmanly nature, he ignored this fact and shamelessly accepted the horse. He said to the Mīrzā that he would give him one of his elephants. He took a servant of the Mīrzā with him but let alone the elephant, he could not send even an insignificant hawk which he had promised to send along with the elephant. The servant of the Mīrzā was sent back without any thing. After some time he reached Jahāngīrnagar and thence he went to the imperial court. (725)

**Jadū Nāyak flies to the hills.** Now I shall give a short account of the army sent by Mīrzā Nathan against Jadū Nāyak, and its achievements. Jadū Nāyak thought within himself that when all these three regiments would join together, he would not be able to meet them. So he marched throughout the whole night and in the morning attacked the regiment of Ḥabīb Khān Lūdī. A great battle was fought and he (Ḥabīb) was about to be routed. But owing to the firmness of Ḥabīb Khān, the rebels were repelled. He (Jadū) returned from that place after mid-day and two *gharīs* before evening he fell upon the regiment of Sayf Khān and Sayf Khān was put to great straits. As Sayf Khān was halting at the fort of Bakū, the rebels owing to their numerical superiority entered the fort, offering a hand to hand fight. But at the strong resistance offered by the men of Sayf Khān, the position was recovered and the rebels took to safety in flight. Next morning they (the rebels) attacked the regiment of Muṣṭafā Khān just as it was going to start on horse back. The battle was fought till mid-day and Muṣṭafā Qulī Beg and his regiment were about to be defeated. At this juncture Ḥabīb Khān with his regiment arrived there from the other side. As soon as the sound of his kettle-drum was heard, the rebels took to their heels, and after suffering these repeated failures, they took shelter in the hills. All these three regiments joined together. (726)

**Jadū Nāyak attacks the fort of Jumriya.** The rebels again came out with the help of the hill-men and raised a fort in front of these three regiments and put them to great straits. Thus they blocked the path of the supply of rations. The scarcity of food put the army to a great hardship and the path of water-supply was also blocked by the rebels. These regiments then thought it expedient to retreat to the bank of the river, and then to come against the rebels after making necessary arrangements for the supply of rations. Accordingly, they marched at night and reached Jumriya in the morning. The rebels also, informed of this, followed them in the morning and they took rest for a while after traversing half the way. They resumed their march in the evening and attacked the fort of Jumriya at midnight. Such a battle took place that it reminded one of the Day of Resurrection and the market of the angel of death became very brisk, and the wounded lay in heaps one upon another. Thus the rebels thrice entered the fort and on all these three occasions these brave soldiers drove them out of the fort by offering a hand to hand fight. When Jadū Nāyak, the chief of the rebels, was wounded, a great confusion arose among the rebels and they suffered a defeat. When two *gharīs* of the night still remained, the kettle-drum of victory and the clarion of good tidings were sounded. In the morning, the report of the victory was sent to Mīrzā Nathan. But the Mīrzā, hearing many sounds of cannon at night, started for the

Thāna of Jumriya and arrived there within one *pahar*. He consoled the wounded men and those who survived martyrdom and appointed a fresh army for their aid. And as the rainy season had begun, the punishment of the rebels was postponed for the next year, and he started for his Thāna and residence at Suālkuchi. After five days, he reached his destination and reported all these events to the Khān Fatḥ-jang, and kept himself informed of (the events happening in) nooks and corners. (727)

**Submission of Dāngar Dev, chief of Khatribhāg.** When the Mīrzā had stayed at his own Thāna for some time, the ryots of Khatrībhāg[19] of the Jāgīr of the Mīrzā, taking advantage of the high flood, refused to pay their revenues. The Mīrzā sent a detachment to Talia under the command of one of his officers named Shaykh Awliya. This regiment went there, raised a fort and engaged itself in the pacification of that region. They sent a message to Dāngar Dev, son of Dumria Gosāin, holding out hopes of Mīrzā's generous treatment. After a protracted negotiation, Dāngar Dev agreed that he would submit to the Mīrzā provided Khwāja Sa'ādat Khān made a covenant through Balabhadra Dās, the Dīwān of Mīrzā Nathan. So at first the aforesaid Rāy (Balabhadra) went to Dāngar Dev and brought him to Talia. Then Khwāja Sa'ādat Khān went and shook hands with him. Mīrzā Nathan presented him with a suitable horse and a robe of honour and allowed him to return to his home after giving him the *Tīka* (ceremonial mark on the forehead used by Hindu chiefs at their installation) of Rājaship of that region. (728)

**Death of Dāngar Dev.** Rāja Satrajit, a vassal Zamīndār, was in the habit of molesting the friendly chiefs. Inspite of great favours shown to him (Satrajit) by Mīrzā Nathan, and the great friendship he had with Dāngar Dev, son of Dumria Gosāin, he (Satrajit) conspired with Kansa Narāyan, helped him with a force and prevailed upon Hardeo Chutia to make a night-attack upon Dāngar Dev. Dāngar Dev, was quite unaware of it and was staying with a small army. Inspite of this, he offered a brave resistance. But before the Mīrzā could receive this information and send an army to his aid, he was killed. In short, the well-wishers of Dāngar Dev brought his four wives and his son to Mīrzā Nathan. The Mīrzā assigned the villages of the Jāgīr of Dāngar Dev to his son and kept him under his fostering care. The wives of Dāngar Dev burnt themselves. (729)

**Promotion of Nathan.** After some time when the rainy season disappeared and the Canopus arose, the water of the rains dried up here and there, the rivers came to their normal state and the horses could move about. The Kūch people then indulged in some raids. The messengers of Mīrzā Nathan who had been sent to the Imperial Court along with the representations of the Khān Fatḥ-jang recommending the services of Mīrzā Nathan and other imperial Manṣabdārs, returned at this time from the Court with the promotion of Mīrzā's rank by an additional increase of 300 personal and 150 horse[20] and with the honour of the title of Shitāb Khān. A peremptory imperial Farmān along with robes of honour on behalf of the Emperor as well as on behalf of Nūrjahān Begum arrived from the capital city of Kashmir to his pargana of Sūnābāzū. (730)

**Nathan's sister comes to Dhāka.** The elder sister of Mīrzā Nathan also accompanied the royal messenger and arrived at Sūnābāzū. On the arrival of the messenger and particularly of his sister, the Mīrzā wrote a letter to his revenue officers to welcome his sister and her son Saiyid Mufattiḥ at the place of their arrival and to extend to them a befitting hospitality. The Zamīndārs were ordered to present their *pēshkash* to them. Accordingly, 'Abdu'l-Malik Seth, who was the Shiqdār (revenue administrator) of fourteen parganās, went first of all to receive them and presented a *pēshkash* of Rs. 1,000 to the Mīrzā's sister on his own behalf as well as on behalf of the Zamīndārs of the parganās. Another sum of Rs. 4,000 which was arranged for them as the expenses of their journey, was paid to them and they were sent to Jahāngīrnagar. When they arrived at Jahāngīrnagar *alias* Dhāka, the Khān Fatḥ-jang took the sister of the Mīrzā who was considered as a foster child by Ruqaiya Sultan Begum, wife of Ibrāhīm Khān, with great respect to his residence, and he extended to her a befitting hospitality. Many of the rare articles of Bengal were presented to them and they were kept at Jahāngīrnagar for two months in order to remove the fatigue of the long journey which they had undergone. (731)

**Assignment of Jāgīrs by the Ṣūbahdār.** After this the parganā of Khuntaghāt and others were assigned to the Mīrzā in lieu of his salary and the parganās of Būsī and Khatrībhāg were given to Mufattiḥ and he was sent to Mīrzā Nathan. Accordingly, the Mīrzā sent his Dīwān Rāy Balabhadra Dās in order to regulate the revenue and the administrative affairs of the Khuntaghāt and other parganās with instructions to make an estimate of the revenues and to make revenue settlements of different places. He was further instructed to arrange for a *Kheda* operation for the capture of wild elephants and to inform the Mīrzā about it, so that he might go personally to seize the elephants. It was also ordered that on the arrival of his sister, all the Zamīndārs and the revenue officers should be presented to her and a hospitality with *pēshkash* befitting this parganā should be extended to her party. Then they should be sent with all satisfactions to Bagrībārī, and information should be sent to the Mīrzā who would go up to Chandankuth to receive them with respect. Rāy Balabhadra reached the aforesaid parganā and executed his work as he was ordered to do. Having pacified that region he (Balabhadra) sent four thousand *pāiks* along with the scouts of elephant-catchers (*Qarāwālān-i-Fīlgīr*) under the command of Shaykh Amānu'llah in order to bring the elephants to the Qamargāh (ring) and to send the news to him. (732)

**Reception accorded to Nathan's sister.** When the sister of the Mīrzā arrived near Khuntaghāt he (Balabhadra) went with the Zamīndārs, and the revenue officers, and particularly with the chiefs of the *pāiks* to receive her and made his obeisance at Kānurhāda,[21] and extended a befitting hospitality to her. Then he returned after receiving robes of honour. When at Suālkuchi the Mīrzā received the news of the arrival of his sister, he started from that place with his famous officers by swift boats, and as he travelled with the current, he reached Chandankuth within a day and a night, and obtained the honour of kissing the feet of his elder sister who occupied the place of his mother. After staying there for three days and nights he came back to Suālkuchi safely on the seventh day. Here, from the bank of the river where they were disembarking, from the boats up to the *Masnad* (i.e the exalted seat of the lady) carpets were laid at three places. The sister was taken to the residence arranged for her stay and her sons were taken to the places meant for them. A befitting hospitality was extended to them for a week and every day they were presented with rare gifts. During this time, when the sister of the Mīrzā and her followers expressed their desire of having some maids and slaves, the Mīrzā promised that in order to meet their wishes he would undertake an expedition to the hills and give them all the captives brought from that place. In short, all the days were passed in joy and pleasure. (733)

**'Kheda' operation in Darrang.** Now I shall give a short account of Shaykh Kamāl. When the season for *Kheda* or the hunting of wild elephants began, he started with his own officers and some Manṣabdārs to Darrang and Bhurabārī with the purpose of catching elephants. He took with him eight thousand *pāiks* and brought the elephants to the Qamargāh to the best of his abilities. But owing to the great toil and the changing climate of that place and the vitiated water of the flood, the Shaykh, with three hundred and seventy men consisting of his own followers and imperial servants, fell ill. (734)

**Dissension among the Mughal Officers.** There were constant quarrels between Shaykh Kamāl and Mīr Ṣafī, the Dīwān, Bakhshī and Wāqi'navīs, and each of them reported to Ibrāhīm Khān Fatḥ-jang against the other. The Khān, therefore, sent to Hājo a recluse named Mīr Shams who had passed a long time in retirement. When Ibrāhīm Khān was not in power, he (Mīr Shams) had promised that he would give up the life of a calender when Ibrāhīm Khān attained the rank of 5000 and live with him. Accordingly, at this time when God the Great raised the Khān to the rank of 5,000 and favoured him with the Ṣūbahdārship of Bengal, he (Mīr Shams) gave up his life of a calender and took up his residence with the Khān. The Khān used to pay annually a sum of Rs. 30,000 to the aforesaid Mīr. Now he (the Khān) sent this man (to Hājo) with the following instructions:—"Owing to the illness of Shaykh Kamāl, I hear the report of the advance of the Assamese. So you are to go to that place with three hundred boats, and after being assured of the safety of the nooks and corners, you should send a detailed report to me about the quarrels between the Shaykh and Mīr Ṣafī." (735)

**An Enquiry held by Mīr Shams.** After twenty five days the Mīr arrived at Hājo and had a friendly meeting with the Khāns. Informed of the true state of things, he desired to invite Mīrzā Nathan from the Dakhinkul and to hold an assembly of all the officers, high and low, in order to investigate into the quarrel between the Shaykh and Mīr Ṣafī. The Shaykh, fearing that his prestige might be lowered, thus suggested,—"What is the use of proceeding in this manner? A crowded meeting may lead to quarrel. The best course is to make private enquiries from some of the intelligent persons who understand these affairs." It was accordingly done. The Mīr retired to a private chamber along with Shaykh Kamāl, Shitāb Khān, Mīr Ṣafī, the Dīwān and Bakhshī, Rāja Satrajit, Rāja Madhūsudan, Mīrzā Ṣāliḥ Arghūn, Mīrzā Yūsuf Barlās, Islām Qulī, Sūnā Ghāzī and Majlis Bāyizīd. Mīr Ṣafī was asked,—"What have you to say against the Shaykh? He replied,—"I am the Dīwān. It is necessary for me to have access to old records. Why then does not the Shaykh submit to me the record of his revenues so that I may be able to realise the excess revenues accordingly. Shitāb Khān is a house-born imperial servant and an experienced man. Please ask him whether I am reasonable or not." Shitāb Khān said, "You are officers of the *Chakla* (district) of the Uttarkul, I come from the *Chakla* of the Dakhinkul. Why do you then cite me as a witness? Why don't you get some other witnesses? The duties of a witness are very delicate. Nowadays no body in the world likes truthfulness. Therefore, the only result of speaking the truth is courting displeasure." Mīr Ṣafī replied,—"I swear by the Emperor that I will abide by the decision of you all, and I will never think ill of any body." Shitāb Khān again said,—"The Mīr says thus because I have not yet spoken anything. The moment I speak, it will displease you first of all and then the Shaykh. What is the use of asking a truth-speaking man like myself?" The Mīr insisted again and took an oath. After this Shitāb Khān opened his lips and turning his face towards the Mīr said,—"I ask you on behalf of the Shaykh to show us if you have any letter from your master communicating the dismissal of the Shaykh and ordering you to take his accounts. If that is so, by the time I kiss it (the letter) and place it over my eyes, kindly order some one to assume charge of the revenue administration of the country and relieve the Shaykh from his office, and then he will go down on his knees and render accounts. It is for you to decide what you should do if you have no letter. Shaykh Kamāl is not so weak and humble a man as to render accounts to you and me." The Mīr got excited and said,—"I am the Dīwān; I want to economise expenses. So the Shaykh must submit the records to me so that I may enter the excess income in the rent-roll." Shitāb Khān replied,—"If your object is to scrutinize the income from the revenues, then you may write to Jawharmal Dās to send a copy of his register to you and then be guided by the register. If you have any doubt, speak plainly and put it in writing that the Shaykh has realised fifty or twenty-five per cent more, so that the Shaykh may be ordered to explain these charges. There is no need of orders from Nawāb Ibrāhīm Khān. I myself, in consideration of the welfare of the Emperor, will dismiss the Shaykh and put the affairs under your control." The Mīr was in a fix and could not give satisfactory reply to it. Shitāb Khān said,—" I told you in the beginning that plain speaking will ultimately lead to this and it (my speech) already has disturbed the mind of the great officers." In short, the Mīr and all others expected that as Shitāb Khān was thirsting for the blood of Shaykh Kamāl, he would prove the Shaykh to be a liar and put him into difficulty, as soon as he (i.e. his conduct) became the subject of discussion. But Shitāb Khān did not deviate from truth and acted according to the right principle. He censured Mīr Ṣafī in such a way that everybody began to praise him for his justice. Shitāb Khān then returned to the Dakhinkul and Mīr Shams stayed there doing his own work. Mīr Ṣafī, without being recalled by the Khān Fatḥ-jang, proceeded to Jahāngīrnagar and stayed on at the court of the Khān Fatḥ-jang." (736)

**Death of Shaykh Kamāl.** Mīr Shams thought in his mind,—" As long as Shaykh Kamāl is at the helm of affairs, the Khān Fatḥ-jang will never appoint me to hold charge of the government of Kāmrūp unless the Shaykh dies." Accordingly, as Mīr Shams was an expert in the science of necromancy, he began to incant magic spells. The Shaykh was affected in such a way that lumps of blood began to come out of his stomach and throat. The Shaykh knew that he would not live long; so he started for Jahāngīrnagar by very swift boats and within a few days he reached the presence of the Khān Fatḥ-jang. After a week he expired. The Khān Fatḥ-jang appointed a revenue officer to take charge of his properties. Shaykh Shāh Muḥammad, the eldest son of Shaykh Kamāl, was honoured with the rank of 300 horse and 150 personal and the parganās of Chand Pratap and other Jāgīrs of his father were assigned to him and then he was sent to the Imperial Officers at Hājo to serve there. (737)

**Witchery of Mīr Shams on Shitāb Khān.** After this, Mīr Shams thought that unless he could do away with Shitāb Khān he would not be able to become the master of the whole of Kūch and Kāmrūp. So he began to exercise his witch-craft over Shitāb Khān too. Shitāb Khān also was affected to such an extent that blood began to come out of his throat. Therefore, Shitāb Khān wrote about it to a Darwīsh at Jahāngīrnagar *alias* Dhāka named Miān 'Āqil Muḥammad in whom he had great confidence. Miān 'Āqil Muḥammad began to pray from Jahāngīrnagar for his recovery and began to exercise his magical influence. By the favour of God he became so successful that at first the mediums of the two necromancers began to fight with each other and the medium of Miān 'Āqil Muḥammad overpowered the medium of Mīr Shams and drove it back to the Mīr. After this the Mīr was attacked with such a serious disease that blood began to flow out of his stomach and he was about to die. He wrote to the Khān Fatḥ-jang about his condition. (738)

**Official Changes.** The Khān Ṣūbahdār appointed Mīrzā Bahrām, the son of the brother of his wife as the Sardār of the Kūch territory, and Mīr Ṣafī was reinstated to the office of the Dīwān, Bakhshī and Wāqi'navīs to look after the revenue administration. They were sent to Kūch.

Begum, the wife of the Khān Fatḥ-jang, wrote a letter to Shitāb Khān,—" As Mīrzā Bahrām is like my own son, so he is to be considered as your son also. Under the circumstances, we are sending him to Kāmrūp, depending on the mercy of God as well as upon your love and kindness. Please manage the affairs of that place in such a way that it may baffle the enemies and please the friends." Accordingly, Mīrzā Bahrām and Mīr Ṣafī started from Jahāngīrnagar and reached Hājo after a lapse of time. The officers of Hājo and Shitāb Khān from the Dakhinkul came to receive him, and after staying there for two or three days, he (Shitāb Khān) returned to the Dakhinkul. When Mīr Shams saw that there was no possibility of his survival and his stay at Hājo in particular was against his interests, so *nolens volens* he started for Jahāngīrnagar against the will of Mīrzā Bahrām and went to the Khān Fatḥ-jang. The Khān cured him after prolonged treatment. (739)

**Quarrel between Shitāb Khān and Mīr Safī.** Now I shall give a short account of the officers of Kūch. When the parganā of Khuntaghāt was assigned by the Khān Fatḥ-jang to Shitāb Khān in lieu of his salary of Rs. 30,000, this sum became due to Shitāb Khān in the season of *Rabī'* (spring crop). When Shitāb Khān put forward a demand for it, a quarrel arose between him and Mīr Ṣafī. The Mīr thought in his mind that as Shitāb Khān did not take his side in his attempt to prove Shaykh Kamāl a liar, so he would take vengeance for it. Therefore, all Shitāb Khān's insistence and complaints and Mīrzā Bahrām's instructions to Mīr Ṣafī proved unavailing. Then Shitāb Khān came from the Dakhinkul to Hājo and asked permission from Mīrzā Bahrām to go to Jahāngīrnagar. Mīrzā Bahrām consoled the aforesaid Khān and sent messengers to Mīr Ṣafī with message: —"If you do not pay him the sum of Rs. 30,000 due to him in the Rabī' season, give him his draft (*sanad*) which he may forward to the Khān Fatḥ-jang and get cashed." But it was of no avail. At last Mīrzā Bahrām said,—"Alright, I shall write a strong letter to Ibrāhīm Khan and the Begum. Please go back to your Thāna this time. If no action is taken on it at Jahāngīrnagar I will not stand on the way of your departure." Accordingly, Shitāb Khān said to Mīrzā Bahrām,—"I will personally go once again to the house of Mīr Ṣafī. If he does either of those two things (i.e. pays the money in cash or gives a draft), it is well and good; otherwise, I go back to the Thāna." Then Shitāb Khān went to his house. While he was going to the house of the Mīr, he was met on the way by Islām Qulī. Islām Qulī was certain that it boded ill for Mīr Ṣafī. He accompanied Shitāb Khān offering him counsels (all the way) and the Khān reached the house of the Mīr. As soon as he entered the mansion of the Mīr, the situation took a serious turn. The followers of Shitāb Khān began by administering a sound beating to the Mīr, and he was ultimately saved by Islām Qulī and Khwāja Sa'ādat Khān, the eunuch of Shitāb Khān. They said,—" Your object is to take Mīr Ṣafī with you to the house of Mīrzā Bahrām. Alright, you wait outside, we will take the Mīr out to your boat." Shitāb Khān, who was holding the neck of the Mīr, loosened his grip and went out without suspecting that Islām Qulī was playing a trick with him. When the Khān had gone out, Islām Qulī ordered his men to turn out Khwāja Sa'ādat Khān by force and began to pelt stones and bricks. The Khān jumped out of his boat, ran towards the *Bēra* (fencing) of the mansion with his men in his front. Every one, small and great, fell upon the *Bēra* and broke it to pieces. When five *Bēras* i.e. a kind of fencing which is constructed in Bengal like a wall,—had been levelled to the ground, the Khān and his men entered the interior and gave a good beating to a Mughal who was going to fire his gun. Mīr Ṣafi broke the mat wall of the kitchen and the *Siḥat Khāna* (privy) and ran on foot to the house of Rāja Satrajit through the bazar. The aforesaid Rāja who was coming to his help, met him on the way and said, " I have come to your help; come back, I shall settle matters with Shitāb Khān." But he did not turn back. He ran away saying,—" I go to your house. Let yourself and Shitāb Khān settle the matter between yourselves. He is creating a great mischief." In short, the Rāja went to the house of Mīr Ṣafī and the Mīr went to the house of the Rāja. During this time Shaykh Shāh Muḥammad, son of Shaykh Kamāl, who was given a Manṣab, had come to Hājo after the death of his father and was staying there. He, in consideration of Shitāb Khān's fair dealings at the time of giving evidence in favour of Shaykh Kamāl inspite of their strained relationship, was in accord with Shitāb Khān. He pretended to help Mīr Ṣafī but private instructions were issued to his men to assist Shitāb Khān. He personally came and took the Khān to his home. After a while the Khān went to the house of Shāh Muḥammad, the former Bakhshī of Hājo, who was a relation of Mīrzā (Bahrām) and a great friend of Shitāb Khān. Shitāb Khān was staying in his house as if in his own home since his arrival from the Dakhinkul. News of this incident was then sent to Mīrzā Bahrām. Mīrzā Bahrām sent his messengers with the following message to the house of Mīr Ṣafī where Rāja Satrajit and Islām Qulī had assembled together with the Manṣabdārs and the Zamīndārs,—" I am the Sardār of the country. If Shitāb Khān has created any trouble, it is my business to take action, not yours. In fact you have created this trouble. One is an imperial Dīwān and the other is a house-born one of the Emperor. They are quarrelling with each other for their salaries. I shall investigate whether any of them has exceeded his limit. If you do not withdraw yourselves from this commotion, I shall hold you responsible for creating this trouble and send you to the Ṣūbahdār." The trouble subsided for the night. Next morning all of them mustered their troops again at the house of Mīr Ṣafī. When this news reached the Thāna of Shitāb Khān during the night, the followers of the Khān came to him one after another by every possible conveyance they could procure, whether it was his war-boat or a fisherman's boat, and failing these, they came up on foot through the hilly route with great difficulty. There arose a strange commotion. Mīrzā Bahrām also ordered his men to get armed, and the imperial elephants were arrayed. At last Satrajit, fearing that the blame would be laid on him, said to Mīr Ṣafī, —" As all the officers, high and low, excepting Mīrzā Bahrām have assembled in your house, take a document attested by all of them with their seal and signature to the effect that the provocation was given by Shitāb Khān." At last Mīr Ṣafī realised the document and sent them all to their respective houses. Shitāb Khān stayed for that night at Hājo and next morning returned to his Thāna and home. This incident was then reported to Ibrāhīm Khān by every one according to his own way. The Khān appointed Khān Sāmān (Steward) Āqā Taqī and Rāja Raghūnāth to enquire into this quarrel and sent them to Hājo. (740)

**'Kheda' operation in Khuntaghāt.** It has been mentioned before that Rāy Balabhadra Dās, the Hindu officer of Shitāb Khān, who was sent to the parganā of Khuntaghāt, had sent four thouasand *pāiks* under the command of Shaykh Amānu'llah with the brother officers of the Khān in order to round up the elephants into the *kheda* or Qamargāh. Therefore, the Khān, assured of the safety of the communication of the Thānas of the Dakhinkul, started for Khuntaghāt by boats by the river Brahmaputtra with a force of three hundred cavalry and five hundred matchlock-men. On the fourth day he reached a place named (left blank in Ms.) where there was a Thāna of Shitāb Khān. Rāy Balabhadra Dās and other *Mutasaddīs* (revenue officers) of that circle came to receive him and offered *pēshkash* according to their means. The Zamīndārs came in batches to pay their respects. The Khān sent a fresh detachment in order to bring news of the *kheda* or Qamargāh and enquired from Shaykh Amānu'llah about the condition of that place. Amānu'llah sent a representation from that place saying, "The *Pālī*, i.e., the guards of the Qamargāh being in different places, are keeping the elephants in their respective areas. More than two-thirds of the enclosures in which the elephants are to be captured have been completed. Please come. By the time you reach this place, the enclosures will be finished. So orders may be given to the tax-collectors to bring the *Ghar-Duwārī pāiks,* i.e., the auxiliary *pāiks*, from their homes to capture the elephants." Accordingly, the hard-working officers were sent to bring the *Ghār-Duwārī pāiks*, and the Khān also proceeded to that place. On the third day, he arrived at the place where these enclosures had been constructed. In the course of his inspection of the work, he found it defective on the side in charge of Bankhī Lashkar. He was given a verbal censure and was brought to senses from his sleep of negligence by the pouring of vinegar in the cup of his intoxication. This opened the eyes of others and they put their greatest efforts in the completion of the enclosures. The Khān, after two days, went personally towards the *Pālī* and made a strict supervision of the *Pālīs* as well. Every day the (the circle of the) *Pālīs* was narrowed down. (741).

**Pacification of the Bhutias.** At this time information was received that all the Pāikpūrs (Bhutias of the border ?) had assembled together and were planning to make a night-attack. The Khān sent a *Kūch* messenger to them, saying,—" God forbid ! But if my *Pālīs* are disturbed, I shall give up the idea of catching elephants, and taking all the soldiers of the Khuntaghāt region, by the favour of God, I will pillage and burn up to Bhūt (Bhutan hills) and will not leave even a bird of your race alive." The Pāikpūrs sent one of their own men to the Khān with this message,—" We are hill-men. It is not easy to capture us. How will you be able to come to our hills ? Therefore, if you give us presents, which are always given to us by the Rājas who come to capture elephants, we shall never create any trouble. First, you should allow the Bhutias to come down for trade ; and secondly, your Sardars should remain with their women within the *Pālī*, so that the villages may not be molested." The Khān said,—" If you want presents from us, then come to us in accordance with your old practices to receive your customary gifts." Then he (the messenger) demanded a guarantee that they would not be deceived. The Khān gave his word. Next morning the camp became full with the Pāikpūrs. The Khān procured from the villages ten big jars of wine called *Būkāis* which is plentiful in that country and gave these to them along with fifty pigs, twenty dogs and fifty maunds of rice of different kinds. They danced for the whole day and night, drank and made merry. If any of them felt the necessity of pairing with his wife, he would do it in the open field without shame or fear in the presence of other men. Next day when they had gone, the Bhutias came down to sell Tāngan horses, musk, *ghazhgha* (a kind of mountain ox) and Bhūt (blankets?). (742)

**Mīr Ṣafī starts for Jahāngīrnagar.** It has been mentioned before that Āqā Taqī and Rāja Raghūnāth were appointed to enquire about the quarrel between Mīr Ṣafī and Shitāb

Khān. Accordingly, they were sent and they arrived at Hājo. But by that time Mīr Ṣafī, without being recalled by Ibrāhīm Khān and without the permission of Mīrzā Bahrām, started for Jahāngīrnagar *alias* Dhāka. (743)

**Account of the 'Kheda' operation.** Now I shall revert to my main theme. It has been mentioned before that the elephant catchers were sent to drive the elephants into the enclosures. From the twelfth day when the *Pàlī* was narrowed down to its extreme, batches of four men took their position, one after the other and they began to drive the elephants from the jungles into the enclosures. Fourteen elephants were brought at night towards the fold. Four *gharīs* after evening they entered the enclosure of Jagat Bīda. The *pāiks*, who were ready there, immediately raised a barrier in the middle of the enclosure of Jagat Bīda, and made the place too narrow. But at the noise of the labourers, the elephants came to the second enclosure named Jabalkadah and began to get out by breaking a corner of the enclosure on the side of Bankhi Lashkar which was guarded by a small number of men. From the time when the region of Khuntaghāt was brought under imperial sway, the *Kheda* of that region was closed. Shitāb Khān secured this Jāgīr by promising that he would undertake a *Kheda* operation and send the elephants thus captured (to the imperial Court). So the True Lord had ordained that Shitāb Khān would not lose his prestige. When the elephants were going out, a band of *pāiks* arrived there and created a noise on that side. Eight of these elephants turned back and entered the third enclosure named Bānch Bhanita. A tumult arose at midnight that the elephants had gone out. The Khān came out of his camp, and inspite of the fact that he had not with him even ten of his trustworthy followers, he, in a furious mood, brought out the Sardārs of the *pāiks* who had allowed the elephants to get out, from the midst of two to three thousand *pāiks*, scourged them heavily and threw them down before him with their hands bound. Khwāja Sa'ādat Khān noticed that a disorder had appeared among the *pāiks* and that it would lead to a mutiny. So he without asking the permission of the Khān released the Sardārs and pacified Bankhī Lashkar who was standing in a trembling condition. Thus the excitement of these men was pacified and proper watch was kept in different places. Next morning when the Khān was saying his prayers, he was informed that the elephants were within the enclosure, and he was taken there to see them. The Khān found that there were eight elephants within the enclosure. He then called the elephant-catchers and encouraged them, and asked them to bring the elephants into the *Markadah*, the place in which the elephants are shackled. They brought the elephants with great difficulty into the enclosure of the *Markadah* and became free from anxieties, because unless the elephants were put within that enclosure there was every possibility of their going out. In short, Shitāb Khān offered his thanks to God with all his heart and soul. He took his seat on a platform which had been constructed there and ordered the elephants to be taken through the gate of the *Markadah* to their place of confinement. Attempt was made during the whole of that day to bring them to that place, but none of the elephants could be chained. At midnight the biggest elephant of the herd came to that gate and was chained. Early in the morning it was taken out of that place and they waited for the entry of the other elephants to that place of confinement. Shitāb Khān named this elephant as Mīrān Prasad. After this, three female elephants came together to the gate and were chained. These were also taken out. On the third occasion a big elephant with a baby was caught. One female elephant struggled so hard that it was beyond description. At last she was caught within the enclosure of the *pāiks*. She was then brought out of it and every body became free from the apprehension that the elephants would escape. Shitāb Khān sent a report of these events to Ibrāhīm Khān. When the report reached the Khān Fatḥ-jang, he became very much pleased and thanked him in reply. (744)

**Death of Mūsā Khān.** Masnad-i-'Alā Mūsā Khān, son of the late 'Īsā Khān was suffering from a serious illness from a long time. Although the Khān Fatḥ-jang placed him under the treatment of imperial physicians it did him no good. Therefore Mūsā Khān deposited his frail existence to its Creator and relieved himself from the worries of life. Ibrāhīm Khān Fatḥ-jang conferred imperial robes of honour upon Ma'ṣūm Khān, the eldest son of Mūsā Khān, about eighteen or nineteen years old. He was relieved of his sorrows and was given the highest honour. Robes of honour were also given to Khwāja Chand, the *pēshwa* (minister) of Mūsā Khān Masnad-i-'Alā, Ramay Lashkar, 'Ādil Khān, the Mīr-Baḥr, and Jānkī Balham, and they were retained as the *pēshwas* of Ma'ṣūm Khān in the same way as they were the *pēshwas* of Mūsā Khān. He (Ibrāhīm Khān) began to take fostering care of him (Ma'ṣum Khān) and devoted his time in the political and financial administration of the country of Bengal. (745)

**Shitāb Khān proceeds against Jadū Nāyak.** Now I shall give a short account of Shitāb Khān. After sending his letter to the Ṣūbahdār about the capture of elephants, he stayed there for a week in order to make the elephants docile. When he received an information that his nephew Mufattiḥ had come from Suālkuchi to the Thāna of Khuntaghāt and was desirous of coming to this place, Shitāb Khān thought in his mind that he would have asked him to come if the elephant-capture had not been finished. But now as that excitement was over and the climate of this place was also very insalubrious, so he decided to march to the Thāna (of Khuntaghāt) and reached there within a very short time. Mufattiḥ honoured himself by kissing his feet. Here also he stayed for a week and then proceeded to Suālkuchi. When he reached Bagrībārī, he thought of proceeding personally against Jadū Nāyak and to extirpate him. Therefore, he made preparations for it. (746)

**Strange things seen in the 'Kheda' operation.** Two strange things were observed at the place where elephants were captured. First, in the jungles where elephants live and where the *pāiks* were posted for *pāli*. i.e., to watch that the elephants might not go away, they used to sit constantly in their *chawkīs* to guard the elephants and would not go to any distant place even for the purpose of drinking water lest the elephants might get away. They used to procure drinking water in the following manner:—There is a king of trees in that jungle. As soon as a branch of this tree is cut off with the stroke of a sword, water begins to flow in such a quantity that two jars may be filled up. But what a clear water it is! In beauty, taste and sweetness, it is just like the transparent and pure water of a river. The only difference is that if a man drinks to his full, he is immediately attacked with fever owing to its extreme coldness and suffers for a long time. If, on the contrary, he drinks to satisfy only half his thirst, it does no harm. The *pālīs* were posted from the beginning in batches of two after every hundred cubits. The general rule observed by them is this:—They cut bamboos and thrust into them at either side a piece of bamboo of the size of one cubit. These are heaped together. Dry straws are placed beneath them and these are spread from one end of a *chawkī* to the next *chawkī*. When the elephants try to get out of the enclosure, one of these (*pālīs*) immediately runs from the left and another from the right with fire in their hands and set fire under these heaped-up bamboo pieces. The fire makes the joints of the bamboos crack in such a way that they produce sounds like the reports of big guns, and at this the elephants turn back into the enclosure. Thus they are stopped from going out. Besides these they use an entire stump of bamboo, half of which is cleft in the middle and a rope is tied to one of its halves. One of these two *pālīs* pulls that rope and it produces a sound at all hours. It is called *Takā*. They also use two pieces of bamboo, one of which is carved and the other is carved in the middle and these are perforated at every two finger's breadth. These are beaten with sticks like a kettle-drum and a sound is produced like that of a pair of big kettle-drum. In the language of the Kūch it is called *Dānk-Dankā*. The second strange thing is this:—There is a stream in that place named Lūpānī. The special characteristic of this stream is that from four *gharīs* before morning till six *gharīs* after morning it rises very high so that in some of the deep places the water comes up to the waist of a man; and then it gradually dries up to such an extent that if a man walks in it, the water would not reach even up to his ankle. Six *gharīs* before evening, it becomes absolutely dry. Then again the water begins to rise up to the end of one *pahar* of the night and after that the water disappears. (747)

**Shitāb Khān marches to Bhujmala.** In short, after five days, Shitāb Khān, relieved of his revenue and other affairs, crossed the river Brahmaputtra and started for extirpating Jadū Nāyak. His first halt was made at Nagarbhera (Nagarbera). After halting there, he marched to Bhujmala. As Mufattiḥ, the nephew of the Khān was seriously ill, so he was sent to Suālkuchī to his mother with the uncle of Shitāb Khān named Mīrzā Madārī. He (Shitāb Khān) marched from that place and proceeded forward. Mufattiḥ arrived at the bank of the river Brahmaputtra. At this time, God the Great favoured Shitāb Khān with a son. So Khwāja Almās, one of the old eunuchs of the Khān, with the hope of getting rewards from the Khān, came from Suālkuchī in great haste on a gondola to convey the news. But it was of no avail. By that time, the Khān had reached his fifth station, and for fear of the hill-men who were blocking the ways, no one could carry this news. At last Ḥabīb Khān, the Shiqdār of the parganā of Jakhalī sent a few words with Dunda, a Gāro Sardār to the Khān. Khwāja Almās returned to Suālkuchī with Mufattiḥ. But this Gāro, with the hope of getting rewards, traversed a distance of seven days' journey within four *pahars* through the hills and delivered the news to Shitāb Khān. It became an occasion of great pleasure to the friends and imperial officers. The trumpet of happy news was played and great rejoicings took place. Although it was a place full of jungles and forests, dainty dishes were prepared and all the men were fed. Saffron was scattered on all and the otto of roses was sprinkled. Then they took rest and the sentinels were ordered to keep guard with care and vigilance. Next morning the march was resumed. Mīrzā Madārī, the uncle of

Shitāb Khān, after nine days' journey up the river, brought Mufattiḥ, the nephew of Shitāb Khān, to his mother in safety, and he wrote to the Khān about their safe arrival. (748)

**Flight of Jadū Nāyak.** When Jadū Nāyak saw that the Khān was approaching him, he blocked the passage of his advance with a force of eight thousand *pāiks* and offered battle. Khwāja Sa'ādat Khān, who was at the van, gave battle and then Mast 'Alī Beg, Nīk Muḥammad Beg, Muṣṭafa Qulī Beg, Mīr 'Abdu'ṣ-Ṣamad, Hātim Khān, Ḥabīb Khān Lūdī and many other experienced and devoted officers dismounted from their horses and joined in the great battle. A wonderful battle took place. Thus Jadū Nāyak compelled this army to retreat three times, and on all these three occasions, these battle-loving heroes, with the aid of their central regiment, put their greatest efforts in storming the enemy's forces and drove them to the defiles of the hills and dense forests. The wounded and the dead lay upon one another. When the Khān saw that the rebels were not falling back, he dismounted from his horse and rushed forward by placing the shield before his face. At the advance of the Khān, the entire army of the centre ran on foot, and the van with the support of the centre repelled the impudent rebels. When Jadū Nāyak was wounded, a great confusion arose among his followers and they sought safety in flight. Then the trumpet of victory was sounded. After this it was ascertained that more than one hundred rebels had been killed, double this number had been wounded and perished in the adjacent places. The rest fled away half-dead. From that place, he (Shitāb Khān) made a quick march in proper order and encamped at a place, one *kos* distant from the field of battle. (749)

**Conquest of the hill-fort of Jadū Nāyak**. Next morning, the Khān, under the guidance of the loyal Zamīndārs, marched to the hills with all his soldiers on foot. After proceeding a distance of four *kos* into the interior, he reached the fort of the rebels on the summit of a hill which was strongly fortified. The passage was blocked by the rebels with numerous logs of wood. The Khān crossed all these obstacles with full force and attacked the fort. The fort was conquered after a hard fighting for four *gharīs*, and then the rebels fled to the jungles. The age began to praise (the action) in significant language and the people of the age became pleased in their thousands of hearts. The trumpet of the announcement of victory was played and then they returned to the camp which was pitched at the foot of the hill. Nine *kos* were covered on foot in the hills and surprising results were achieved. (750)

**Pursuit of Jadū Nāyak.** It was then decided to send Nīk Muḥammad Beg with a force of three hundred experienced horsemen on foot, two thousand Kūch infantry and five hundred matchlock-men to go up to the hills in pursuit of the rebel (Jadū Nāyak) and to capture him wherever he might be found and the Khān was to proceed by the foot of the hills. Accordingly, Nīk Muḥammad Beg started up the hills to execute this work with large equipmonts of war. The Khān ordered the Sardārs of the Kūch *pāiks* to prepare fifty *Larakcha*, i.e., a kind of palanquin made of green bamboos and carried by men on shoulders like a *Duli* (litter). These were sent with Nīk Muḥammad Beg and one hundred and fifty strong Kūches were appointed with instructions that if any of the noble officers of the army failed to climb the hills, they should carry him in one of these *Larakchas*, so that in time of need he might come out of it and join his comrades in battle. In short, Nīk Muḥammad Beg proceeded to the hills in an auspicious moment on Sunday. Shitāb Khān also proceeded by the foot of the hills. After marching for five *kos*, the camp was pitched and as the army had been divided into two and as two-thirds of it had gone to the foot of the hills and one-third remained with the Khān along with their elephants, so a stockade was raised to pass the night with care and vigilance. Nīk Muḥammad Beg, reaching the interior of the hills, set fire to three places where the rebels had constructed forts with the help of the hill-men and the Rājas of the upper-hills. In all these three places, many rebels were killed and wounded and a heavy punishment was inflicted on them. (751)

**Capture of Jadū Nāyak.** Then Jadū Nāyak took shelter with Rāja Nilrangily who was the ruler of the fourth series of hills of the upper-hill regions. As he went with his family, Rāja Nilrangily immediately gave him shelter. After this, when he saw that the (imperial) army had reached his hill to attack him, he kept Jadū Nāyak under confinement and offered resistance to the imperialists according to his own power. On the first day, as the army reached there after marching a great distance through many hills, the fort could not be conquered and the army had to remain in suspense. At night, the enemies made a night-attack. But as the brave fighters were ready for battle, the Kūch *pāiks* whose Sardārs were friendly to Nīk Muḥammad Beg, fought a great battle. The hill-men, unable to stand, returned to their fort suffering a defeat. Next morning, envoys were sent to carry on negotiations. Nīk Muḥammad Beg, through the loyal Zamīndārs, sent this message to Rāja Nilrangily :—" Why are you allowing your hill to be destroyed ? We will never give up the pursuit of this fellow, even if he climbs all these hundred hills. Therefore, if you send him alive as a prisoner to us along with his wife and children, you will get large rewards from our master, and you will be made the chief of all the Rājas of the upper-hills. The *Qalīcha* (the carpet of the throne), the winning of which is considered as a great distinction by you, will be given to you and the *Tika* (sacred mark) of Rājaship will also be given to you before we return." He then replied,—" I will hand over Jadū Nāyak with his family and followers to you, provided you give golden robes of honour to me and to my wife, reward of Rs. 300 for my relations, and the *Qalīcha* and the *Tika* of the Chief Rājaship over all the Rājas." Nīk Muḥammad Beg agreed to these terms. After these agreements, he put on the robes of honour along with his wife in the presence of Nīk Muḥammad Beg. He received the stipulated sum, the *Qalīcha* and the *Tika* of Rājaship. Nīk Muḥammad gave him leave to return as early as possible. (Two words blurred in the ms. here). The men of the Rāja brought Jadū Nāyak as a prisoner and handed him over to Nīk Muḥammad Beg. The news of the arrival of the Rāja and his return after receiving the robes of honour and the despatch of a regiment with him to bring Jadū Nāyak were communicated to Shitāb Khān. As Jadū Nāyak was secured soon after the despatch of that letter, he (Nīk Muḥammad) also started from that place and reached Shitāb Khān with his army and captives and obtained eternal honour. (752)

**Shitāb Khān returns to Suālkuchī.** Owing to the peculiar climate of that place and a kind of insect called *gāndhī*, all the soldiers suffered from a sort of sore from which yellow water began to flow like that of water-melon. All of them became marked with blisters and bruises. Every one of them suffered from four to five months. The Khān then ordered five Sardārs of Jadū Nāyak to be trampled under the feet of elephants. Next morning he started for Suālkuchī along with Jadū Nāyak, Manui Dalai, a relation of Jadū Nāyak and their families, and reached there in fourteen marches. (753)

**Shitāb Khān rewards his officers.** The men who rendered good services, particularly those who were in the company of Nīk Muḥammad Beg were honoured with two-and-a-half fold, five-fold and ten-fold increase in their salaries. Nīk Muḥammad Beg was presented with a robe of honour and an 'Irāqī horse of high breed. Fourteen warriors whose names are given below were each rewarded with a horse by Shitāb Khān. They were, Miān Khwāja Aḥmad, Sayf Khān, Ḥabīb Khān, Mīr 'Abdu'ṣ-Ṣamad, Ḥabīb Khān, the second, 'Ālam Khān, brother of Ḥabīb Khān, Shaykh Awliyā. Shaykh Amānu'llah, Khwāja Aḥmad, Niẓāmu'd-Dīn, Ruknu'd-Dīn, Shīr Khān Kākar, Shaykh Chamrū and 'Alī Khān Rohila. In short, every day and night was passed in holding assemblies of musical entertainments, story-tellers, poets and readers of books. After some time Manui Dalai obtained his freedom through the mediation of some men by paying a ransom of Rs. 5,000. He was entrusted to Ḥabīb Khān, the Thānadār of Tappa Jumriya, in order to see whether he was loyal or not. Shaykh Amānu'llah was again sent to Khuntaghāt. Letters were written to Bankshī Lashkar and other Sardārs of Khuntaghāt asking them to arrange for another *Kheda* for which they would be rewarded. Robes of honour were sent with Shaykh Amānu'llah for all the seventeen Sardārs of the elephant-catchers and the Sardārs of the camp-followers. Balabhadra Dās who was at Khuntaghāt was ordered to make his utmost efforts to arrange for the second *Kheda.* Accordingly, the aforesaid Rāy summoned the Sardārs, gave them the robes of honour, encouraged them and sent them with Shaykh Amānu'llah to the *Kheda,* i.e., *Qamargah* for capturing wild elephants. A force of twenty matchlock-men was also sent in their company and he (Balabhadra) remained busy in the management of his own affairs. (754)

**Rebellion of Shāhjahān.** Now I shall give a short account of Ibrāhīm Khān Fatḥ-jang and particularly of Aḥmad Beg Khān, the Ṣūbahdār of Orissa. The following peremptory imperial Farmān was issued to Ibrāhīm Khān :—"News has come from the Deccan that on the departure of Prince Parvīz from the imperial Court, Prince Shāhjahān, being annoyed, has left Burhānpūr and entered into the wilderness. It is not known where he is going. Therefore, do not neglect the affairs of Orissa and of Aḥmad Beg Khān. Arrange the affairs of that region in such a way that no harm may reach that region from the wrath of the light of the lamp of greatness (Shāhjahān)." Accordingly, Ibrāhīm Khān Fatḥ-jang used to write always advisory letters to Aḥmad Beg Khān and he kept himself informed of the nooks and corners. He kept his ears open to hear the report of the arrival of the august army of that prosperous prince, because, although Ibrāhīm Khān Fatḥ-jang had no other alternative except obeying orders, yet owing to his loyalty to the dynasty of Ṣāḥib Qirānī (Taimūr) he was greatly devoted to the Emperor of the world Jahāngīr Bādshāh. He resolved that he would prove his loyalty by attaining marytrdom and thus leave the country of Bengal to the august Prince Shāhjahān. No measure was taken to obstruct the passage of the prince and he took an indifferent attitude. Aḥmad Beg Khān was more indifferent than him, as will be described below.[22] (755)

## CHAPTER VI

*The rebellion of Shāhjahān, the prince of the world and its people. His march from the Deccan to Bengal. His clash and battle with the imperialists. Death of Ibrāhīm Khān and occupation of Bengal by Shāhjahān.*

**Shāhjahān arrives at Cuttak.** The sum and substance of this long affair is this:—When Aḥmad Beg Khān[1] heard that the august prince had reached Bānpūr,[2] he, being a servant, had not the courage to obstruct the prince. So the mountain pass,[3] in which a force of three hundred to four hundred thousand soldiers may be held up by a regiment of five hundred matchlock-men, was crossed by the prince with his five to six thousand cavalry without any battle and he proceeded from Orissa to Bengal. Every place he halted at was devastated. The prince of the world arrived safely at Khurda. Rāja Purushottam, Rāja Pancha,[4] Rāja Nilgīrī, Bajādhar and other Zamīndārs of Orissa presented themselves and obtained the honour of kissing the ground. The wise and intelligent prince halted for a few days with his court at Cuttak and managed the affairs of that province.[5] The report of his victorious advance produced a commotion among the Zamīndārs of that region. One of the relatives of the King of Portugal named Captain Chanika,[6] i.e., a Firingi Sardār, who was holding a post equivalent to that of an imperial Ṣūbahdār, and was the viceroy of the King of Portugal at Hugli, Pipli and other parts of the province of Orissa, thought that his best interests would be served by kissing the feet of the prince. So he came with five sea-elephants, and rare gifts of jewels and jewelled appliances worth about Rs. 100,000 and obtained the eternal honour of kissing the ground. His Royal Highness the Qībla of the world kept him in attendance for three days with his consent. Every day he was presented with robes of honour and valuable gifts of India, Kashmir, 'Irāq, Persia, Rūm and of other places, the like of which he had never seen before. On the day of his departure he was given a special robe of honour, an 'Irāqī horse and a Turkish horse with bejewelled saddle and rein and a sword, and he was given farewell with many favours. Muḥammad Taqī,[7] who was one of the devoted loyal servants was honoured with the Ṣūbahdārship of Orissa and was given the Manṣab of *Panj-Hazārī*, 5,000 horse and the title of Shāh Qulī Khān. He was left in Orissa along with a large number of loyal officers and then he (Shāhjahān) marched forward. (756)

**Aḥmad Beg flies to Akbarnagar.** Aḥmad Beg Khān went to Bardwān to Mīrzā Ṣāliḥ, son of Mīrzā Shāmī and he proposed to go to Akbarnagar *alias* Rājmaḥal along with Mīrzā Ṣāliḥ.[8] Mīrzā Ṣāliḥ did not agree to this and remained there with the desire of strengthening the fort. Aḥmad Beg went his own way and proceeded to Akbarnagar. The prince of the world and its people, Shāhjahān, reached Midnapūr in safety and happiness. He conferred upon Muḥammad Shāh the title of Shāh Beg Khān and left him at Midnapūr. From that place, he made a swift march from stage to stage and reached the vicinity of Bardwān. (757)

**Shāhjahān occupies Bardwān.** Mīrzā Ṣāliḥ, through the influence of his evil star, took his stand to fight against the prince, the Qibla of the world, and commanded the garrison. The august prince reached the fort of Bardwān. The fort was attacked from every side by the Sipāh-Salār 'Abdu'llah Khān Firūz-jang,[9] Rāja Bhim,[10] Dariyā Khān Rohila, Shajā'at Khān *alias* Saiyid Ja'far, Nāsir Khān *alias* Khwāja Ṣābir,[11] Rao Manrūp, Rāja Sārdūl, Lashkar Shīr Khwāja, Khwāja Dāwūd and Khwāja Ibrāhīm, brother and nephew of Khwāja 'Uṣmān, Babū Khān, and Bahādur Khān, son of Dariya Khān. They secured a commanding position over the fort by proceeding under the cover of artificial barriers (*sībā* and *ṣābāt*), and Mīrzā Ṣāliḥ was put to great straits. He was spending his days and nights in pleasure in enjoying the dances of women and public singers. His soldiers, offered a great resistance from their trenches. When the brave warriors (*bahādurān*) of the prince of the world and its people, led their attack by placing the *gardūns* in their front and the garrison was pressed very hard, Mīrzā Ṣāliḥ awoke from his sleep of negligence, and under the guidance of his wife and through the mediation of Her Highness Mumtāz Maḥal, he came alone to the gate of the royal residence by tying the rope of humiliation around his own neck. Dārāb Khān[12] took him and placed him under the feet of the Qibla of the world and its people (Shāhjahān). That senseless and foolish man deserved punishment, but in consideration of the value of recognition of old servants he was honourably received and was ordered to be kept in confinement. He was then taken on an elephant in his retinue. Bardwān was assigned to Khān Dawrān as a Jāgīr in lieu of his salary, and his brother Dūrmuz Beg was left in charge of Bardwān. From that place they proceeded to Rājmaḥal. (758)

**Ibrāhīm Khān proceeds to Akbarnagar.** Now I shall give a short account of the affairs of Aḥmad Beg Khān. When he left Mīrzā Ṣāliḥ and reached Akbarnagar, he wrote the details of his arrival to Ibrāhīm Khān Fatḥ-jang at Jahāngīrnagar and sent it in great haste by a swift boat. The messenger reached the Khān with great promptness and delivered the message to the Khān. The august Khān sent his Bakhshī Mīrzā Bāqī to the Thāna of Phūldūbī with a force of one thousand trustworthy and experienced picked soldiers. And after making satisfactory arrangements for the safety of the Thānas of Jessore, Tippera, Bhalwa, Sylhat and Kachār, he (the Khān) proceeded to Akbarnagar with the rest of the imperial army. Khwāja Idrāk, who was his personal assistant and the Chief officer of his household, was left in charge of his *Maḥal* (harem) at Jahāngīrnagar with a force of five hundred cavalry and one thousand matchlock-men. He made swift marches from stage to stage and reached Akbarnagar within eleven days. The Sepulchre[13] (*maqbara*) of his son which was strongly fortified was strengthened as a fort of defence and the command was given to his nephew Mīrzā Yūsuf. Leaving Jalā'ir Khān and other high imperial officers at the fort of the Sepulchre, he went to the bank of the river Ganges and pitched his camp. Akbarnagar *alias* Rājmaḥal, which had a strong fort, being far from his war-boats, was abandoned by him. (759)

**Ibrāhīm Khān refuses to surrender.** The prince of the world and its people, after traversing the stages and stations, made a victorious and fortunate halt at the city and fort of Akbarnagar. I'timād Khān *alias* Khwāja Idrāk (son of) Aṣaf Khān Marhum (?) *alias* Mīrzā Ja'far was sent as envoy to the Khān Fatḥ-jang with many favourable terms. In short, the purport of the message was this,—" As that old devoted slave, due to his relationship with Nawab Āṣafjāh,[14] is considered to be our own relation, so under the circumstances, it is proper that he should come to our presence and obtain the honour of kissing our feet. He should remain in Bengal with prince Awranzīb in his company, so that we may proceed with fortune and prosperity for the conquest of the city of Patna, assured of the safety of the rear." Khwāja I'timād Khān, an attendant of Āṣaf Khān Ja'far went to the Khān Fatḥ-jang and tried to win him over by various means. But the Khān Fatḥ-jang, true to his salt, began to speak thus keeping himself within the rules of decorum,—" I consider it as a felicity for both the worlds to sacrifice a hundred thousand dear lives like mine at the dust of the feet of the Qibla of the world, and to make myself happy by kissing the ground and obtaining the honour of sweeping the dust at the Court of the son of my Qibla. But the salt (of my master) stands on the way of my adopting such a procedure. I see the temporal and spiritual welfare of that light of the world is this that he should seek the pleasure of the true Qibla (Jahāngīr) and should not transgress (from the path of duty) even by a hair-breadth." In short, he expressed many words showing his external and internal fidelity and bade adieu to I'timād Khān.

When I'timād Khān returned to kiss the threshold of the prince of the people, he reported the discussions he had with

Ibrāhīm Khān. His Royal Highness* then, at the advice of his Sipāh-Sālār (commander-in-chief) 'Abdu'llah Khān Firūz-jang, ordered a regiment under the command of Dārāb Khān to besiege the fort of the Sepulchre. They dug trenches at different places and advancing under the cover of artificial barriers, they mined the fort from three sides. (760)

**Battle on the bank of the Ganges.** Dariyā Khān, Bābū Khān Barīj and a detachment of Afghān army were ordered to cross the river Ganges opposite Panti[15] and to proceed *via* Tājpūr Purnea against Ibrāhīm Khān. Accordingly, Dariyā Khān crossed the river Ganges during the day with the boats of the *Bepārīs* (traders) and pitched his camp in the sandy plains. This news reached the Khān Fatḥ-jang. The Khān sent Aḥmad Beg with a force of two thousand imperial cavalry and one hundred elephants against Dariyā Khān. Aḥmad Beg Khān started in the early part of the day and without stopping at any place he marched for the whole day and night and arrived there early morning before the horses of Dariyā Khān and other men of the army could cross the river. All of them were on foot. Dariyā Khān and his regiment, sure of their death, girded up their loins to fight on foot, and placing an imperial private elephant named Jatājūt in their front, advanced forward. As soon as they ascended a hillock from its foot where they were staying, they rushed upon Aḥmad Beg and the regiment sent by Ibrāhīm Khān, by wrapping the coffin-cloth on their heads. Aḥmad Beg Khān all alone fell upon some men and plunged into their midst, but it was of no use. They, welcoming death, took their stand like a mountain of steel. Every step they advanced was like the movement of a steel mountain where there was no sign of any cleavage for the entry of any human being. No sooner did they come and exchange a few blows than the regiment (of Aḥmad Beg) took to flight. But as the regiment of Aḥmad

* Prince Shāhjahān is always addressed by the author of this book as His Majesty حضرت شاهنشاهی and آنحضرت To avoid confusion with Jahāngīr, I have translated it as His Royal Highness.

Beg was on horseback and the other army was on foot, they did not go in pursuit of them and they remained standing there. The regiment of Aḥmad Beg Khān which came with such violence, gradually became scattered like the constellation of the Bear and disappeared. After retreating to some distance he (Aḥmad Beg) passed the day in that place. Then considering that it would be difficult for him to show his disgraceful face before Ibrāhīm Khān and other imperial officers, he marched back during the night against Dariyā Khān and attacked him in the morning. During this engagement, almost all the horses and followers of Dariyā Khān had joined him. At this second defeat, Mīrzā Aḥmad Beg was pursued by the Afghāns of Dariyā Khān and many of his men were sent to the house of annihilation. On this occasion Aḥmad Beg Khān, utterly routed, returned to his uncle with great disgrace. Ibrāhīm Khān censured him very severely. The effect of such censure for a well-bred man was more deadly than the fatal wound of a shining sword. Then he (Ibrāhīm Khān) personally proceeded with the whole of his army. (761)

**Second army of Shāhjahān cross over the Ganges.** When the news of the two victories of Dariyā Khān and the defeat of Aḥmad Beg Khān reached the august and fortunate prince, His Royal Highness sent Rāja Bhim and then Sipah-Sālār 'Abdu'llah Khān, to join Dariyā Khān and the first army. Then Ibrāhīm Khān sent Mīr Shams with a fleet of three hundred swift war-boats and also a large number *Jaliya* boats of the Firingis under the command of Manmil in Mīr Sham's company, with instructions to offer such opposition that 'Abdu'llah Khān and Rāja Bhim might not cross the river. When the whole imperial army was proceeding to that side, the Khān Fatḥ-jang, being the master of the fleet of the province of Bengal, should have personally gone there at that time and do what he could. But as the True Lord desired that the sovereignty of the land and the age should be conferred upon that chosen one of Him, what could the wish of a descendant of the prophet (*nabī-zāda*) do ? In short, as from the very beginning Mīr Shams, along with Manmil and other

Firingis, was seeking to be linked to the threshold of the Court of the Prince, the asylum of the world, he (Mīr Shams) acted very indifferently and came back after having a short skirmish with some people who wanted to cross the river and did not execute the real work. By that time 'Abdu'llah Khān and Rāja Bhim had crossed the river and joined Dariyā Khān and the first army. They then proceeded forward. (762)

**Death of Ibrāhīm Khān.** In short, they advanced from either side throughout the whole night; and one *pahar* after daybreak, a battle took place in the vicinity of the villages of Maldah and Akbarpūr. A desultory opposition was offered but it was of no use. Although Aḥmad Beg Khān had a regiment with him, the soldiers lost heart and acted like dumb creatures. Besides this, the army which was with Ibrāhīm Khān Fatḥ-jang consisted of inexperienced men who had never seen any battle. His experienced soldiers were sent to the fort of the Sepulchre, to the fleet of Mīr Shams and to the different Thānas with his Bakhshī Mīrzā Bāqī and others. He was offering opposition singly, with the object of attaining glory and fulfilling the imperial obligations. None of his companions was prepared to die. They caused the death of the faithful and brave Ibrāhīm Khān. He got killed in an affray with an Afghān who did not know that he was the Sardār, and he thus attained martyrdom. (763)

**Occupation of the fort of the Sepulchre.** Now I shall give a short account of the affairs of the fort of the Sepulchre. When in compliance with the orders, the Sipah-Sālār 'Abdu'llah Khān and Rāja Bhim proceeded to the aid of Dariyā Khān and others of the first army, and Ibrāhīm Khān Fatḥ-jang was killed, royal orders were issued to Wazīr Khān to proceed to the trench of Dārāb Khān and to urge upon the soldiers of the trenches to attack the fort. Khidmat Parast Khān *alias* Riẓā Bahādur Chela who had the honour of being a foster-son, was ordered to proceed to the place where the mining operations (*naqbahā*) were being carried on, with instructions to set fire to all the three mines at the same time. Wazīr Khān came to the trench of Dārāb Khān and urged the aforesaid Khān (to attack the fort). Dārab Khān, replied, —"This is an affair of capturing a fort; it is not a battle in the open field." Inspite of this, Wazīr Khān's men went to all the trenches and ordered the soldiers to attack the fort. The devoted soldiers turned their faces towards the field of battle with great sincerity and offered a bold fight from all sides. Khidmat Parast Khān ordered them to set fire to all the three mines at once. Fire of death began to rain from above the fort. The dead began to lay in heaps upon one another and the market of the angel of death became very brisk, and the remembrance of God attained its prominence. The brave fighters (*jawānān*) with foams on their lips, and intoxicated with bravery considered dying together as a great festival, and made their efforts to enter into the fort. The garrison within offered their resistance in defence of the fort. When the fire of the wicks reached two of the mines simultaneously, two towers and walls of the centre were blown up from the ground to the summit of the pleiades and reached the floor of the eighth sky. The valiant heroes (*bahādurān*) of the field of battle without waiting for the disappearance of the smoke from the surroundings of the fort entered the gate of the fort. 'Ābid Khān Dīwān, Riẓā Bahādur, Shīr Khwāja, Rāo Manrūp, Rāja Sārdūl, Saiyid Muẓaffar, Mīrzā Jalāl and his brother, many other officers, high and low, and Khwāja La'l, a eunuch of the royal household, who arrived at this time from the August Presence in order to make enquiries about the fort, entered it along with the loyal officers (of the prince). More than three or four hundred men entered the fort of the Sepulchre from the side which had been breached. Mīrzā Yūsuf, however, commanded very remarkably. Jalā'ir Khān, Mīrzā Isfandiyār and Mīrzā Nūru'llah took a very firm stand. They offered a brave resistance and considered the Royal (Shāhjahan's) force to be their enemy, and they fought to their best abilities in this struggle at the fort and became triumphant. Thus 'Ābid Khān and many others drank the cup of martyrdom. That Khwāja also became a traveller to the Kingdom of Heaven. Khidmat Parast Khān and some others saved themselves by jumping down from the towers and walls of the fort. Saiyid Mūẓaffar and many others were taken prisoners. When one *pahar* of the day still remained Jalā'ir Khān completed a mud wall with the labour of Bengalee boatmen on the side which had been breached. By the time of sunset, however, news came that Ibrāhīm Khān Fatḥ-jang had attained martyrdom, the imperial land-force had suffered a defeat and the Royal army (Shāhjahān's army) had plundered the camp of Ibrāhīm Khān Fatḥ-jang, and that. Mīr Shams along with Masnad-i-'Alā Ma'ṣūm Khān, son of Mūsā Khān bin 'Īsā Khān Masnad-i-'Alā, all the Zamīndars, and Manmil and other Firingis were returning to Jahāngīrnagar with the entire fleet. Then a great confusion arose in the fort of the Sepulchre. Every body, who had either a war-boat or any other boat at the foot of the fort, embarked on it and proceeded to Jahāngīrnagar. Those who had no boat had either to court disgrace by falling under the feet of one another or by being imprisoned in the hands of the Royal soldiers (i.e. soldiers of Shāhjahān). When the news spread that the inmates of the fort were voluntarily evacuating the fort, an attack was led from the trenches from all sides and the brave and experienced fighters of the prince of the world and its people entered the fort and played the trumpet of victory and the clarion of the tidings of a happy conquest. 'Abdu'llah Khān sent the news of his victory and the death of Ibrāhīm Khān Fatḥ-jang. The Royal trumpet of victory was (again) sounded. Mīrzā Yūsuf, Jalā'ir Khān and all the officers, of the fort of the Sepulchre, high and low, joined Mīr Shams and others and went to Jahāngīrnagar with the swiftest possible speed. Mīrzā Aḥmad Beg Khān and other imperial officers of Jahāngīrnagar returned to that place by the land route. Begum, the wife of the late Ibrāhīm Khān and Khwāja Idrāk engaged themselves in arranging boats for starting from Jahāngīrnagar, with their belongings loaded on boats, by the Brahmaputtra towards Patna till they could receive aid from Patna and particularly from the imperial Court. (764)

**'Kheda' operation in Khuntaghāt.** Now I shall give a short account of the territory of Kūch. When Shitāb Khān sent Shaykh Amānu'llah to Khuntaghāt for the purpose of arranging a second *Kheda* or *Qamargāh* for seizing elephants, he went there and arranged for a *Kheda* operation. Four big elephants along with a female fell within the enclosure. Inspite of the fact that the elephants had entered the enclosure of the *Markadah* (a kind of enclosure for catching elephant) from which they could never expect to get out and free themselves from their bondage, one of these which was the strongest, threw down the female elephant into the ditch and using her as a bridge, three elephants went out by sheer force. The fourth elephant, which was bigger than the one lying low on the ground, was detained. After thirteen days it was caught in a trap and was brought from that place to Shitāb Khān. The news of the martyrdom of Ibrāhīm Khān Fatḥ-jang having spread in all the Thānas, a great confusion ensued. (765)

The third volume of the Bahāristān is thus brought to its close.

# BOOK IV

(Begins with an ornamental preface in praise of God, the Prophet and Emperor Shāhjahān, extending over a page and a half. It contains a prayer for the prosperity of his empire and rule and is named as "*Wāqi'āt-i-Jahān Shāhī*" or Chronicles of Shāhjahān. This preface contains no historical matter, and is left out in translating).

# CHAPTER I

*The victorious march of the august prince Shāhjahān from Akbarnagar* alias *Rājmaḥal to Jahāngīrnagar* alias *Dhāka.*

**Burial of Ibrāhīm Khān.** The sum and substance of this happy event is this:—It has been mentioned at the end of the third volume called Ibrāhīm Nāma, that Ibrāhīm Khān Fatḥ-jang had attained martyrdom, and Sipah-Sālār 'Abdu'llah Khān Fīruz-jang had obtained a decisive victory which may be called one of the greatest of military triumphs. The report of this victory was sent to the prince of the world and its people, and the head of Ibrāhīm Khān was brought to be honoured with the honour of kissing the ground. The illustrious officers came one after another in accordance with their ranks and obtained the eternal honour of kissing the threshold. Though the late Khān was disobedient and disloyal, His Royal Highness, through his own sense of recognition of merit in others and of Ibrāhīm Khān's faithfulness (to his master), ordered the dead-body of Ibrāhīm Khān to be brought with honour from the field of battle instead of hanging his head at the gate of the fort of Akbarnagar. His body and the head were buried together in the fort by the side of the sepulchre of his son according to the desire expressed by him. (766)

**Shāhjahān demands the surrender of Patna.** The figure of Sipah-Sālār 'Abdu'llah Khān, riding on a lion with a naked sword in his right hand and the severed head of Ibrāhīm Khān in the left, was ordered to be painted on a standard. According to this command, the expert painters painted the aforesaid figure on two standards with agility and alertness, and produced them before His Royal Highness. One standard was given to one of the old and devoted Aḥadīs with orders to proceed to Patna with this flag fixed on his reins and to carry a peremptory Farmān to Mukhliṣ Khān, brother of Fidā-i-Khān. The Farmān ran :—" Surrender the fort of Patna to our officers if you desire your own welfare, or, like Ibrāhīm Khān, you will have only yourself to thank for your own punishment." Rāja Bhim was appointed to be the Chief officer (Sardār) of Akbarnagar. Khwāja Sa'ādat and many others were given Jāgīrs up to Mungyr in lieu of their salaries and they were sent in advance. Ṣipah Sālār 'Abdu'llah Khān was honoured with the Manṣab of 7,000 horse, of the rate of two horses and three horses (*dū-aspa, sīhaspa*).[1] He was also presented with royal robes of honour along with jewelled sword and sword-belt, and a horse with jewelled saddle and reins. Dariyā Khān Rohilla was honoured with the Manṣab of 5,000 with 5,000 horse and the title of Shīr Khān Fatḥ-jang. He was also presented with a royal robe of honour and an elephant named Jatājūt. His son Bahādur Khān was raised to the Manṣab of 4,000 with 3,000 horse, and was presented with a horse and a robe of honour. Bābū Khān Barīj was honoured with the title of Dilāwar Khān and the Manṣab of *sih-hazārī* (and) 2,500 horse. Of the rest of the officers who took part in the battle with the Sipah Sālār, some were honoured with the Manṣab of 200 some with 150 and the others with 120. (767)

**Shāhjahān summons Shitāb Khān.** After leaving this place the first halt was made at the village of Maldah. Mīrzā Mulkī[2] was ordered thus :—" Draft a peremptory Farmān to Shitāb Khān, one of the special servants of our Court, who is staying at the Ṣūbah of Kūch and who was brought up from childhood under our feet, and bring that draft to us." Mīrzā Mulkī prepared a simple draft according to his own intelligence and brought it to the alchemic notice (*kimiya-āṣar*) of His Royal Highness. It was not approved, and a letter was written in his own elegant style (may dear lives be sacrificed to it ;). A Mercury-like Secretary copied the letter, and brought it to his presence, closed and sealed with the special seal of the lion. The contents of the letter were :— " As that peerlessly faithful one is staying in that region, so our august mind is quite sure of the peaceful condition of that place. The day this command reaches him, he should keep in that place whomsoever he considers safe and the rest should be sent to the Court with Bahrām Barlās, the Chief officer of that place. He should wait till the arrival of a man to take charge of the Ṣūbardārship of that place, and after that he should come to kiss the threshold. Up to that time, the administration of that region will remain in his hands and our favours in respect of him will increase from day to day. We have sent a special robe of honour in order to distinguish him, so that, being honoured over all, he may be enthusiastic in the discharge of his duties." Other Farmāns were sent respectively to Mīrzā Bahrām Barlās, Rāja Lakshmī Narāyan and Rāja Satrajit to the following effect:—" You should not step beyond the orders and advice of Shitāb Khān, who is one of the special devotees of our Royal Court. Be up and doing in your work. The satisfaction of that unique one of the assembly of the Court should be considered as your perennial stock. His praises and accusations should be considered as leading to the most weighty consequences." The aforesaid Farmāns along with the robe of honour which was meant for Shitāb Khān, were sent with one of the servants of Ibrāhīm Khān who at this time entered as an Aḥadī of the prince. He agreed to proceed alone to Kūch. Accordingly, he was included in the circle of the Aḥadīs, was raised to the Manṣab of 250 horse, and the title of Yakka Bahādur was conferred upon him. Then he was granted leave to proceed, and he was given one of the flags on which the figure of Sipāh-Sālār 'Abdu'llah Khān Fīrūz-jang was painted. (768)

**Strained relations between Shitāb Khān and Mīrzā Bahrām.** Now I shall give a short account of the state of affairs of the people of the Ṣūbah of Kūch. When the news of the arrival of the prince of the people reached Kūch, Shitāb Khān, who by way of courtesy used to pay courteous visits to Mīrzā Bahrām, kept himself off and remained in his own house. Therefore, Mīrzā Bahrām began to talk thus about the decreases in the frequency of the visit of the Khān,—" What is the reason of this decrease in the frequency of his visits ?," and made his talk reach the Khān's ears. Thereupon, Shitāb Khān, after making satisfactory arrangements in the communication of his Thānas, came to Hājo to the house of Mīrzā Bahrām and stayed on for ten days. At the prolonged stay of the Khān, the Mīrzā again became suspicious and through his far-sighted caution, he forwarded this message to him :—" I do not understand the object of your coming to Hājo and your stay here." The Khān replied,—" When, apprehensive of these suspicions, I withdrew myself from your company and kept within my doors, you began to complain. Now when I have come and am staying by your side with a few men with the object of putting a stop to the accusation of the enemies, they are creating this friction." When they were busy in this dispute, the news of the death of Ibrāhīm Khān Fatḥ-jang got publicity in the city of Hājo. Mīrzā Bahrām sent messengers to Shitāb Khān, the writer of this book, inviting him to come to his house. This humble self sent this message in reply,—" When you entertain so much suspicion about me, I have also become very highly suspicious of you. But if Rāja Lakshmī Narāyan, Rāja Satrajit and Rāja Madhūsudan from among the imperial servants of this frontier, and Rāja Raghūnāth and Āqā Taqī who have come to investigate into our quarrel, come and swear by the Lord of lords that nothing untoward will happen, then I may go to you ; otherwise, what necessity is there to go to you and to court an evil name ? " Mīrzā Bahrām, with many entreaties, sent the aforesaid comrades to this most insignificant Shitāb Khān. They pacified his heart with oaths and then he went with them to Mīrzā Bahrām. The aforesaid Mīrzā was sitting armed with his regiment waiting for the arrival of the comrades. This humble Shitāb Khān also, through far-sighted caution, went with his own followers. These comrades too, who took their oaths, came with their own followers, so that no untoward action might take place. Rāja Lakshmī Narāyan, in particular, with whom this humble self had sworn into a brotherly relationship, came armed and equipped with his men. Mīrzā Bahrām, who had evil designs in his mind, got alarmed, and seeing his death to be apparent and clear, he withdrew from his designs. He began to talk and ended his discourse with these words,—" The holy Qur'ān should be placed before us in order to prove our purity of mind and sincere friendship." Both parties agreed to this. When the Qur'an was brought to the assembly, and respect was shown to it, first of all Mīrzā Bahrām took the oath thus :—" Wherein the well-being of Shitāb Khān is concerned, I will consider his good to be my good and his evil to be my evil." Then it was the turn of the humble Shitāb Khān to take the oath. This humblest of creatures, while taking the oath, said,—" I will be a partner in the good and evil of Mīrzā Bahrām subject to loyalty to the master." At this, Mīrzā Mahandī, a young officer of Ibrāhīm Khān, who was staying with Mīrzā Bahrām began to say,—" Whom do you call your master ?" Shitāb Khān, the writer of this book, said in reply,—" Whom do the servants consider their master ?" Then he got excited, became harsh and said,—" In this way you spoil your affairs at the words of foolish men." On this occasion Rāja Satrajit pacified both sides and wanted to bring about a reconciliation. After this, all dispersed to their homes and Mīrzā Bahrām remained in his own. (769)

**Kāmrūp officers receive Shāhjahān's Farmāns.** After sometime, news came from the Shiqdār of Bagrībārī, the Jāgīr of this humble Shitāb Khān, that a manṣabdār named Yakka Bahādur, who was sent to this region by the prince of the world and the people, Prince Shāhjahān from Maldah after the death of Ibrāhīm Khān Fatḥ-jang, had arrived at that place. He was waiting to go to Hājo in the way, he (Shitāb Khān) directed. The humble Shitāb Khān sent immediately five boats as swift as the wind which could race even with the east wind, with orders to bring the aforesaid Yakka Bahādur to Hājo without any delay. After five days the Bahādur reached Hājo. This humble self ordered velvet canopies to be erected on the bank of the river which flows by the foot of the fort of Hājo. Yakka Bahādur was asked to wait there with the royal Farmāns and souvenirs so that the Khāns might come and make their obeisance. In short, it was arranged in that way. This humble self sent message to Mīrzā Bahrām and to all the imperial officers and he himself went on a horse to receive the Royal Farmāns with respect and honour as previously arranged. At the aforesaid place where Yakka Bahādur was sitting under the *shāmiyānas* (canopies) he and all others, high and low, dismounted from their horses and elephants and began to observe the rites of obeisance from a distance of one arrow-shot. Reaching near Yakka Bahādur, Shitāb Khān, the author of this book, made three obeisances and prostrations of gratitude (*taslim-wa-sijda*) and then he placed the Farmāns respectfully with his two hands over his head and again performed the rites of obeisance and prostrations of gratitude, and put on the robe of honour. After offering royal salute for the third time, he took the Farmān for Mīrzā Bahrām and thrust it on the head of the aforesaid Mīrzā and he was made to perform his obeisance with his face turned towards Jahāngīrnagar. Then Rāja Lakshmī Narāyan and after him Rāja Satrajit were made to observe the rites of obeisance. After this he (Shitāb Khān) had a friendly interview with the messenger of the Court of the asylum of the world and then he returned to his abode. (770)

**Plight of Mīrzā Bahrām.** The following message was sent to Bahrām Mīrzā (by Shitāb Khān),—" Although your properties along with those of Ibrāhīm Khān have been ordered to be confiscated to the State, my sincere heart does not desire to bring any injury upon you in view of our oaths. You will do well to leave your elephants in the herd and yourself should proceed to His Royal Highness in order to try your luck, and see what orders are given about you. I shall spare no pains in rendering to you every possible help that lies in my power by writing letters of intercession and endeavouring for your welfare." At this time five hundred horsemen of Ibrāhīm Khān, who were with Mīrzā Bahrām as auxiliaries, surrounded his house demanding their salaries. They became violent and did not allow him to move out. This humble self (Shitāb Khān), out of his good nature and in consideration of

Ibrāhīm Khān's benevolent treatment of all the officers of Jahāngīr, sent his Bakhshī Badrīdās with one thousand cavalry and five thousand infantry to the *chawkī* of the mansion of Mīrzā Bahrām, with this message to those people:—" This behaviour of yours will not only throw your demands to the winds of destruction but will make you lose your jobs in future and in the meantime it may also bring death and destruction upon you. If you come away from the environs of the mansion of Mīrzā Bahrām at my command and do not surround him again, it is well and good. I will not only retain you in the service of the Emperor but will also arrange for the payments of your salaries from the imperial treasury for the period of two months that you served under the late Ibrāhīm Khān." Those people turned to the right path and came away. Thus Mīrzā Bahrām was saved. (771)

**Āqā Taqī appointed Dīwān of Kāmrūp.** When the administration of new affairs and the transaction of business could not be accomplished without an imperial Dīwān and Bakhshī, it was considered expedient to appoint Āqā Taqī,[3] an experienced officer of Ibrāhīm Khān Fatḥ-jang, who came to investigate into the quarrel between Mīr Ṣafī and Shitāb Khān, and he was honoured with the office of the Dīwān, Bakhshī and Wāqi-'navīs of the Ṣūbah of Kūch, and recommended for the Manṣab of 400 with 100 horse, and a representation was sent (to the prince). (772)

**Shāhjahān visits the shrine of Nūr Quṭb.** Now I shall pull the reins of the bay-horse of my pen and make it trot again to the royal road of my object. At the second stage, the prince, the protector of the people, encamped at the bridge of Sarā-i-Pathārī.[1] But as Pāndūa was on the way, His Royal Highness went to the shrine of His Holiness Shaykh Nūr Quṭb 'Ālam, and after performing the necessary rites of pilgrimage, he recited a *Fātiḥa* (benedictory prayer) and then proceeded forward. Four thousand rupees were given as offering to the *Khādims* (the servants in charge of the tomb) of that sublime monastery. On the third day the august camp was pitched at Dihīkūt and on the fourth day, halt was made at Ghoraghāt. I'timād Khān *alias* Khwāja Idrāk was sent in advance to condole with the Begum, the wife of Ibrāhīm Khān, and to pacify Aḥmad Beg Khān, Mīrzā Yūsuf, Jalā'ir Khān, Mīrzā Isfandiyār, Mīrzā Nūru'llah, and all the officers of Jahāngīrnagar. (773)

**Shāhjahān issues Farmāns to Kāmrūp officers.** On his way to Ghoraghāt, the representation of the humble Shitāb Khān, which was sent from Kūch with one of his old servants named Bahbūd, was received by the victorious prince at a place near Budhī-Budha in the parganā of Kalābārī. While he (the prince) was riding with fortune and prosperity on the howdah of an elephant, as a protector of (even) atoms, he himself read the representation and proceeded onward enquiring from that servant about the condition of the humble Shitāb Khān. As soon as he reached his destination, auspicious Farmān was issued in reply to the representation along with six other Farmāns to the following men about whom the humble Shitāb Khān had prayed for the issue of Farmāns for their consolation. These were Rāja Lakshmī Narāyan, Shaykh Shāh Muḥammad, Rāja Satrajit, Rāja Madhūsudan, Rāja Raghūnāth and Āqā Taqī. Āqā Taqī, who had now become an officer of the Court, was recommended for a Manṣab of 400 with 100 horse ; and on the dismissal of Mīrzā Bahrām, Shitāb Khān had assigned his (Bahrām's) Jāgīr to him and had prayed for the issue of an encouraging Farmān to the following effect:—" At the request and recommendation of Shitāb Khān, his Manṣab and Jāgīr are confirmed and we distinguish him with the post of the Dīwān, Bakhshī and Wāqī-'navīs of the Ṣūbah of Kūch." Accordingly, the aforesaid Farmān with the above contents was issued and it was sent to him within the night with the servant of the humble Shitāb Khān. (774)

**Shāhjahān arrives at Jahāngīrnagar.** Next morning the Royal camp was pitched at an intervening place. On the sixth day after departure from Akbarnagar *alias* Rājmaḥal, the Royal camp was pitched at Yūsuf Shāhī *alias* Shāhzādapūr. From there, on the fourth day, i.e., nine days after departure from Akbarnagar he (the prince) arrived in safety and happiness at Jahāngīrnagar. As the eunuch (*khwāja-sarā*) I'timād Khān had arrived there ahead of him and pacified all the officers, high and low, the Khāns went out to receive him to a distance of one to two *kos* one after the other in accordance with their rank, and obtained eternal distinction. Every one of them was honoured with the presents of robe of honour, horse, shawl and other things according to his rank. Begum, the wife of the late Ibrāhīm Khān, with her whole family, became honoured by kissing the ground. The dust of the arrival of that valiant champion of the field of bravery and manliness, the light of the whole of Hindustān, was made the collyrium of her eyes, and she extended her hospitality (to the prince). His Royal Highness stayed at the delightful residence of Ibrāhīm Khān in the fort of Jahāngīrnagar *alias* Dhāka for a period of seven days, and after making satisfactory arrangements (*band-u-bast*) for all the Thānas of Bengal and Kūch, he proceeded for the conquest of Patna.[5] (775)

**Official changes in Bengal.** Dārāb Khān with whom the prince was displeased for the opposition offered by his father Khān Khānān 'Abdu'r Raḥīm, was now pardoned (by the prince) because he (Dārāb) had allied himself with the prince and also because it was the nature of the prince to recognise merit in others and help them readily. He was raised to the Manṣab of 6,000 with 5,000 horse and was presented with a robe of honour, a horse and a bejewelled sword and sword-belt. The Ṣūbahdārship of Bhātī was given to him. A son of Dārāb Khān named Ārām Bakhsh was raised to the Manṣab of 1,000 horse, and a son of Shāh Nawāz Khān named Shakarshikan was also given the Manṣab of 1,000 with 1,000 horse and were taken in the Royal retinue.[6] One son and a nephew (brother's son) of Dārāb Khān were raised to similar Manṣab and were left with Dārāb Khān. Mīrzā Mulkī was raised to the Manṣab of 500 and 200 horse and was appointed to the office of the Dīwān.* Mīrzā Hidāyatu'llah, son of Khwāja Waisi was appointed to the office of the Bakhshī and Wāqi-

'navīs of Jahāngīrnagar and was promoted to the Manṣab of 400, with 150 horse. Malik Husayn, nephew (sister's son) of Ihtimām Khān was retained in the office of the Treasurer-general of Bengal (*Khazānchīgīrī-i-Kull-i-Bangāla*). A group of officers of the august stirrup was appointed to help Dārāb Khān. 'Ali Khān Niyāzī was appointed to be the Sardār of the Ṣūbah of Jessore, and he was honoured with the Manṣab of 2,000 and 1,500 horse. Mīrzā Ṣāliḥ was appointed to be the Sardār of Sylhat with his original Jahāngīrī Manṣab Mīrzā Bāqī, the Bakhshī of the late Ibrāhīm Khān, was given the Manṣab of 500 with 400 horse and was appointed to be the Thānadār of Bhalwa. 'Ādil Khān and Pahār Khān, the admirals of Ibrāhīm Khān, were retained in their former posts of admirals of Jahāngīrnagar *alias* Dhāka. 'Ādil Khān was left with Dārāb Khān, and Pahār Khān was taken with the victorious stirrup and was allowed to serve with Khidmat Parast Khān *alias* Riẓā. (776)

**Shāhjahān visits Qadam Rasūl.** Then he (the prince) with fortune and prosperity proceeded to Akbarnagar with the fleet. The Sipah-Sālār 'Abdu'llah Khān Fīrūz-jang and all the officers of the State were sent by land. The first halt was made at Khiẓrpūr on the bank of the river. A pilgrimage was made with many prayers at Rasūlpūr where the foot (print) of His Holiness the Chief of the Universe lay (enshrined). It (i.e,. the foot-print of the Prophet) was obtained by Ma'ṣūm Khān Kābulī from the merchants who brought it from Arabia on payment of a large sum of money and was placed at Rasūlpūr. For this reason the place was named Rasūlpūr and it is also called Qadam Rasūl (may the blessings and peace of God be upon him). One thousand *darbs* (half rupees) were paid to the *Khādims* (servants) of that holy monastery. (777)

**The Mag Rāja sends his loyal message.** Immediately after the arrival of His Royal Highness at Jahāngīrnagar, the Rāja of the Mags, who possessed ten thousand war-boats, fifteen hundred elephants and one million infantry, hearing the report of the prince's victorious arrival, sent his envoys to

His Royal Highness with rare gifts worth Rs. 100,000 as *pēsh-kash.* And with great humility he made a representation that he should be considered as a loyal vassal and he swore by God the Great that he would serve loyally whenever he would be summoned for any work. Therefore, His Royal Highness sent a valuable dress of honour along with many precious gifts to the Rāja of the Mags and a peremptory Farmān was issued confirming the sovereignty of his territory and asked him to be firm in his words and to attain eternal glory by helping the State officers at Jahāngīrnagar. In short, the envoys of the Rāja of the Mags were granted leave to depart. (778)

**Shāhjahān proceeds to Patna from Akbarnagar.** From there (Qadam Rasūl) he (the prince) proceeded onwards in a befitting manner and the second halt was made at a place opposite Bikrampūr. Wazir Khān[7] was left at Jahāngīrnagar for a period of seven days in order to prepare and to bring the rent roll of the whole of Bengal. On the third day the Royal encampment was made at Kalākūpa. The fourth halt was made on the river at Jatrapūr. From there they reached the confluence at 'Alā-i-pūr in four stages. But at this place many boats were sunk by a terrible storm; and the Royal boat was about to capsize but it was saved by the protection of the Divine protector who always gives His kind protection to that chosen one of Him. From there, Akbarnagar was reached in five stages. After staying there for three days, he proceeded to Patna with Her Highness Nawāb Mumtāz Maḥal, the Begum, and a few of the near ones of the heavenly pavilion. All the other ladies (*mahalha*), the store of jewels (*jawāhir-khāna*), the stores and State factories (*kārkhānjāt*) and the heavy baggage were left at Akbarnagar. At the time of the start for Patna Rs. 20,000 were sanctioned for building a *maḥal* (harem) at Akbarnagar. Muḥammad Ṣāliḥ was appointed to the office of the Bakhshī and Wāqi-'navīs of the Ṣūbah of Gawr. The office of the chief Inspector of Buildings (*Dārūghagī-wa-Mushrif-i-'Imarāt*) of Akbarnagar was also assigned to the aforesaid (Ṣāliḥ), because of his faithfulness. He was given peremptory instructions to complete the *maḥals* as soon as possible. On the day prior to his departure from that place, the elephant Miān Baṣīr was made to fight with the elephant Pahlawān Tātārī. These two mountain-bodied elephants fought with each other for more than one *pahar* and fought very well. Both of them stood the fight equally well till they were separated. But one tusk of Miān Baṣīr was broken. His Royal Highness was greatly mortified at this. Miān Baṣīr, Pahlawān Tātārī, Hindān Khān and other small and great private elephants, one hundred and twenty in number, were left at Akbarnagar. From that place he (the prince) proceeded forward and the Royal camp was pitched at Pantī. Wazīr Khān also, after settling the affairs of the whole of Bengal, obtained the honour of kissing the ground. (779)

**Mukhlis Khān evacuates Patna.** As soon as Mukhliṣ Khān[8] heard at Patna about the arrival of His Royal Highness, he, unable to resist, proceeded to Ilahābās (Allahabad) with the belongings of the State factories (*karkhānjāt*) of Sultan Parvīz as far as he could carry. Within a short time, he joined Mīrzā Rustam Khān at the fort of Allahabad. (780)

**Zāhid Khān sent to Kūch as its Sūbahdār.** Zāhid Beg Bukhārī was conferred the title of Zāhid Khān and was sent to assume the Ṣūbahdārship of Kūch. He was given the rank of 3,000 (*sih-hazārī*) with 3,000 horse, and the aforesaid Ṣūbah was assigned to him as a Jāgīr in lieu of his salary. A large number of imperial officers and many of the officers of the Ṣūbah of Bengal, who were appointed with Zāhid Khān, were ordered to depart (with him). (781)

**The officers at Hājo receive the Farmāns.** Now I shall give a short account of Shitāb Khān and the officers of the Ṣūbah of Kūch who were staying at Hājo. First of all, Bahbūd, the servant of Shitāb Khān, who had carried the representations to the august prince, returned with the Farmāns as mentioned before. Shitāb Khān, with the loyal officers, went to the bank of the river which was at a distance of one *kos* from the fort. Every one honoured himself by observing the necessary rites of obeisance. The Khāns, in order of precedence, placed their Farmāns on their heads, and performed their obeisance and prostrations of gratitude. From that place they returned to their respective homes and every one acted in accordance with the orders. Shitāb Khān sent his whole family with his sister's son to Jahāngīrnagar and gave him strict orders to reach (the destination) without delay. They delayed a great deal on their way and travelled a journey of ten days in twenty-five days. They reached Jahāngīrnagar at a time when His Royal Highness had already left a week ago. (782)

**Shitāb Khān proceeds to Jahāngīrnagar.** Now I shall give a short account of Shitāb Khān. On the third day after the arrival of the first Farmāns with his servant Bahbūd, the Mīr Bāḥr (admiral) of Shitāb Khān named Jamāl, who went to His Royal Highness to Jahāngīrnagar with a representation, returned with another peremptory Farmān which was issued at the time of his (the prince's) departure from Jahāngīrnagar. Shitāb Khān went to receive it and performed the necessary rites of obeisance. Before he heard the news of his transfer or of the despatch of Zāhid Khān he made satisfactory arrangements for the territory of Kūch with great zeal and loyalty. Saiyid Mufattiḥ, his sister's son, was appointed to be the Ṣūbahdār of Hājo. Rāja Lakshmī Narāyan and Shaykh Shāh Muḥammad, son of the late Shaykh Kamāl, along with the son of Sarḥad Khān *alias* Shaykh 'Abdu'l-Wāḥid, Rāja Satrajit, Rāja Madhūsudan, Mīrzā Ṣāliḥ Arghūn, Mīrzā Yūsuf Barlās and all the imperial officers were placed under the leadership of his Hindu officer Rāy Balabhadra Dās and Mūhammad Taqī, the Dīwān, Bakhshī and Wāqi-'navis of the territory of Kūch. A week before his departure, Khwāja Badridās, his personal Bakhshī, was appointed to be the chief officer of Jahāngīrābād *alias* Gilahnay, with a force of 600 cavalry and 500 matchlock-men. Shaykh Afẓal and other officers, high and low, of the Ṣūbah of Jahāngīrābād, were directed to obey the aforesaid (Badridās) and to consider the discharge of imperial affairs equivalent to the highest devotion to God. Accordingly, Badridās went to Gilahnay and stayed there. After this the humble Shitāb Khān took with him seventy selected elephants from his own stable as well as from the stable of Mīrzā Bahrām in order to present them to His Royal Highness, the Qībla of the world. One big elephant, two baby-elephants and one female elephant from among his own elephants and other gifts were sent in advance as *pēshkash* by land with his land-army consisting of more than one thousand cavalry and two thousand infantry. He (Shitāb Khān) started for Jahāngīrnagar by boat at an auspicious hour. A robe of honour, a horse and an elephant were given to Saiyid Mufattiḥ, and the loyal officers were greatly encouraged and asked to remain in his (Mufattiḥ's) company. On the third day he reached Rangāmatī. Here he heard that Shaykh Afzal was withdrawing his neck from the yoke of obedience and was refusing to remain with Badridās. He stayed there for a day, brought the aforesaid Shaykh to the right path, and after giving some advice to Badridās he proceeded on his way. On the fourth stage, he reached Patladah. There he came to know that the Qībla of the people of the world had started from Jahāngīrnagar *alias* Dhāka for Akbarnagar. Therefore, he proceeded more swiftly and reached Jahāngīrnagar after four days. (783)

**Shitāb Khān starts from Jahāngīrnagar.** Mīrzā Mulki, the Dīwān, Mīrzā Hidāyat Beg, the Bakhshī and Wāqi-'navīs and Malik Ḥusayn, the Treasurer-general of Bengal, came to see Shitāb Khān and they had a friendly interview. At the time of the departure of Shitāb Khān, he gave two *Tāngan* horses of beautiful black and white colour and of high breed to the Dīwān as well as to the Bakhshī along with five seers of aloe-woods. One *Tāngan* and two seers of aloe-woods were given to Mīrzā Malik Ḥusayn. Next morning he paid friendly visits to their homes beginning early in the morning from the house of Mīrzā Mulkī and ending in the evening with the house of Hidāyat Beg. Next day he went to see Dārāb Khān with his friends as previously arranged. Mīrzā Mulkī and Mīrzā Hidāyat Beg also went with him. Dārāb Khān came out of the doors of his Dīwān-Khāna (hall of audience) and embraced Shitāb Khān. They sat outside for a while and then Dārāb Khān went in with Shitāb Khān, the Dīwān and the Bakhshī. After some exchange of ideas, they took leave of one another. Dārāb Khān gave him some oral messages to be delivered to His Royal Highness. Then they bade good-bye to one another and Shitāb Khān returned to his residence and arranged for his departure. At the time of his departure he sent for the *Mahājans* (money-lenders) with whom he had dealings and took Rs. 30,000 from them, and carried with him many rare gifts as *pēshkash* (to the prince). He started, leaving his family at Jahāngīrnagar. (784)

**Shitāb Khān learns of the appointment of Zāhid Khān.** At the ninth stage he reached a village in Chilajūwār in the parganā of (Sūnā ?)-bāzū. At this stage the advance-boats of Zāhid Khān came up and he was informed that Zāhid Khān had been appointed to the Ṣūbahdārship of Kūch and he was proceeding to Kūch by land *via* Ghoraghāt and his men were sent by boat. This news was unpleasant to the superficial observers and particularly to the men of sense and intelligence. Some of the Zamīndārs and *pāiks* of Kūch, who were in the company of Shitāb Khān, and who had received many favours from Shitāb Khān, said,—" What has happened that Kūch has been given to another man ? As long as we live we will not leave your happy company. If you do not believe us, order at this very moment to put all the Sardārs in chains. We shall not leave you till you yourself remove the shackles from our feet and drive us off from your service. We apprehended that Zāhid Khān would put our families to trouble when he found that we accompanied Shitāb Khān even after the receipt of the report of his arrival. Inspite of this our mind was at rest. Because, (we expected that) he (Zāhid Khān) would also recognise that when these people were serving that Chief of the Ṣūbah so faithfully, they would also be faithful in his service. If he (now) does not think like this, we shall also not care for him and we shall proceed with you to the prince and explain our condition and we (hope) you will get for us a letter of pardon issued by His Royal Highness to Zāhid Khān." At this, Shitāb Khān, the author of this pleasant history, who is entitled Ghaybī as already mentioned, became pacified, as everything that these people said had the lustre of truth. He gave robes of honour to all the Sardārs and retained them in his service with great encouragements. Then he proceeded onwards. (785)

**Shitāb Khān Visits the shrine of Saiyid Aḥmad.** At the sixth stage from that place, he arrived at Malatipūr, a village of Tanda, where the shrine of His Holiness Mir Saiyid Aḥmad-Al-Ḥusaynī is situated. There is no doubt whatsoever about his greatness and miraculous powers. From the time he adopted the life of a recluse he never moved from that place and he lived there till his death. For his own subsistence, he never thought of any other means except resignation to the will of God. If any of the inhabitants of that village planted any fruit tree or cultivated vegetables in his house, he would not allow him to stay there and would say,—"As you have no faith in reliance on God, go and stay in some other place." As he was endowed with Divine favours, he had a miraculous power which by the favour of God and by the blessings of his asceticism still survived in that place. If up to the time of the evening prayer even a hundred men would come to him, every one of them would be supplied with a dish of food. If any body had a horse with him, he would be supplied from his (saint's) house five seers of grain and a load of grass for the horse. The travellers were not allowed to cook for themselves. People of that region have a great faith in him. The writer of this Iqbāl Nāma-i-Ghaybī who is well-known as Shitāb Khān, and who is a faithful disciple of the chief of the Shaykhs, the unique among the saints, the cream of the chosen-ones of God, His Holiness Shaykh Farīd Shakarganj, paid his homage to Mīr Saiyid Niẓāmu'd-Dīn, spiritual successor (*Ṣāḥib-i-Sajjada*) of this place. Then he performed his pilgrimage at the shrine of His Holiness Mīr (Saiyid Aḥmad) and obtained everlasting happiness. It was settled that the annual feast (*'urs*) of His Holiness Mīr (Saiyid

Aḥmad) should be celebrated next morning and then they would start. (786)

**Zāhid Khān seizes the elephants of Shitāb Khān.** At this time a letter came from Khwāja Badridās, the Bakhshī of Shitāb Khān, which disquieted the mind of the Khān. The purport of the news was this:—"When I was sending the imperial elephants and the *pēshkash* by the land route and these had reached Jahāngīrābād *alias* Gilahnay, Shaykh Afẓal, owing to his brainlessness and the absence of the Mīrzā, thought of seizing the elephants. Knowing that the soldiers who accompanied the elephants had fallen behind and thinking that I was staying with a small force, he fell upon me. But as the Royal fortune was powerful, the soldiers, who had fallen behind came up at that moment. While he (Afẓal) was attempting to kill me and to execute his plan by setting fire to my house, they saved me from his clutches and corrected the aforesaid Shaykh by chastising him. Therefore, representations will reach you every moment one after another, till the elephants reach that place." These last words gave some relief to Shitāb Khān. He decided to send a trustworthy officer to bring the elephants. But next morning, another letter came from Shaykh Khwāja Aḥmad, the commander of the land-army, with the following communication:—"When we reached Bakī (one letter is blurred in the Ms.) Darbār Khān, son of Zāhid Khān arrived at that place and seized by force four female elephants which were meant for the special use of His Royal Highness and carried them back to Kūch. When from that place we came to Ghoraghāt and met Zāhid Khān, the aforesaid (Khān) seized all the elephants and took them by force back to Kūch." Therefore, Shitāb Khān became very much enraged and sent one of his devoted officers Nīk Muḥammad Beg with a few lines to Zāhid Khān,—"If you have received any order to the effect that elephants sent by Shitāb Khān to the Royal Court should be taken back by Zāhid Khān for use in Kūch then send that order to me and take the elephants with you; otherwise, be true to the salt of the sovereign and send the elephants to the Court. Failing this, take it for granted that I am (personally) going to your place." Nīk Muḥammad Beg was thus instructed,—" If Zāhid Khān steps beyond the bounds of reason, act in such a way that your name may be immortalised in history as long as the world exists. Deal him such a stroke of the dagger in his stomach that it may become the talk of ages." In short, being in a whirpool of perplexity, Shitāb Khān did not move from his place till the receipt of reply from the Court (of Shāhjahān). A representation was sent to the Royal Court and he kept his eyes and ears opened. (787)

**Doings of Shāhjahān.** The representation, which was sent by Shitāb Khān after his arrival at Jahāngīrnagar from Kūch, reached the Royal presence, and a reply arrived (which brought in the following items of information). The world-conquering and justice-dispensing Emperor, (i.e. Shāhjahān) having traversed the stages and stations from Pāntī entered the delightful oity of Patna. The Sipāh-Sālār 'Abdu'llah Khān Fīrūz-jang was sent in advance to Jaunpūr[9] with the whole of the devoted Mughal officers. The illustrious Khān started for Jaunpūr at an auspicious moment and reached there in seven marches. He then sent a representation about the state of affairs of that region. Accordingly it was resolved to start for Jaunpūr after making satisfactory arrangements for the Ṣūbah of Bihar. Wazīr Khān was ordered to assign Hājīpūr and its vicinity along with Darbhanga as a Jāgīr to the Sipāh-Sālār in lieu of his salary. The whole of the Ṣūbah of Bihar was parcelled out among the devoted officers in lieu of their salaries and nothing was left for the Imperial Exchequer. Wazīr Khān acted in accordance with the orders. (788)

**Surrender of the fort of Rohtas.** A peremptory Farmān was issued to Saiyid Mubārak[10] at the fort of Rohtas,—" If aided by fortune, you honour yourself by kissing the ground, we shall distinguish you with high Manṣab and shall assign to you the whole of Karāmānikpūr,[11] your home land." For this reason, Saiyid Mubārak, helped by,his star, came to the Royal presence and obtained the honour of both the worlds by receiving Royal favours. His Royal Highness gave him a grand dress of honour, a jewelled sword-belt and a sword, and a special elephant. He was distinguished with the Manṣab of *Chahār-Hazārī*, with 4,000 horse, and was taken in the Royal retinue. The post of the *Qil'a-dār* (commander of the fort) of Rohtas was given to Saiyid Muẓaffar,[12] a devoted servant of the victorious stirrup; he was honoured with the Manṣab of 700 with 500 horse, and was granted leave to go to take charge of the fort. (789)

**Shāhjahān's displeasure on Shitāb Khān.** At this time the representation of Shitāb Khān reached His Royal Highness, and it produced certain resentment in his mind. Mu'taqid Khān was ordered thus:—"As both of you are friends, write to Shitāb Khān thus:—"Your (Shitāb Khān's) arrival at Akbarnagar was expected before the death of Ibrāhīm Khān. Instead, when we have come to Patna with pomp and power, you still send your representation saying that you have reached Jahāngīrnagar and are preparing to start for our presence. It is well and good. It has been settled that after the festival of illumination we shall proceed to Jaunpūr. If during this period you can reach this place to kiss the ground before our departure, it is well and good: otherwise we shall not accept your obeisance (*kūrnish*)." In short, this letter containing the Royal orders was received by Shitāb Khān on the night of the *Shab-i-Barāt* at Malatipūr where he was in a bewildered condition on account of his elephants. That humble self did not know what to do. He was in a perturbed condition due to the troubles about the elephants, and this communication confounded him. He prepared for death and did not know what to do. (790)

**Shitāb Khān joins the Prince.** Thus helpless at these uncertain state of things, he, at last, started for Patna on the 18th of Sha'bān and made a forced-march heedless of his own conditions. A journey which could not be covered with the swiftest speed within less than twenty to thirty days, was covered by him within eight days. Thus God, the Great, granted this faithful servant the honour of serving his Qibla and kissing the feet of the master of the world and its people at Patna. The time fixed for the departure to Jaunpūr was postponed to 27th (Sha'bān) on account of an illness of Her Highness Mumtāz Maḥal Begum. The Royal camp moved in the first *pahar* of the night of the 27th. Shitāb Khān the author of this Iqbāl-Nāma, the lowest of the house-born ones (*khāna-zādān*) and the meanest of the followers, after one and a half *pahar* of the aforesaid night, arrived at the *ghāt* of Patna. In the morning His Royal Highness halted on the way to say his morning prayers. When after finishing the prayers he was preparing to proceed, then Shitāb Khān made his obeisance with an offering of twelve *ashrafis* (gold-coins) and twelve rupees. He (Shāhjahān), being a nourisher of atoms, kindly allowed him (Shitāb Khān) to kiss the august feet, and granted honour to this pale face which had for a long time been deprived of this honour and dignity. The dust of the holy feet of His Royal Highness was applied as collyrium to his eyes. As Shitāb Khān had taken a vow that as soon as he would meet His Royal Highness, he would go round him (like pilgrims) nine times, so he began to go round him. His Royal Highness, through his kindness to the poor, ordered Shajā'at Khān thus :—" Stop him. He need not go round." Shajā'at Khān stopped him, but by that time he had already finished three circumambulations round his Qibla and Ka'ba and had obtained the felicity of both the worlds. Rāja Bhim represented thus :—" Long live your Royal Highness ! who is this man ? " The prince of the world and the people said with his pearl-scattering tongue,—" His name is Nathan. This is the devoted servant in Bengal about whom I told you." Then he (the prince) began to say,—" He grew up from childhood with us. He is one of our confidential and devoted servants." As he was saying these words, this humble self performed the rites of obeisance and prostrations of gratitude. The march was then resumed with safety and happiness ; and after proceeding for a short distance enquiring about his (Shitāb Khān's) conditions, he (the prince) ordered him to ride. He again performed his obeisance and prostrations and then rode on a horse. The first halting station of the land-route was reached five *gharīs* after morning and halt was made at that place. At this station, a representation came from the Sipah-Sālār 'Abdu'llah Khān that he was proceeding to Ilāhābās and that he had not received any news of Parvīz and Mahābat Khān and of the arrival of the officers of His Majesty (Jahāngīr). Therefore, march was resumed next morning by boats. By the land-route it was a distance of twelve *kos* and by river fourteen *kos*. The destination was reached one *pahar* before evening. The third halt was made at Munīr.[13] Although the march was resumed next morning, His Royal Highness drove for a pilgrimage to the shrine of His Holiness Shaykhu'l-Mashayekh Makhdūm Shaykh Sharfu'd-Dīn Yaḥiyā Munīrī, and the sublime royal feet were anointed with the dust of supplication. The *Fātiḥa* (benedictory prayer) was recited and a sum of one thousand *darbs* (half rupees) was given to Miān Shaykh Tāj in order to distribute them among the servants (*Khādimān*) of this holy monastery. (791)

**Shāhjahān reaches Baliyā.** Saiyid Muẓaffar was sent from this halting place to take charge of fort of Rohtas and he (the prince) proceeded forward by boat. Khān Dawrān *alias* Bayrām Beg was honoured with post of the Ṣūbahdār of Bihar and he was granted leave to proceed to Patna. He was raised to the Manṣab of *Panj-Hazārī*, 5,000 horse, and a robe of honour, a horse and a special elephant were given to him. His Royal Highness then started and reached his halting place towards the close of the day. The moon of the month of Ramaẓān being visible at this station, the fasting was begun. But it was so extremely hot that not a single day passed without the death of eight, or nine or ten men, four or five horses, one or two elephants and five to ten camels in every station. Men and beasts suffered great hardship and very few men could keep fast. Though Kings are not answerable for (non-observance of) prayers and fasting and are responsible only for their dispensation of justice, yet His Royal Highness through his love of God and his desire for Divine favours, kept his fast inspite of this torture of heat.

In fact he did not miss a single fast. In the sixth stage, he arrived at the parganā of Baliyā. (792)

**Rāja Narāyan Mal and his brothers honoured.** Rāja Narāyan Mal Ujjainia came with all his relations and brothers and obtained the felicity of both the worlds by kissing the Royal ground. He was given the Manṣab of *Panj-Hazārī*, 5,000 horse, and his brother Pratāp was raised to the Manṣab of *Sih-Hazārī* with 2,000 horse. The rest of his brothers were honoured with the Manṣab of *Du-Hazārī*, with 1,000 horse and every one of them received robes of honour and horses. (793)

**Mīrzā Bahrām sent from Hājo to Dhāka.** Now I shall give a short account of Saiyid Mufattiḥ, the nephew of Shitāb Khān and of his Hindu officer Rāy Balabhadra Dās and Āqā Taqī, the Dīwān, Bakhshī and Wāqi-'navīs of Kūch and what they did after the departure of Shitāb Khān. First of all Mīrzā Bahrām Khān was sent to Dārāb Khān with Mast 'Alī Beg a confidential officer of the Khān (Shitāb), and one month's salary of the five hundred horsemen of Ibrāhīm Khān was paid, as was arranged by the author known as Shitāb Khān. As there was no work in that region these soldiers were sent to Dārāb Khān. On every third day, Saiyid Mufattiḥ with all the imperial officers used to go out for pleasant excursion and hunting. The Thānas at different places were also in a peaceful condition. Therefore, Āqā Taqī used to send his reports giving the details of every day to the Royal Court along with the representations of Mufattiḥ. (794)

**Promotion of Shitāb Khān.** A groom, who came from Kūch, and who passed by Shaykh Khwāja Aḥmad, brought a letter from Shaykh Khwāja Aḥmad containing this news :— " Before Nīk Muḥammad Beg, could reach (his destination) Zāhid Khān seized two other female-elephants. The father and the son carried six elephants with them. We have arrived at Akbarnagar with the elephants and *pēshkash,* and we are soon reaching you with them." In short, the groom in great haste arrived on the day when the Royal camp was pitched in the parganā of Chausa (Chaunsa)[14] and delivered the news. This most insignificant Shitāb Khān submitted the letter to His Royal Highness and represented the state of affairs. It gave pleasure to the Royal mind. At this station, Shitāb Khān was honoured with a horse and a special robe of honour and he was promoted to the Manṣab of 2,500 (with) 1,500 horse. A Farmān of displeasure was issued to Zāhid Khān to the effect that as he and his son had taken away six elephants without permission, they must send back to Court the three female elephants so highly praised by Shitāb Khān. (795)

**Shāhjahān witnesses the swimming of elephants.** Next morning His Royal Highness with fortune and prosperity personally came to see the elephants crossing the river. At first orders were given to make the elephant Fatḥ-jang, the chief of the private elephants, swim, which the master and Qibla had the greatest desire to see. Accordingly, the servants of this prosperity increasing work-shop brought out the aforesaid elephant with the female-elephants and attempted (to make him swim) till mid-day; but it was of no use. The elephant refused to get into the river to swim. In short, His Highness the Qibla of the inhabitants of the world returned to his camp which was pitched on the other side of the river Ganges. He again came one and a half *pahar* before evening and personally tried for two or three *gharīs*. When all attempts to bring the elephant to deep water had in fact, proved futile, the humblest of the devoted servants, Shitāb Khān, advanced with his boat and represented thus to His Royal Highness,—"Long live your Royal Highness! Is the object to make the elephants cross or is it to tire yourself?" His Royal Highness replied,—"The object is to make the elephants cross." (One word blurred in the Ms. here.) This humble self said,—"Please give me another boat for my help along with the boat on which I am; Your Royal Highness will see in a moment how I make the elephant cross this terrible river." The master of the world and its inhabitants favoured him with a boat and getting the Royal boat moored to the bank of the river, he took his stand as a spectator. Shitāb Khān, the meanest of authors, asked the crowd, which had gathered round the elephant to make it cross, to disperse from that place. The elephant-driver was directed not to trouble the elephant and to let it stand at ease. Then a large quantity of sugar-canes was brought and placed before the elephant. After a short while, when the anger of the elephant cooled down and it began to eat the sugar-canes, the elephant-driver was ordered to bring the elephant into the river, and he was instructed that as soon as the elephant showed its inclination to come out of the water, it should be made to lie down just as is done at the time of bathing. The elephant-driver acted accordingly. After an hour it was taken to the pasture and was brought to a deep sheet of water and made to lie down again. In short it was thus pacified. When the elephant was immersed in water upto its eyes and before it could suspect that it would be forced to swim, two ropes were tied to the boats and the other ends were fastened with the halter on the elephant's neck. The boatmen were then ordered to row the boats. The ropes of the boats were very weak. As the elephant did not raise his feet from the bed of the river, the ropes snapped through its weight. Then it was thus represented (to the prince):—" If I am permitted, I will tie a thick rope to the collar of the elephant and make him cross the river." Permission was given accordingly. This humble self bound the animal again with this rope and made an attempt in the same way. When the feet of the elephant were detached from the river-bed, the boats were set in motion, though the elephant struggled against it. This humble self represented to His Royal Highness that he should himself follow the elephant with his special boat and frighten it with his special lance so that it might swim swiftly and cross the river safely. When the elephant reached the middle of the river, His Royal Highness shouted to Shitāb Khān to tie the waist of the elephant with ropes, so that it might not perish. He replied that it would be done according to the orders of the master. In short, by the time of sunset the elephant crossed the river Ganges in safety and reached the other side. This humble self represented :—"By the time Your Royal Highness break the fast at your camp, I shall take the elephant in safety to that part of the bank of the river where there is no silt and will inform you after having it tied in a dry place." The master of the world and its inhabitants went to his *Maḥal.* This humble self brought the elephant out of the water one *gharī* after evening and after keeping it at the village of Baliyā in the parganā of Maḥmūdābād, went to the gate of the *Maḥal* and sent news about the elephant. His Royal Highness, the Qibla and Ka'ba, through his fostering care for this house-born one, honoured him (Shitāb Khān) with permission to kiss the Royal feet. This humble self after performing the rites of salutations and the prostrations of gratitude took his meal in the company of some comrades. (796)

**Shitāb Khān transports 1010 elephants over the Ganges.** In the last *pahar* of the night the kettle-drum of march was sounded. This humble self was summoned to the door of the *Maḥal* and a Royal command was issued that Khidmat Parast Khān should remain there till candle-light with thirty boats and after transporting all the elephants he should follow the Royal camp. When Khidmat Parast Khān complained that the boats had already departed, His Royal Highness, was displeased and said,—"Remain with Shitāb Khān and transport the elephants over the river after securing boats from whichever place you can." Khidmat Parast Khān, being helpless, procured twenty eight *kūsa* and *dhūra* boats and began to transport the elephants in the company of this humble Shitāb Khān. After transporting one thousand and ten elephants, big and small, they started for the Royal camp and reached there after plying for the whole night at a time when march was being resumed. Eighty three elephants were left behind. But it was of no avail. The boat-men of the boats of this humble self and Khidmat Parast Khān, after transporting the elephants for the whole day and plying the boats for the whole night had become so tired that it became difficult to reach the Royal boat which had already started. With great difficulty, the boats of Khidmat Parast Khān and Shitāb Khān reached His Royal Highness at a time when he was going to take his food in the *Maḥalgīrī* boat (boat where the ladies stay). This insignificant Shitāb Khān wrote a representation about the transport of elephants and sent it into the *Maḥal.* The contents (of the representation) were:—"Long live His Royal Highness! As we had commands to transport as many of the elephants as practicable till evening and then to come to Your Royal Highness, we have come accordingly. Otherwise we could have transported the other eighty three elephants as well. If it is ordered now to go back, we may go to transport those elephants also." It was thus ordered:—"Kajast Khān should go with four *kūsas* to transport these elephants and you are to follow the Royal camp." Shitāb Khān then performed the rites of obeisance and prostrations of gratitude, and remained in attendance. (797)

**Siege of Allahabad.** In the fifth stage, the Royal camp arrived at the mouth of the river Gumtī.[15] A representation came from the Sipah-Sālār 'Abdu'llah Khān Fīrūz-jang:—"As soon as I reached Jhūsī I sent a force of five thousand horse, at the rate of two horse and three horse (*dū-aspa, sih-aspa*) under the command of Nāṣir Khān to the other side of the Ganges towards Aryal[16] to the territories of the Zamīndārs of Barhār[17] in order to bring the family of this devoted servant. As Mīrzā Rustam Khān Qandahārī is putting up a strong defence at the fort of Ilāhābās (Allahabad) and the devoted officers have crossed the river and raided up to Karā Mānikpūr, I am keeping the fort of Ilāhābās[18] under siege waiting for orders. The early arrival of your Royal Highness at Jaunpūr has become a necessity so that the shadow of the standard of Royal favours may fall upon the heads of the devoted servants." Accordingly, His Royal Highness proceeded from the *mohanā* or mouth of the river Gumtī and came to Jaunpūr, traversing a journey of ten days within a period of four days. (798)

## CHAPTER II.

*Arrival of His Royal Highness Prince Shāhjahān at the delightful city of Jaunpūr and his preparation for the conquest of the fort of Ilāhābās.*

**Shāhjahān's plans for the capture of Allahabad.** A short account of this amazing event is this :—The master and Qibla of the inhabitants of the world rode on an elephant named Fatḥ-i-Jahān and entered the city safely in an auspicious hour and alighted at the delightful residence in the fort of Jaunpūr.[1] Next day, Rāja Bhim was honoured with the present of a special elephant and he was ordered to cross the river Ganges opposite Aryal along with all the Rājputs and Zamīndārs and to establish a Thāna there. Sipah-Sālār 'Abdu'llah Khān was directed by a letter to cross the river Ganges opposite Ilāhābās and to lay a close siege to the fort of Ilāhābās. Shajā'at Khān and Mu'taqid Khān Bakhshī were ordered to proceed to Jhūsī and to remain ready for the support of the Sipah-Sālār. Shīr Khān Fatḥ-jang *alias* Dariyā Khān Rohilla, Dilāwar Khān Barīj, Bahādur Khān, Haydar Khān and other Afghāns, a force of twelve thousand horsemen, were sent to a place on the Ganges opposite Karā Mānikpūr with instructions not to allow the world-conquering army of Jahāngīr to cross the river. In short, the Khāns proceeded in haste to different places and fortified their stations. Every one of them transported a regiment of theirs over the river in order to attack the suburbs of Charkhata in the territory of Hasand.[2] Nāṣir Khān, went to bring the family of the Sipah-Sālār 'Abdu'llah Khān. The imperial armies of Jahāngīr Shāh pressed the Zamīndārs of Barhār from all sides to capture the aforesaid family, but to no purpose. The aforesaid Zamīndārs, after the arrival of Nāṣir Khān, handed over the family to him. Though Nāṣir Khān was pursued by the imperial army, he offered a strong fight and brought the family to the Sipah-Sālār. Howsoever His Royal Highness tried to win over Mīrzā Rustam Khān by conciliatory methods asking him to surrender the fort to the loyal officers, it did not produce any effect. Day after day he continued to defend the fort bravely. Therefore, Mīr Shams and Ma'ṣūm Khān, son of Mūsā Khān Masnad-i-'Alā along with the Zamīndārs of Bhātī were sent under the command of Khidmat Parast Khān to the Sipah-Sālār 'Abdu'llah Khān with instructions to teach a proper lesson to the defenders of the fort of Ilāhābās with the help of the artillery of the fleet. Khidmat Parast Khān went and joined him, and reduced the garrison to great straits by bombardment. (799)

**Shitāb Khān appointed chief officer at Akbarnagar.** Shitāb Khān, the most insignificant of the house-born ones, was distinguished among the people of the world, with the Manṣab of *Chahār-Hazārī*, 4,000 horse, and he was also favoured with a horse and a special robe of honour. In an auspicious hour he was granted leave to proceed to Akbarnagar *alias* Rājmaḥal. Many wise admonitions were given to this loyal servant; and the following Royal order was issued: "Five *Maḥalgīrī* boats specially meant for the use of the ladies of chastity, which were left at Akbarnagar in accordance with Royal command, should be sent to Patna. I'timād Khān should follow the Royal *Maḥals* (harems) and after reaching Patna in safety, he should proceed to the fort of Rohtas with the *Maḥals* and stay there with care and vigilance. You (Shitāb Khān) will be responsible for the good or bad management of the region up to Shāhzādapūr Yūsuf Shāhī on the side of Bhātī, Bardwān on the border of Orissa, the vicinity of Bāhir Bund[3] on the border of Kūch, and Pantī on the border of Hind (upper India). Be enthusiastic in your sphere of work and hopeful of good results. Every moment our daily growing favours concerning you, will increase. Exert yourself in a way that the elephants which you have brought from Kūch may reach the Royal presence soon. It will bring rewards to you." At the time of granting leave of departure, one hundred *muhars* (gold coins) were given (to Shitāb Khān) to offer at Ghāzīpūr to His Holiness Saint

Shaykh 'Abdu'llah. At the fourth stage when he reached Chaunsa, he went to Ghāzīpūr by boats and obtained the honour of attending on the saint. He presented the Royal offering first and then offered fifteen *ashrafīs* on his own behalf. This insignificant man (Shitāb Khān) then proceeded on his way and reached Patna on the fifth day. There, he had a friendly interview with Khān Dawrān. Khān Dawrān extended a fitting hospitality to this humble man for two days. Next day, at the request of this humble self, he came to his residence and became a guest. After dinner, otto of roses was sprinkled. Five beautiful Tāngan pie-bald horses were presented to Khān Dawrān and then they took leave of each other. When the elephants reached Patna, four of them which fell ill, were left with Khān Dawrān, and the rest along with the *pēshkash* of cash and things of the worth of Rs. 76,000 were sent to the Royal Court with Muṣṭafa Qulī Beg and Gopāl Dās, a Hindu officer. He then proceeded on his way. Miān Shaykh Khwāja Aḥmad was sent on his own behalf to Akbarnagar with a force of two hundred horse and three hundred matchlock-men in order to despatch the *Maḥlgīrī* boats in advance. I'timad Khān was directed by a letter to proceed with the ladies (*Maḥalhā*), leaving all the private elephants with Shaykh Khwāja Aḥmad, the son of the Pīr of Shitāb Khān. Shitāb Khān also advanced swiftly. As soon as I'timād Khān came out with the ladies, Shaykh Khwāja Aḥmad got the *Maḥalgīrī* boats ready and I'timād Khān proceeded on. The humblest (Shitāb Khān) reached Buda Katgal and honoured himself by making his obeisance (*kūrnish*) to the royal harems. And then bidding farewell (to them), he arrived at Akbarnagar. After making necessary arrangements, a representation was sent to the Court reporting his arrival. It reached His Royal Highness (duly). (800)

**Ibrāhīm Khān's wife stays at Akbarnagar.** In the city of Akbarnagar was the mansion of Begum, wife of the late Ibrāhīm Khān, and it was built just in front of the tomb of her son. The revenues of the three adjacent bazars were given to her officers and I commanded my men not to loiter around her mansion. On the night of the appearance of the new moon and on the days of *'Īd* and *Barāt,* I went to the door of the *Maḥal* of the Begum first of all and sent my benediction and then I went to the *'Īdgāh* (place of *'Id*-prayer). Due to my genial nature, I considered it a great privilege to serve her. (801)

**Shāhjahān receives presents from Shitāb Khān.** It has been mentioned before that this humble writer had sent to Jaunpūr with Muṣṭafa Qulī Beg and Gopāl Dās, the elephants which were the exclusive property of the State as well as those brought by him from the Ṣūbah of Kūch along with his *pēshkash,* intended for His Royal Highness, the august princes, Her Highness Nawāb Mumtāz Maḥal and the other princes. The price of these things including the elephants, horses, cash and articles was Rs. 76,000. In fifteen marches they reached the royal threshold and presented the elephants along with the *pēshkash* to His Royal Highness. His Royal Highness, through his fostering care for this house-born one, renamed the elephant Sārdul as Shāh Pasand and included it among his private elephants, and valued it at Rs. 30,000. The whole of the *pēshkash* was approved and accepted. Muṣṭafa Qulī Beg was honoured with a robe of honour and he was asked to remain in attendance at the Royal Court. (802)

**Parvīz and Mahābat Khān prepare for battle at Karā.** Now I shall give a short account of Sultan Parvīz, Mahābat Khān and all the loyal officers of the Emperor Jahāngīr who were staying at Burhānpūr. Reports reached (them) to the effect that the world-conquering prince had gone to Bengal, the Khān Fatḥ-jang had been sent to the house of non-existence because he refused to surrender, the Ṣūbahs of Orissa, Bengal, Kūch and Bihar had been brought under the absolute possession of the Prince, and that he (the Prince) himself, after reaching Jaunpūr, had sent 'Abdu'llah Khān in advance to besiege the fort of Ilāhābās, and that Dariyā Khān Rohilla entitled Shīr Khān Fatḥ-jang, having reached

Mānikpūr, had plundered the revenues of Charkhata and set fire to the place. Therefore, after making satisfactory arrangements for the peace of the Ṣūbahs of Aḥmadnagar, Aḥmadābād, Khāndesh, Mālwa and Ajmīr, they (Parvīs and others) made a forced march towards this region. Leaving the capital city to their left, they reached Charkhata *via* Kalpī and then marched to Mānikpūr. The Prince (Parvīz) sent an august order (*Nīshān-i-'Alā*) to Rustam Khān, and another was issued to Mukhliṣ Khān thus:—"Are you not ashamed of your grey beards that at this age of yours you have evacuated a place like Patna without any resistance? In short, before our arrival, if you can not compensate for this loss, you will have only yourself to thank for your own punishment." Therefore, Mukhliṣ Khān, in view of his impending disgrace, took one *tola* of poison and committed suicide, and he thus saved his honour and retired to the kingdom of Heaven. The news reached the regiments on both sides.

The camp of Sultan Parvīz and Mahābat Khān was pitched at Karā opposite Mānikpūr. Then a band of loyal Afghāns informed Shīr Khān Faṭḥ-jang *alias* Dariyā Khān of the arrival of the imperial army, and they suggested,—"First of all let us march from this station to the bank of the Ganges and pitch our camp there. We shall not allow the army of Parvīz to cross the river." Shīr Khān Fatḥ-jang, who was addicted to incessant drink, was highly intoxicated. He did not approve of this plan. He foolishly, began to say,—"Let them cross. When Mahābat crosses over, I will teach him such a lesson that henceforth he will never again gird up his loins for battle." In short, howsoever these men pressed their far-sighted views, it did not produce any effect. Mahābat Khān prepared to cross the river by collecting the boats. (803)

**The officers of Allahabad surrenders.** When the inmates of the fort of Ilāhābās were put to straits by the Sipah-Sālār 'Abdu'llah Khān, they began to surrender (one after another). First of all, Zabardast Khān Dakhinī submitted to the Sipah-Sālār, and after accepting a Manṣab of 2,000 with 1,000 horse, he joined the devoted officers of the prince. After him, Siyāsat Khān, the *Kotwāl* of the fort of Ilāhābās, came and joined the Royal army. He was honoured with the Manṣab of 250 with 100 horse. In this way every day, the Aḥadīs and Sipāhis of the Amīrs began to join the fortunate army of the august prince in batches of hundred and two hundred. The other side became weaker day by day. (804)

**Siege of Chunādah.** Therefore, it thus occurred to the Royal mind, which is an eternal spring of the Lord :—" Several attempts were made to win over Gopāl Jādūn (Jadū), the commander of the garrison at Chunādah,[1] by sending admonitions and giving hopes of Royal favours ; but due to his pride and arrogance he refused to surrender the fort to the officers of the State. It is proper that before the armies of the Emperor Jahāngīr take a firm stand, this fort of Chunādah should be besieged and captured." Accordingly, a force of fifteen thousand ready-mounted cavalry was despatched under the command of Wazīr Khān along with Rāja Narāyan Mal Ujjainia with his brothers and Zamīndārs. Rāja Narāyan Mal, son of Rāja Bhatmal Bishan with his followers, Sarandāz Bahādur and many of the old servants of the prosperous stirrup accompanied him. Wazīr Khān was given an elephant, a horse, and a special robe of honour and a horse and a robe of honour were given to each of the other officers. Rāja Narāyan Mal Ujjainia was given a horse, a robe of honour and a jewelled *phūl katārā* (a kind of dagger). Rāja Narāyan Mal Bishan was given a horse, a robe of honour and a jewelled camphor box (*kāfur-dān*). They went and besieged the fort and put the garrison to great straits. (805)

**Pahār Singh joins Shāhjahān.** During this time Kanwar Pahār Singh, son of Rāja Bīr Singh Dev Bundela, who had a quarrel with his father, left his company and joined the forces of the august prince, along with his five brothers, eight thousand horse and fifteen thousand infantry. He distinguished himself by kissing the ground. His Royal Highness, due to his fostering care for the humble, raised

Pahār Singh to the Manṣab of 5,000, with 5,000 horse and he was presented with an elephant, a horse, a robe of honour a sword-belt and a jewelled sword. His second brother was raised to the Manṣab of 3,000 with 2,500 horse, and he was favoured with a horse and a robe of honour. Each of the other three brothers was raised to the Manṣab of 2,000 personal and 1,000 horse, and a horse and a robe of honour were presented to each. They were retained in service with great encouragement. (806)

**Shāhjahān sends his family to Rohtas.** It also occurred to the Royal mind that the august Princes Sultan Dārā Shukoh and Sultan Awrangzīb along with the ladies of the harem should be sent to the fort of Rohtas. Accordingly, the princes and the ladies were sent in an auspicious hour to the fort of Rohtas with Mīr 'Abdu's Salām, the Khānsāmān (High Steward). Mīr 'Abdu's Salām undertook this work according to Royal orders and reached the fort within nine days from Jaunpūr. Saiyid Muẓffar came to the foot of the fort and honoured himself by making obeisance (*kūrnish*) to the august princes and the ladies of chastity, and then he went up to the fort in the company of the prosperous stirrup. He sent a representation to His Royal Highness about the arrival of the princes and the Begums at the fort (of Rohtas). This put the Royal mind at ease. (807)

**Shāhjahān removes his camp to Bahādurpūr.** Mahābat Khān procured a large number of boats from Surun and other parganās of the upper regions, and within one night he crossed the river with six thousand brave horsemen and halted on that side by raising a fort. The regiments of Jahāngīr crossed one after another and engaged in raiding. Shīr Khan Fatḥ-jang was suddenly roused from his sleep of intoxication and finding it inadvisable to resist with his single regiment, he sent a representation (to Shāhjahān) stating the details of the arrival of Mahābat Jang and fell back. While Shīr Khān was retreating with the Afghān regiment, the Sipah-Sālār also raised the siege of the fort of Ilāhābās and proceeded towards Jhūsī. He made a representation to the prince of the people of the world, and said:—"As effective arrangements have been made at Rohtas, and as the armies of Jahāngīr Shāh had crossed the river leaving no impediment on our way, so expediency and far-sighted caution demand that the Royal camp should move from Jaunpūr and halt at Bahādurpūr[5] making the river Ganges as a base for defence." For this reason His Royal Highness marched from Jaunpūr to Benares. 'Abdu'llah Khān, Shīr Khān, Rāja Bhim and all others were written to, to come to the Royal presence. As soon as he arrived at Benares it was decided to cross the river Ganges and to pitch the Royal camp at Bahādurpūr. Accordingly, the river was crossed and the camp was pitched. A peremptory Farmān was issued recalling Wazīr Khān along with all his followers. Gopāl Jadū had been reduced to a helpless state and was about to surrender the fort when the order reached Wazīr Khān. Yet Wazīr Khān, on the receipt of this strict order of recall, had to raise the siege, and returned to the Royal presence at Bahādurpūr. The Sipah-Sālār 'Abdu'llah Khān Fīrūz-jang with his followers, Shīr Khān Fatḥ-jang with all the Afghāns, Rāja Bhim with the Rājputs, Shajā'at Khān and Mu'taqīd Khān, the Bakhshī with all the Saiyids came one after another. All of them were ordered to cross the river and to have the honour of kissing the ground. In accordance with this order they crossed the river in order of precedence and obtained the honour of both the worlds by kissing the ground. The fleet of the Zamīndārs of Bhātī, which was in the stirrup of the world-conquering prince Shāhjahān, was kept equipped and ready for battle. An august Farmān was issued to Dārāb Khān to send immediately to His Royal Highness, Manmil, Durzisuz[6] and all other Firingis along with their fleet consisting of the *ghurābs, jaliyas, postas, parkūsas,* and *machwas* in the company of trustworthy collectors (*Muḥassilān*). (808)

**Review of the army.** Now I shall give a short account of the army of Parvīz. After the arrival of Mahābat Khān and the retreat of Shīr Khān, Sultan Parvīz also crossed the river Ganges with his whole army and pitched his camp there.

A military review was held and the soldiers were counted. The total strength of the army of Parvīz was eighty thousand brave horsemen, one thousand nine hundred elephants, and hundred thousand experienced infantry. This news was reported to the prosperous and august prince Shāhjahān. Then the Royal Bakhshīs were ordered to hold a review of the fortunate Royal army. Accordingly, seven days and nights were spent in inspecting the army. It was ascertained that there were one hundred and eighty thousand iron-clad horsemen, one hundred and ninety thousand brave infantry, two thousand four hundred war-elephants, seven hundred of which were in a state of heat, five hundred war-boats and fifteen hundred cannon.[7] It became a source of blindness to the eyes of enemies. (809)

**Birth of Sultan Murād.** Now I shall give a short account of Her Royal Highness Nawāb Mumtāz Maḥal Begum. As she was big with child, she gave birth to it at the fort of Rohtas. At an auspicious hour when the Venus and the Jupiter were in the ascendant, a fortunate son was born.[8] The wise astrologers gave the name of Sultan Murād Bakhsh to that light of the world. In order to celebrate a happy festivity at the appearance of that pearl of the casket of sovereignty and kingship, a representation was sent to the master and Qibla of the inhabitants of the world. His Royal Highness held an assembly of joy for three days and nights, and wrote to the Begum that if she required anything to be done, she might summon the most devoted Shitāb Khān by issuing a writ (*Nishān*). Accordingly, a *Nishān* was issued by Her exalted Ladyship to this most insignificant slave Shitāb Khān demanding the undermentioned articles of scent for the celebration of the birth of the prince of lofty fortune at the fort. It was written that the necessary cost of these things should be arranged by this insignificant Shitāb Khān and the purchases should be made by Begum, wife of the late Ibrāhīm Khān and then Shitāb Khān should carry them to the fort to Her Highness the exalted Lady. These were the things:— Thirty seers of white ambergris of the sea, two maunds of *khashkhas*, two thousand pods musk of Khata and Khutan (Tartary and China); five maunds of the essence of amber; two thousand bottles of the essence of Egyptian willow (*bid-i-mushk*) (*salix sygostomon*), extracts of the flower of the jujube tree, (*'araq-i-fitna*) and the essence of orange-flowers (*araq-i-bahār*) ; ten thousand bottles of the rose-water of Yazd and fifty maunds of saffron. (810)

**Battle on the bank of the Ganges.** Mīr Shams, Masnad-i-'Alā Ma'ṣūm Khān and all the Zamīndārs, who were sent with their fleet under the command of Khidmat Parast Khān, met the army of Parvīz which was halting on the bank of the Ganges without any fort. They put the army of Parvīz to great straits by killing men and beasts with the discharge of the artillery from the fleet. Not a single day passed without wounding and killing from five hundred to one thousand men, and four to five hundred horses, elephants, cows and asses. During this time Manmil, Zarrisuz and other Firingis, who were called from Jahāngīrnagar with their fleet from the company of Dārāb Khān reached this humblest author and house-born (*khāna-zād*) Shitāb Khān at Akbarnagar and they proceeded to the Royal camp. They joined the victorious army within the shortest possible time and they fought against the armies of Parvīz and Mahābat Khān for seven days in such a way that it is beyond description. Thus three times they pillaged the stores of the camp of Parvīz including even his wearing apparels. Every day they were honoured with royal favours. The Zamīndārs raised a rampart with towers on the bank of the river from one end to the other in front of the army of the prince of the people, and mounting selected cannon in different positions they did not allow a single soul of the army of Parvīz to move on that side of the river. A wonderful battle took place. (811)

**Shitāb Khān appointed Censor.** The representatives of this humblest of men were sent every day with the mail-runners (*Dāk-chawkiān*) to the sublime Court. Owing to great confidence reposed on this devoted slave by His Royal Highness, an order was issued expressing the desire that every letter that goes from the Royal camp to Bengal and every letter that comes from Bengal to the Royal camp should be censored by his slave. Accordingly, the Farmāns to the officers and the representations of the life-sacrificing devoted servants and of the *Karorī* and the letters of the agents and tax-collectors of the Amīrs which were written to their masters were censored and then allowed to pass from one side to the other. One day a letter of Khān Dawrān which was written from Patna to Dārāb Khān containing some complaint against the master and Qibla, the *Pīr* and *Murshid* (spiritual guide i.e. Shāhjahān), fell into the hand of this most insignificant creature in the course of censorship. This letter was sent to the Most Exalted Royal Highness who is a pure self and a necessary existence, along with a representation of his (Shitāb Khān's) own which he had to make. (812)

**Shitāb Khān permitted to bring his family.** When the family of this humble author lived at Jahāṇgīrnagar *alias* Dhāka, he had no son. If any son was born he did not survive. During this time before the arrival of His Royal Highness, God, the Great, favoured this most insignificant creature with a son from His invisible treasure while he was in the Ṣūbah of Kūch. So he had a great longing to see the child. Therefore this representation was sent to the master and Qibla, the *Pīr* and *Murshid* :—" I had no son. This time, on the occasion of the auspicious arrival of Your Highness, God, the Great, has favoured me with a son. As my family is at Jahāngīrnagar, I pray that either I may be permitted to bring my family to Akbarnagar or after making satisfactory arrangements at Akbarnagar I may be allowed to go to see the son of the slave of Your Highness and then return (to Akbaṛnagar)". His Royal Highness, due to his kindness to the humble and his fostering care for the house-born ones, issued a Royal command that this most insignificant creature should bring his family to Akbarnagar. Accordingly, the Royal command, which is an interpreter of Divine secrets, was communicated to Dārāb Khān and he was asked to send the family of (Shitāb Khān). As Dārāb Khān had vicious ideas in his mind and as he was not favourably disposed towards the master and Qibla he played tricks and did not send the family of this humble self. He said :—" This Farmān was issued in reply to your representation. When a Farmān is issued to my name asking me to send the family of Shitāb Khān to Akbarnagar, then I will send them." I sent this letter of Dārāb Khān to His Royal Highness along with a representation of my own concerning this matter. A letter was written to my wife and children to come to me in the manner directed by me. At this stage my revered sister became an enemy of mine. Neither did she come, nor did she allow my family to come. This gave me great mortifications and I was put to shame before my master and Qibla as will be narrated below. (813)

**Change of Officials.** Now I shall revert to my original theme. When His Royal Highness became aware of the state of affairs he appointed Wazīr Khān to be the Ṣūbahdār of Patna and recalled Khān Dawrān along with his sons, brothers and nephews to the Royal Court. On the arrival of Wazīr Khān at Patna, Khān Dawrān proceeded to kiss the threshold of the master and Qibla. (814)

**Encounter with Parvīz at Jhūsī.** During this time the spies brought news that Ilahyār Khān, Naẕr Bahādur, Muḥammad Zamān *Karorī* and Sultan Parvīz were staying with some other men at Jhūsī. Therefore Khān Dawrān, Khwāja Ibrāhīm, brother of Khwāja 'Uṣmān, Khwāja Dāwūd, son of Khwāja Sulaymān, and nephew of Khwāja 'Uṣmān, prayed thus :—" If we are permitted, we shall go against them and if they resist they will be sent to the lane of non-existence and their heads will be brought to the Royal Court. If they show their humility and surrender to the officers of the State, then we shall bring them (alive) with consolations and hopes of mercy." His Royal Highness, the Qibla of the people of the world, did not approve of this plan and prohibited them (from doing so). But these men, who deserved death and destruction, in league with one another, proceeded without Royal orders. They started at mid-day, and after marching for the whole night, they reached Jhūsī after one and a half *pahar* of the next day in such a state that their horses were powerless to move any further. In short, Ilahyār Khān, Naẕr Bahādur, Muḥammad Zamān and others, hearing the sound of their kettle-drum, came with fresh vigour on strong horses to fight. As soon as they came in front of them they rushed with open swords and attacked them. After a short skirmish, Khān Dawrān attained martyrdom. Khwāja Ibrāhīm and Khwāja Dāwūd, being wounded, fell back with the son of Khān Dawrān leaving the field to the men of the opposite party. On the evening of the third day this news reached the Royal camp, and superficial observers were affected by some consternation. But the bustle of the soldiers in the army (of Shāhjahān) was so great as to be beyond description (and the effect of this news, therefore, was soon effaced.) (815)

**Shitāb Khān intercepts two letters of Dārāb Khān.** Now I shall give a short account of the state of affairs of the Ṣūbah of Gawr. During this time two letters from the *vakil* of Dārāb Khān, who was staying with his son Arām Bakhsh in the Royal camp, were sent from the Royal camp to Dārāb Khān through Akbarnagar and fell into the hand of this humblest of the house-born ones. These two letters were in the hand-writing of Khān Khānān *alias* 'Abdu'r Raḥīm, father of Dārāb Khān. Another letter (which fell into his hand) was of Dārāb Khān addressed to the agent of his son Arām Bakhsh. These letters were sent to the Court along with his (Shitāb Khāns) own representations expressing his fidelity and miseries, and many words relating to the welfare of the State were included therein. Accordingly, His Royal Highness, due to his extreme kindness and fostering care for the house-born ones, issued an auspicious Farmān to this house-born (Shitāb Khān) with many encouraging and kind words. The Prince was always thinking how to recall Dārāb Khān to the Court. (816)

**Supply of money and materials by Shitāb Khān.** In the Farmān issued to this humble author Shitāb Khān, the house-born, it was written that he should not neglect the supply of rations to the Royal army and particularly to Wazīr Khān for relaying the same to the fort of Rohtas, and that he should act in such a way that this demand may soon be satisfied and he might get his reward. It was also directed that he should not show any slackness in sending the revenues of the State and in the supply of gunpowder, lead and iron. Accordingly, this most insignificant man sent from the beginning till end three hundred and twenty thousand maunds of corn to Patna to Wazīr Khān. Every time fifty to sixty boats of the capacity of carrying five hundred to one thousand maunds were despatched to Patna. Four thousand maunds of gunpowder, and eight thousand maunds of lead, iron and stone shots (*gulahā-i-sangī*) were supplied. A stock of five hundred maunds of gunpowder, four to five hundred maunds of lead and iron were always kept ready at the fort of Akbarnagar. The Royal factory was situated at the centre (of the town). Everyday men were sent to different places to the *Karorīs* to collect revenues from all sides. Rs. 700,000 were remitted to Wazīr Khān at Patna in eight instalments. At the time of sending the first instalment, all the roads were inundated with the heavy rains of the season. So the revenues had to be sent by boat. It was greatly feared that if by chance the boat capsized with the revenue, it would not be possible to appear before the master and Qibla (to answer for it). Therefore, God the Great, through His kindness, revealed to my mind a way by means of which the revenue could be despatched. I thought within my mind that the depth of the water nowhere would be more than two hundred yards. Then I ordered for one hundred ropes, each two hundred yards in length, of the thickness of the middle finger. After this I ordered for five-hundred small gourds which are used in India for the purpose of swimming. When these things were brought, I ordered that the sum of Rs. 100,000 which was to be sent as the first instalment, to be put into a hundred bags of Rs. 1,000 each, and one end of a rope to be tied to the neck of each bag and the other end to five of the gourds. The boat was then directed to be covered with planks, and instead of putting the money in a box, the bags were directed to be placed on the plank and these hundred ropes to be placed in a heap over these bags with these five hundred gourds. After this arrangement it was expected that trustworthy men would be able to carry the money with proper guard and vigilance. Some fishing boats were also arranged to be sent with fishermen who could dive to a depth of two hundred yards, so that if by chance the boat sank, these fishermen would immeditely be able to go with their boats to the place wherever they would see these gourds floating and bring out the bags of gold like buckets and carry them to their boats. And if perchance these bags got entangled in any object or sand deposits, these fishermen would be able to dive to the bottom and bring the bags up to their boats by removing those obstacles. In short, on all these eight occasions, through my firm faith, I was successful in sending the wealth of my master, the Qibla, the *Pīr* and *Murshid*. It became a source of happiness and thousands of thanks were offered to the Lord with heart and soul. (817)

**Enquiries as to the correctness of the rent-rolls.** Another Farmān reached (Shitāb Khān) to the following effect:—"Tājpūr Purnea was given as a Jāgīr to Shīr Khān Fatḥ-jang in lieu of his salary. But Shīr Khān has some doubts as to the assessment of its revenue. It has been represented that Shīr Khān would accept that assignment if a correct statement of the revenues of those two places are made by a trustworthy officer of yours. Therefore, we have issued this Royal command (to you) to make a thorough enquiry into the conditions of the ryots of those two *maḥals* so that neither the ryots and the Jāgīrdār may be put to hardship nor the imperial revenues fall short, and then you are to send a report to the Court." Accordingly, a confidential Afghān officer named Yāra Khān was deputed to those two parganās along with Khwāja Todarmal, the Mīr Sāmān of this humble self with these instructions,—"I shall send another party to make secret enquiries about the real state of affairs over and above yourself. I may even go personally. After understanding the situation, prepare a correct register of revenues of those two parganās with the consent of the ryots, the signature of the Qānūngūs, and the deed of agreement (*qabūliyat*) of the Chawdhūris, verified and attested by the agents of Shīr Khan Fatḥ-jang." They started for that place. Although I had confidence in them yet another party was secretly appointed to see that they may not conspire with the officers of Shīr Khān. They went there and began to survey and inspect the villages so that after ascertaining the facts they might be able to finish the preparation of the rent-roll. (818)

**Shāhjahān's name read in the " 'Īd " Sermon.** When the day of the festival of sacrifice (*'Īd-i-Qurbān*) came, in the morning all the officers went to the place of prayer. The preacher was instructed to read the sermon in such a way, that when he would come to the commendation of His Majesty the Caliph, the Shadow of God, Jahāngīr Bādshāh, he should read " Nūru'd-Dīn Muḥammad Jahāngīr Bādshāh and Abu'l-Mẓaffar Shāhjahān Bādshāh Ghāzī Bin Nūru'd-Dīn Muḥammad Jahāngīr Bādshāh " and then finish the sermon by offering the *Fātiḥa* (benedictory prayer) for the long life of His Royal Highness. In fine, the preacher finished the sermon in that way. At the time when the name of His Royal Highness (Shāhjahān) was uttered, inspite of the fact that this preacher had been given a robe of honour by each of the Emperors, I threw my dress of honour embroidered with pure gold on the shoulder of the preacher, and *rezagi* (two-anna, four-anna and eight-anna pieces) of Rs. 500 were scattered as a sacrifice before the preacher. Many of the needy people removed their difficulties of livelihood by means of this and they became happy. Voices of greetings reached the sky. After returning home, I performed the Qurbānī (sacrifice of animals). A great banquet was held throughout the whole day and night with the pleasant entertainments of beautiful singers and dancers of lovely grace and story-tellers of pleasant disposition. Many of the workers of the factories were favoured with gifts. (819)

**Maintenance charge for the elephant Gaj Dula.** According to royal regulations, every confidential and old servant is in charge of one of the private elephants of the Emperor. Therefore, a private elephant named Gaj Dula, which was very much liked by His Royal Highness, was in my charge and it was kept at the guard-house of the Royal camp. Accordingly, I had to send the expenses for its food. Therefore, with a view to see that my agent may not behave in the same way as other agents, who keep the private elephants in starvation with the plea that no expenses were being received by them from their masters, every time I sent a representation to the Court of my *Pīr* and *Murshid*, the Qibla of the people of the world, I used to send fifteen *la'l-i-jalālī ashrafīs*,[9] within the cover of the representation. I used to mention in the representation,—"So many *ashrafīs* are sent for the maintenance of the private elephant. They may be ordered to be handed over to my agent, to be spent on the maintenance of the elephant." His Royal Highness (may a thousand humble writers like Shitāb Khān be sacrificed for him), by way of kindness to the humble and the poor, and due to his fostering care for the house-born, used every time to send for my agent Bhimsen and deliver the maintenance allowance of the elephant to him with his august hand with strict orders to take proper care of the private elephant. This was a source of great pleasure to the Royal mind, and it was considered as an eternal honour by this humble self. (820)

**Shitāb Khān demands the revenues of Crown-lands.** During this time Dārāb Khān sent his men to Akbarnagar in order to demand the pay of the Qānūngūs of the head-quarters (*Qānūngūyān-i-Ṣadr*). This humble self, became annoyed at this and wrote to Dārāb Khān thus:—"The Crown-lands in your *Chaklā* (revenue division) yield a revenue of Rs. 700,000. A Royal command was issued to the effect that this amount should be sent to Shitāb Khān who would remit the amount to Court. But you are not paying your attention to the Crown-lands (*Khāliṣa*) and you are demanding the salary of the Qānūngūs. Please arrange to send the sum of

Rs. 700,000 soon to Akbarnagar so that it may be remitted to the Royal camp." I then sent back the men of the aforesaid Khān. (821)

**Reinforcement sent to Orissa.** During this time the following letter came to this humble man from Orissa from Shāh Qulī Khān,—" It occurs to my mind that if at any time His Royal Highness summons me to wait upon him, I do not find stipendiary officer of this Ṣūbah of the type who can accompany me. From the purport of your letters written to me, and from the contents of the royal Farmāns which were issued with favourable references about you, I consider you to be a unique person of the State. Therefore, by way of far-sightedness, I would make you the request to send me five thousand cavalry. Of these, please recommend whomsoever you consider fit for the imperial Manṣab. Please fix the salaries of those whom you consider fit for my service and pay them all their expenses. Please write about what is spent by you in sending them here, so that it may be paid off by a bill of exchange (*hundūwī*)." Accordingly, I ordered the imperial Bakhshīs and my Hindu officers to recruit men. One of my Hindu officers named Bhimsen was appointed to be the Bakhshī of the Royal Ahadīs and of the department of the Personal artillery of His Royal Highness. The man, who held this post so long, was appointed to be the Bakhshī of these five thousand cavalry requisitioned by Shāh Qulī Khān. Then I sent a representation to the Royal Court about this affair along with the correspondence of Shāh Qulī Khān. His Royal Highness approved of the arrangement with praise. (822)

**Basta parganā plundered.** The following peremptory Farmān was issued to this sincere devotee Shitāb Khān:—" It has been represented to us by Khwāja Sa'ādat (son of) the late Mīrzā Najfī, Jāgīrdār of the parganā of Basta, that Saiyid Muḥammad has come to this region from Orissa without permission from Shāh Qulī Khān to the parganā of Basta, the Jāgīr of Sa'ādat. He (Saiyid Muḥammad) has seized the revenue collectors and taken by force the money they had with them. He has taken possession of the parganā and is collecting its revenues. If immediately after this Royal Farmān is received, he (Saiyid Muḥammad) gives up his evil ways in accordance with the orders and admonitions of that unique servant of the Court (Shitāb Khān) and submits to him, he should then be sent to the Court. If it becomes apparent that under no circumstances he would submit, then he would have, by all means, only himself to thank for his own punishment and his head should be sent to the Court." Accordingly, an Aḥadī was sent to summon Saiyid Shāh Muḥammad with a letter of necessary admonitions. I waited to see what he would do, and then to hold him responsible for his own punishment by taking necessary steps, depending on the favour of God and the eternal fortune of the master and Qibla. (823)

**Three unsuccessful attempts of Shāhjahān.** Now I shall give a short account of the state of the prosperous army (of Shāhjahān). One day Khidmat Parast Khān, Mīr Shams and Masnad-i-'Alā Ma'ṣūm Khān went with all the Zamīndārs and the fleet of the Firingis and attacked the army of Rāja Gaj Singh who was in the company of Sultan Parvīz. As the Rājputs possess no other weapons of war but the lance and the sword, so as soon as one volley was fired from the cannon, and the boats were driven to the bank, the Rājputs, unable to stand the cannonade, left the bank and retreated to a great distance. The soldiers of the fleet disembarked from their boats, seized all the tents of Gaj Singh and brought them to the boats. When the Rājputs made another assault, the cannoniers (*tūp-andāzān*) fired their cannon and killed a large number of them, and remarkable results were achieved. Next day similar attack was made on the camp of Parvīz. On the third occasion, the bed and the wearing apparels of Sultan Parvīz were plundered by Khidmat Parast Khān and his companions and were brought to His Royal Highness. They were praised for this act and were distinguished with Royal favours. In short, every day the Royal fleet began to give an effective blow to the soldiers of Sultan Parvīz and

Mahābat Khān. Then one day an army of Rājputs, Mughals and Saiyids joined together and decided that they would allow the fleet of the Zamīndārs of the army of prince Shāhjahān to proceed (up the river) and then they would fall upon it from the rear in a narrow part of the river and thus deal it a heavy blow. Accordingly, with the aid of the *Bīldārs* (delvers or miners and sappers) they raised a fort on the bank of the Ganges and equipping it with artillery and making its towers and walls all fire, pure and simple, they waited ready. The fleet of the Zamīndārs came in its usual course and began to fire cannon. The soldiers of the army of Parvīz made a retreat and allowed the fleet to proceed, and at last at the time of its return they led an attack on it in a narrow part of the river and began to discharge arrows, guns, and cannon in such a way that it enveloped the resplendent sun in darkness and the bright day was converted into a dark night. In short, although all the men of the fleet came out of this ordeal by making a hard struggle and driving the boats thrice to the bank with shields before their faces, yet two *kūsas* along with their boat-men were captured by the opponents and their soldiers were killed. Khidmat Parast Khān, Mīr Shams, Masnad-i-'Alā Ma'ṣūm Khān and other Zamīndārs, Manmil, Durzisuz and other Firingis returned with their booties which had been seized in the first assault and presented these to the Qibla of the people of the world. They were honoured with Royal favours. After a short time the boatmen of those two boats, who were captured, were sent adrift with their boats, to float at random down the river. The hands of the boatmen were cut off and their feet were tied to the posts of the boat. The current of the river brought the boats with the boatmen down the river and the boats passed by the Royal camp. The loyal officers were surprised at this. Some of the soldiers of the fleet hurried to the rescue of those helpless men in the boat in order to bring them to the shore. But human hand has no control over the wrath of God. All on a sudden there arose a whirlwind and both these boats with the boatmen sank in the river and no trace of them was found. This act produced a vindictive attitude in the Royal mind and the firing of cannon went on from both sides. (824)

**Jawharmal Dās appointed Dīwān of Bengal.** When a representation from Dārāb Khān containing allegations about the improper behaviour of Mīrzā Mulkī, the Dīwān of Bengal, reached the Court, Rāy Jawharmal Dās, the Dīwān and personal assistant of the late Ibrāhīm Khān Fatḥ-jang, who was working as the Superintendent of the elephants in the Royal camp, was appointed to be the Dīwān of the whole of Bengal. He was given the Manṣab of 500 with 300 horse, and was honoured with the gift of a horse and a robe of honour. A *tūgh* (horsetail standard), a standard, (*'alam*) and a kettle-drum were sent with Rāy Jawharmal to Shitāb Khān, the most humble author and the meanest of the faithful slaves, with instructions to hand them over to Shitāb Khān after which Rāy Jawharmal was to proceed to Jahāngīrnagar. A peremptory Farmān was issued to this humble Shitāb Khān,—" The private elephant named Batpā which was brought from the Ṣūbah of Kūch is given by us to that faithful and devoted (Shitāb Khān) as prayed for by him. Yakjihat Khān has been ordered to hand over the elephant to his (Shitāb Khān's) agent Bhimsen. As he (Shitāb Khān) is conversant with the management of the affairs of Bengal and of the tax-collectors and the *mutaṣaddīs* (accountants) of the late Ibrāhīm Khān, so he should depute his own officers to different places to summon them (the revenue officers of Ibrāhīm Khān) and inspect the accounts of every one of them. The amount due from everyone of them should be remitted to the State-treasury (*Sarkār-i-Khāliṣa Sharīfa*)." Rāy Jawharmal Dās arrived at the fort of the Sepulchre of the late Ibrāhīm Khān and the news of his arrival with the *tūgh*, the standard and the kettle-drum was communicated to this humble house-born one. This insignificant creature proceeded with great humility to welcome him and after performing the rites of obeisance and the prostrations of gratitude to the Eternal, he received the *tūgh*, the standard and the kettle-drum one after the other. Every time he honoured himself by making three obeisances and prostrations of gratitude. After this he had a friendly meeting with Rāy Jawharmal Dās who had sincere and brotherly relation with him from a long time past. He was brought to his house. Although the aforesaid Rāy showed his shyness, a great hospitality was offered to him. Next morning at the time of his departure, he was given a sum of Rs. 5,000 on five trays, a female elephant and a suitable horse. Although the Rāy offered excuses, yet *nolens volens,* he accepted these things and bade farewell. He proceeded to Jahāngīrnagar, reached the place at an auspicious hour, and met Dārāb Khān. He then engaged himself in his work and sent a representation to the Royal Court about his arrival. (825)

**Battle on the bank of the Tons.** Now I shall stop my pen from narrating these events and shall revert to my original theme. Mahābat Khān was always endeavouring to cross the river Ganges by every possible way. Accordingly, with the guidance of some Zamīndārs and particulary, with the help of the boatmen, he crossed the river Ganges in its upper region with a band of officers of the Court of Jahāngīr. Therefore, the Royal officers considered it expedient to oppose them making the river Tons[10] as the base of their operations, so that the route to the fort of Rohtas might be safeguarded. With this plan in view, they marched during the night from Bāhadurpūr and halted at a place making the river Tons as a base for defence. But the fleet of Bengal and of the Firingis was kept in the Ganges. Khidmat Parast Khān *alias* Riẓā Bahādur was sent to guard the fort of Rohtas. Therefore, Mīr Shams did not act as loyally as was expected from him. He did not report to the master and Qibla about the wicked intentions of Mā'ṣūm Khān, the Zamīndārs, Manmil and the Firingis so that they might be kept under surveillance at the Royal camp. This group of people under the pretext that their fleet was posted in the big river (Ganges) sent their subordinates along with the boatmen to raise a fort at the Royal camp and they remained behind. A continual fighting with cannon and gun was carried on, on the bank of the river

Tons. Every day a regiment of Sultan Parvīz used to attack the Royal army. (826)

**Dārāb Khān evades meeting Shāhjahān.** It occurred to the mind of His Royal Highness that Dārāb Khān should be summoned to this battle. Accordingly an august Farmān was issued to Dārāb Khān asking him to come immediately to the Royal camp, leaving Jahāngīrnagar in charge of his son with a number of officers. It was settled that the battle would be fought after his arrival at the Royal camp. But as Dārāb Khān was not sincere and honest in his loyalty to the master and Qibla, he avoided coming to the Court with the false plea of an impending Mag raid. He sent his son to the Court with a force of one thousand horsemen and two hundred war-boats of Bengal. His son made a swift march from stage to stage carrying also the land-army in the fleet. (827)

**Desertion of the Zamīndārs and the Firiṇgis.** Mīr Ṣafī, a detestable man who did not deserve any favour, was appointed by His Royal Highness to be the Atāliq (tutor) of the august princes. At this time, after the departure of Mīr ʻAbdu's-Salām to Rohtas in the stirrup of the great princes and ladies of the Royal harem, the aforesaid Mīr Ṣafī was appointed to be the Khān-Sāmān and the controller of the Crown-lands (*khāliṣa sharīfa*). He was also staying in the fleet on the plea of supplying provisions to the stores and State factories (*kārkhānjāt*). He conspired with the son of Narāyan, brother of Rāja Satrajit, Zamīndār of Bhusna, and thus in league with each other, they entered into a conspiracy with Maʻṣūm Khān. Then, in league with Manmil and other officers, high and low, they sent a representation to Sultan Parvīz and wrote a letter to Mahābat Khān, thus:—"If we are given assurance of the imperial favours of Jahāngīr, then, at this juncture when it is not possible for the army of the world-conquering prince Shāhjahān to execute their main functions without the fleet, we shall run away with the fleet and after imprisoning Dārāb Khān we shall create a disturbance in the Ṣūbah of Bengal. From that side we shall advance with an army and fall upon the army of prince Shāhjahān from the rear." Mahābat Khān, informed of this, sent a letter of his own along with a *Nishān* (letter of a prince) of Sultan Parvīz giving assurance to Mīr Ṣafī and particularly to Ma'ṣūm Khān, the Zamīndārs, Manmil, Durzisuz and other Firingis. A robe of honour was sent to every one of them with their messengers. When these letters came to these short-sighted people, they sent their secret agents to the prosperous (Shāhjahān's) army, and recalled their boatmen who were engaged on the bank of the river Tons in the construction of the fort and the *Damdama* (a raised battery). After this they sailed away with their fleet. (828)

**The deserters plunder the City of Patna.** Next day the report of the desertion was brought to His Royal Highness, the Qibla of the people of the world. His Royal Highness sent an Afghān named Aḥmad Khān, who had been serving in the fleet from a time previous to Khidmat Parast Khān *alias* Riẓā Bahādur, along with an officer in waiting, by a swift gondola to Shitāb Khān and Dārāb Khān with this verbal message:—"These faithless people have deserted us by throwing the dust of disgrace upon their heads and faces. It is proper that they should be seized by every possible means, severely punished for their faults and sent back to their work. Whoever will be able to accomplish this task, will certainly be distinguished with high honour, and will be entrusted with the administration of the Ṣūbahs of Bengal and Bihar." In short, the aforesaid Aḥmad Khān along with the Royal attendant proceeded by a boat and came all the way getting mixed up with the fleet of those faithless people (*namak-harāmān*). Owing to the large number of their boats, they thought that this was also a boat of theirs. They could not distinguish this boat from those of theirs. When they reached Patna, Wazīr Khān, due to his negligence, could not defend the city. As soon as they reached (Patna), they fired a volley, moored their boats at the bank and disembarked. They set fire to the city and the bazar and plundered the people as far as they could. (829)

**Shitāb Khān warns Dārāb Khān.** During this interval, Aḥmad Khān and the royal attendant, who were in their boat, proceeded to Akbarnagar and reached there on the day of *'Āshūrā* (i.e. the 10th of Muḥarram). They came to this humble self Shitāb Khān who was the Ṣūbahdār of that place and took their stand before the terrace on which he was standing and distributing royal alms to the poor and the needy. I recognised them and asked them where did they come from, in this way. They said,—" We are coming from the Court of the master and Qibla." I thought that they had brought Royal Farmāns. I came down to them with great respect. After having some confidential talk with them I sent them away. I wrote the following few words to the son of Dārāb Khān who was proceeding to the Royal Court and had reached the mouth of the Hajrāhatī[11],—" I thought of accompanying your fleet to fight against the enemies. But as it (the expedition) was not arranged according to my plan, so I remained behind. As you will not be able to achieve success in a contest with them, it is better for you to return to the Khān (Dārāb) before the arrival of the enemy and to strengthen Jahāngīrnagar. This will be equivalent to offering a hundred battles to them. If you find that the enemies are following you, tie the legs of the boatmen with ropes and keep them with such care that they may not abscond and you personally remain with your boats in the narrow stream of the Hajrāhatī and keep the land-army ready on its either side, so that the enemies may not attack you from the main river. After this, proceed by the main stream of the river and join Dārāb Khān as early as possible and help your father who could not come to the aid of the master and Qibla." I wrote to Dārāb Khān :—" As I have no fleet at Akbarnagar, so I desired to go by a boat to your son Mīrzā Afrasiyāb in order to fight a good battle under the Atāliqship of your son, against the rebel Zamīndārs who had deserted the master and Qibla. But as I was not sure whether the men of Mīrzā (Afrasiyāb) would agree to my proposal, I remained in my own place. I wrote to him a letter of admonition which I considered necessary to write. Excuse my rudeness, but had I been at Jahāngīrnagar with the equipments which you have, you would have seen how I would have dealt with Ma'ṣūm Khān. Even now, the Khān, after taking a firm stand, should act in such a way that he (Ma'ṣūm Khān) may find no other alternative than to send mediators, offering his submission. It should also be known for certain that the well-being of the honourable Khān and the life of Nawāb Khān-Khānān depend on the type of services that may be rendered by the Khān to the sovereign (Shāhjahān). A disaster will befall them the very day any untoward behaviour is indulged in by the Khān." (830)

**Shitāb Khān defends the city of Akbarnagar.** In short, after granting leave to Aḥmad Khān and the royal attendant to proceed to Jahāngīrnagar, I sent my messengers to summon Mīrzā Fatḥu'llah, grandson of the late Ibrāhīm Khān. When he was brought I did not find it advisable to detain him. I sent Muḥammad Ṣāliḥ, the Wāqi-'navīs, with a force of three hundred horsemen and (? the word giving the number effaced in the Ms.) musketeers to guard the mansion of the Begum, the wife of Ibrāhīm Khān to keep information about hours of arrival of the fleet of the Zamīndārs, so that they might not attack the family of the late Ibrāhīm Khān. In short, this army remained there for the whole of the day and night. Next morning another force of equal strength along with twenty elephants was sent under the command of an eunuch of this humble author Shitāb Khān, named Khwāja Sa'ādat in order to relieve Muḥmmad Sāliḥ and his regiment and to send them to their respective homes. Accordingly, on the arrival of Khwāja Sa'ādat Khān, the Begum sent a large quantity of food to Mīrzā Muḥammad Ṣāliḥ, Khwāja Sa'ādat and their followers, with many excuses. When all these men were busy in taking food, the rebel Zamīndārs, the accursed Ṣafī and the Firingis of the enemy's country (*Firingiān-i-Dāru'l-ḥarb*) appeared on the scene with their fleet and raised a great commotion. But as from the previous day this insignificant creature was ready with his officers, high and low, fully armed and equipped, so he came out and rushed to that place. The Zamīndārs, attempted to leave their boats under the cover of a heavy cannonade. They attempted to moor their boats in a safe place and then to enter the city and the bazar for the purpose of looting. But when they saw that this most insignificant creature (Shitāb Khān) was ready with a force of three thousand horsemen and five thousand matchlock-men in two regiments, with elephants posted in his front with the intention of attacking their boats and smashing them under the feet of the elephants as soon as the boats were brought to the bank, they did not venture to come to the bank but kept up a continuous fire from (the boats) till the last *pahar* of the day. Then, finding no other alternative, they gave up firing and went their way. But this insignificant creature, Shitāb Khān, kept ready on horseback till candle-light lest the enemies played some tricks and renewed the fight. (831)

**Shitāb Khān tries to win back the deserters.** When they reached the village of Tipūra, they sent their messengers by a gondola to me (Shitāb Khān) with a copy of the *Nishān* of Sultan Parvīz. Being in doubt of its authenticity I sent this message to them :—" You have not acted well by displaying such improper behaviours. Either to-day or to-morrow you will see what will happen to Parvīz and Mahābat Khān, and you shall have to throw the dust of repentance on your head and face. Even now if you desire your well-being, you may repent of your misdemeanour and submit yourselves through this humble self to the master and Qibla. Acting as a mediator, I will secure pardon for your faults and will arrange for your stay with me and for the stay of your followers at the Royal Court." Their messengers then returned. After receiving this message they proceeded onwards for Jahāngīrnagar. After travelling for the whole night, they reached Hajrahatī at the mouth of the river Atrāyi next morning. Three *pahars* before this, the son of Dārāb Khān had proceeded to his father with his fleet and his land-army, and he thus joined his father at Jahāngīrnagar. Two *pahars* after his arrival, these people reached the *Mohāna* or mouth of the river at Khīẓrpūr, and surrounded Jahāngīrnagar. (832)

**Shāh Muḥammad won over by Shitāb Khān.** Now I shall give a short account of the affairs of Saiyid Shāh Muḥammad. It has been mentioned before that in accordance with the Royal command, I sent two Aḥadīs to admonish him and to bring him to me. When a long time elapsed and nothing could be achieved by the Aḥadīs, I sent Rāy Kāsīdās, the Superintendent of the mint (Dārūgha-i-Dāru'ẓẓarb) at Akbarnagar along with a confidential officer of mine. I wrote a letter to Shāh Muḥammad to the following effect giving him hopes and promises of safety:—" At this time when the Zamīndārs of Bengal, being faithless, (*harāmkhūrī*) have deserted the Royal stirrup, and a Royal mandate has been issued to extirpate them, why do you, under these circumstances want to make yourself culpable and notorious by fighting for a single parganā ? Come immediately to me. If you act according to my direction, I will secure for you a Manṣāb of 3,000 personal and 3,000 horse. The assignment for your original Manṣab of 700 and 300 horse will be made from the State-domain (*Khāliṣa*), and the assignment for the rest of 2,300 personal and 2,700 horse will be given to you from the Estate of Bhusna of Rāja Satrajit who is not in need of maintaining a fleet." In short, Kāsīdās and the officer of this humble self went and brought Saiyid Shāh Muḥammad to Akbarnagar after a good deal of persuasion. After an interview, I won him over by oral assurances and then I sent a representation giving the details of Saiyid Shāh Muḥammad's arrival at this place and waited for the Royal command. (833)

## CHAPTER III.

*The arraying of soldiers by His Royal Highness to fight against Parvīz and Mahābat Khān and other armies of Jahāngīr Shāh. Some misfortunes of the victorious army (of Shāhjahān). Re-strengthening of the Ṣūbah of Bengal and particularly of the Ṣūbah of Orissa.*

**Mahābat Khān and Parvīz cross the river Tons.** A short account of this amazing and sad incident is this: When the battle on the bank of the river Tons dragged on and the construction of the fort and ramparts were given up by the royal officers owing to the desertion of the Bengal Zamīndārs, Mahābat Khān attempted to cross the river wherever it. was fordable. Therefore, he went up the river to attempt to cross it. Although he went up the river keeping close to its bank, the world-conquering army of the fortunate prince Shāhjahān, the conqueror of the world, followed him (Mahābat Khān) by the opposite bank of the river. When they reached Khīragarh[1] a battle of cross-bows and cannon took place between the two parties. Not a single day passed without the death of one to two hundred men on both sides. A strange commotion took place and not a single day passed on which hundred to two hundred horsemen of the officers of Jahāngīr Shāh did not attack the Royal army (of Shāhjahān). On the date of the month ( the space for the date and the name of the month left vacant in the Ms.) in the last *pahar* of the day, Mahābat Khān, with the guidance of the loyal Zāmīndārs of Jahāngīr, crossed the river Tons with a force of four thousand horse and seven hundred famous elephants. Thereupon, Rāja Bīr Singh Dev Bundela, also snapped asunder the thread of his calculation when Mahābat Khān passed by the side of his regiment. He crossed the river Tons with a force of seven thousand horse, twelve thousand infantry and two hundred elephants and encamped in front of Māḥābat Khān. The other regiments of Jahāngīr Shāh began to cross one after the other and by nothing more than two-thirds of them crossed the river. This news reached the Royal camp in the evening. The superficial observers were distressed at this. But His Royal Highness, the prince of the world and its inhabitants, i.e., the world-conquering prince Shāhjahān, who is himself boldness and courage personified, depending entirely on the aid of God for his temporal and spiritual welfare, did not think thatwise in his divinely inspired Royal mind. With renewed hopes of divine favours, he engaged himself in preparing for the war in a joyful and happy mood and stood ready for battle by raising a barrier. Sultan Parvīz also crossed the river with all the armies of Jahāngīr and encamped with Mahābat Khān. (834)

**Disposition of Shāhjahān's army.** Then an august command was issued by His Royal Highness to the great Bakhshīs in order to array the armies of life-sacrificing officers in the following order:—Shīr Khān Fatḥ-jang who held the Manṣab of 5,000 with 5,000 horse, Khwāja Ibrāhīm, brother of Khwāja 'Uṣmān, of the Manṣab of 4,000 with 4,000 horse, Bahādur Khān, son of Shīr Khān, of the Manṣab of 4,000 with 3,500 horse, Dilāwar Khān of the Manṣab of 3,000 with 2,500 horse, and other brothers of Shīr Khān and Dilāwar Khān who jointly held Manṣabs of more than 14,000 with 10,000 horse, and all the Afghāns were posted in the van in front of the army of the Sipah-Sālār 'Abdu'llah Khān. Three hundred experienced elephants were posted in the front. Four hundred elephant-wagons ('*arāba*), one thousand bullock-carts in which fifty to sixty bullocks were employed in carrying the big cannon, and five thousand matchlock-men of the infantry were posted under the command of Rūmī Khān who had a force of one thousand horse of his own. Another contingent of four thousand musketeers of the royal cavalry (*barqándāz-i-sūwār-az-khāṣa-i-shāhī*) was attached to his company. They were posted with

Shīr Khān Fatḥ-jang and the Afghāns in the van in front of all. The Sipah-Sālār 'Abdu'llah Khān, who held the Manṣab of 7,000 with 7,000 horse, was posted in the centre in support of the Afghāns. Nāṣir Khān, who held the Manṣab of 4,000 with 3,000 horse, Aḥmad Beg Khān of the Manṣab of 4,000 with 3,000 horse, Mīrzā Isfandiyar of the Manṣab of 2,000 with 2,000 horse, Mīrzā Nūru'd-Dīn of the Manṣab of 1,000 with 1,500 (500 ?) horse, and Sa'ādat Yār and other brothers of Īlahyār Khān, who held the Manṣab of 2,000 with 1,500 horse along with all the Mughal Manṣabdārs except Shīr Khwāja and Sarandāz Bahādur, and with the private Aḥadīs were attached to the company of 'Abdu'llah Khān. The whole army consisted of twenty thousand horse and three hundred elephants. Rāja Bhim, who held the Manṣab of 6,000 with 5,000 horse, was posted to the right wing along with all the picked Rājputs of the stirrup except Rāo Manrūp, numbering more than eighteen (thousand ?) horse, three hundred elephants and two thousand musketeers of the infantry. Rāja Pahār Singh, who with his brothers (jointly) held the Manṣab of 22,000 was posted to the left wing along with Rāja Ratanpur and other loyal Zamīndārs, with a force of seventeen thousand ready cavalry (*sūwār-i-hāẓirī*) and three hundred elephants. Shīr Khwāja and Sarandāz Bahādur were entrusted with half the number of the private Aḥadīs and were appointed as *Ughchīs* of the armies of the right and the left wings, so that in time of need they might come to the aid of the Rājputs by discharging arrows from both sides and thus join in the battle. Shajā'at Khān *alias* Ja'far was posted at the advance-reserve (*Iltamish*) with all the Saiyids. He was given two hundred private elephants and was stationed in between the army of the Sipah-Sālār (and the vanguard) so that in time of need they might come to the aid of the Mughals. He himself (Shāhjahān) with fortune and prosperity took the central position with fifty thousand picked horsemen of his own and two hundred special elephants. Rāo Manrūp was posted in the reserve with some picked Rājputs consisting of a force of five thousand experienced horsemen and one hundred experienced elephants swift like fire. (835)

**Plan of the imperial army.** Therefore, when this news of the array of regiments by the world-conquering prince reached Sultan Parvīz and Mahābat Khān, they also arrayed the regiments of Jahāngīr in the following order, and became ready for war. They posted at the van twenty thousand Saiyid horsemen along with half the number of the private elephants of Jahāngīr and Parvīz which numbered more than four hundred. Rāja Bīr Singh Dev Bundela, who possessed a force of seven thousand horse of his own, was posted in the right wing along with all the Zamīndārs of the regions of the capital (Agra), Allahabad and Kalpī; and five thousand matchlock-men and one-fourth of the other half of the elephants were attached to his company. Rāja Gaj Singh was posted to the left wing along with all the other Rājputs except Rāja Jay Singh, grandson of Rāja Mān Singh, and another one-fourth of that other half of the elephants was attached to this regiment. Rāja Rāj Singh also brought an auxiliary force of five thousand matchlock-men. Khān 'Ālam was posted to the advance-reserve with the entire Mughal contingent and another one-fourth of that other half of the elephants. Sultan Parvīz and Mahābat Khān took their stand in the centre with the remaining one-fourth of the elephants. Rāja Jay Singh was posted in the reserve (*ṭarah*) with five thousand horse and fifty experienced elephants of Mahābat Khān. Thus they arrayed their regiments and remained at ease. But both the sides kept waiting for an auspicious hour in order to begin the battle at a fortunate moment. (836)

**The battle begins on the 26th October, 1624.** The True Lord, the Grantor of desires of His chosen slaves, in consideration of the desires of both sides and the safety of their Sardārs had preordained the ultimate end by His eternal pen. In short, although almost all the astrologers and particularly Rashīd Sharfu'd-Dīn Munajjim Ghāzīpūrī declared that the hour was not propitious for battle and strongly advised His

Royal Highness not to get upon his horse even, yet at the suggestion of some short-sighted officers, on Saturday, the 13th Muḥarram, 1034 A.H., corresponding to the 4th day of Abān which is called Shahryūr (26th October, 1624, A.D.), His Royal Highness came out to the field of battle as soon as he heard that Sultan Parvīz and Mahābat Khān had come to the battlefield considering this hour to be auspicious. The Royal feet of divine splendour became defiled with the dust of the field. As soon as the armies met, the Saiyids of the van of Parvīz rushed forward. One regiment posted in front of the Khān ('Abdu'llah) fired their artillery upon the enemies. Shīr Khān Fatḥ-jang with his Afghān contingent did not move from his post. All the *'arābas* (wagons) placed at the van fell into the hands of Parvīz. Seeing this state of affairs, Rāja Bhim, the Sardār of the right wing, rushed to the van and engaged in battle. Although his Rājput followers did not give him a satisfactory support, yet he took a firm stand with a band of soldiers and offered a bold and sincere fight. After putting a large number of men to the dreadful sword, he retired to the kingdom of Heaven with twenty-one fatal wounds. (837)

**Feats of the elephants.** The elephant named Shāh-pasand which was sent as a *pēshkash* by this insignificant man (Shitāb Khān) was in the regiment of Rāja Bhim. It showed splendid feats the like of which had never before been shown by any elephant during this long period of time. It threw down two elephants of the army of Parvīz and killed them, more than one hundred horses along with their riders were hurled down and levelled to the dust of disgrace; ten or fifteen of the foot-soldiers who crowded round the elephant to cut off its legs were trampled to death. Then after receiving more than two or three thousand wounds from arrows, it breathed its last and fell on the field like a mountain along with the two elephant drivers who had already been killed. The feet of one of these drivers were struck to the rope at the neck of the elephant and the other was tied to the *phānd* (halter). They lay dead on the elephant. Shīr

Khwāja, who was ready at the *Ughchī* of the right wing, shot a heavy shower of arrows and produced a great tumult in the battlefield by hurling large spears (*kaybūrhā*). He was about to disperse the Saiyid regiment. But at the death of Shīr Khwāja, who went to the lane of non-entity like a lion, the regiment of the *Ughchī* took the way to safety. Seeing this state of affairs, the Afghāns put forth their efforts. The elephant-drivers of the elephant named Jatājūt performed splendid services. Thus wherever this elephant was driven, there arose a confusion in the regiment of Jahāngīr. If it was confronted with an elephant, its opponent could not stand against it and ran away. As soon as it was faced with another elephant, the driver of Jatājūt would bring down the driver of the other elephant with a blow from his lance and the elephant Jatājūt throw the other elephant down on the ground and on several occasions its opponent was killed. If it would attack a regiment, the regiment would run away in confusion. The infantry had not the audacity to oppose it. Then the Saiyid regiment surrounded the elephant from two sides and poured on it showers of arrows. Thus both its drivers attained martyrdom and the elephant died after receiving two to three thousand wounds from arrows. When the *piādas* (foot-soldiers) were making mincemeat of its four legs with their swords, the elephant lay low in the field. In short, if the Afghāns had shown one-fourth of the boldness and strength shown by the elephants Jatājūt and Shāh-Pasand and if Shīr Khān Fatḥ-jang had taken a firm stand, the victory would have been won by the royal officers. But they showed absolute indifference. (838)

**Flight of 'Abdu'llah Khān.** Thus thought the Sipah-Sālār 'Abdu'llah Khān:—" Shīr Khān Fatḥ-jang and Rāja Bhim are my associates. Being false to my salt and without being ashamed (for it) before the Incomparable Lord, I behaved in that way with Jahāngīr Bādshāh. Now I have behaved in this way with the world-conquering illustrious prince Shāhjahān and have not sacrificed myself by placing my head at the dust of the hoof of the horse of that Royal cavalier of the field of bravery and manliness, in a battle where he himself with fortune and prosperity was standing in my support. As I have exhibited my unsteadiness, I should turn my reins to the lane of safety." He turned his reins towards the Afghāns and took the way to his adversity along with his army. (839)

**Pahār Singh deserts Shāhjahān.** At this state of affairs, Kunwar Pahār Singh, son of Rāja Bīr Singh Dev Bundela, who quarrelling with his father, had joined the prince of the people of the world, and who was honoured with royal favours as mentioned before and was appointed to command the left wing, also proved faithless, as is the eternal trait of these ill-fated Bundelas. He went over to the side of Parvīz and fought against the Royal army, and by throwing the dust of disgrace on his own head and face and on those of his ancestors, displayed his mean nature. (840)

**Shāhjahān narrowly escapes death.** During this time the horse of His Majesty named Yūz-i-Baiẓā was struck by a bullet from a gun. But this high-bred horse stood the shot and did not fall down. It did not even shake its body. By this time the life-sacrificing grooms brought another horse. That bold lion rode on this horse named Jaymurat and began to encourage the life-sacrificing officers who were around him. Every one of these devoted men who had showed his boldness in presence of that Royal cavalier of the field of battle, was infused with renewed enthusiasm with divine aid. In the mean time this second royal horse was also wounded by an arrow and an ill-fated assailant came to attack His Royal Highness. His Royal Highness with his sublime self stood to fight with him. A blow of the sword which that depraved man aimed at that male lion (Shāhjahān) was averted by him with the shield of divine protection and that rebel was sent to hell. At this time a soldier appeared behind the back of His Royal Highness and while he was engaged in throwing down his other opponent, this ill-fated man took aim at him. At this juncture, God the Great, gave guidance to Kamālu'd-Dīn Mīr Tuzuk Bāshī (Superintendent of the muster), an old servant of this State who was in charge of the arsenal. He came to his rescue and with the greatest possible swiftness he brought the assailant of His Royal Highness down from the saddle of his horse by one stroke of his sword and thus achieved a great distinction. By sunset, everybody left the field scattering the dust of faithlessness on his face. His Royal Highness remained firm like a mountain in the battlefield with a band of devoted followers whose names are mentioned below. Kamālu'd-Dīn, Hayāt Khān, Yūsuf Beg, Khwāja Yakdil, Khwāja Viqār, a few of the canopy bearers, a few private Aḥadīs and servants in-waiting remained with him like bold lions. The Amīrs of Jahāngīr went in pursuit of a band of spiritless people and then went away with the impression that they have achieved a victory. (841)

**Shāhjahān retreats to Patna.** In short, two *gharīs* after evening, the loyal officers who were in the Royal stirrup represented to him thus :—"The field is not yet out of your Royal Highness's hand. A group of cowards have run away seeking the way of safety and the army of Jahāngīr has gone in pursuit of them. Now what is the use of standing in this desert ? It befits Your Royal Highness to proceed from this station to Patna and then to act in the manner that seems advisable. " Being helpless, they proceeded (to Patna). Throughout the night they traversed the hilly ways of Khiragarh. The Sipah-Sālār 'Abdu'llah Khān and some others, who had left the battlefield before His Royal Highness, were met on the way. Being ashamed of themselves, they accompanied him. The royal horse which was wounded in the battle died on the way. The jewelled saddle of that horse was of the value of Rs. 300,000. As the Sipah-Sālār ('Abdu'llah Khān) offered a horse of his own for His Royal Highness's ride, the saddle was presented to him. The aforesaid Khān thought in his mind that if the saddle was put on any horse the groom might run away with it. So he broke the saddle into pieces and kept it with him with great care. The hills of Khiragarh were crossed in the morning, and the march was continued till next evening without stopping at any place. Then reaching a village, His Royal Highness slept for a while under a tree putting his head over his special quiver-case. The other people also took a little rest wherever they could. Then when His Royal Highness resumed the march, every body joined his stirrup in front and behind. The march was made throughout the whole night. In the morning when they reached near Sahsaranùn (Sasaram ?),[2] they halted at an adjacent village for the purpose of ablution. Khwāja Rashīd Khān and some other attendants obtained a goat and roasted some meat. But no body had the courage to request His Royal Highness to partake of this food. Therefore, the gnostics Shaykh Tāj and Shaykh Naẓīr, who were the special favourites of God and who with great willingness kept the company of His Royal Highness and Shaykh Naẓir in particular who never left the Royal camp from the beginning till end, urged upon him to take a portion of it. His Royal Highness, in order to please these two saints, took a little of it. (842)

**He reaches Rohtas.** From that place His Royal Highness proceeded alone to Rohtas. 'Abdu'llah Khān, Shīr Khān and all the other Amīrs were ordered to proceed by the right way to Patna. He himself with fortune and prosperity reached the fort of Rohtas. After staying there for three nights and two days, His Royal Highness thought within himself about the great faithlessness shown by his paid officers, and about their pride, arrogance and deliberate negligence, which ruined the cause of their master and the Qībla. He decided to send 'Abdu'llah Khān and Shīr Khān to two different directions with all the necessary equipments they require and to see how they behave. And he himself decided to stay for a few days more at the fort of Rohtas. But this plan was not approved by Her exalted Ladyship (Mumtāz Maḥal). She represented to His Royal Highness:—"Both these men are shameless, they ought to die by taking poison and should not show their face to Your Royal Highness. Your Royal Highness can judge that if these two men had performed their duties, Your Royal Highness would not have been faced with this difficult situation. As your desire to achieve this object, by the will of the Lord of Honour, has been concurrent with your august arrival, the object will be realised and it will pacify your Royal mind." His Royal Highness highly approved of this and decided to proceed to the capital city of Patna. (843)

**His arrival at Patna.** After making satisfactory arrangements for the fort, prince Murād Bakhsh, who was of three months old, was entrusted to the care of some of the ladies of harem and nurses. Khidmat Parast Khān, Saiyid Muṣṭafa Barha and Kanhar Dās, brother of Rāja Bikramajit were left in charge of the fort. Kotwāl Khān, father-in-law of Khidmat Parast Khān, who was weak and wounded, was also appointed as the custodian and Kotwāl of the lower and upper regions of the fort. He himself along with the rest of the ladies and the treasure-house (*jawhar-khāna*) started for Patna and reached there on the third day. Wazīr Khān with his fellow officers came out and made his obeisance. The entry into the delightful fort and the city of Patna was made in an auspicious hour and the august alightment was made at the palace of Parvīz. (844)

**The imperialists cross the river Son.** Now I shall give a short account of Sultan Parvīz and Mahābat Khān and of the army of Jahāngīr. On that night after pursuing the fleeing royal army for a period of two *pahars*, they pitched their camp and halted. They stayed there for a week and engaged in searching and capturing the deserted royal elephants and the belongings of the soldiers. After securing a large booty, they marched on the eighth day from that place and encamped at a distance of three *kos*. Both sides engaged spies to obtain news of their opponent's activities. Sultan Parvīz and Mahābat Khān made a march upto the river Son and began to cross it. (845)

**Shāhjahān decides to proceed to Akbarnagar.** When the news of the crossing of Jahāngīr's army was reported, the Royalists represented this to His Royal Highness and as an expedient measure it was decided to proceed to Akbarnagar and to offer battle by fortifying the pass (*dar-band*) at Garhī. Accordingly, His Royal Highness (may a thousand persons like Shitāb Khān be sacrificed for him) issued an auspicious Farmān to this insignificant Shitāb Khān,—" The day you are honoured with receipt of this peremptory Farmān, you are to proceed to Garhī and raise a fort blocking the passage to Bengal in such a way that not even a bird can cross through it. Make the place very strongly fortified and put forth your efforts to finish the work within the shortest possible time, so that it may be completed according to the desire of the officers of the State." Therefore, this insignificant creature hastened to Garhī and laid the foundation of a lofty fort. Ten thousand men consisting of builders, labourers, and diggers (*bildārān*) were engaged. Every twenty yards was assigned to one of the officers and the work was expedited. No Royal palace was built therein. It was due to two reasons. First, if a building were built in a state of hurry, the native population were likely to be panic-stricken at these alarming news, and, secondly the builders and the labourers of private buildings being all engaged in the construction of the fort, they could not be employed for this work. When the affairs took a different turn, I sent a message to Saiyid Shāh Muḥammad asking him to go to the *dar-band* and to see that no disturbance or obstruction might occur in the work of the construction of the fort. He showed signs of vacillation. Then, in consideration of the welfare of the State, I sent a sum of Rs. 4,000 from the State Treasury to Saiyid Shāh Muḥammad and Muḥammad Ṣāliḥ Wāqi'-navīs as subsidies. They drank and became intoxicated. (846)

**Quarrel between Shitāb Khān and Shāh Muḥammad.** At mid-day when I was enjoying my siesta at my home, all on a sudden Saiyid Shāh Muḥammad came armed to the *ghāt* of the river at Akbarnagar and began to shoot arrows at the boatmen of my boats. The elephant named Miān Baṣīr, which was taken to the river with its trappings for a swim, was seized by him; and he raised a tumult and said: " Shitāb

Khān is planning to cross the river Ganges and to take with him the entire treasury of Akbarnagar and the royal elephants. As long as I live I will not allow any body to go." He began to speak and do much nonsense like these. When this news was reported to me, I sent some men to him with a message,—" Where did you get these news of my project of departure ? It is quite clear that I am sleeping in my home, my boatmen are in the lane and market, the boats are in the ghāt without their boatmen, the royal elephants are in the grazing ground, and the treasury is with the *Khazānchī* (treasurer). How can this affair take place ? Therefore, give up your drunkenness and send back the elephant to Miān Baṣīr at once; otherwise, I will send you my elephant Tātār Pahlawān who has broken the tusk of Miān Baṣīr. It will immediately make you repent of your boastings and break your teeth knocking you against the second tusk of Miān Baṣīr." I said many other words of abuse to him. When the aforesaid Saiyid Shāh Muḥammad was in a state of intoxication, Muḥammad Sāliḥ, the Wāqi'-navīs, came to his senses and tried to prove that this matter had no foundation. But he did not repent of it, and he went against me. However, he took Saiyid Shāh Muḥammad to his home and sent the elephant Baṣīr with its trappings to me. As it was a strange situation, so in consideration of the welfare of the master and Qibla, I overlooked the offence of Saiyid Shāh Muḥammad and reported the details to my master and Qibla, the *Pīr* and *Murshīd.* It was presented to His Royal Highness and was read by the courtiers. His Royal Highness then started for Patna. (847)

**Dārāb Khān joins the deserters.** Now I shall give a short account of the affairs of Dārāb Khān and Ma'ṣūm Khān. Ma'ṣūm Khān under the lead of Mīr Ṣafī came along with the Zamīndārs and halted at the *Mohāna* or mouth of Khiẓrpūr where the river Dūlāy falls into the Lakhya. From that place he proceeded to Jahāngīrnagar and besieged the city and the fort. He wrote to Mīrzā Ṣāliḥ of Sylhat asking him to come at once and join them. He came and joined them.

Dārāb Khān was besieged. Dārāb Khān was unable to do anything and as it was his desire to join the officers of Jahāngīr, he did not put forth any effort and as an expedient measure he took an oath of allegiance to them. They also promised safety to Dārāb Khān. But being suspicious they kept themselves alert so that he might not abscond by some tricks. Dārāb Khān did not entertain any such plan in his mind. Rather, he was anxious to join Sultan Parvīz and Mahābat Khān. But for nine days he remained under suspense with the fear that when he would meet them, he might lose his head and the honour of the Khān Khānān[3] might be at stake. In fact why should not the salts of both sides produce their own effects. (848)

**Shitāb Khān reported to have rebelled.** His Royal Highness reached Pantī in six marches. He heard a rumour that this insignificant house-born one had turned a rebel. Although His Royal Highness did not believe it, yet at the instance of interested people and for the sake of precaution, Miān Shaykh Tāj was sent to this meanest of the slaves with an auspicious Farmān written with the Royal hand. The contents were,—"Let it be known to that unique and sincere devotee that something about him has reached the Royal ear which was never expected of him. Although our far-sighted mind does not entertain any doubt as to the sincere loyalty of that devoted servant, yet, in short, we have said to Bandagī Miān Shaykh Tāj what we had to say about that rumour talked about by the people. Whatever representation he has to make, he should do immediately without concealing any fact. As at present we do not consider any one else as he, and as he is suspicious of the behaviours of his comrades, so on the arrival of this epistle he should put in fetters Ṣāliḥ and Shāh Muḥammad including the other officers, high and low, and keep them in confinement till our arrival." In short, Miān Shaykh Tāj also arrived at the parganā of Akbarnagar. But being doubtful about his reception by me, he did not personally come to me. He sent the Royal Farmān with Khwāja Sandal I'timād Khānī with a message,—"I am a Darwish. If he sends for me, making God as a witness, then I can go." The aforesaid Khwāja came to me with the Royal Farmān and reported this to me. Although I had great liking for him, I abused him and said,—" O, inexperienced man! If Miān Shaykh Tāj could not put faith in me, you yourself ought to have gone yesterday to the Royal camp and sent Shaykh Tāj to me and should have represented the matter to His Royal Highness through his favourite courtier I'timād Khān. As you did not do that, you ought to have remained at the *Chabūtra* of the Kotwālī and informed me about it so that I could have gone with great humility to receive the Farmān of the prince and attain eternal happiness. It is clear that you are also of the same opinion; otherwise how could this fun be enacted?" In short, I sent him back immediately to the *Chabūtra* of the Kotwālī and then I walked on foot up to that place. I received the Farmān with respect and placing it on my head, I made my obeisance and performed the prostrations of gratitude. Being distinguished with the honour of both the worlds, I returned to my home. Then I immediately sent the aforesaid Khwāja to Miān Shaykh Tāj with a letter in which I wrote:—" If you do not come to me during the night, know it for certain that you will be responsible for creating disorder in Akbarnagar. I will leave the fort and the treasury without a Sardār and will proceed on foot to wait upon His Royal Highness. Then whatever is to happen will happen." Accordingly, Miān Shaykh Tāj came in haste during the night and entered the fort of Akbarnagar when two *gharīs* of the night still remained, and had a friendly interview with me. Soon after this a representation of him along with a representation of this humble self was despatched. The representation was to the following effects:— " I was to go to kiss the threshold, but Miān Shaykh Tāj detained me here. Now I shall proceed most respectfully to wherever I am ordered to go and will attain eternal distinction by rubbing (the forehead) on the dust of the feet of my master and Qibla." As Miān Shaykh Tāj had obtained leave of His Royal Highness to go home, he decided to go ahead and then to join the Royal stirrup at Jahānābād or Sulaymānābād. Therefore, whatever *sukhpāl, kahārs* (bearers), and necessary things of the store and kitchen and of the wardrobe were required by him were supplied to him. He was also given Rs. 1,000 as a present and then he was sent to his destination. I waited for the reply of my representation in order to receive the orders. In short, when the representation of Miān Shaykh Tāj and that of this humble self reached the Royal threshold, His Royal Highness, after going through these, laughed and said,—" Did we not say that this report was without any truth ? In fact, if such an act is committed by Shitāb Khān, (i.e., if he goes against the princes, with whom he was brought up) we would think that the princes had done something improper, (which incited him to commit such an act), because he was brought up and trained under our feet. We believe that even if we kill him, his dead body will fall towards us and not to any other direction. There is no room for his faithlessness." (849)

**Shāhjahān at Akbarnagar.** In short, next morning the march was resumed. In great haste a reply to the representation of this slave Shitāb Khān was written with the Royal hand,—" We desire from that true and loyal servant the following procedure of services. He should remain in the fort and should not stir out. He should distinguish himself by kissing the feet at the gate (*deorī*) of the *Maḥal.* He should know that we are reaching with safety and prosperity. He should not worry about this slight ill-luck which had befallen this State." The peremptory Royal Farmān reached five *gharīs* after morning. His Royal Highness arrived at Akbarnagar with fortune and prosperity when it was past one and a half *pahar* of the day. This humble self was under the impression that as His Royal Highness had safely come by boat so he would enter the fort by the postern gate (*khirki*) adjacent to the private *Maḥals.* This humble self also was standing at the postern gate of the fort with the view of illuminating his forehead with the honour of kissing the ground. But when I saw him disembarking with prosperity from the boat and riding on a State horse and proceeding towards the gate of the fort, I ran on foot and from a distance when my eyes fell upon the august face of that Royal cavalier of the field of battle, the pearl of the casket of sovereignty, the conqueror of the world, the master, the *Qibla*, the *Pīr* and *Murshīd*, I began to make my obeisance and performed the prostrations of gratitude. At the benevolent Royal orders, I obtained the honour of kissing the stirrup of the lamp of the seven climes and attained eternal distinction. I offered nine *muhrs* and nine *ashrafis* along with another one hundred *muhrs* and one hundred rupees as an offering to His Royal Highness. From that place, His Royal Highness, the protector of the world, entered the fort of Akbarnagar, enquiring on the way about the condition of his house-born one. After reaching the gate of the Royal residence he enquired about the completion of the Royal *Maḥals* (harems). This humblest of the house-born ones represented :—" The work was begun with great exertions, but after receiving strict orders for the construction of the fort at the *dar-band* of Garhī, I, with the view of putting a stop to false rumours, thought it expedient to stop the work of the construction of the *Maḥals* and to complete the fort of Garhī soon. Therefore, the construction of the buildings had been postponed." His Majesty became displeased with Muḥammad Sāliḥ, the Dārūgha (Inspector of buildings). This humble self once again represented :—" Muḥammad Sāliḥ is not to blame. This humble slave is guilty of the offence." By way of kindness he entered that *Maḥal*. The special carpets (*farsh-i-khāsa*) which remain in the *Maḥals* of rulers, was in this *Maḥal* where Shitāb Khān was living for the time being and on a previous occasion His Royal Highness also had stayed in this building. His Royal Highness alighted in State at the *Ghusalkhāna* (parlour) which is a private sitting place and sat on the seat of State (*Takht-i-Dawlat*). After a short while he rose and went to inspect the *Maḥals*. When he found that little work was being done, he became very much enraged and ordered Nawbat Khān, the *Kotwāl*, to punish Muḥammad Sāliḥ by inflicting a hundred stripes on him at the market place. When I saw His Royal Highness in great rage, I lost my courage for the moment (to say anything). Afterwards when he (Muḥammad Sāliḥ) was carried away, and His Majesty the Qibla of the world returned to the sitting room after inspecting the *Maḥals*, I prostrated myself before him and represented,—" This slave is to be blamed for the non-completion of the buildings. Sāliḥ is unjustly punished. I pray that this punishment be given to this mean slave and he should be released. May God, the Great, grant long life and prosperity for thousands of years to Your Royal Highness, the Qibla of the devoted people to rule over us and to pardon the sufferers of calamity by means of his kindness and fostering care to the poor." But by the time the order of his pardon was conveyed (to proper place) Sāliḥ had already received forty stripes as preordained by the decree of Fate. So he got the remission of sixty stripes. His Royal Highness, the Qibla of the inhabitant of the world, went with fortune and prosperity to the court-yard of that building and standing there asked,—" What happened to the bungalow which was situated here ?" I represented :—" It made the court-yard narrow and its presence spoiled the beauty of the other mansion, so I arranged in this way." His Royal Highness inspected the place and ordered it to be used for the residence of the princes and Her Highness, the Begum. For the purpose of a special bedroom, a partition was ordered to be raised between these two bungalows. The *Farrāshes* immediately ran, brought the partitions and fixed them up. But His Majesty, the Qibla of the inhabitants of the world asked this slave Shitāb Khān, —" Do you know anything of Dārāb Khān ?" I represented, " Your Royal Highness be pleased to take your seat and order the place to be vacated by others. Then I shall represent to you." It was accordingly done. After this I represented,—" I myself on the first day represented to you on the boat at the time of your departure for Jaunpūr that Dārāb Khān was alienating himself. I saw nothing good in his motives. If he had any sympathy (for your cause) he would have by this time requested your Royal Highness for reinforcements to serve in Bengal and he himself would have arranged for sending aid for your service. Your Royal Highness knows that Dārāb Khān could not be successful in his struggles against the Zamīndārs. Much as I wrote to him to send the treasures of Jahāngīrnagar to me to be forwarded to the Royal Court, he did not comply. Now if he wants to send away this treasure he is unable to do so. Either Sāliḥ, son of Shāmī with his four hundred cavalry would not allow him to do so, or the Zamīndārs may also block his way. In short, due to his evil origin, he has made an alliance with them and has turned away from your Royal Highness." In short, His Royal Highness, the Qibla of the inhabitants of the world, became a little mortified at his disloyalty and at the loss of the Ṣūbahs of Bengal, Sylhat, and Orissa from his control. This insignificant creature represented :—" I consider the seven climes of this world to be a (worthy) sacrifice for one single hair of your Royal Highness. Bengal and Bihar are not of such value that their loss should cause grief to the ocean-like heart of your Royal Highness. To-day or to-morrow, by the grace of God, the whole of Hind will come with auspiciousness to your hands inspite of the perverted enemies." Therefore, a great regard was paid to the faith of this house-born one. After an hour Her Highness the Begum and the august princes arrived. Then he went to the *Maḥal* and this humble self was granted leave to go to his home. As soon as he entered the *Maḥal*, I came out to the other side of the door of the *Ghusalkhāna* (parlour) and sitting there I began to write letters to my people at home. At this time, His Royal Highness came out. I got up. His Royal Highness by way of showing kindness to the poor, asked me,—" What are you writing about ?" I represented :—" I am writing a letter to the house-born ones of your Royal Highness." He took the letter and began to read. When he came to the line where I had written to my sister :—" If you do not kill my wives and daughter by giving them poison, I shall hold you responsible on the Day of Judgment," he asked me, "What is the reason of writing such things?" I represented,—"It is known to your Royal Highness that as long as this house-born one is in the stirrup, Dārāb Khān will be after dishonouring him. Then when I am sacrificing my life as an offering to your Royal Highness, what is the use of the existence of my children?" In short, out of sympathy, a few drops of tears fell from his august eyes. Crores of lives like that of Shitāb Khān deserve to be sacrificed to each of these drops of tears. Strict orders were given to construct the Royal *Māhals* at an early date, so that His Royal Highness could stay there. The *jharūka* for the high and the low and the private *Ghusalkhāna* were completed within three days and nights and these delightful houses were occupied at an auspicious moment. Royal orders were issued to the Mutaṣaddīs to manage the works of every factory under the direction of this humblest slave, Shitāb Khān. Accordingly, all the thirty-six workshops of furniture (*Karkhānjat-i-Rukhwatī*) which were in use were set in order and I offered a sum of Rs. 17,000 from my private purse without a single *dām* (a copper coin) from the State. It was accepted. (850)

**Hunting excursions at Akbarnagar.** His Royal Highness used to go out for hunting every day to the adjacent places of Akbarnagar and he used to enjoy the sight of the kills effected by the hawks, falcons and panthers. One day the Royal order was issued to the effect that His Royal Highness would cross the river Ganges and hunt in the island. Accordingly, the great Bakhshīs were ordered to inform Shitāb Khān to send a force of two hundred experienced and famous horsemen to the other side of the river one *pahar* before morning and he (Shitāb Khān) himself was to accompany the Royal stirrup. No other man was allowed to cross the river. In the meantime 'Abdu'llah Khān represented,—"If no other man is allowed to go, two hundred horsemen of long service should accompany the Royal stirrup. His Royal Highness with his pearl-scattering tongue, said,—"Who else is there more old and faithful than Shitāb Khān? He is in our august service from childhood up till now, and he knows our nature." The Sipah-Sālār remained silent and the other rivals also writhed within their hearts like a broken-headed snake. His Majesty, the Qibla of the inhabitants of the world, then returned to bed. This insignificant creature, in accordance with the orders, began to transport his picked and noted men from midnight, and after that he came to the gate of the *Maḥal* and sat there. When four *gharīs* of the night still remained, he summoned Dil Qabūl Khān, the officer in charge of the private *Maḥal* and sent a representation:—"Very little of the night is left. It will be best if your Royal Highness would take the trouble of proceeding." His Royal Highness came out safely and happily, got inside a *sukhpāl* at the gate of the *Maḥal* and came to his boat. After crossing the river safely, he began to hunt from the early morning. This humble Shitāb Khān was ordered to let loose the private animals to (hunt). So he let loose a falcon after a partridge and followed it. At this time there appeared a tiger. His Royal Highness wanted to kill the tiger with his gun from the back of an elephant. At this time this humble Shitāb Khān arrived at that place. Fearing that some accident might take place, he went beyond the rules of decorum, swore in the name of the Lord of lords and requested His Royal Highness not to attempt such a thing from the saddle of the elephant. He then represented,—"If it is in the desire of Your Royal Highness to kill this tiger, order me to bring the female elephant which is being trained for hunting tiger, so that you may ride on it and hunt." His Majesty graciously, said, "The elephant is not at Akbarnagar at this time, it must have been taken out to the grazing field. By the time the elephant is brought over, the tiger will run away. Then what is the gain?" I represented,—"Through the favour of God and through the benign influence of the Royal grace, this humble self will be responsible for keeping the tiger at bay. Until the female elephant provided with the howdah arrives here, Your Royal Highness may keep yourself engaged in hunting bustards (*charz*)." Therefore, the heralds (*naqībān*) were ordered to bring the female elephant. The elephants which were in the Royal stirrup were given to this humble self and His Royal Highness went to enjoy the hunt of the hawks and falcons. This humble self kept the tiger at bay with the help of the elephants. Until the female elephant was brought, His Royal Highness sent men every moment to enquire about the tiger from this insignificant creature. On each occasion I represented that the tiger was in its place. When the female elephant was brought, His Royal Highness came from the other side riding on it. This humble self advanced towards His Royal Highness and showed him the tiger. His Royal Highness fired his gun. In short, as it was not destined to die, the shot did not take effect. The tiger went from that place to another forest. It was again followed and a second shot was fired. This time it passed through the skin and the tiger was wounded. The tiger again ran away from that place and took shelter under a heap of grass. It was then followed to that place and a Qamargāh (hunting ring) was formed. As no other man had the audacity either to shoot an arrow or to fire a gun without permission, so this mean house-born one (Shitāb Khān) represented to His Royal Highness:—" Every time this tiger roars, the elephants are frightened, and do not remain firm in their positions and a great confusion arises among them. If it was permitted, the tiger could have been transfixed with ten arrows by this time." His Royal Highness with a smile of admiration, said,—" The permission is given. Let us see what kind of arrows are shot by our servants." This most insignificant creature made his obeisance and performed the prostrations of gratitude. A search for the tiger was made but no trace of it could be found. Inspite of diligent searches the whereabouts of the tiger could not be traced. As there was no help for the situation, the pursuit was given up and His Royal Highness returned to the Royal palace. (851)

**Sympathy shown to Shitāb Khān.** At night in the *Ghusalkhāna* His Royal Highness was graciously pleased to say,—" Shitāb Khān! It is our desire that in order to secure your young ones, we shall send you to Jahāngīrnagar with an advance army of two thousand brave and experienced horsemen, divided into two regiments." Therefore, I illuminated my forehead by making obeisance and prostrations of gratitude. For the Royal favours shown to me from moment to moment which deserve to be recognised by the sacrifice of my own person, I expressed my gratitude by performing the rites of obeisance according to imperial regulations. His Royal Highness addressing this house-born one told all the nobles-in-waiting about his services of young days as far as he could remember. This became a source of honour and distinction to this house-born one. Then His Royal Highness went into the *Maḥal.* (852)

**Bridge built on the Ganges.** Next morning Royal orders were issued to Shitāb Khān to go personally to the fort of the pass of Garhī and to stay there so that the fortification of that path of communication might be well secured. This humble self performed three obeisances and prostrations of gratitude and with his heart and soul he deemed obedience to Royal command to be his temporal and spiritual happiness. But at last it occurred to the Royal mind that there were many other works to be done by this humble Shitāb Khān. So it was ordered that this insignificant man should remain at the Royal threshold and a force of three thousand and five hundred matchlock-men should be sent under Kamālu'd-Dīn Huṣayn entitled Jān Niṣār Khān so that he might go along with Rūmī Khān and stay at the aforesaid fort. This slave was ordered to supply Mīr Shams with all materials he required to construct a bridge over the river Ganges. Therefore, I supplied Mīr Shams I'timād Khānī with every thing he required. He, with the help of the workers and boatmen of mine, completed the bridge within four days and nights. (853)

**Officers sent to realise revenues.** During this time Shīr Khān complained that he was not receiving his allowance from his Jāgīr of Ghoraghāt. He prayed for permission to send one hundred horsemen to the help of the revenue officers of that place. An order was issued to this slave Shitāb Khān to post one of his confidential officers at the bridge in order to count these hundred horsemen of Shīr Khān and allow them to cross over the bridge. Accordingly, I sent my eunuch there. Shīr Khān Fatḥ-jang also went to the bridge and transported his hundred horsemen over in collaboration with my eunuch. Then he (Shīr Khān) returned to his residence. Dilāwar Khān was also granted leave to depart with instructions to come back after securing some money from the Jāgīr. Kamālu'd-Dīn Ḥusayn was also recalled from the fort of Garhī and sent to the Jāgīrs of Rāja Bhim in order to bring whatever (money) he could realise. The officers of this humble self who went to the pargana of Tājpūr Purnea ascertained its revenues to be Rs. 120,000. It was assigned to Shīr Khān in lieu of his salary of Rs. 240,000 as a grant for six months. He did not accept it. It was then ordered to be assigned to some other men. But with the object of pleasing Shīr Khān, none of the officers was willing to take it. Wazīr Khān represented the details (to Shāhjahān), that every one to whom it was assigned raised some objections. His Royal Highness, said,—" I know that they are doing so for the sake of Shīr Khān. Alright, give it to Shitāb Khān. He does not care for any one else but our person. He will accept it in lieu of his allowance." Accordingly, it was given to this humble self. I accepted it on condition that I am permitted to go there personally to punish the Zamīndārs and to make them obedient to my officers. But as this humble self was entrusted with many other works so His Royal Highness did not sanction it. At last it was assigned to Saiyid Shajā'at Khān. (854)

**Shitāb Khān's officers leave Hājo.** Now I shall give a short account of the affairs of Kūch. When Zāhid Khān reached Kūch, my nephew Mufattiḥ and my Hindu officer, Balabhadra Dās, relinquished their charge of the Ṣūbah of Kūch and everything connected with it in favour of Zāhid Khān and they prepared to return. Zāhid Khān for the sake of preparing a correct account of the allowance of his Jāgīr stood on their way. After a dispute, when the agents of this humble Shitāb Khān rendered an account, Zāhid Khān had nothing to complain and then he gave them the permit (*Rukhsat-nāma*) to depart. They started from that place and reached Ghoraghāt. But as the conditions had changed, my sister's son, acted according to the saying,—" Buy the sister's son with pure gold or kill him with a blackstone." I showed him great favours and through the grace of God and the fostering care of His Imperial Majesty, he was made the ruler of Kūch and great Amīrs were made to follow him. A position like this was never seen even by his grand-father Ẓiāu'l-Mulk, but inspite of all these things, at the instigation of his mother, he did not show any consideration either to the favours shown by this humble self or to the grace of the master and Qibla. He in collusion with that mean Hindu (Balabhadra) and some *Sipāhis* (soldiers) played some tricks and did not come to Akbarnagar. He remained in the vicinity of Maldah. His Royal Highness due to his benevolent nature did not take notice of it; otherwise if I had represented to His Royal Highness, a Royal order would have been issued to Kamālu'd-Dīn Ḥusayn, who was sent to the Jāgīrs of Rāja Bhim, to bring him by force. But as it was the will of God that this humble self should be dishonoured, he (Mufattiḥ) behaved in that manner. (855)

**Allegations against Shitāb Khān.** One day when His Royal Highness was sitting on his throne, Wazīr Khān came and represented:—" Shitāb Khān has obtained Rs. 30,000 from the pargana of Mangalkūt. The revenue-sheets (*nushkha*) of other districts (*maḥallāt*) have not yet been submitted for inspection to ascertain the amount received from those districts. When an enquiry was made, he refused to submit them. He says that he would submit his explanations when it would be demanded by Your Royal Highness." His Royal Highness, said,—" What has Shitāb Khān to represent? Does he admit the charge?" Then an order was given to summon Shitāb Khān. This humble self was present behind the throne. He came and stood before him. He was questioned about the allegations made by Wazīr Khān. He represented,—" He (Wazīr Khān) is speaking the truth in a way. Because whatever (revenue) falls short in the Crown-lands (*khalisa*) must be written in the name of some one. But the prayer of this house-born one is this, that the harvest of the autumn season (*Faṣl-i-Kharīf*) is already over. This slave also suffered the same changes of circumstances as every other officer in Bengal. At the time of the assignment of the spring collection, Wazīr Khān, said:—' If you demand your allowance from the spring collection, (there is no means of paying you, as) there has already been a loss of four crores in the Crown-lands, and every one will have to share the loss.' Therefore, let that gain of the servant go to hell which brings loss to the wealth of his master. I passed over the spring-crop. The time for the collection of the third season of the autumn crop which has been assigned in lieu of salaries, has not yet come. This humble self had to protect the Ṣūbah of Kūch till the arrival of Zāhid Khān and had to govern the Ṣūbah of Gawr keeping a strict eye over its surroundings; and in addition, he had to supply provisions for the elephants of Kūch which were sent to the Royal Court. How was it possible for him to manage all these expenses? Therefore, he decided to meet all these expenses from the State treasury. In near future, when the autumn crop will be collected he will repay this money to the State treasury. For these reasons he had to spend this sum. Now even this autumn collection, owing to the transference of his Jāgīr, is also going to fail. Any order (considered suitable) may be passed in this matter." His Royal Highness, said,—" Who transferred your Jāgīr?" I represented, " It was transferred in accordance with (Royal) orders. Mangalkūt, the chief pargana of the Jāgīr had been assigned to the Sipah-Sālār. Dartia and Katakpūt which were my principal Jāgīrs and which were assigned to me on their transference from Her Exalted Ladyship Mumtāz Maḥal Begum, have been reassigned to her. The Kotwālī of Akbarnagar has been assigned to Nawbāt Khān. Now, being content with Dunapūr and some other second and third rate parganas, I am unable to maintain my estate." Therefore, an order was issued that Wazīr Khān should abstain from favouring the Sipah-Sālār and should make assignments to this humble devoted slave to his satisfaction. It was further ordered that no one should ask for the repayment of the money spent by him from the Royal treasury. The accounts of friends are in their hearts." Wazīr Khān had nothing further to say. This humble self made three obeisances and performed prostrations of gratitude and distinguished himself amongst all with the honour of both the worlds. (856)

**Bananas kept for Shitāb Khān eaten by Awrangzīb.** At night, in the *Ghusalkhāna* when he (Shāhjahān) was favouring some of his courtiers with the gift of bananas named *Martaban* (a kind of sweet banana) from the Royal table, the share of this humble house-born Shitāb Khān was ordered to be kept within the *Maḥal.* As soon as I went there, His Royal Highness himself remembered about them and ordered them to be brought up. The eunuchs delayed in bringing them. At last Khwāja Shamshād brought two bananas from the *Maḥal.* On enquiry it was learnt that prince Sultan Awrangzīb had eaten the rest. His Royal Highness became enraged. This humble house-born one made his obeisance and represented,—" It is a great fortune to this humble house-born one. The first good-luck is that this humble self is distinguished over all by Your Royal Highness remembering him at the Royal table; the second good-luck is that the provision from the Royal table kept for this humble one has been taken by the son of his master and Qibla." At these words His Royal Highness, the Qibla of the inhabitants of the world, became highly pleased and showed great sympathy. (857)

**Conspiracy against Shitāb Khān.** His Royal Highness's favours concerning this humble author Shitāb Khān began to increase from day to day, and it turned some of his friends into enemies. Therefore, at the instigation of most of the courtiers, Nawbat Khān, the Kotwāl, brought one of the bow-makers and alleged that the desertion of Ḥakīm Ṣāliḥ, the

Superintendent of the arsenal, was effected with the knowledge of one of the officers of Shitāb Khān named Dūst Muḥammad. His Royal Highness the Qibla of the people enquired of it from this humble self. Very much annoyed at this (allegation), I represented thus:—"I have in reality no employee named Dūst Muḥammad. One Mughal horseman named Dūst Muḥammad, who was my officer, died a month ago. If this allegation can be proved, I shall hold myself responsible for the desertion of Muḥammad Ṣāliḥ." At last when His Royal Highness asked that bow-maker, he represented,—"Dūst Muḥammad was a servant of Fath Shāh, the Shiqdār (revenue officer) of Akbarnagar. He took by force five bows from me without paying for them. Now he has left the service of Fatḥ Shāh as well. Smarting under the loss, I brought this allegation." This humble Shitāb Khān ran and fell upon the Royal feet. His Royal Highness (may a thousand lives be sacrificed for him) with great leniency, ordered the infliction of a hundred stripes on the bow-maker. Nawbat Khān was severely censured and was turned out of the assembly. (858)

**Farmāns sent to Dhāka and Hājo.** At night in the *Ghusalkhāna* a peremptory Farmān was entrusted to me to be sent to Dārāb Khān by any means possible. In compliance with the command, I sent it to Dārāb Khān. I was further instructed to write letters to Zāhid Khān, Shaykh Shāh Muḥammad, Rāja Satrajit and other Zamīndārs of the frontier of the Ṣūbah of Kūch. Therefore, in accordance with the command, I wrote these letters in the presence of His Royal Highness as dictated by him. Rāja Satrajit was particularly written to thus:—"What are you thinking in your mind? By the will of God and by the fortune of His Royal Highness, either to-day or to-morrow the supporters of Parvīz will be brought either as prisoners to be confined in the fort of Rohtas or their heads will be cut off and hung at the gate of the fort of Jahāngīrnagar." The ill-fated Satrajit sat over this letter with the plea that its disclosure would lead to disorder. (859)

**Death of Saiyid Mubārak.** Saiyid Mubārak Mānikpūrī, who had surrendered the fort of Rohtas to the Royal officers, was at this time favoured with the Jāgīr of the parganas of Sulaymānābād and Jahānābād yielding an income of two hundred thousand rupees (per annum). He was granted leave to go to his Jāgīr. As he (Shāhjahān) had to go to the Deccan and as his (Mubārak's) Jāgīr lay on his way, he was instructed to secure a good sum. Accordingly, Saiyid Mubārak reached the pargana of Jahānābād and began to collect the revenues. Chandra Bhān and other Zamīndārs and particularly (the Zamindar of ?) Jhakra-Barda came and waited upon him and remained in his service. In the meantime they received the news that His Royal Highness was marching with fortune and prosperity. Therefore (the Zamindar of ?) Jhakra-Barda without the knowledge of Chandra Bhān led a night-attack against Saiyid Mubārak. Saiyid Mubārak, under the false belief that (the Zamīndār of ?) Jhakra-Barda would not attack him, was staying alone with his camp followers in a way against the rules of military leadership. He came out with his son, his son-in-law and two servants to the field before the fort and after a short skirmish he attained martyrdom along with three servants. One horseman saved himself and came out of the field. But his escape was of no avail. When the death of the Sardār became known, every one began to fly from his post. In short, he (the Zamīndār of Jhakra-Barda) seized all the belongings of Saiyid Mubārak and fearing the approach of the Royal army fled away. (860)

**Shāhjahān decides to return to Burhānpūr.** In short, His Royal Highness the Qibla of the people, prince Shāhjahān, stayed at Akbarnagar for a period of twenty-four days. After this the following arrangements were made for the well-being of the State. As the entire army of Jahāngīr was advancing upon Bengal so before they (Jahāngīr's army) could return to the Deccan, His Royal Highness would go to Burhānpūr by the same route by which he came, and take possession of the Ṣūbahs of Aḥmadnagar, the Deccan, Khāndesh, Gujarāt and Mālwa. The march was planned accordingly. Astrologers who had knowledge of the stars were summoned to find out an auspicious hour. One astronomer named Chakrpatī (Chakravarti ?), who was also an expert physician, was in my service. He possessed a sound knowledge of the science of Astrology and was undoubtedly an expert in his science. Therefore, I presented him on this occasion (to Shāhjahān). The master and Qibla of the people called that astrologer and ordered him to be seated before him. He answered all the questions that were asked by His Royal Highness. It was decided to march from Akbarnagar on the 22nd Rabi'u'l-Awwal. His Royal Highness then retired to bed and the loyal officers in-waiting were granted leave to go to their respective houses. This humble self also went to his home and slept. (861)

**Shitāb Khān allows his property to be looted.** Next morning I thought within myself that Mufattiḥ and Balabhadra Dās had not come. How then would it be possible to start without the conveyances and have the goods and chattels carried ? Therefore, I went to the store houses, opened their doors and shouted,—" O, comrades ! Take whatever you require before others receive information." First of all, all my servants, particularly the group of stipendiary servants, who in fact were not to accompany me, began to loot the goods. This humble author Shitāb Khān stood by. I was amazed to find that this herd of ungracious people did not stop to consider how, having eaten the salt of the master, they could agree to ruin the property of their master. They began to loot the goods in such a way that even an enemy would not do so in looting the property of his adversary. Even the enemy shows some consideration for his neighbours. At this sight I became greatly mortified and astonished, and tears came out of my eyes. But these people raised a tumult, the like of which was never seen or heard. I became perplexed. When nothing was left except some apparels which had been kept separate, I went to make my obeisance to His Royal Highness. I represented to him,—" As I have no beast of burden to carry my goods, I have consigned all my goods and chattels to the plunder of the vicissitudes of time. A small portion was kept to be carried with me, but I find no conveyance even to carry that." His Royal Highness, the Qibla of the people favoured me with two female elephants for carrying the goods. Her Exalted Ladyship the Begum along with the princes, who are the pearls of the casket of sovereignty and kingship, were sent ahead of others. At night in the *Ghusalkhāna* great favours were shown to me. But Mīrzā Sharīf, the Superintendent of the elephant-stable sent away the female elephants during night. In the morning he sent me two baby elephants which could carry only four maunds of goods with great difficulty. This humble self at the time of the morning prayers went to the gate of the Royal residence and stayed from that time near the august stirrup till the Qibla of the people rode out to start. (862)

**One thousand deserters killed.** When I saw that the Sipah-Sālār was ordered to return to the city and to kill whoever is found there, I sent back one of my officers named Nīk Muḥammad Beg to bring Sa'ādat Khān and other officers of mine and to force them to march by every possible way. When His Royal Highness with fortune and prosperity reached the destination and started for hunting, I also took leave to go to my quarters and to return after making necessary arrangements. His Royal Highness agreed to it and I went to Akbarnagar with one of the Aḥadīs in my company. Mīr Shams was ordered to dismantle the bridge on the river Ganges. He executed the order. As Nīk Muḥammad went ahead of me and as he was preparing to start with all (men) high and low, so I became ready soon after my arrival and proceeded to the Royal camp. I reached there at a time when His Royal Highness was sitting at the door of the Royal tent and was endeavouring to fix its door. When the Royal tent was satisfactorily fixed, he went into the *Maḥal*. At night the *Ghusalkhāna* was prepared. Kamālu'd-Dīn Ḥusayn came from the rear and represented,—" I saw the Sipah-Sālār preparing a row (*khiyābān*) of the heads of the people killed (by him). The head of Arām Bakhsh, son of Dārāb Khān, was placed in its centre. The torch-bearers (*mash'alchiān*) were made to stand within the row of heads and he himself was taking his food sitting in its centre. His Royal Highness asked,—"How many of the deserters from the Royal camp have been killed to-day. ?" Kamālu'd-Dīn Ḥusayn represented,—"I saw four hundred and thirty heads before the Sipah-Sālār. I killed fifty-two men. More than three hundred were killed by Sarandāz Bahādur, and Rūmī Khān has killed about two hundred men." In short, according to this account it was manifest that about one thousand deserters and disloyal people had received their retribution (*qiṣāṣ*) on that day. Then His Royal Highness retired to bed. **(863)**

**Hunting excursions.** Next morning the march was resumed. The whole journey was spent in the enjoyment of the hunt of hawk and falcon till the next stage was reached. At night the *Ghusalkhāna* (parlour) sat (as usual). His Royal Highness sat there for one *pahar* and distributed the games to the life-sacrificing servants. Then he went into the *Maḥal*. The third encampment was made at Tipūra. The whole journey was spent in hunting. As the horse on which this humble house-born Shitāb Khān was riding was drenched with perspiration due to the weight of the *pākhar* (a kind of steel armour that covers the body of the elephant) which was on it, so His Royal Highness the Qibla, by way of kindness asked me to take out the *pākhar* and to put it on the pack-saddle of the Royal elephant. I dismounted from the horse and made my obeisance and performed the prostrations of gratitude. Ḥusaynī Bahādur Chila, who was riding in front of the pack-saddle occupying the place of the chief elephant-driver, placed the *pākhar* on the pack-saddle of the Royal elephant and thus the next station was reached. Not a single day passed without some Royal favours being shown to this unfortunate and humble Shitāb Khān. The confidence into which this insignificant man was taken, was not enjoyed even by the princes. The trust reposed on me was beyond description. In every way His Royal Highness showed his favours to me. (864)

**Shitāb Khān deserts Shāhjahān.** It has been mentioned before that by the grace of God, His Royal Highness imbibed such a turn of mind that he would prefer to be separated from the princes but not from Shitāb Khān. Myself, as well as the whole world were of this way of thinking that every one with all his belongings and family should sacrifice himself as an offering to the dust of the feet of His Royal Highness and distribute their belongings to the poor, for the well-being of the master and Qibla and for felicity in both the worlds. I wanted to do accordingly. But it was not ordained to be so. I was disgraced in both the worlds. I was separated from His Royal Highness in the following manner and was thrown into the well of calamity. After the audience at the *Ghusalkhāna*, although I was posted at the *chawkī* (guard-house), I came to my camp. All on a sudden, it thus occurred to my mind,—" You are following the Royal stirrup but all your people are in bondage." It was just like the famous saying of His Holiness Shaykh Muṣliḥu'd-Dīn Sa'dī Shīrāzī.

*Qiṭa'* :

" That man, having no sense of honour,
Shall never see the face of good-luck,
He who chooses comforts for his own self
And leaves his wife and children in hardship."

In short, when I was overwhelmed with this idea, I started on foot with sixteen of my intimate followers who accompanied me. Having reached the river Ganges, by the favour of the Lord of Honour, I crossed over it and came to Malatipūr to my *Pīr-Zāda* (son of the spiritual director) Miān Saiyid Niẓāmu'd-Dīn and obtained the honour of kissing his feet. Then next morning at the time of march, the fact of my departure was reported to His Royal Highness. At first he was greatly aggrieved. At last when people began to speak ill of this humble self, His Royal Highness through his innate benevolence, said,—" He has not gone without our permission." May God grant him long life and sovereignty! May a hundred thousand lives like mine be sacrificed for one single hair of His Royal Highness who had shielded me in such a way! (865)

This volume has thus been brought to its end. It has grown into a thing to be remembered for several thousands of years.

THE END

# APPENDICES

# NOTES

## BOOK I

### INTRODUCTION.

1. Zamzam is the sacred well of Mecca, also called the well of Isma'īl. It is in *al-haram-al-sharīf* S.E. of Ka'ba opposite the corner of the sanctuary in which the Black Stone is inserted. Zamzam literally means "abundant water". Muslim tradition connects the origin of this well with the story of Abraham. It was opened by the angel Gabriel to save Hagar and her son Isma'īl who were dying of thirst in the desert. Hagar was the first to catch its water by building a wall of stone around it. It was held in reverence from a very remote age and even in pre-Islāmic period the Persians used to visit this place. (For details see Encyclopaedia of Islām.).

### CHAPTER I.

1. Jahāngīr Qulī Khān known as Lāla Beg was the son of Niẓām, Humāyūn's Librarian. He entered the service of Akbar who placed him among the attendants of Prince Salīm. He was given the title of Bāz Bahādur when Jahāngīr was a Prince. After one month of Jahāngīr's accession to the throne he was raised from the Manṣab of 1,500 to that of a 4,000 horse and appointed governor of Bihar. After the death of Quṭbu'd-Dīn, governor of Bengal, in an encounter with Shīr Afgan, he was appointed to succeed him and his rank was raised to 5,000 personal and horse. But owing to the unhealthy climate of Bengal he died within a short time of his assumption of office. (Iqbāl Nāma, 33, 34; Memoirs, I. 21, 142, 208; Ma'āṣir, I. 512-14.).

2. Islām Khān was the grandson of Shaykh Salīm Chishtī and a foster brother of Jahāngīr. His original name was 'Alāu'd-Dīn. He first entered the service of Akbar. When Jahāngīr ascended the throne his rank was raised to 2,000 and he was conferred the title of Islām Khān. At the transference of Jahāngīr Qulī Khān from Bihar to Bengal he was appointed Ṣūbahdār of Bihar. Then he was appointed as the governor of Bengal in May 1607 to succeed Jahāngīr Qulī. (For the date of his appointment see note 10.). His appointment to Bengal was very much resented by the nobles of the Court as they considered him to be too young for that responsible office. His age at this time was thirty-eight, being one year's younger than the Emperor. The Emperor loved him for his bravery and indomitable spirit, and was addressed

by him as "My son". Later on we find that he had fully justified his appointment by suppressing all the rebel chiefs of Bengal and bringing the whole country under the complete subjugation of the imperial power. (For details see Memoirs, Rogers, I, 31, 32, 144, 171, 208.).

3. Akbarnagar or Rājmaḥal is situated on the western bank of the Ganges about 20 miles north-west from the ruins of Gawr in the Maldah district. The original name of this place was Āk-Maḥal or Āg-Maḥal. There are different explanations of the name of this place. According to Beveridge "Āk-Maḥal" which is a Turkish word means "The white palace." According to 'Abdu'l-Laṭīf a contemporary traveller' the place was called "Āg-Maḥal" or "the town of fire", because of the frequent outbreak of fire in the houses of the town which were made of straw and *hogla*. While others say that the Sultans of Bengal and Bihar used to rest here after accomplishing the first stage of their journey from Gawr to Bihar. The place was therefore named as Āg-Maḥal or Advance station. The town was founded by Mān Singh, who changed the name to Rājmaḥal alias Akbarnagar. Previous to this the place was known as Āg-Maḥal. In 1608 A.D. the seat of the government of Bengal was transferred by Islām Khān from Rāj Maḥal to Dacca. It was again made the capital of Bengal during the viceroyalty of Prince Shujā'. (Martin's Eastern India, II, 10, 13, 67; Sarkar's "'Abdul-Laṭīf's Travels in Bihar", J.B.O.R.S., V, 1919, 601; Blochmann, J.B.A.S., 1873, 218; Bengal, Past and Present, XXXVI, 1928, II; Rennell's map No. 15.).

4. Ihtimām Khān whose name was Malik 'Alī was a commander of 250 horse during the reign of Akbar. He was for some time the Kotwāl of Agra and Jahāngīr sent him against the rebellious Khusrau. He was also sent to Malwa against the rebellion of Badī'u'z-Zamān, son of Mīrzā Shāhrukh, in order to bring him to the Court. Later on he was appointed to the post of the 'Mīr-Baḥr' or admiral of the imperial fleet in Bengal. At the time of this appointment he was raised to the rank of 1,000 personal and 300 horse (Memoirs, I. 127, 144; Iqbāl Nāma, 9.). According to Mīrzā Nathan he was given the rank of 700 horse, and 1,000 personal, which is contrary to the account given in the Tuzuk, p. 68. Mr. Sri Ram Sharma is evidently wrong when he says that Ihtimām Khān was "raised to the command of a thousand horse." (vide Journal of Indian History, Vol. XI, p. 339).

5. Wazīr Khān originally known as Muqīm was given the title of Wazīr Khān by Akbar and the Viziership of his dominions although according to Ma'āṣir, (iii, 932), he does not seem to have had any real power, and he was soon superseded. Jahāngīr also "selected him for the same title, rank and service." But he was not given full authority. The office was jointly held by Jān Beg and Muqīm in the first year of Jahāngīr's reign. Later on this office of Vizier was given to 'Ināyat Beg

and Wazīr Khān was sent to Bengal as the Dīwān of the province. Then the Emperor, being displeased with his work, dismissed Wazīr Khān from the Dīwānship of Bengal and recalled him to the Court on the 2nd Zu'lhijja, 1016 A.H. = 19th March 1608 A.D. It seems that he was removed from office soon after Islām Khān was appointed Ṣūbahdār of Bengal. He presented himself before the Emperor on the 17th Jumād I, 1017 A.H. = August 29th, 1608. (For details see, Memoirs, I, 13, 20, 22, 139, 147 ; Ma'āṣir, III, 932-33.).

6. His full name is Abu'l-Ḥasan Shihāb Khānī. He was appointed on the same date when Wazīr Khān was recalled. But he reached Bengal almost at the same time with Islām Khān. (Memoirs, I, 139.).

7. His full name was Shaykh Ibrāḥīm, son of Quṭbu'd-Dīn Khān Kūka. In the first year of Jahāngīr's reign, he was given the rank of 1,000 personal and 300 horse, and the title of Kishwar Khān. Later on he was appointed governor of the fort of Rohtas. On the 5th year of Jahāngīr's accession he was promoted to the rank of 2,000 personal and horse, and posted as the Fawjdār of Uch. In the expedition against 'Uṣmān of Sylhat he was sent to help Shajā'at Khān the Mughal commander. He was killed in this battle in 1612.

8. Chaund was the name of a pargana situated to the west of Sasaram. Abu'l-Faẓl calls it Jaund. (Akbar Nāma, Text, 148 ; Beveridge, I, 327.). Beams says that it is in Sarkar Rohtas, (J.A.S.B., 1895, 81.).

9. Rohtas is situated on the Sōn in the district of Shāhābād. It is one of the oldest fortresses of this division. Originally it was built by a Hindu Prince named Rohitaswa after whom it derives its name which was corrupted into Rautas and Rohtas. Mān Singh, the Mughal Viceroy, selected this place as a place of safety for his family and treasures and he constructed the buildings which are to be found now (Martin, Vol. I, 404, 432 ; Rennell's map No. 9.).

10. If we are to accept the date given here of the departure of Ihtimām Khān from Agra to Bengal we shall have to locate the date of Islām Khān's appointment at some time previous to 30th June, 1607 A.D. Neither the Tuzuk nor the Iqbāl Nāma definitely give the date of the death of Jahāngīr Qulī Khān, the predecessor of Islām Khān. Jahāngīr records in the account of his Third New Year's feast from Accession that the report of the death of Jahāngīr Qulī Khān reached him on the 20th Muharram 1017 (?) A.H. (7th May, 1608), and on the receipt of this report he appointed Islām Khān governor of Bengal (vide Translation of the Tuzuk, Vol. I, 142.). But the text of the Tuzuk (Aligarh edition, pp. 67, 68.) gives the year as 1014 A.H. The translator of the Tuzuk considers 1014 to be a wrong date and substitutes 1017

in its place. The Iqbāl Nāma (p. 33) records these events in the accounts of the beginning of the third year of Jahāngīr's reign which commences on Thursday, the 2nd, Zu'lhijja 1016 A.H. (20th March 1608). The author has not given the exact date of the death of Jahāngīr Qulī and the appointment of Islām Khān. But in the next page he has given the date 4th Rabi'u'l-Akhir when the author was honoured with the title of Mu'tamid Khān. The month of Rabi'u'l-Awwal following the Zu'lhijja of 1016 A.H. falls in the year 1017. So it appears from these authorities that the report of the death of Jahāngīr Qulī reached the Emperor sometime during the period between the two dates mentioned above and he made the appointment of his successor. In substance the Iqbāl Nāma follows the Tuzuk.

The Bahāristān says that Islām Khān, after his arrival in Bengal made recommendation to the Emperor to appoint new civil and military officers to serve in Bengal and in compliance to his requests the Emperor appointed Ihtimām Khān as the Mīr Baḥr and granted him leave to depart on the 5th, Rabi'u'l-Awwal, 1016 A.H. (30th June, 1607). In the next paragraph we find that the Emperor had reviewed the fleet on the 9th of the same month and Ihtimām Khān left for Bengal on the same date. In paragraph 64 of the Bahāristān we find that the Bengal fleet had entered the river Ichhamati near Dākchara in the district of Dacca on the 27th, Rabi'u'l-Awwal, 1017 A.H. (11th July 1608 A.D.). Had the appointment of Islām Khān been made on the 20th Muharram 1017 (7th May 1608), it would have been impossible for him to enter the Ichhamati on the date mentioned above. He had already spent one rainy season at Ghoraghāt and was proceeding towards Dacca at a slow speed fighting the rebel Zamindars on his way. If we read the date of the Tuzuk referred above as 20th Muharram, 1016 A.H. (16th May, 1607), we may reconcile the dates of the events recorded in the Tuzuk and the Bahāristān. The sequence of events and dates that followed the appointment of Islām Khān in Bengal clearly shows that his appointment was made sometime in May 1607 and not in 1608 as is generally believed. The dates deduced from the texts of the Tuzuk and the Iqbāl Nāma seem to be wrong. The Bahāristān, being an account of an eye-witness who had taken a prominent part in all the expeditions of Islām Khān, is to be preferred to other authorities.

11. Khān Jahān originally known as Pīr Khān, son of Dawlat Khān Lūdī, was a famous warrior of Akbar's reign. He served successfully under Raja Mān Singh, Prince Daniyal, and Prince Salīm. In the second year of Jahāngīr's reign he was given the rank of 3,000 personal and 1,500 horse, the title of Ṣalābat Khān, and the distinction of sonship (*farzandī*). He enjoyed the highest royal favour and wielded a very great influence at the Court. In A.D. 1608 he was given the title of Khān Jahān and raised to the rank of 5,000 personal and horse. He accom-

panied the imperial army to the Deccan expedition. In the 12th year of Jahāngīr's reign his rank was raised to 6,000 personal and horse. During Shāh Jahān's reign, Khān Jahān Lūdī fled from Court, was pursued, and killed. (Memoirs I, 87, 89, 128, 129, 139, 161, 296, 299, 372.).

12. Prince Jahāndār was born of a concubine of Akbar about the time of his death in 1605. Gladwin says he was born as a twin with Prince Shahryār. But this is contrary to the account given in the Tuzuk. The tutorship of this prince was assigned to the governor of Bengal. After the death of Jahāngīr Qulī Khān, the tutorship of this Prince was assigned to Islām Khān. Later on owing to the insecure political condition of Bengal, Islām Khān sent him back to the imperial Court in the fourth year of Jahāngīr's accession. He waited upon the Emperor on the 25th, Jumad I, 1017, A.H. (6th September, 1608, when Jahāngīr found him to be a "born devotee". (Memoirs, I, 20, 143, 156; Preface of the Tuzuk, 17, Alig. Edn.). In Roger's translation of the Tuzuk, p. 156, f.n. 1, Prince Jahāndār is said to have been found a born-idiot by Jahāngīr after his return from Bengal. Gladwin also suggests that he was sent to Court because he showed some signs of insanity. This is opposed to the testimony of the Tuzuk and the Bahāristān. This misconception about Prince Jahāndār, arose out of a wrong translation of the word مجذوب (majẕūb) which was used by the translator in the sense of an idiot. But the proper meaning of the word is, "Attracted by Divine grace and renouncing all worldly concerns; to give oneself entirely over to piety and contemplation", (vide Steingass). The context also points out this to be the proper sense of the word.

## CHAPTER II.

1. Rāja Kalyān Singh has been described in the Tuzuk (Text, 199, Translation, I, 402) as a son of Todar Mal. He served for some time in Bengal. In the 6th year of Jahāngīr's accession he was promoted to the rank of 1,500 personal and 800 horse. In the same year he was appointed governor of Orissa with an increase in rank of 200 personal and horse. On the 7th Ramaẓān 1026 A.H. (8th September, 1617) he waited upon the Emperor to explain some charges of misconduct brought against him. An enquiry was made by Āṣaf Khān and he was found to be innocent. He was then given a robe of honour and a horse and was appointed to help Mahābat Khān in Bangash. (Memoirs, I, 192, 199, 202, 389, 402.). Mr. Sri Ram Sharma in his article 'Bengal under Jahāngīr' (Journal of Indian History, Vol. XI, 339, f.n. 15.) accepts Rāja Kalyān to be a son of Mān Singh on an alleged statement of Nathan opposed to the Tuzuk. But on f. 4. b. l. 2 and also in Chapter X

of the Bahāristān, Nathan calls him a son of Todar Mal راجه کلیان ولد تودرمل I believe the first statement made by Nathan is either a mistake of his own or an error committed by copyists. The second statement being in conformity with the accounts given in the Tuzuk should be accepted. It may also be seen from the Memoirs, I, p. 266 that the legitimate heir of Mān Singh at the time of his death was Bhāo Singh the other living heir being Mahā Singh, son of Jagat Singh, who predeceased Mān Singh.

2. Sarāi Bandagī, a halting station near about Allahabad.

3. Rānī Gawr evidently means the Rānī who hailed from Gawr, i.e. Bengal and probably refers to the princess of Kuch Bihar who was married to Rāja Mān Singh.

4. Jhūsī or Jūsī is situated on the eastern or left bank of the Ganges, just above its confluence with the Jumna at Allahabad. (Rennell's Beng. Atlas, map No. 13.).

## CHAPTER III.

1. Chajūha or Chahūba? Chachular, about 25 miles down Jhūsi (Rennell's sheet No. 14.) may be the place intended.

2. The word '*Gawar*' probably means a set of unruly people. The tribe of Gawars, if there is any, could not be identified.

3. 'Uṣmān has been variously described by several authorities. Ain (II, 147) describes him as the son of Sulaymān; Ma'āṣir, (I, 165), as Sulaimān's brother and Katlu's son. Dorn, (I, 183) calls him brother of Dāwūd Khān, King of Bengal. Blochmann (Ain, II, 147.) calls him son of 'Isā Khān. Tuzuk (p. 101) calls him 'Uṣmān, the Afghān. Akbar Nāma, Firishta and Iqbāl Nāma do not say anything definite but call him simply an Afghān leader. Gladwin, Vincent Smith and Beni Prasad follow the Tuzuk. His true genealogy is this:—

'Isā Khān Lūhānī Miān Khel, Chief Minister of Katlū Khān, occupied the throne after the death of Katlū and reigned for five years. He left five sons, (1) Khwāja Sulaymān who ruled for a short period, and died in A.H. 1002 (A.D. 1593) leaving a son named Khwāja Dāwūd; (2) Khwāja 'Uṣmān, reigned from A.H. 1002-1021 (A.D. 1593-1612); he died leaving two sons Mumrīz and Ya'qūb; (3) Khwāja Walī, who occupied the throne of 'Uṣmān, against the consent of the military chiefs and his other brothers; (4) Khwāja Malhī; and (5) Khwāja Ibrāḥīm (vide Sir Jadunath's article 'The last pathan hero of Bengal', *Prabāshī*, XXI, pt. 2, 153; Dorn's History of Afghāns, II, 115.).

Taylor in his Topography of Dacca (71), says, " On the death of the Emperor Akbar, in 1605, Osman Khān, one of their chiefs, collected 20,000 of his countrymen, and was proclaimed King. With this force he overran the lower parts of Bengal, and kept possession of this part of the country, until 1612, when after a long contested battle on the banks of the Subanreeka in Orissa, he was slain, and his army defeated by Shajā'at Khān and Ethamam Khān, two Mughal officers, who had been sent against him by Islām Khān, the Governor of the Province. Gladwin states that it was after this victory, that Islām Khān, removed the seat of government from Rajmahal to Dacca." The statement quoted above is quite contrary to the texts of the Bahāristān. 'Uṣmān was defeated and killed not in Orissa but in Sylhet, his last stronghold and refuge. The transfer of the capital of Bengal was made to Dacca long before 'Uṣmān's death, i.e., in 1608 A.D., immediately after the appointment of Islām Khān to the viceroyalty of Bengal.

Details of the early career of 'Uṣmān are to be found in the Akbar Nāma. Driven from Orissa, he finally found shelter with 'Isā Khān Masnad-i-'Alā, who, throughout the reign of Akbar ruled in the districts of Mymensingh, Tippera and the northern part of the Dacca district as an independent ruler. After the death of 'Īsā in 1599 A.D., 'Uṣmān who had been accommodated in Bukainagar, about 12 miles direct east of Mymensingh and 2 miles south-east of Gouripur, allied himself with Mūsā Khān and other rebellious chiefs of Eastern Bengal, and it was to suppress this opposition to imperial authority, that the present expedition was planned. 'Uṣmān is last heard of in the Akbar Nāma (Beveridge, p. 1214) as crossing the Brahmaputtra and defeating the Mughal *Thanadar* Bāz Bahādur Qalmāq. This event may be dated in the winter of 1602 A.D. A battle took place between 'Uṣmān and the Mughal troops under Mān Singh on the bank of the Banar river in the north-east corner of the Dacca district. Defeated, 'Uṣmān retreated within his proper boundary, beyond the Brahmaputtra. When about October, 1603, Kedār Rāy of Bikrampūr fell fighting with the Mughals, Mān Singh planned an expedition against 'Uṣmān, who probably had again overstepped his boundaries and crossed the Brahmaputtra. 'Uṣmān was again compelled to fall back within his own boundary and the Mughal Thānas were strengthened and left in charge of able men.

Details of the incident of 'Uṣmān's crossing the Brahmaputtra again and killing Sajāwal Khān, the Mughal Thānadār of Alapsingh, just before the arrival of Islām Khān on the scene, are not to be met with any where. 'Uṣmān appears to have kept quiet during the troublesome and eventful years of 1604-1607, and began to be active again just before the time when Islām Khān took over charge.

4. Alap Singh or Alap Shāhī is a big pargana in the district of Mymensingh, now in the possession of the Acharyya Chaudhuri family of Muktagachha. Its area is about 560 square miles. The Dacca-Bahadurabad Railway line is practically its eastern boundary and the pargana lies west of the section from station Dhalla to station Pearpur, passing through Mymensing. The present police stations of Muktagachha, Fulbāria and Trisal are within it. (Final Report, Appendix, C., Parganā Map of the proposed Central district; Rennell's Bengal Atlas, map No. 6.).

5. Bhāti usually means the entire region of Eastern Bengal. With regard to the extent and situation of Bhātī, Abu'l-Faẓl says that the tract of country comprising the eastern portions of Dacca and Mymensing and the western portions of Tippera and Sylhet is the region which is called Bhātī. (For details see Dr. Bhattasali's Bengal Chiefs struggle for Independence; Bengal Past and Present; p. 8, Vol. XXXVIII, July, Dec. 1929; Blochmann, J.A.S.B., 1873, p. 226).

6. Mūṣā Khān was the son of 'Īsā Khān the Chief of Bhātī. His father 'Īsā Khān was the master of vast territories comprising half of the present Tippera district, half of the present Dacca district, the whole of the Mymensingh district minus Susang and a portion given to 'Uṣmān. Mūsā Khān and his brothers inherited these territories and led the opposition to Islām Khān's advance. Mūsā Khān inherited his father's title Masnad-i-'Alā (Sublime Throne). According to popular tradition this title is believed to have been given to 'Isā Khān by the Emperor Akbar. According to *Rājmāla* (p. 192) this title was given to him by Amara Mānikya, a powerful king of Tippera who ruled from 1577 A.D.—1586 A.D. There is no historical evidence in support of the popular belief that the title was conferred upon 'Īsā Khān by Akbar, nor do we find any other evidence corroborating the statement of Rājmāla. 'Īsā Khān was an ally of the Rāja of Tippera, and he may have as well assumed this title himself, in imitation of the Afghān nobilities of his days who took similar titles, namely, Haẓrat-i-'Alā by Sulaymān Karrānī, and Shīr Shāh, and Masnad-i-'Alā by Tāj Khān Karrānī. (J.B.O.R.S., IV, 188; Bengal: Past and Present, 1928, XXXV, 33, and XXXVIII, 25.)

7. Shaykh Ghiyāṣu'd-Dīn known as Ghiyāṣ Khān was promoted at the request of Islām Khān to the rank of 1,500 personal and 800 horse, and was given the title of 'Ināyat Khān, in A.H. 1017/A.D. 1609. In the sixth year of Jahāngīr's reign in recognition of his approved services in Bengal, he was promoted to the rank of 2,000 personal. Later on he became the Bakhshī of the Aḥadis (special household troops) on March 18, 1618. He died in October 1618. (Memoirs, I, 158, 160, 199; II. 14. 43.)

8. In the second year of Jahāngīr's reign on Monday, the 14th Jumād. II., A.H. 1015 (17th October, 1606), Hāshim Khān, son of Qāsim Khān. was promoted to the rank of 3,000 personal, and 2,000 horse and appointed governor of Orissa. In the sixth year of accession, he was appointed governor of Kāshmir. He stayed there for two years and towards the latter part of 1022 A.H. (1613 A.D.) he was recalled and Safdar Khān was appointed governor of Kāshmir. (Memoirs, I, 127, 183, 199, 203, 256.)

9. Irādat Khān the brother of Āṣaf Khān was given the rank of 1,000 personal and 500 horse and was appointed to the post of the Bakhshī or Pay-Master of the province of Bihār, on 14th, Jumād, I, 1016 (6th September, 1607). In the sixth year of Jahāngīr's reign, he was promoted to the rank of Mīr-Sāmān (Chief Steward). In the twelfth year of his accession his rank was raised to 1,500 personal and 600 horse, in the thirteenth year it was raised to 2,000 and in the fifteenth year he was appointed governor of Kāshmir. He died in 1059 A.H. (1649 A.D.) at an advanced age. He rose up to the rank of 6,000. He worked very faithfully under Shāh Jahān also (Memoirs, I, 306, 372, II, 15, 175; Pādishāh Nāma, III, 718; Ma'āṣir, I, 174-79).

10. Jahāngīr records this promotion of the Rāja in his Tuzuk (p. 98). "At the request of Islām Khān, Rāja Kalyān was appointed to the government of the Sarkār of Orissa and had an increase in rank of—200 personal and horse." (Memoirs, I, 202).

11. Afẓal Khān was the son of Abu'l-Faẓl; he was appointed governor of Bihār in 1017 A.H. (1608 A.D.) to succeed Islām Khān when the latter was transferred to Bengal. His original name was 'Abdu'r-Rahmān. In the second year of Jahāngīr's accession, he was raised to the rank of 2,000 personal, and 1,500 horse, and was given the title of Afẓal Khān, and in the same year it was increased by an addition of 500 horse. After his appointment to the governorship of Bihār he was given the country of Sangrām (Kharakpur) as a fief for a year. In the eighth year of accession he returned to Court and offered gifts and elephants to the Emperor. He died at the capital in the year of his return.

12. These are evidently proper names for certain famous guns, which were given such names after famous persons or places conquered, or which the gun was considered capable of conquering. The big iron gun now lying at Visnupur in the Bankura district is known by the name of Dalamardan, or conqueror of big hosts. The fourth name could not be properly made out.

13. The Chero Chiefs have always been troublesome in the hilly region about Rohtas. They were the ruling chiefs of Palamau, situated

beyond the southern limits of Bihar. (For details see Sarkar's Aurangzib, III, 35-45.).

14. Jahānābād is a subdivision of Hooghly district situated in 22° 53′ N. and 87° 47′ E. on the Dwara-Keswar river. Its modern name is Arāmbāgh. The name was changed in 1900 in order to avoid confusion with the town of Jahānābād in the Gaya district.( Bengal district Gazetteer, Vol. XXIX, 243; Blochmann, J.A.S.B., 1873, 218).

15. Tanbūlak or Tamlūk a subdivision of the Midnapur district in Bengal. It is situated on the Rupnarayan river. (Bengal Gazetteer, XXVI, 220 ; Rennell's Map No. 7).

16. Sūnābāzū is a pargana in the district of Pabna, situated to the north of the town of Pabna. It was originally a part of the Bhatūria Bāzū Pargana (Bengal district Gazetteer, XXXVII, 90 ; Rennell's map No. 9).

Bhatūria is the name of a very ancient pargana, now mostly included under the Thānas of Tarash and Chātmohar in the Pabna district. Bettoria on Rennell's map No. 9 is really the Chakla that went by this name and is very much bigger division than a pargana. Sūnābāzū and Bhatūria are adjacent parganas, Sūnābāzū being on the south-east of Bhatūria.

In the absence of any definite topographical direction, it is not easy to identify Kalābārī. Mr. Sri Ram Sharma has confused Kalābārī with Kaliabar of Assam which was not yet conquered by the Mughals (Journal of Indian History, XIII, 339). See also note No. 7, Ch. V.

17. Ghorāghāt is situated on the right bank of the river Karatoya, to the west of the Rangpur district. It was the frontier district towards Kuch Bihar and Kuch Hājo or Kāmrūp kingdoms. It is at present included within the district of Dinājpur. It is 28 miles due north of the town of Bogra and 18 miles due east from Hili, a station on the North Bengal line of the E. B. Railway. There are good roads leading to Ghorāghāt from both these places. The place has lost all its former grandeur, but it is still the site of a Government Police Station and a few zamindary courts, (Martin's Eastern India, II, 679-682). Buchanon says that the town, at the time of its greatest prosperity extended along the river bank for about 10 miles, while the average depth was about 2 miles. He saw the ruins of a big mosque and some smaller mosques were standing in his time (1808), but he could not trace the ruins of any palace or civil buildings. The *Dargāh* or shrine of Isma'īl Ghāzī was a famous place and it stood at the south-eastern corner of the fort. Isma'īl Ghāzī was a famous captain of the time of Barbak Shāh and was put to death under royal orders in 1474 A.D. (J.A.S.B. 1874. 215: "Notes on Shah Ismaīl Ghāzī."

by G. H. Damont, Blochmann, J.A.S.B., 1873, 215; Rennell's map No. 9).

18. Pratāpaditya was the Rāja of Jessore and one of the most powerful Bengal Chiefs, contemporary to Jahāngīr. Westland in his "Report on Jessore" (p. 31) says that Rāja Prtāpaditya was subdued by Rāja Mān Singh during the reign of Akbar and "he conveyed him in an iron cage towards Delhi. The prisoner, however, died on the way, at Benares." This view of Westland is entirely wrong and opposed to the contemporary accounts given in the Bahāristān which show that he survived Akbar and offered some resistance against the imperial power during Jahāngīr's reign. The details of his career have been fully given in the pages of this book.

19. 'Alā-i-pūr is situated on the Ganges, 12 miles south-east of Putia in the district of Rājshāhī. It was included within the parganā of Lashkarpūr held by a Pathan Jāgīrdār named Lashkar Khān, during the reign of Akbar who usually resided at 'Alā-i-pūr. When Lashkar Khān rebelled, the parganā of Lashkarpūr was given to Pitambar the Zamindār of Putia. Even at present the tenants of 'Alā-i-pūr are given precedence over all other tenants of the parganā at the *Punyaha* day, i.e., the people of this village head the procession of rent-payers. (Bengal, Past and Present, 1928, XXXV, 37; Bengal district Gazetteer, XXXIII, 177).

## CHAPTER IV

1. The twelve Bhuyāns are called by Mīrzā Nathan as Twelve Bumias بومیان of Bengal. They were a set of powerful chiefs who rose to power from 1576 A.D., after the fall of Dāwūd, the last Karrani King of Bengal. Authorities differ as to the number of these Bhuyāns, some holding that they were twelve, and others less than twelve. It is very difficult to fix their number at twelve. (See Dr. Wise, Bara Bhuyāns, J.A.S.B., 1874, 197-214; Blochmann, J.A.S.B., 1873, 223, and his Aīn-i-Akbarī, I, 342, foot note; Beveridge, J.A.S.B., 1904, 57). In the Bahāristān we come across the following chiefs who were struggling for independence in the reign of Jahāngīr and who opposed Islām Khān's attempt at subduing them. They were (1) 'Uṣmān and his brothers; (2) 'Īsā Khān's sons Mūsā, Dāwūd, 'Abdu'lla and Māḥmūd and 'Īsā Khān's brother's son 'Alāu'l Khān; (3) Ma'ṣūm Khān Kābulī's son Mīrzā Mūmin Khān; (4) Dariyā Khān, son of 'Alam Khān; (5) Mādhav Rāy, Zamīndār of Khalsī; (6) Rāja Rāy, Zamindār of Shāhzādapūr; (7) Binūd Rāy of Chandpratāp; (8) Bahādur-Ghāzī, Sūnā Ghāzī, Anwār Ghāzī; (9) Pahlawān, Zamīndār of Matang; (10) Ḥājī Shamsu'd-Dīn; (11) Majlis

Quṭb, Zamīndār of Fatḥābād; (12) Rām Chandra, Zamīndār of Bakla (Backerganj); (13) Pitambar and Ananta of Chilā-Juwār; (14) Ilāh Bakhsh of 'Alā-i-pūr; (15) Ananta Manikya of Bhalwa. Mīrzā Nathan does not definitely tell us who were these Twelve Bhuyāns. The other two chiefs, Rāja Satrajit and Rāja Pratāpaditya submitted to Islām Khān and accepted imperial vassalage without much resistance.

The expedition against Pratāpaditya was sent by Islām Khān when the former broke certain terms of treaty. Although local patriotism ascribe many wonderful achievements to Rāja Pratāpaditya as the leader of the Bengal Chiefs' struggle for independence, the verdict of history is quite opposed to them. It was not Pratāpaditya but the other minor Zamīndārs under the leadership of Mūsā Khān and 'Uṣmān who during the early part of the reign of Jahāngīr carried on the struggles begun under the leadership of 'Īsā Khān against Mughal aggression. But unfortunately local writers have idolised Pratāpaditya as the hero of Bengal's fight for independence and the real leaders of the struggle, like 'Īsā Khān and Kedār Rāy, and subsequently, Mūsā Khān and 'Uṣmān fell into the background.

2. Bhusna is still a place of considerable importance and the headquarters of a Police Station in Faridpur district, about 20 miles southwest of Faridpur, just on the border of Jessore district. Satrajit son of Rāja Mukunda was one of the most unreliable Zamīndār ally of the Mughals. He inherited all the treacherous qualities of his father who had murdered the sons of Mūsā Khān by inviting them to a feast. During the reign of Shāhjahān when Satrajit was posted to serve in Assam he carried on secret negotiations with the Ahoms and betrayed the Mughal cause on several occasions. When the Bengal governor came to know of his nefarious activities he was ordered to be captured. He was ultimately captured at Dhubri and sent to Jahāngīrnagar where he was executed about the year 1636. (For details see Translation of the Rizāẓu's-Salāṭīn, footnotes on pp. 42, 265, 266; Blochmann, 'Aīn, I, 374 and Notes on the Geography and History of Bengal, J.A.S.B., 1873, 228; Pādishāh Nāma, Vol. II, 79-80).

3. There is some confusion here which requires elucidation. The diary of 'Abdu'l Laṭīf brought to light and published by Sir Jadunath Sarkar, in the *Prabāsī* 1326 B.S. pp. 552-53, records as follows:— "Islām Khān, Nawāb of Bengal marched on the 30th March, 1609 (?) from Faṭḥpūr and reached Rāna-Tandapūr, where Salīm Khān, Chief of Hijlī, in Orissa, the brother of Indra Narāyan Rāja of Pāchet, and the cousin of the Rāja of Mandaran saw him and presented elephants, both big and small, numbering 109 in the aggregate. Shaykh Kamāl, the trusted and favourite servant of the Nawāb, presented them. (Translation)."

In the Bahāristān we find this expedition starting against Bir Hamīr, Shams Khān and Salīm Khān who are called "the Zamīndārs of Birbhūm, Pāchet and Hijlī." In the actual description the author does not definitely state where the territory of Bir-Hamīr lay. But in para 362 of the translation where the author gives an account of another punitive expedition against these Zamīndārs he calls Shams Khān Zamīndār of Birbhūm, Bir-Hamīr, Zamīndār of Pāchet, and Salīm Khān, Zamīndār of Hijlī. This account gives us the exact territorial limit of these three Zāmīndārs. Indra Narāyan named by 'Abdu'l Laṭif is probably Bir Hamīr's brother.

The Darnī hills at the outskirts of which the fort of Shams Khān was situated may be the Dorunda hills of Chotanāgpūr. Another hilly place called Doomree is shown on Rennell's Map No. 7, lying 50 miles west of Nagar, the capital of the Muslim Rājas of Birbhūm. The site of this captial is within a strong intrenchment, about 32 miles long. Nagar of Rājnagar is only about two miles east from the western boundary of the Birbhūm district, beyond which begins the hilly region of the Santal Pargana.

Pāchet is situated at a little distance from the southern bank of the Dāmodar river, about 12 miles south-east of Barakar (Rennell's Map No. 7).

Hijlī, once an important place, but now a mere village under the Contai subdivision of the Midnapūr district, is situated on the mouth of the Rasūlpūr river, about 6 miles direct east of Contai.

4. Tipūra and Titūlī. There is a village called Titūlī or Tituliya in the district of Maldah, situated about 23 miles to the east of the city. There is a trunk road leading from Tituliya to Ghoraghāt *via* Nishānpūr. (Rennell's Map No. 5). But this evidently cannot be the place intended, as the pargana of Gawr had not yet been reached. These two appear to be unimportant places, not shown on the map.

5. Chilajuwār is a small pargana included in the pargana of Bhaturiā Bāzū. It is situated on the Ganges near about the station of Sara-Ghāt. Its real name is Chila. Juwār is a termination denoting a part or unit of a parganā (Bengal, Past and Present, 1928, XXXV, 36).

6. Chātmahal was originally the capital of Ma'ṣūm Khān Kābulī. Its real name is Chāt Mohar; it is situated on the river Barul, 19 miles north of Pabna. The Railway station of this name on the Sara-Sirajganj Railway is about 3 miles south of the real place. (Bengal, Past and Present XXXV, 34; Rennell's Bengal Atlas, Map No. 16, Bengal district Gazetteer, XXXVII, 116).

7. Khalsī is shown about five miles east of Jafarganj near the Ganges where the Dhaleswari river took its rise (Rennell's Bengal Atlas, Map No. 16).

8. Gawr was the ancient capital of Bengal. Originally it was the capital of one of the Hindu Kings of Bengal named Lakshman Sen after whom it was known as Lakshmanawatī which was corrupted by the Muslims into Lakhnawty. When the Muslims conquered Bengal, Lakhnawty remained the capital of the province for a long time. According to Aīn (II, 51) it was renamed by Humāyūn as 'Jannatābād' i.e., the city of paradise. The ruins of its old forts and buildings are still in existence. It is situated between the Mahananda and the little Bhagirathi rivers to the south of Maldah (Martin's Eastern India, III, 68-80; Rennell's Map No. 5).

9. 'Atā Khāl, at present known as Maluar Khāl is shown on modern maps as branching off from the Chitra river and falling into the Bhairab in the Narail subdivision of the Jessore district, by about a mile east of Narail. Bhushna, the capital of Satrajit is considerably to the north of this area and this gives rise to the presumption that a much longer extension of this water-course towards the north, went by the name of 'Atā Khāl three hundred years ago.

10. He waited upon Jahāngīr on the 25th Jumād, I, 1017 A.H. (5th September, 1608). (Memoirs, I, 156.).

11. One Shāhpūr is situated at a distance of about six miles north from the town of Naogāon in the district of Rajshahi. It is on the west bank of the river Jabuna (Rennell's map No. 6.). This place is not on the Atrai and is very much more than two and a half stages from Chātmohar. Moreover, there is no reason why Nathan should go northwards to such a great distance from Chātmohar. In spite of the text which places Shāhpūr up the Atrai, the meeting of the forces of Nathan and of the reinforcements sent subsequently to help him at Ekadanta, seven miles north-east of Pabna, shows that Nathan moved eastwards from Chātmohar towards the retiring rebels and not away from them. A Shāhpūr is mentioned under Thāna Shāhzādapūr in the Pabna Gazetteer, p. 88, which shows that it is a diara Khās Mahal i.e. the original Shāhpūr was washed away by the river. This is probably the place where Nathan went.

12. The Atrayi or Atrai was one of the great rivers of North Bengal. It was one of the main channels by which the waters of the Tista discharged into the Ganges. It enters the district of Pabna from the district of Rājshāhī flowing through the Chalan *Bil* and falls into the Baral near Nun Nagar. The diversion of the waters of the Tista eastwards has wrought great havoc on both the Atrayi and the Karatoya and both

of them have practically dried up in their lower reaches. In the Pabna district, many silted up channels of the Atrayi can still be traced.

13. Nāẓirpūr is situated on what the modern maps call the Nandakuja river, known further eastwards as the Gomani river, about four miles north-east of the headquarters of the Gurudaspur Police Station at the south-eastern corner of the Rajshahi district. The place is about 12 miles east of Natore. The Nandakuja and the Gomani rivers appear to be only remnants of the old Atrayi. The place must have been very jungly three hundred years ago to be the scene of successful *Kheda* operations. It should be mentioned here that there is a pargana called Nāẓirpūr under the Faridpur Police Station of the Pabna district, which is centrally situated amidst Chātmohar, Ekadanta and Shāhpūr, and this may be the Nāẓirpūr of our narrative. (Pabna Gazetteer, p. 89.).

14. Ekadanta is a well-known place, about seven miles north-east of modern Pabna.

15. The Doāb or the region between two rivers is probably the land lying between the Atrayi and the Karatoya.

16. Sunārgām has been read as *Sāzkām* by Prof. Sarkar (Vide *Prabāsī, Bhādra,* 1329 B.S., 644.). But the Ms. I used distinctly writes سنارگام Sunārgām. The Bahāristān says that after the second defeat of Mūsā Khān at the battle of Katrabū he fled to Sunārgām. Both these places are within the district of Dacca and adjacent to one another. I, therefore, think that the place mentioned here is Sunārgām or Sunārgāon, not Sāzkām as suggested by Prof. Sarkar. It is a well-known pargana of the Dacca district lying between the Meghna and the Lakhya rivers. (Rennell's Bengal Atlas, Map No. 17.). For a fuller details of Sunārgāon reference may be made to Cunningham, Archaeological Survey of India Reports, XV, 137; Dr. Wise, J.A.S.B., XLIII; Taylor's Topography of Dacca, 70.

## CHAPTER V.

1. The Andal Khān is the same as the Ariyal Khān river, of the Faridpur district. It was formerly a channel of the Ganges down which the water of the Ganges flowed, and it is still its main distributary in the interior of the district. Its upper reaches is known as the Bhubaneswar. (Gazetteer, Faridpur Dt. Ed., 1925, 11; Rennell's Bengal Atlas, Sheet No. 1.).

2. The town of Sripūr was situated on the bank of the Kāliganga river at a distance of about eighteen miles from Sunārgāon. It was carried off by the Padma. The site of Sripūr is marked on Vanden

Broucke's Map where it is called Ceerpoor Firingi. Rennell has not shown this place in his Map. (Taylor's Topography of Dacca, 70 ; Wise, Notes on Sunārgāon, J.A.S.B., 1874, p. 76.).

3. Bikrampūr is a pargana in the district of Dacca. It was bounded on the north by the Dhaleswari, on the east by the Meghna, on the west by the Padma and a part of the pargana of Chandrapratāp, on the south by Idilpūr. At present the southern portion of Bikrampūr is included within the district of Faridpur. The Mughal historians of this period always name Sripūr and Bikrampūr together. (Taylor's Topography of Dacca, 100 ; Jarrett, Ain, II, 138 ; Rennell's Bengal Atlas, sheets No. 1 and 17.).

4. The Karatoya is an ancient river mentioned in the Mahābhārat as a sacred river. It was the boundary line between the old kingdom of Paundravardhana, the country of the Pundras, and the kingdom of Kāmarūpa. It is shown in Van Den Broucke's map of Bengal as flowing into the Ganges. This must have been the course of the river in Mīrzā Nathan's time. But that course has undergone a great change. Before the great flood of 1787 it discharged the water of the Tista into the Atrai and then into the Ganges. But when after this flood the main stream of the Tista changed its course and broke away to the east, the portions of the Karatoya falling within the district of Pabna gradually silted up and at the present time it is of minor importance. One channel which joins the Baral east of Pabna is still called the Old Tista and the Karto or Karatoya. In Rennell's Map (No. 9.) it is shown as passing through Rangpur and Bogra with Ghoraghāt on its right. This river during the early Mughal days was also the frontier line between the Kuch Kingdom and the Mughal Bengal. (For a discussion of the old course of Karatoya—see Bhattasali : Muḥammad-i-Bakhtiyār's expedition to Tibet, Indian Historical Quarterly, 1933, pp. 49-62.). A great deal of confusion prevails as to the source of this river. It rises from the extreme north-west jungles of Jalpaiguri and passing through the boundary of Dinajpur and Rangpur districts meanders through Rangpur and Bogra. In the south of Bogra it receives the Halhalia and the united stream is called Phuljhur. It leaves Bogra at Chandaikona and flowing in a southerly direction joins the Ichhamati at Nalka. The Phuljhur flows south past the village of Ullapara, a few miles below which it joins the Hurasagar at Narina after a course in the district of Pabna of about 40 miles. After this junction, it takes the name of Hurasagar and passing close by Shāhzādapūr and Bera joins the Jamuṅa near Nakalia. (For details see Martin's Eastern India, III, 359-364 ; Bengal District Gazetteer, XXXVII, 13-14.)

5. Amrūl is a pargana in the district of Rajshahi. It was included within the Sarkār of Barbakābād, so called from Barbakshāh, Sultan

of Bengal, and extending from Sarkār Lakhnawatī along the Padma to Bogra. (Blochmann, J.A.S.B., 1873, 215; Ain, I, 137.). On enquiry from the Collector, Rajshahi, it is learnt that at present this pargana is within the Thanas of Bagmara (in the Sadar subdivision), Natore, Atrai (Naogaon subdivision) and Naogaon in the district of Bogra. It lay on either side of the Eastern Bengal Railway from Natore to Santahar.

6. The text calls this place Ambūl امبول But from the context it is evident that the place meant is the pargana of Amrūl.

7. & 8. Ibrāhīmpūr, Kalābārī and Budhī Budha. In locating these places, we have to remember that Ihtimām Khān started from Sunābāzū i.e., present Chātmohar in Pabna district and was moving west *via* Atrai river towards the pargana of Amrūl, say towards the railway station of Atrai. "The major portion of the parganas of the Jāgīr of Ihtimām Khān was in this part of the country," says the text; —i.e., near about the pargana of Amrūl. So Ibrāhīmpūr appears to have been situated not far from Atrai and Kalābārī was only three *kos* or about six miles west of Ibrāhīmpūr. Under Police Station Nandalāli, directly west of Atrai there appears one Kalābārī, south of the Atrai river. near an important place called Bandaikhara Kasba. This may be our author's Kalābārī; and Budhi Budha, if not identical with Bandaikhara, should be somewhere in this locality. Sir Jadunath Sarkar reads Budhi Budha (*Prabāsi*, *Bhadra*, 1329 B.S.) as Udi Burha but the place was not identified. N.K.B.

9. Shāhzādapūr is a well-known place in the district of Pabna. It is situated on the west bank of the river Karatoya (Rennell's Bengal Atlas, Map. No. 16.) For the antiquities of the place see "On the antiquities and traditions of Shāhzādpūr" (by Maulvi 'Abdu'l-Wali, J.A.S.B., Part I, No. 3, 1904.).

10. Chāndpratāp is a big pargana in the Manickganj Subdivision of the Dacca district. It spreads over the northern and the southern sides of the river Dhaleswari. It is named after Chānd Ghāzī one of the Bhuyān chiefs of Bengal. (Rennell's Bengal Atlas, Map No. VI; *Dhākār Itihās*, I, 24-29.). The name of Binūd Rāy بنود the Zamīndār of Chāndpratāp, has been read by Sir Jadunath as Nabud Rāy (vide his article on "The fall of the independent Zamindars of Bengal", *Prabāsī*, 1329, B.S., p. 639.).

11. Kangal or Katgal. Probably 'Kanhtal', a pargana in Sarkar Ghoraghāt. (Blochmann, Ain II, p. 36.).

12. The Khurdah Rāj family was founded by Rām Chandra Deb one of the influential Zamindars of Orissa. In recognition of his valua-

ble services rendered to the Mughals when Mān Singh was deputed by Todarmal to survey the lands of Orissa, Rām Chandra Deb was created the first hereditary Rāja about the year 1580 A.D. His territory included the free-hold of a large area extending from Mahanadi (the northern boundary of Cuttak) to Khemti near Ganjam. He was also appointed the hereditary guardian of the temple of Jagannāth. Khurdah was the mountain stronghold of this Rāj and hence they are known as the Khurdah Rājas. Purushuttam Deb ascended the throne of his father in 1609 A.D. The descendants of this family held their mountain stronghold up to 1818. But as a result of their rebellion against the British in 1818, they lost Khurdah and retired to Puri. Khurdah is at present a Government Khās mahal. (For details see, Stirling, Asiatic Researches, XV, 294 ; Hunter, Orissa, II, 190 ; L. M. Ghosh, Indian Chiefs, 450.).

13. Rāja Keshodās Mārū first entered the service of Akbar as a commander of 300 horse. When Jahāngīr ascended the throne he was promoted to the rank of 1,500 personal and horse and after sometime to 2,000 personal and 1,000 horse. The statement made by Nathan that he was raised to the rank of 4,000 and given a standard in recognition of his meritorious service in Puri is not mentioned in the Tuzuk. (Tuzuk, 146 ; Memoirs : Trans : by Beveridge, 1-19, 21, 79, 296, 297, 390, 410.). Some authorities (Memoirs I, n. 170 ; Puri District Gazetteer, 37 ; Banerjee's History of Orissa, II, 35.) confuse Keshodās Mārū with Keshodās Rāthor, son of Jaymal of Marta who was shot by Akbar when he was defending Chitor, although the Aiṅ (I, 502, 506.) enters them separately as commanders of 300 and 200 horse.

14. Three campaigns were led against Khurdah during Jahāngīr's reign :—(1) Siege of the temple of Jagannāth by Keshodās Mārū in 1609, (2) Rāja Kalyān's raid in 1611, (3) Mukarram Khān's expedition in 1617 and its annexation to the imperial dominion (Tuzuk, 193, 214, 215.).

15. Kāmta or Kamatā originally denoted the western part of the Brahmaputtra valley up to the Karatoya and it was included within the ancient kingdom of Kāmarūp. The Mughal historian sometimes use the terms Kāmrūp and Kāmta as synonymous. Here Kāmta is used to signify the portion of Kuch territory lying to the west of the Manās river, and Kāmrūp to its east. (For details see Gait's History of Assam, 42-44 ; Baruah's Early History of Kāmarūpa, 284.).

Lakshmī Narāyan (spelt in the Ms. as Lachmī Narāyan), son of Nara Narāyan was the Rāja of the territory of Kuch Bihar lying to the west of the Manās river up to the vicinity of Ghoraghāt. Gait says "The friction between the cousins (i.e. *Parikshīt and Lakshmī Narāyan*) continued to increase, and at last, in 1612, Lakshmī Narāyan went in person to Dacca and begged the Nawāb to intervene", (History of Assam, 65). But it was not so. Lakshmī Narāyan did not go to Dacca. He paid his homage to Islām Khān at Ghoraghāt in 1608, through Rāja Raghūnāth and promised his help in the campaign against his cousin. The Kūch campaign was due more to Parikshīt's refusal to accept imperial vassalage than to the request of Lakshmī Narāyan. It is no doubt true that Lakshmī Narāyan incited the Mughals to conquer Kāmrūp in order to feed fat his ancient grudge.

16. Parikshīt (spelt in the Ms. as Parichit) is the son of Raghū Dev. He was the Rāja of the Kūch territory to the east of the Manās. Here his territory is called Kāmrūp as distinct from Kāmta the territory of Lakshmī Narāyan. (For details see Gait's History of Assam, 63-68 and S. K. Bhuyan's *Kāmrupar Buranjī*, p. 6-12.).

17. Raghūnāth was the Zamīndār of Susang. Susang is situated on the north-east border of Mymensingh district. (Rennell's Map No. 6.). Rāja Raghūnāth was badly treated by Parikshīt and his family was imprisoned by him. He then readily submitted to the Mughals and applied for help to the Bengal viceroy. After the defeat of Parikshīt the family of Raghūnāth was released (Pādishāh Nāma, II, 65.). This fact is not mentioned by Mīrzā Nathan. But from the enthusiasm displayed by Raghūnāth in the subjugation of the Kūch territory, it seems that the Pādishāh Nāma is right.

18. This fact has been wrongly represented in Mughal North East Frontier Policy, p. 134 says—"Thereupon, an Imperialist officer, Abdul Wahed by name, was sent at the head of an army to Kāmrūp. After a short encounter, Parikshīt was defeated. In the vain hope of securing redress for the unwarranted attack on his realm, he proceeded to Fatehpur (*en route* to the Mughal capital). But no useful purpose appears to have been served by the journey." The facts, as will appear from the text translated above are very much different and Parikshīt's journey to seek redress for his grievances is entirely imaginary.

19. "*Kuthi-i-Farangi*", is a kind of long coat of mail worn under the breastplate. It has an opening at the front. (For description vide Ain, 112, No. 61 and on plate XIV, No. 50; Irvine, 69.).

20. Budnagar is probably Madhnagar, now a Railway Station on the E. B. Ry., about 8 miles north of Natore.

21. Siyālgarh, Kudiā Khāl and Katasgarh. About a mile to the west of Sirājganj, a well-known Railway terminus on the Brahmaputtra (Jamuna) river, (Dt. Pabna), there are three contiguous villages, Sialkol, Khurda-sialkol and Chak-sialkol on the western bank of the Ichha-

mati river. But possibly Siyālgarh has to be sought for further north along the Karatoya, in the Bogra district.

The passage of the Brahmaputtra river through the Jamuna channel has changed the configuration of the part of the country through which the Mughal army was operating to a very great extent. Modern maps therefore are of very little use and we have to fall back upon Rennell's Bengal Atlas, sheet No. 6 for the topography of the advance of the Mughal army and the fleet towards Bhāṭī. As will be seen from the map, only three rivers are concerned, e.g. Atrai on the west, Karotoya in the middle and Ichhamati in the east. A copy of this map is attached to the text for ready reference. Islām Khān was at Ghoraghāt and Ihtimām Khān's fleet was somewhere near Bandaikhara. Islām Khān was marching south towards Shāhzādapūr by the right bank of the Karatoya river and had halted at Siyālgarh three marches south of Ghoraghāt. Siyālgarh was therefore on the Karatoya south of Ghoraghāt possibly within the present Bogra district. He expected Ihtimām Khān to go up to Siyālgarh with his entire fleet avoiding the Bhuyān-infested south. Thus Ihtimām Khān was compelled to seek for a short cut from the Atrai to the Karatoya. From the map it will appear that there were only two such short cuts e.g. the Nagar river and another river to its east which is not named on Rennell's sheet but which is in reality the Bhudai. The Nagar is shown as starting from Atrai about ten miles north-east of Natore and it strikes the Karatoya at Sibganj only about fourteen miles south of Ghoraghāt; so probably this is not the sought for short cut. The other river Bhudai starts from the Karatoya about 3 miles south of the town of Bogra, forming the southern boundary of the village of Shujābād. This place is about 32 miles south of Ghoraghāt. Shujābād is on the west bank of the Karatoya, and against it, on the east bank of the same river is the village of Ghanchaitara near which must be situated the village of Siyalkot mentioned in Babu Prabhash Ch. Sen's History of Bogra, p. 20, 2nd Ed. Siyālgarh of our text and Siyalkot mentioned in the History of Bogra appears to be identical. It will be seen from the map that the road bifurcates here, one going straight east to Bukāinagar and Jangalbārī, the strongholds of 'Uṣmān and Mūsā Khān, and the other going south to Shāhzādapūr. Islām Khān was evidently waiting at this junction and expected Ihtimām Khān to come up by the Bhudai. If our contention is right, Kudia appears to be a mistake for Bhudai. It may be remembered in this connection that Bhudai falls into the Atrai inside the Chalan *bil* and the Gadai or the Mūsā Khān river (this name is very significant, and shows that this region was under the sway of Mūsā Khān, son of 'Īsā Khān) is only a southern continuation of the Bhudai and Gadai may easily be written Kudai or Kudia by Persian writers.

For Katasgarh, see infra, N. K. B.

22. Shaykh Nūr Quṭb known as Quṭbu'l-'Ālam was the son of the saint 'Alā u'l-Ḥaq the spiritual successor of Makhdūm Ākhī Sirāju'd-Dīn a famous saint of the district of Maldah. Shaykh Nūr Quṭb was greatly patronised by Sultan Ghiyāṣu'd-Dīn who is said to have studied theology with him at Rājnagar in Birbhum. After the death of Sultan Ghiyāṣu'd-Dīn, Pandua was occupied by Rāja Ganesh with the help of this saint. But later on Rāja Ganesh became very cruel and began to persecute the Muslims. At this the Shaykh, being disgusted with the inhuman behaviour of the Rāja, appealed to the Sultan of Jaunpur (i.e. Shamsu'd-Dīn Ibrāhīm) for help and protection. The Sultan invaded Bengal and put the Rāja to such a strait that he appealed to the saint to stop the invading army from further advance and promised that he would allow his son to be converted to Islām. The saint agreed to his proposal and ordered the invaders to withdraw and converted his son. After this the Rāja wanted to reconvert his son to Hinduism "by having him passed through a cow made of gold, the material of which was divided amongst the Brahmins who conducted the ceremony." But his son being under the influence of the saint did not apostatise and succeeded his father in 1414 A.D. under the name of Jalālu'd-Dīn. The Shaykh died in 1415 A.D. He was buried at Pandua near his father's tomb who died in 1384 A.D. The place is visited by many people as a place of pilgrimage and offer their prayers for the benefit of their souls. The shrine is called *Shash Hazārī*, because an endowment of 6,000 *bighas* of land are attached to it for the upkeep of its buildings and to meet other necessary expenses in feeding the poor. (Bengal district Gazetteer, XXXV, 17, 19, 86, 96; Riyāẓ, 113-117; J.A.S.B., XLII, 255.).

23. Ādīna Mosque, was built by Sikandar Shāh, the eldest son of Hājī Ilyās in 766 A.H./1374 A.D., at Ādīnah, at a distance of two miles from Pandua. This is one of the most remarkable specimens of Pathan architecture in Bengal and according to Fergusson the ground plan and dimensions are exactly similar to those of the great mosque at Damascus. "The outer walls of brick enclosed a quadrangular space 500 feet long north and south, by 300 feet wide east and west. Of these walls, the northern, eastern and southern were pierced with windows; the western wall had no opening, but a chamber containing the tomb of Sikandar Shāh projected from it on the outside just beyond and north of the centre of the wall. Inside and following the outer walls, with which they were connected by spring arches, was a series of cloisters enclosing an open quadrangle. The eastern cloisters through which, by an insignificant door, the building was entered, were 38 feet wide from outer wall to inner court. This space was subdivided by means of brick arches on stone pillars into 127 squares, each of which was covered by a small dome 20 feet high. The northern and southern cloisters were

constructed on the same pattern, but being shorter contained only 39 squares similarly covered with domes. The innermost squares opened on to the inner quadrangle by arches. The western side of the quadrangle was the mosque proper, the inside of the western wall having the usual niches.

In the centre of this side was the nave of the mosque with the pulpit. It was 64 feet from east to west and 32 feet from north to south and was surmounted by a dome, of which the height from the floor to the centre was 62 feet. South of the nave, and connected with it by arches, were cloisters similar to those of other sides of the building. In these the common people worshipped: north of the nave, and similarly connected with it, were cloisters carried to a greater height, the pillars of which supported a floor at a height of eight feet from the ground level. This platform called the Bādshāh-ka-Takht (the royal platform) was 40 feet wide and 80 feet long. The niches in its western wall were four in number and there were two doors, communicating directly to the chamber of Sikandar's tomb. This chamber, 38 feet square, which was covered by nine domes, was on the same level as the royal platform to which it gave access. It was built on a plinth, eight feet high, there being stone steps to the ground level."

The greater portion of this building is in ruins. The outer walls the royal platform with its domes, the pulpit and a part of the outer chamber are in existence. (For details see Maldah Gazetteer, 1918 Ed., 16, 94, 97 ; Riyāẓ, 105).

24. Pandua is an old capital of Bengal in the Barind or Barendrabhum situated in 25° 8′ N., and 88° 10′ E., at a distance of 6 miles north-east from Old Maldah, on either side of the main road from Old Maldah to Dinajpur. During the Muslim rule the capital was transferred from Gawr to Pandua by Sultan 'Alāu'd-Dīn about the year 1353 A.D. (For details see Maldah District Gazetteer, 1918 ED. 10, 11, 12, 16, 22, 68, 72, 86, 89, 92 ; Riyāẓ, Tr. 97, 98. Rennell's Map No. 9.)

25. Dihikut was the name of a Mahal under the Sarkar of Jannatabad or Lakhnawati (Ain., II, 131).

## CHAPTER VI

1. Majlis Quṭb was Zamīndār of Faṭhābād, modern Faridpur. In the early part of the Mughal rule Fatḥābād was the Jāgīr of Murād Khān. But after his death in 1589 A.D., his sons were treacherously murdered at a feast to which they were invited by a Hindu Zamindar named Mukundaram of Bhusna, and their territory was seized by him. The details of Majlis Quṭb's acquisition of this Zamindary from the

possession of Mukundaram are not recorded. Abu'l-Fazl speaks of Bhusna falling into the hands of enemies and it is quite probable that Fatḥābād was taken possession of by the rebel leaders at the same time, and apportioned to Majlis Quṭb. (For details see Dr. Bhattasali's articles, Bengal, Past and Present, 1928, XXXV, 36; Faridpur district Gazetteer, 1925 Ed., 23).

2. *Thathari* is a kind of big chariot used in war-fare in front of a regiment as a defensive barrier, under the shelter of which the soldiers advanced to attack a fort. It is also termed as *Gardūn*. The text says in f. 240a, تهتری یعنی گردون کلان "*Thatari*, i.e., a big wheel or chariot."

3. There is a place called Bowleah (Rennell's Atlas sheet No. 6) situated at a distance of about seven miles to the south-west of Shāh-zādapūr in the district of Pabna. But it seems this is not the place mentioned here. For the probable site of this place see the next note.

4 & 5. Trimohāna of the Khāl Jogini and the Mohāna of Katas-garh.

In para 50, we find Islām Khān reaching Baliyā in three marches and halting there. This place has been identified with Bowleah of Rennell's Sheet No. 6, about 7 miles south-west of Shāhzādapūr. The distance, however, appears to be too short for three marches. Ihtimām Khān took 15 days or more to cover this distance owing to the zigzag course of the river. The *Mohāna* of Khāl Jogini was reached from this place in the course of a morning. Katasgarh was reached from this place by Islām Khān in two marches (para 53). From para 55, it will be found that the *Mohāna* of Katasgarh must have been the name of the mouth of the channel which led to Jatrapūr. It should therefore preferably be identified with the great confluence of rivers at Jafarganj which led to the river Ichhamati and to Jatrapūr. The position of the *Mohāna* of Khāl Jogini and of Baliyā can be surmised from the position assigned to the *Mohāna* of Katasgarh, and Khāl Jogini is probably represented by the confluence near Singhasan. Baliyā was very close to this place. The encroachment of the great Brahmaputtra river (Jamuna) has effaced all traces of these places— N. K. B.

6. No trace of this fort is to be found at present at Dacca. The place where this fort was built is now occupied by the Dacca Central Jail and the Civil hospital. The places round about this fort is still known as *Gird-i-Qal'ā*... (*Dhākār Itihās,* I, 338; Taylor's Topography of Dacca, 94).

7. Jatrapūr is situated on the bank of the Ichhamati river, about 30 miles to the west of Dacca. There is a trunk road leading from

Jatrapūr to Dacca *via* Nawābganj and Churan (Rennell's Bengal Atlas, Map No. 16).

8. The Ichhamati (spelt in the Ms. as عیسمتی 'Īsāmatī) river rises from the Dhaleswari near Sāhibganj and falls into the Dhaleswari on the east of Madanganj in the Dacca district. Formerly this river arose from a point to the south of Jafarganj opposite the factory of Nāthpūr and went as far as Joginighāt of Munshiganj. But now the course is considerably changed. (*Dhạkār Itihās,* I, 48; Rennell's Bengal Atlas, Map No. 16).

9. Dākchara may also be read as Dākjara. There is a place called Dhākjara situated at a distance of about three miles to the north-west of Jatrapūr. This is probably the place meant here.

10. Padmavatī is another name of the river Padma.

11. The Mātibhanga or Matabhanga is a distributary of the Ganges. It branches off about 10 miles down from the Jalangi, which rises from the Ganges to the south-east of Sardah in the Rajshạhi district. (Rajshahi district Gazetteer, and the district map.)

12. Kutharuiyā is the old name of the Kirtinasha, i.e. the portion of the Padṃa which passes through Bikrampūr and joins the Meghna. The original name of this river was Rathkhola then it was changed into Brahmabadhia and then to Kutharuiya and lastly to Kirtinạsha, or 'destroyer of memorable works' from the ravages it wrought amongst the buildings of Raja Raj Ballav at Rajnagar in the Farid-pur district. (*Dhākār Itihās,* I, 42; Taylor's Topography of Dacca, 9).

13. There is a place called Kudaliyā at the confluence of the Padma and the Jabuna near Goalanda. This place is generally known as the 'Mohana of Baiskudaliā.' But the text shows that this is not the place mentioned here. According to the text the place is situated somewhere between Kalākūpa and Patharghata. There is a village named Kudaliā near Narayanganj and also a place called *Char* Kudaliā on the northern bank of the Dhaleswari, north of Patharghata. One of these places is probably the Kudaliyā of our author.

14. Balra is on the bank of the Ichhamati, about 24 miles west of Dacca.

15. Kalākūpa is on the bank of the Ichhamati river, about 17 miles to the south-west of Dacca. (Rennell's Bengal Atlas, Map No. 12).

16. Shīrpur Murcha is situated on the west bank of the river Karatoya to the south of the town of Bogra. Rennell spells it, Seer-pour (Map, No. 6, Bengal Atlas). It was included within the Sarkar Bāzūhā. The word *Bāzūhā* is the plural of the Persian word *Bāzū,* 'an

arm'; the Mahals in this Sarkar extending from Barbakabad across the Brahmaputtra up to Sylhat was called a *Bāzū*. (Blochmann, J.A.S.B., 1873, 216).

17. Patharghata is on the south bank of the Dhaleswari river, about 6 miles south of Dacca. (*Dhākār Itihās*, I, 43; Rennell's Map No. 16).

18. Jahāngīrnagar is the name of the city of Dhāka given by Islām Khān Chishtī after the name of the Emperor Jahāngīr. He made it the capital of Bengal as he found it to be the most convenient place to deal effectively with the rebellious Zamīndārs of Bhātī or Eastern Bengal and the Mags and the Firingi pirates who often used to raid the imperial territories. Previous to this the Mughal capital of Bengal was at Rājmahal or Akbarnagar.

There are conflicting views as to the date of the transfer of capital to Dacca. Stewart in his History of Bengal suggests that the capital was transferred in 1608 A.D., and Gladwin says that it was transferred in 1612, after the defeat and death of 'Uṣmān, the Afghān. Dr. Sudhindra Nath Bhattacharya in his article "On the transfer of the capital of Mughal Bengal from Rajmahal to Dacca". (Dacca University Studies, Vol. I, 1935, pp. 36-63) makes confusing inferences and gives a wrong chronology of events said to have been based on the Bahāristān. He prefers the date of Gladwin and suggests that the transfer was 'a piecemeal act' as if all the parapharnalia of the capital were removed one after the other from Rajmahal to Dacca within a period of about two years. The contributor of this article has failed to understand many of the important facts of the Bahāristān which have important bearing on this question. He believes that Dacca was 'a temporary armed camp gradually changed into permanent civil station....'

Jahāngīr in his Tuzuk mentions, "When Islām Khān made Dhāka (Dacca) his abode and made the subjection of the Zamīndārs of that neighbourhood his chief object, it occurred to him that he should send an army against the rebel 'Uṣmān and his province" (Tuzuk, 102; Rogers and Beveridge, Memoirs, I, 209). From this passage it is quite clear that Islām Khān made Dacca the capital of Bengal before 1612 A.D., i.e. before the expedition against 'Uṣmān to Uhār was undertaken. Further the trend of the text of the Bahāristān shows that Islām Khān proceeded from Rājmahal to Dacca with the determination of making it the capital of the province, and all his civil and military high officials followed in his train. There is no evidence in the Bahāristān to hold that 'from a military settlement Dacca became the seat of the civil government, and finally emerged as the official capital of the Bengal *subah*' as Dr. Sudhindra Bhattacharyya suggests. On his march to Dacca when Islām Khān reached Baliyā he sent ahead three of his officers, namely, Shaykh Kamāl, Tuqmāq Khān and Mirak Bahādur Jalā'ir, along with sufficient equipments to build a fort at Dacca. They came and constructed the fort as ordered before the arrival of Islām Khān. This fort is the nucleus of the 'New Dhāka' so often mentioned by Mīrzā Nathan to distinguish it from the 'Old Dhāka.' The palace of Islām Khān was also within this fort. The Bahāristān says that the imperial fleet entered the Ichhamati river near Dākchara (a place situated at a distance of about thirty-three miles to the west of Dacca) on the 27th, Rabiu'l-Awwal, 1017 A.H. (11th July, 1608 A.D.); and on the day following the entry of the fleet into the Ichhamati, Islām Khān occupies the fort of Mūsā Khān at Dākchara. (Dr. Sudhindra Nath Bhattacharyya has again misquoted the Bahāristān and places this event on 9th June 1610; vide Dacca University Studies, Vol. I, 1935, 47). From Dākchara Islām Khān proceeded to Balra (about twenty-four miles to the west of Dacca) and thence to Kalakupa (about seventeen miles south-west of Dacca) where he occupied a fort of the rebels. From here he started for Dacca by land and reached there before the arrival of his fleet. Although Mīrzā Nathan has not given the exact date of the arrival of Islām Khān at Dacca, we may very reasonably deduce from the date of the occupation of Dākchara that he made his formal entry into the city of Dacca towards the end of the month of July 1608. Making all allowances for the obstacles on his way it could not have taken him more than a fortnight to reach Dacca from Dākchara, a distance of about thirty-three miles. (Dr. Sudhindra Nath Bhattacharyya is wrong in asserting on the authority of the Bahāristān 'that Islām Khān reached Dacca only early in June 1610;' vide Dacca University Studies, Vol. I, 1935, 60).

Mīrzā Nathan mentions the name of 'Jahāngīrnagar *alias* Dhāka' as soon as Islām Khān entered Dacca and from this time we find that Dacca is always mentioned by him by that name. From these facts stated in the Bahāristān and corroborated by circumstantial evidences of the Tuzuk, it appears that the formal transfer of the capital from Rājmahal to Dacca took place in July 1608 and not in 1612 as suggested by Gladwin and others.

19. The Kawādharī or Gawādharī is a canal which joins the Ichhamati at Rasūlpūr and the Dhaleswari at Paragong, at a short distance to the south-west of Dacca. The canal runs parallel to the Tulsi creek and there is a place called Guadery at its confluence with the Dhaleswari. (Rennell's Map No. 16).

20. Demrā khāl is situated to the north-east of Dacca at the confluence of the Lakhiya and the Baloo rivers. (Rennell's Bengal Atlas, Map No. 12).

21. Dulāy river rises from the Baloo river and falls in the Buri Ganga near Faridābād of Dacca. It is more of a canal than a river. One branch of it passes through the city of Dacca and joins with the Buri Ganga near Bābū Bazar. In 1830 A.D. an iron suspension bridge has been constructed over it connecting the city with Dulāyganj. At present it is in a moribund condition and is not navigable. (*Dhākār Itihās*, I, 76 ; Rennells' Map No. 12).

## CHAPTER VII

1. Katrabū is also called Kartabhū or Katrapūr. It is situated on the river Lakhiya opposite Khiẓrpūr, at present known as Katarab. (*Dhākār Itihās*, I, 448, Rennell's Bengal Atlas, Map No. 6). The river Lakhiya rises from the Brahmaputtra at a point to the west of Egārasindur and falls into the Dhaleswari river to the south of Narayanganj. The northern position of this river is called Banār. (*Dhākār Itihās*, I, 44 ; Rennell's Map No. 12).

2. Pandar or Bandar was a naval station situated in the Ichhamati river in the district of Dacca. (Rennell's Map No.·12 ; *Dhākār Itihās*, I, 488.)

3. Qadam Rasūl is on the eastern bank of the river Lakhiya opposite Narayanganj. It is believed that a foot-print of the Prophet Muḥammad was instituted here in a mosque by Munawwar Khān a descendant of 'Īsā Khān so the place is named as Qadam-Rasūl or the 'Foot-print of the Prophet.' Mīrzā Nathan says (vide para 777) that the foot-print was instituted by Ma'ṣūm Khān Kābulī who purchased it from some merchants who had brought it from Arabia. (For details see Aulād Hasan's Antiquities of Dacca, 59 ; Rennell's Bengal Atlas, sheet No. 12).

4. Chura or Churan is situated on the south of the river Ichhamati at the place where the Churan creek rises from the Ichhamati. (Rennell's Bengal Atlas, Map No. 12).

5. Khiẓrpūr is situated to the north-east of Narayanganj, about 9 miles off from Dacca. It is on the Lakhiya river, about 3 miles from Sunārgāon. (*Dhākār Itihās*, I, 453 ; Rennell's Bengal Atlas, Map No. 6).

6. Kanwarsar or Kumarsar (spelt as Kanwarsar in the ms.) is Cablenesser of Rennell's Map No. 12. It is situated to the south of Narayanganj and to the north of Firingi Bazar. The place is surrounded on three sides by the Dhaleswari and the Lakhiya rivers and by a small stream on the west.

7. Kūpa is probably the same place as Kalākūpa.

8. Biquliā Char. There is a place called Vikuliā within the jurisdiction of Kapasia Thana district Dacca. But no *char* of this name is to be found at present. There might have been an island of this name in the Meghna but no trace of it exists at present.

9. *Farangiān-i-Harmād* is used here to mean the European i.e. Portuguese pirates. The word *Harmād* is a corruption of the word Armada. The Portuguese pirates were generally termed as '*Farangiān-i-Harmād*' or the 'Europeans of the Armada.'

10. The Rāja of the Mags was probably Rāja Manrājgiri of Arracan to whom the king of Burmah sent two ambassadors with presents requesting his aid against the king of Pegu. He was called by the Portuguese Xilimxa. Mīrzā Nathan also calls him Salīm, the Rāja of the Mags. We do not know why he styled himself as Salīm which is a Muslim name. (Chittagong Hill Tract Gazetteer, 1909, I, 28; *Jessor-Khulnār Itihās*, II, 298.)

11. Gawsawal Firingi of our text, is Sebastian Ganzalves, a Portuguese pirate-chief who held his sway over the island of Sandwip during this period. (For details of his career see Campos' History of the Portuguese in Bengal, 81-87, 154-157; Phayry's History of Burma, 173-76; A. Bocarro-Decada 13 da Historiadu India, parte 2, Lisbon, 1876, pp. 440-444). Anik Farank or Ank Frank of the Bahāristān is probably the son of Anaporan, the younger brother of the king of Arracan. Anaporan, who took shelter with Ganzalves after his war with his brother, was secretly murdered by Ganzalves. Ganzalves took possession of all his wealth and got his widow married to his younger brother Antonio Carvalho. It seems that Anik Farank makes an alliance with the Mughals to vindicate the wrongs done to his father. (Vide Sir Jadunath's article in *Prabasi*, 1329, B.E., p. 664).

12. Kharagpur or Currucpour is in the district of Mungyr, Bihar. It is situated to the south of the Ganges. (Rennell's Bengal Atlas, Map No. 2).

13. Ujjainia here means Bhojpūr of Bihar. The originators of the state of Bhojpūr are the ancestors of the Dumraon Rāj family, who came from Ujjain of Malwa. Rāja Sindhol Singh, who had first settled in Bihar, abdicated the throne in favour of his son Rāja Bhoj Singh who named the territory as Bhojpūr after his own name. (Vide L. M. Ghose's Indian Chiefs, 437). Rāja Madhūkar, who helped the pretender Khusraw, must have been one of the Chiefs of this family. Jahāngīr has not mentioned the name of this Chief. He gives the name of the pretender as Quṭb belonging to Uch who secured the aid of the

Ujjainis with the promise of making some of them ministers of his State as soon as he would become victorious. (Rogers and Beveridge, Memoirs, I, 173-176).

14. The Punpun (Pompon river) comes from the Ramgar district, Bihar. There are two rivers of the same name known as Little Punpun and Great Punpun. Both the streams flow from the south in a north-eastern direction and join the Ganges near Fatwa in the district of Patna. (Rennell's Bengal Atlas, Map No. 3; Martin's Eastern India, I, 12, 13).

15. Ibrāhīmpūr. There is a rather well-known and large village of this name under Nabinagar P.S. of the district of Tipperah, 3½ miles south of Nabinagar and five miles inland from the eastern bank of the Meghna. It is about 28 miles north-east of Sonārgaon. This may be the place meant, but this appears to be too far off. Moreover, it is not an "island" by which term Ibrāhīmpūr is qualified in para 86. It was probably an island in the Meghna, now no longer existent. N.K.B.

## CHAPTER VIII

1. Sahaspūr has been wrongly spelt in the Ms. as Sahaspir. It is, I believe, is the Mahal of Sahaspūr included within the Sarkar of Sulaymānābād, as mentioned in the Aiṅ. II, 140.

2. Tājpūr Purnea is a Sarkar extending over Eastern Purnea east of the Mahananda, and western Dinajpur. It includes 29 mahals or circles. The town of Tajpur is situated on the bank of the river Nagore. There is also road-ways leading from Tajpur to Purnea, Dinajpur and Maldah. (Blochmann, J.A.S.B., 1873, 215; Rennell's Map No. 5).

3. The Kusī river flows from the hills of the northern mountains of the Nepal range, and passing through the district of Purnea it falls into the Ganges. The river has undergone a considerable change of its course from what has been described by Rennell. (For details see Martin's Eastern India, III, 10-16; Rennell's Map No. 9).

4. Dihīkūt. See note No. 24, Chapter V.

5. Ananta Manik of Bhalwa. Bhalwa or Bhulua is the modern Noakhali in Eastern Bengal, situated on the east bank of the Brahmaputtra. Bhalwa has been mis-spelt in two places in the Ms. as تبلوه. Probably this is a mistake committed by the copyist. There is a village of this name a few miles west of modern Noakhali town which contains the ruins of a 17th century fort. The history of the chiefs of

Bhulua is very obscure. The accounts of Dr. Wise, of Babu Ananda-nath Roy, and Babu Kailash Chandra Sinha (Rājmala) have very little of history in them. Kailash Babu makes Amarȧ Manikya contemporary of Islām Khān. But Amar died in 1586 A.D. The contemporary chief of Bhulua during Islām Khān's invasion was Ananta Manikya the successor of Lakshmana Manikya. (For details see Bhattasali's 'Bengal's Chiefs' struggle,' Bengal, Past and Present, 1928, XXXV, 37-39; Rennell's Map No. 1 and Noakhali District Gazetteer, 102).

6. The Dāktiyā Khāl or the Dackiteeah river of Rennell rises from the hills of Tipperah and falls into the Brahmaputtra near Chandpūr. (Rennell's Map No. 1; Noakhali District Gazetteer, 5).

7. The Feni rivers rise from the hills of Tipperah. One of them is known as the little Feni or Dākātiā river which passes through the plains near Comilla and enters the Noakhali district near Sikandarpūr and flows through the western portion of the modern Feni subdivision to the Brahmaputtra. The other is known as the big Feni which enters the Noakhali district at its eastern limit and forms the boundary between the districts of Chittagong and Noakhali. (Rennell's Map No. 1; Noakhali District Gabetteer, 6).

8. *Charandharan.* According to Wilson's Glossary, 'Charhandar' means a servant accompanying a cargo of goods. But it cannot be this. I think *Charandharan* is an officer of the imperial wardrobe in charge of the shoe department. There was a department in the royal household known as *Charandharī Khāna*.

9. Bukāinagar is in the district of Mymensingh situated to the south-east of Kishoreganj. In Rennell's Map No. 6, it is included within the Pargana of Mominshāhī on the west of the Brahmaputtra.

## CHAPTER IX

1. Lāur hill is on the north-west border of Sylhat, about 14 miles from the town of Sunamganj. There is a trunk road leading from Bukāinagar to Lāur. (Rennell's Bengal Atlas, Map No. 6).

2. Ḥasanpūr is situated on the east bank of the Brahmaputtra. Its present name is Haybatnagar. It is on the south-west of Kishoreganj at a distance of six miles, and about eight miles to the south-east of Gaffargaon railway station. Bukāinagar is 23 miles north of Ḥasanpūr. (Rennell's Bengal Atlas Map No. 6).

3. Shāh Bandar is situated on the Ichhamati opposite Narayanganj, about thirteen miles from Dacca. This place is also known as

Firingi Bazar after the settlement of the Firingis at this place during the rule of Nawāb Shayesta Khān in 1663. (*Dhākār Itihās*, I, 486; Taylor's Topography of Dacca, 103).

4. Yārasindūr or Egārasindūr is on the east bank of the Brahmaputtra in the Ḥusaynshāhī pargana, district Mymensingh. It is situated to the south of Ḥasanpūr at a distance of about 10 miles, just opposite Tuk. (Rennell's Map No. 6). The name of this place has been spelt in the Ms. as یارسندور 'Yarsindur,' and یارەسندور 'Yarasindur.'

5. Tuk is situated on the eastern bank of the Brahmaputtra near the point where the Lakhya river rises. It was used as a naval base of the Mughals. It is at a distance of about 35 miles from Dacca, to the north-east. (Rennell's Map No. 6).

6. Baniāchung is a zamindary within the district of Sylhat, at present included in the Habiganj subdivision. (Rennell's Bengal Atlas, sheet No. 6).

7. Sylhat or Srihatta district is situated in the lower valley of the Surma river in Assam. It is bounded on the north by the Khasi and Jaintia hills, on the east by Kachār, on the south by the State of Hill Tipperah, and on the west by the districts of Tipperah and Mymensingh. In Akbar's time it was known as Sarkār Silhat consisting of 8 mahals or subdivisions. According to Marco Polo, the *Ain* and the *Tuzuk* Sylhat was notorious for supplying eunuchs which was banned by Jahāngīr in 1608 A.D. (For details see Sylhat District Gazetteer, 11; Blochmann, J.A.S.B., 1873, 216; Memoirs I, 150. Rennell's Map No. 6).

8. Tājpūr. There is a village of this name in North Sylhat, 15 miles from the town. But the Tājpūr mentioned here must be somewhere between Bukāinagar and the Lāur hills. It has been pointed out by Sir Jadunath Sarkar in his article "The last pathan hero of Bengal" (*Prabasi*, 1328 B.E., p. 147), that there is a place called Tājpūr with ruins of an old fort at a distance of about 6 miles to the north-east of Bukāinagar. I think this is the place mentioned here. Mr. Shree Ram Sarma is entirely wrong in identifying this place with Tajpur of Upper Assam. (See his article in the Journal of Indian History, Vol. II).

9. The position of Matang could not be definitely located. But from the text it appears that it was situated somewhere near about Ṭaraf.

10. Taraf is situated on the north-east of the pargana of Sarail, at a distance of about 34 miles from it. It is in the south-west portion of the district of Sylhat, about 10 miles from Habiganj in the south

eastern direction. There is a road leading from Sarail to Taraf. (Rennell's Bengal Atlas, sheet No. 6).

## CHAPTER X

1. Jessore is spelt in the Ain and the Bahāristān as جسر 'Jasar'. It was also known as Rasūlpūr and was included as a Mahal in the Sarkār of Khalifatābād (Ain II, 134). I have adopted the modern spelling in my translation.

2. Bakla or Ismā'ilpūr was the name of a small Sarkār comprising portions of Bāqirganj and Dhāka districts. It contained four Mahals and was situated to the north-east of Fatḥābād or Faridpūr. (Ain, II, 134, Blochmann, J.A.S.B., 1873, 217).

3. *Jharūka* also called *Jharūka-i-darshan* is the custom of showing the face of the Emperor to his subjects every morning from his palace balcony. This is an imperial prerogative introduced by Emperor Akbar. Abu'l-Fazl writes,—" His Majesty generally receives twice in the course of twenty four hours, when people of all classes can satisfy their eyes and hearts with the light of his countenance. First, after performing his morning prayers, he is visible from outside the awning to the people of all ranks, whether they be given to worldly pursuits, or to a life of solitary contemplation, without any molestation from the mace bearers". (Ain, I. 156).

*Chawkī* is the custom of making the nobles mount guard round the palace and formally salute the palace. It is an imperial prerogative introduced by Akbar. Abu'l-Fazl writes,—" Mounting guard is called in Hindi *Chawkī*. There are three kinds of guards. The four divisions of the army have been divided into seven parts, each of which is appointed for one day, under the superintendence of a trustworthy Mansabdar. Another, fully acquainted with all ceremonies at Court is appointed as *Mīr 'Arẓ*. All orders of His Majesty are made known through these two officers (the *Mīr 'Arẓ* and the commander of the palace). They are day and night in attendance about the palace, ready for any orders His Majesty may issue. In the evening, the imperial *Qūr* (standards) is taken to the State Hall. The mounting guards stand on the right; the ranks of the guards to be relieved are drawn up on the other side. His Majesty generally inspects the guards himself, and takes notice of the presence or absence of the soldiers. Both ranks salute His Majesty. If His Majesty is prevented by more important affairs from attending, one of the princes is ordered to inspect the guard. From predilection and a desire to teach soldiers their duties, as also from a regard to general efficiency, His Majesty pays much attention to the guards. If any one is absent without having a proper excuse, or from laziness, he is fined one week's pay or receives a suitable reprimand." (Ain, I, 257).

*Qūr* is a collection of flags, arms and other insignia, which follow the king wherever he goes. Abu'l-Fazl mentions:—" At Court reception the Āmīrs and other people stand opposite the *Qūr*, ready for any service; and on the march they follow behind it, with the exception of a few who are near His Majesty. Elephants in full trappings, camels, carriages, *naqāras*, flags, the *kaukabahs*, and other imperial insignia, accompany the *Qūr*, while eager mace-bearers superintend the march, assisted by the *Mīr Bakhshis*." (Ain, I, 50, and 110.).

4. Pitambar is the founder of the Putia Rāj family of Rajshahi. He was the Zamīndār of the pargana of Chilajuwār situated on the Ganges near about the station of Saraghāt. He was the ruler of a considerable portion of Pabna and Rajshahi districts. His descendants still retain the old Zamindary. (Bengal Past and Present, 1928, XXXV, 36; Rajshahi District Gazetteer, 176.).

5. *Bhuyi* is an elephant driver who sits behind upon the rump of the elephant, and assists in quickening the speed of the animal. In Akbar's time his pay was 110 *dāms* per month and the *Māhūt* or the driver who sits on the neck of the elephant used to get a salary of 200 *dāms* (Ain, I, 125.).

6. Mahadpūr Baghwān:—There is a place called Baghwān situated on the Bhairab river, about 20 miles to the north of Krishnanagar. Mahadpūr or Mahatpūr is situated to the north of Krishnanagar at a distance of about six miles (Rennell's Bengal Atlas, Map No. 1.).

7. Bāgha was the name of a Mahal included within the Sarkār of Sharifābād (Ain, II, 139). This is probably the village of Bāgha situated on the other side of the Tribeni of the Hugli district at the confluence of the Jumna.

8. Salka. The Salka creek is marked on Rennell's sheet No. 1 as starting from the Ichhamati river about 22 miles north of Buranhatty. The starting point of the stream has been taken to be the Thana of Salka by the late Mr. Satish Chandra Mitra in his *Jasohar-Khulnar-Itihās* (History of Jessore and Khulna), p. 374. That the Mughals were first held in check at the Thana of Salikha was well-known, as Ram Ram Basu, writing in 1802, has also referred to the name and the incident. (Quoted in ibid., p. 373.). N. K. B.

9. Khwāja Kamal known as Kamal Khūja was a pathan soldier in the service of Pratāpadītya. At first he was the chief of the life-guards of the Rāja. He gradually rose to the position of the commander of an

army and was in charge of one of the chief forts of the Rāja. A fort was built by the Rāja which was named after him as Garh Kamalpur. (*Jessore and Khulna Itihas*, II, 127-128.).

10. Budhan or Burhan is probably the Burronhutty of Rennell's Bengal Atlas, Map No. 1. It is situated on the east of fort William, at a distance of 38 miles. The river Ichhamati flows by its eastern side. There is a pargana called Burhan in the district of Jessore. (Vide *Jessore-Khulna Itihas*, I, 136.). Ain (II, 141) shows it as a mahal under the Sarkār of Sātgaon, comprising the modern district of 24 parganas, western Nadiya, South-western Murshidabad and extended in the south to Hatiagarh below Diamond Harbour.

11. River Jessore i.e., the Bhairab river which passes by the city of Jessore (Rennell's Map No. 1.).

12. Kharawan Ghāt was probably the name of a certain Ghāt or ford on the Ichhamati river. It seems to have been situated on the north-east of the fort of Jessore. But I have not been able to trace the place in the maps I have consulted.

13. Here the portion of the Jumna flowing by the western side of the fort of Jessore is called Bhagirathi. Kagraghāt is situated at a distance of 40 miles from Mīrzā Nagar of Jessore. Rennell calls it Cogreeghāt (Map No. 2.). The river is divided here into three branches; one of these may be named as Kagarghāt khāl. In folio 274-a of the Bahāristān it is mentioned that there is "a place named Kagraghata three *Kos* ahead of Jessore towards Hijlī."

14. دویست has been read by Sir Jadunath as 40 (*Prabāsi*, p. 6, 1327 B.E.) but it means 200, not forty.

15. The word in the Ms. is written as *hila* حله but the proper reading is *Chilta* چلته which means a coat of mail or any armed covering.

16. *Harmad* هرمد i.e. the people of the Armada, a term applied to the Portuguese pirates.

17. Katky Brahmins were the Brahmins imported by Pratāpadītya from Cuttak, to perform the religious rites in the temple of Gopalpūr. (Sarkār's article, "The fall of Pratāpadītya," *Prabāsi*, Kartick 1327 B.E.). Mr. Shri Ram Sharma has misread this word as *Kathika* and translates it as 'story-teller'. The Ahom Kings of Assam also brought Katky Brahmins to their Court and maintained them at the State's expense. Their descendants still bear the surname of *Katky*.

18 Bankura is the name of a village on the west bank of the river Kalindi near Kaliganj. Remains of a temple of Siva are to be found

in this place. There is a quarter called Bangālpāra to the north of this place, which I believe derived its name from the existence of so many Bungalows constructed by the Mughals during their stay.

19. Chandra Kuna has been confused with Chadraguna of Chittagong hill tracts by Mr. Shri Ram Sharma (Journal of Indian History, VIII, 331.). It is a well-known municipal town in the district of Midnapur, 28 miles north-east of the district town. It was the seat of a petty chief during the early days of Mughal rule in Bengal and its chief Hari Bhan is even mentioned in the Tuzuk-i-Jahāngīri as a rebel in 1617. The pargana of Chandrakuna lies round the town and the pargana of Burda adjoins it on the east. Jhargram, which is the centre of a large estate lies 18 miles to the south-west of Chandrakuna and may be the Jhakra of our author. N. K. B.

20. Ibrāhīm Khān Kākar was an Afghān officer who was raised to the Mansab of 2,500 personal and horse and was given the title of Dilāwar Khān in recognition of his meritorious services. Jahāngīr pays many compliments to him in his Tuzuk. (For details see Memoirs, I, 29, 30, 49, 59, 62, 77, 105, 248, 286, 298.).

21. Rāja Kalyān was appointed governor of Orissa (July 6, 1611) 21 Rabi' II, 1020 A.H. (For details of his career see Memoirs, I, 192, 199, 202, 326, 389, 390, 402.).

22. This is the second expedition led by Rāja Kalyān against Purushottam Dev of Khurda. The first campaign was led by Rāja Kesho Dās Mārū (see para 39, Chapter V) when the temple of Jagannath was desecrated.

23. Shāh 'Alā or the saint 'Alāu'l-Ḥaq was the spiritual successor of saint Ākhī Sirāju'd-Dīn whom tradition says he served with such humility that he allowed the hot cooking pot of his spiritual father to be carried on his head so that he became bald. Ākhī Sirāju'd-Dīn is said to have paid several visits to Mecca on foot and 'Alāu'l-Ḥaq accompanied him carrying the cooking pot of his father in the journeys. His shrine is at Pandua not at Gawr as mentioned by Nathan. The shrine is known as "Shash-Hazārī" shrine, because an endowment of 6,000 *bighas* of land are assigned as an endowment for the upkeep of the shrine.

24. Chandnī Ghāt is a well known ford of the city of Dacca on the bank of the Burhi Ganga river. It is probably named after the special boat of Islām Khān called Chandnī.

25. Uhār has been read as Adhar by many scholars. There are different opinions as to the location of this place. Stewart in his History of Bengal supposes that it was on the bank of the Subarnarika in Orissa

Blochmann (Ain I, 520) says on the authority of Makhzan-i-Afghānī that the fight took place 100 *kos* from Dacca and in a place called Nek Ujayl, and he points out in a note that there are several Ujayls in Eastern Bengal. Possibly 'Adhar' is Udhar or Uzhar, and a corruption of Ujayl. The Riyazu's-Salatin does not mention the site of the battle. But the translator Maulavi 'Abdu's-Salam, in his foot note No. 2, p. 175, has confused the issue and has drawn groundless inferences. In foot note No. 1, p. 176, he surmises that the battle took place on the bank of the Lakhya river close to Khiẓrpūr and Baktarpūr. Some authorities suggest that 'Uṣmān's residence was at *Kohistan-i-Dhāka* i.e. the hilly regions of Dacca and *Vilayat-i-Dhāka* i.e. the country of Dacca and these places are identified with Ran Bhawal or the Madhupur jungle. But from the text of the Bahāristān we find that 'Uṣmān took up his residence in Sylhat at a place called Uhār. In para 183 of this translation it further says that 'Uṣmān marched for battle from Uhār and in two marches he arrived at Dawlambapūr in Chawallis pargana and there he pitched his camp for battle on the bank of a *jalah* or marsh. Now the Chawallis pargana is situated within south Sylhat and the distance from the actual site of the field of battle to the stronghold of 'Uṣmān is said to have been covered by the Afghan army in twenty-four hours in course of their retreat and after reaching Uhār they buried the dead-body of 'Uṣmān between two hills (vide para 207 of the translation). Therefore it appears that Uhār must have been the name of a place in the southern extremity of Sylhat surrounded by hills which the modern maps of the district do not show.

26. Shajā'at Khān, known as Shaykh Kabīr, belonged to the family of Shaykh Salīm and was honoured by Jahāngīr with the title of Shajā'at Khān when he was prince. In the first year of Jahāngīr's accession to the throne, he was raised to the rank of 1,000 and then he was deputed to fight against Mīrzā Muḥammad Ḥusayn of Ahmedabad. In 1607 A.D. he was promoted to the rank of 1,500 personal and 1,000 horse. He was then appointed for some time to serve in the Deccan. In the month of March, 1611 he was recalled from the Deccan and was appointed to serve in Bengal. (For details see Memoirs, R. and B., Vol. I, pp. 29, 44, 113, 192, 209-14, 227 ; Ma'āṣiru'l-Umarā, II, 630.).

27. Kishwar Khān known as Shaykh Ibrāhīm was the son of Quṭbu'd-Dīn Khān Kūka. In 1606 he was given the title of Kishwar Khān and the rank of 1,000 personal and 300 horse. He was appointed governor of the fort of Rohtas in 1608. Two years after i.e., in 1610, his rank was increased to 2,000 personal and horse and he was appointed Fawjdār of Uch. Then he was deputed to serve in Bengal in the expedition against 'Uṣmān of Sylhat where he died. (For details of his early career see Memoirs, R. and B., Vol. I, pp. 76, 144, 170, 209.).

28. This incident has been mentioned by Jahāngīr in his Tuzuk. (Memoirs, I, 147.).

29. Sarāil is the name of a pargana in the district of Tipperah. It is also called Satara Khandal. The later name is at present given to a part of the main pargana around the subdivisional town of Brahman Baria. Sarāil is situated between the Meghna and Titas rivers and is about 26 miles long and 13 miles broad. (Rennell's Map No. 6; Bengal Past and Present, 1929, XXXVIII, 12.).

30. Pankiyā پنکیا is, I believe, a wrong spelling for Meghna میگنا committed by the copyist. In Book III, Chapter V of the Bahāristān it is mentioned that when Mīrzā Nathan went from Dhāka to meet Ibrāhīm Khān at Udaypūr with the hill-chiefs of Assam, he passed through the river Pankiyā and as the river was in high flood he could not carry the elephants with him and he had to leave them in an island in the midst of the river. It clearly shows that this river cannot but be the Meghna. The river Pankiyā mentioned in the Ms. must be a misspelling of the Meghna.

31. Tūpia, may be read as Putia also. There is a place named Putiagaon in the district of Sylhat situated within the jurisdiction of the Thana of Habiganj. This may be the place mentioned here.

32. Kadam Tala is probably Kadamtali of Tarup *mauza,* Thana Habiganj, District Sylhat. (Village Directory of Sylhat.).

33. The name of the Rāja of Kachar has not been given by our author. Probably he was Rāja Satrudaman, a contemporary of the Ahom King Pratap Singh. Satrudaman is the hero of a Bengali novel called "Ranachandi". But this novel contains many historical discrepancies. (For details see Gaits' History of Assam, Chapter X, 1st edn., pp. 247-48.).

34. Dawlambapūr, a village in the Chawallis pargana which is situated in South Sylhat. (See *Srihatter Itibritta,* Vol. I, 151.).

35. Sending of this message has been stated in the Tuzuk (Rogers and Beveridge, I, 210.).

36. Iqbāl Nāma (p. 62) says that 'Uṣmān led his charge on the vanguard of the Mughals placing his heated elephant Bakhta in front, and he himself, owing to his abnormal corpulence and heavy weight of his body, was riding on that day on the howdah of another elephant. Jahāngīr calls Bakhta by the name of Gajpat. (Memoirs I, 211.).

37. Jahāngīr mentions that the man who fired the gun at 'Uṣmān was not known. He says, "However much they enquired for the man who fired it, he could not be found." (Memoirs, I, 212.). But here we

find the name of the soldier who struck 'Uṣmān and 'Uṣmān was killed not by a gun-shot but by the shot of an arrow.

38. *Mahua* tree resembles the mango tree ; its wood is used for building purposes. The fruit which is also called *Gilaundah* yields an intoxicating liquor. ( Ain I, Blochmann, 70.).

39. *Pākhar* is a kind of steel covering for elephants. But here it seems that the same armour is used for horses as well. ( Ain, I, Blochmann, 129.).

40. *Bahili* or *Bhili* is a class of infantry. These were men of the wild tribes who lived in the rugged country between Ajmere and Gujarāt. Their principal weapon, which they brought with them when in the Emperor's service, was the long bow of bamboo called *Kamanth*. (Irvine, 170.).

41. Iqbāl Nāma (p. 64) says that an auxiliary force consisting of 300 horse and four hundred musketeers arrived there with Mu'taqid Khān and 'Abdu's-Salām. But according to Mīrzā Nathan, Mu'taqid Khān was with Shajā'at Khān from the beginning of this expedition. The Memoirs (I, 212) also gives the same number of the soldiers but it agrees with Mīrzā Nathan that this regiment was placed under 'Abdu's-Salām.

42. Salīm Khān was the son of Shīr Shāh who succeeded his father with the title of Islām Shāh. The Mughals, owing to their bitter hostility against the Afghāns, never address them as Shāh but always call them Khān. In the Akbar Nāma Shīr Shāh and Salīm Shāh are invariably called Shīr Khān and Salīm Khān. Salīm Khān ascended the throne of his father on the 15th of Rabi'u'l-Awwal, 952 A.H. (27th May, 1545) superseding the claim of his elder brother 'Ādil Khān, the heir apparent nominated by Shīr Shāh. The internecine feuds which followed the accession of Islām Khān and which had weakened the power of the Afghāns, are referred to in this passage.

43. According to Iqbāl Nāma (p. 64), the Afghāns had handed over 49 elephants as *peshkash* to the Mughal commander. The Memoirs (I, 213) also says, "They brought forty-nine elephants as an offering."

44. Ainiya could not be definitely located. From the text it seems that the place was situated at a distance of about thirty miles from Dawlambapūr in Chawallis pargana of South Sylhat.

45. The Emperor and the great nobles were provided with tents in duplicate, one set being sent on to the next camping ground while the other set was in use. The tents thus sent on were known as *pīsh khāna* (lit. advance-house) or advance tents. (Irvine, 195 ; Bernier, 359 ; Ain, I, 47.).

46. Jahāngīr mentions the date to be the 6th of the month of Safar, 1021 A.H. corresponding to 8th April, 1612 A.D. (Tuzuk, 104; Rogers, I, 214.).

47. The Iranian Ambassador Yadgār 'Alī Sultan arrived at Jahāngīr's Court in March, 1611 and had an audience with the Emperor on the 9th April. This Farmān must have been issued about this date. The Afghān prisoners were produced before the Emperor on the 17th Rajab, 1021 A.H. corresponding to 13th September, 1612 A.D. (Vide Tuzuk, 93, 112; and Memoirs I, 193, 230; Iqbāl Nāma, 49.).

48. The office of Wāqi'-navis, or writer of events, had been introduced by Akbar. His duty was to report to the Emperor whatever happened in the district to which he was appointed. Abu'l-Fazl says, "His Majesty's object is, that every duty be properly performed; that there be no undue increase, or decrease in any department; that dishonest people be removed, and trustworthy people be held in esteem; and that active servants may work without fear, and negligent and forgetful men be held in check." This office existed even before the Mughals under the title of *Barīd* reference to which is found in the Tārikh-i-Firūzshāhī. But it was not so systematically organised as was done in Akbar's time. Dr. Fryer, in his 'New Account of East India and Persia', calls these officers 'Public Notaries' or 'Public Intelligencers'. He says, "This cheat (i.e. the practice of false musters) is practised all over the realm, notwithstanding here are public Notaries placed immediately by the *Mogul*, to give Notice of all Transactions; which they are sure to represent in favour of the Governors where they reside, being fee'd by them, as well as paid by the Emperor; so that if a defeat happen, it is extenuated; if a victory, it is magnified to the height; Those in this office are called *Vocanoveces*." (For details see, Ain, I, 258; Blochmann, J.A.S.B. 1872, 51.).

49. The fact of Islām Khān's dismissal recorded here is contrary to what is mentioned in Tuzuk. Jahāngīr says, "I promoted Islām Khān to the rank of 6,000 personal, and honoured Shajā'at Khān with the title of 'Rustam of the age', as well as increased his rank by 1,000 personal and horse." But in one place Jahāngīr mentions, "I had summoned him (Shajā'at Khān) from the Deccan for the purpose of sending him to Bengal to Islām Khān, in reality to take his place permanently, and I entrusted him with the charge of that Ṣūbah". (Tuzuk, 93; compare also Tuzuk, 94, 104; Rogers and Beveridge, I, 192, 214.). There may be some truth in what is said by Mīrzā Nathan.

50. The name of this brother of Yadgār 'Alī Sultan has not been mentioned either in the Tuzuk or in the Bahāristān.

51. These regulations were promulgated in the 6th year of Jahāngīr's reign. (Memoirs, I, 205.).

52. *Salām* and *Taslīm* are forms of salutations observed at the Mughal Court. "*Taslīm* consists in placing the back of the right hand on the ground, and then raising it gently till the person stands erect, when he puts the palm of his hand upon the crown of his head, which pleasing manner of saluting signifies that he is ready to give himself as an offering." Another form of salutation observed at the Court is called *Kurnish.* Abu'l-Fazl describes the *Kurnish* thus:—"His Majesty has commanded the palm of the right hand to be placed upon the forehead, and the head to be bent downwards. This mode of salutation, in the language of the present age, is called *Kurnish,* and signifies that the saluter has placed his head (which is the seat of the senses and the mind) into the hand of humility, giving it to the royal assembly as a present, and has made himself in obedience ready for any service that may be required of him." (Ain, I, 158.).

53. *Qūr,* see supra, note No. 3.

54. The reduction of Islām Khān's Mansab has not been mentioned in the Tuzuk.

55. Sarsābād, one of the Mahals in the Sarkār of Jannatābād or Lakhnawtī. ('Ain, II, 131.).

56. Dunapūr is situated on the left bank of the Ganges in the district of Patna, Bihar. (Rennell's Map No. 9.)

57. Asurainagar. The Ms. spells it as Asurabatgar. I have not been able to identify this place. The word may also be read as Asurnagar or Asurainagar. There was a king named Asurāi ruling in some parts of Sylhat, who was brought under subjection by Chilarāy, brother of the Kūch king Nara Narāyan. Asurnagar may be the name of the capital of Asurai who seems to be a Kachari king. (See Gait's History of Assam, 53 and his article on the Koch kings of Kāmrūpa, J. A. S. B., Vol. LXII, Pt. I, No. 4, 1893.).

## CHAPTER XI.

1. The Kuch territory commonly known as the state of 'Koch Bihar' was originally founded by a petty chief named Biswa Singha, son of Hariya Mandal in 1515 A.D., after the fall of the Khen dynasty. After the death of Biswa Singha in 1540 A.D., his eldest son Malla Dev ascended the throne and assumed the name Nara Narāyan. During the reign of Nara Narāyan the Kuch territory reached its highest expansion. This king with the help of his brother Chilarāy led successful campaigns against the Rājas of Assam, Kachar, Jaintia, Manipur, Sylhat, Tippera and the chiefs of Khairam and Dimarua. All these Rājas were com-

pelled to pay tribute to him. But it seems he could not hold them long in subjection. The extent of his dominions during the reign of Akbar the Great was as described by Abu'l-Fazl,—"Its length is 200 *kos* and its breadth 40 to 100 *kos*." Further on he says, "On the east is the river Brahmaputtra, on the north is lower Tibet and Assam, on the south is Ghoraghāt, on the west is Tirhut." After the death of Chilarāy, his son Raghūdev rebelled against Nara Narāyan. Nara Narāyan, being a kind hearted uncle, made a compromise with his nephew and ceded to him the territory lying to the east of the Manās and kept the western portion for himself and his successors. This was in 1581 A.D. On Nara Narāyan's death in 1587 A.D. his son Lakshmī Narāyan succeeded to the throne of the western Kūch territory. Raghūdev died about the year 1603 A.D. and his son Parikshīt ascended the throne of the eastern Kūch territory, against whom Islām Khān had to send an expedition. (For details, see Gait's History of Assam, 46-69; Assam Census Report, 1891, 212 and Bengal Census Report, 1901, 382; Barua's Early History of Kamrupa, 284-301; Akbar Nāma, III, 349, 1067; Cooch Bihār State and its Land Revenue Settlements, by Mr. H. N. Chowdhury, 232; Gunabhirām Baruah's *Assam Buranji*; *Bansabali*, J.A.S.B., LXII; S. K. Bhuyan's *Kamrupar Buranji*, 6-12.).

2. Barampūr. There is a village called Birampūr within the pargana of Sunārgāon. Probably this is the place referred to here. (*Dhākār-Itihās*, p. 15.).

3. According to Pādishāh Nāma (II, 65) this expeditionary force consisted of 6,000 horse, 10,000 to 12,000 infantry and 500 boats. But the account of the Bahāristān is more accurate, as the author himself took a leading part in the expedition.

4. (Page 223.) Bhawāl is a big pargana in the district of Dacca. This pargana is bounded on the north by the pargana of Alapsingh, on the west by the pargana of Atia, on the east by the river Lakhya and the parganas of Sunārgāon and Maheswardi. The city of Dacca is situated to its south. It was divided into two parts Ran Bhawāl (the northern portion) and Bhawāl proper. Bhawāl proper belonged to the Ghāzī Zamīndārs from a long period before the rise of 'Īsā Khān. Ran Bhawāl was under 'Īsā Khān. During Islām Khān's governorship the whole of this pargana was wrested from the Zamīndārs and included within the limits of Dhāka as an imperial domain. (Rennell's Map No. 6; Bengal: Past and Present, Vol. XXXVIII, p. ii; *Dhākār-Itihās*, I, 4-8).

4. (Page 228). Bajrāpūr is on the right bank of the Brahmaputtra about 6 miles down from Shīrpūr. (Rennell's Map No. 5). "Mughal North-East Frontier Policy." p. 138 f.n. says, "The Ms. is indistinct

and the real place meant is not clear." The name of this place has been read as Peerpoor. But the Ms. used by me is quite distinct and it is written as بجراپور "Bajrāpūr."

5. Patladah is on the right bank of the Brahmaputtra, opposite the Karai Bari hills. (Rennell's Map No. 5). It was included within the Sarkār of Ghoraghāt. (Ain, II 135).

6. Salkūna is on the left bank of the Brahmaputtra between Patladah and Karaibari. Rennell spells it 'Talconaw' (Bengal Atlas sheet No. 5).

7. The Pādishāh Nāma (II, 65) says that in every camping ground they used to protect themselves by raising an enclosure of earth and reeds از نی وخاک as is usually done by the soldiers of the Kuch country.

8. Dhubri is on the right bank of the Brahmaputtra. It is at present the headquarters of the district of Goalpara, Assam. (Rennell's Map No. 5). According to Pādishāh Nāma (II, 65) Parikshīt had posted a force of about 500 cavalry and 10,000 infantry for the defence of the fort of Dhubri.

9. Gilah or Gilajhar (the forest of *Mimosa scandens*) is situated on the west side of Gadādhar, about ten miles from where that river joins the Brahmaputtra. It was the capital of Rāja Parikshīt. (For details see Dr. Francis Buchanon's General View of the History of Kamrupa; Martin's Eastern India, III 472; *Kamrupar Buranji*, 6-7). Pādishāh Nāma, (II, 66) calls the capital of Parikshīt "Ghila" which is the correct pronunciation of the word.

10. Bhitar Band and Bāhir Band are two parganas of Kūch Bihar State lying on the right bank of the Brahmaputtra and to the west and south-west of Rangpur. (Rennell's Map No. 5.).

11. *Dabalghah* is a steel headpiece, with a vizor or nose-guard. Specimens of this armour are preserved in the Indian Museum. Figures of several of these are given in W. Egerton's "Hand-book," Nos. 703, 704 on plate XIII, No. 703 on p. 134, No. 591, on p. 125. Its usual name is *Khud* but Mirza Nathan uses the word *Dabalghah*. It has also been mentioned in the Ain (Blochmann, I, III, No. 52, and plate XIII, No. 43). This is a Chaghatai word for helmet. (Irvine, 65, 307). The Akbar Nāma (Lucknow edn.), III, p. 17 spells *Dabaḷghah* as *Walghah*.

12. Mīrzā Nathan being disgusted with the behaviour of Shaykh Kamal calls him "*Shaykh-i-pirpēsha*," a professional pir in contempt.

13. The ordinary meaning of the word *Ṣābāt* is a covered passage connecting two houses. As a military term it means a trench or

approach made in besieging a fortress. According to Briggs, "Firishta," II, 230 (siege of Chitor) the *Ṣābāt* were constructed in the following way:—"The zigzags, commencing at gunshot distance from the fort, consist of a double wall, and by means of blinds or stuffed gabions covered with leather, the besiegers continue their approaches till they arrive near to the walls of the place to be attacked." (For details see Irvine, 274-277; Firishta, Lucknow edition, Maqala II, 257; Akbar Nāma, Lucknow edition, I, 114, II 243; Badāoni II, 107).

14. *Sība* is a high erection commanding the walls of a fort. Sometimes they were constructed with the branches of trees, and guns were mounted on them. This is a Turkish word, meaning "a place surrounded by walls," (Steingass, 714). But here it is used in the sense mentioned above. (For details see, Irvine, 271, 277-280).

15. *Khākrīz* or Glacis mentioned here was a kind of earthen mound so raised as to bring the enemies into the most direct line of fire from the fort. Irvine says, that the word *Khākrīz,* means "foot of the wall," "the glacis," does not seem to have been in use in India. (Army of the Indian Mughals, 264). But from the description of Mīrzā Nathan it appears that the glacis was in use in India. Although the word *Khākrīz* sometimes means "foot of a wall," but I think it is here used in the sense of a glacis.

16. Pādishāh Nāma (II, 65) says that the siege of Dhubri lasted for only a month. It is incorrect.

17. *Bīldārs* means diggers, delvers, pioneers (Steingass). They were employed in excavation work and in breaking the walls of enemy's fort. Their duties in the field of battle were similar to those of the Sappers and Miners of the present day Indian army. Sometimes they are confused with axeman but they are not so. Bīl means a spade, hoe, or mattock, and Bīldār is a digger. (Irvine, 173-174).

18. "*Purani Asam Buranji*" (p. 199) and "*Kamrupar Buranji*" (p. 9) refer to the defeat and capture of Fatḥkhān and the feats of the elephant Ranbhunwar. They add that Parmānanda Daloi, an officer of Parikshit, was on the elephant and was killed.

19. *Chahār-āyina,* literally 'four mirrors.' It is a kind of defensive armour consisting of four pieces, a breast plate and a back plate, with two smaller pieces for the sides. They are connected together with leather straps. (Irvine, 66, 67; Ain, I, 112 and figure No. 49 on plate XIII).

20. Khuntaghāt is situated on the south bank of the Brahmaputtra and is included within the modern district of Goalpara.

21. Kharbuza Ghāt is in Mechpara *mauẓa*, district Goalpara.

22. Gajādhar river, i.e. the Gadādhar river which rises from the Bhutan Hills and falls into the Brahmaputtra near Dhubri. (Rennell's Map No. 5). The name of the river has been spelt as گجادهر 'Gajādhar' in the Ms. wherever it is mentioned.

23. There was a small territory called Dimarua situated on the south bank of the Brahmaputtra in the Kāmrūp district towards Gāro hills. But the chief mentioned here does not seem to belong to this territory. In chapter III of Book III Nathan says that Karaibari was the home land of the sons of Dumria, a relative of Rāja Parikshīt. So it seems that Dumria mentioned here was a chief of this region. According to the *Purani Asam Buranji* (p. 199) and *Kamrupar Buranji* (p. 9), the name of the Kūch admiral was Purandar Lashkar, son-in-law of the Rāja. He led this naval encounter against the imperial fleet commanded by Kuber Khān's son. Mīrzā Nathan has not mentioned the name of the Mughal admiral engaged in this encounter.

24. Pādishāh Nāma (II, 66) says that Parikshīt started for attacking the fort of Dhubri with a force of 20 elephants, about 4,00 cavalry and 10,000 infantry.

25. Mughal North-East Frontier Policy, 142, wrongly states "400 musketeers were imprisoned." But Nathan says "they were all killed or imprisoned." He gives no figure of the casualties and captives.

26. "Mughal North-East Frontier Policy" is wrong when it states —"He was at once captured" (p. 143). Mīrzā Nathan explicitly says that Nitāy was carried by the *kāndis* like a piece of board. Here he uses a word دوار like a piece of board. This word has also another meaning 'a royal seat or a throne' (Steingass). The sentence may be translated thus "he was carried by the '*Kāndis*' like a royal seat or throne."

27. I have translated the word *Hasham* as 'equipage'. But this word conveys a wider meaning than this. It includes every one connected with the army who is neither a *Manṣabdar*, *Tābīnān*, nor *Aḥadis*. (For details see Irvine, 23, 160-174 ; Ain, I, 251-254).

28. Mīrzā Nathan has not given the name of the place of Parikshīt's refuge. According to Padishāh Nāma (Vol. II, 67), he fled to Barnagar.

29. Sūnkūs or Sonkos river rises from the Bhutan hills and falls into the Brahmaputtra at a point to the west of Bhitar Band pargana. There is another river of this name to the east of the Gadādhar which

rises from the Bhutan hills and joins the Gadādhar a few miles up from its confluence with the Brahmaputtra. Probably this is the 'Little sunecoss' of Dr. Hamilton. The big Sunkus falls at the Brahmaputtra down Dhubri, the other Sunkus up from Dhubri. Here the river referred to is the Little Sūnkūs which the Mughals had to cross after the fall of Dhubri in pursuit of Parikshīt. (Rennell's Map No. 5). Mr. Shreeram Sarma in his article "Bengal under Jahangir" (Journal of Indian History, December, 1934) calls this river Funkus which is entirely wrong.

30. River Dulāyi is probably the branch of the Manās which is known as the Gharabhangi or Dilāyi. (Martin's Eastern India, III, 375).

31. The river Banās or Manās rises from the Bhutan hills and falls into the Brahmaputtra, opposite Goalpara, (Rennell's Bengal Atlas, sheet No. 5).

32. Pāndu is situated on the left bank of the Brahmaputtra, about 5 miles from the modern town of Gauhati.

33. The river Barnadī rises from the Bhutan hills and falls into the Brahmaputtra, east of Gauhati. It has been spelt in the Ms. as Baḍnadī but I have adopted the spelling as spoken and written in the Assamese language.

34. Mānchabāt could not be identified. It may be the name of some place called Manasarbat or the way leading to Manās river.

## CHAPTER XII

1. This passage has been wrongly translated in "Mughal North East Frontier Policy, p. 146. It says "As the Kamrup king boasted of royal dignity 800 years old . . ." The text says بادشاہیت صدسالہ "Sovereignty of a hundred years," not 800 years as supposed by the learned author. At the end of this sentence a few words of the Ms. are mutilated.

2. Jahāngīr says that Islām Khān died on Thursday, the 5th Rajab, 1022 A.H.|21st August, 1613. (Memoirs, I, 257).

3. Ẓafar Khān was appointed governor of Bihar in 1021 A.H./1612 A.D. (Memoirs, I, 231).

4. Kukra-desh or Khukhara, in the jungles of Bihar, was famous for its diamonds found in river-bed. It was annexed in 1615 A.D. during the governorship of Ibrāhīm Khān. Jahāngīr says that the

name of the Rāja of Khukhara was Durjan Sāl. (Memoirs, Rogers and Beveridge, I, 314-15).

5. One *Miṣqāl* = a weight of a dram and three-sevenths.

6. The order for the appointment of Qāsim Khān as the governor of Bengal was issued by the Emperor in the month of Sha'abān 1022 A.H. i.e. September, 1613 (Iqbāl Nāma, 72).

## BOOK II

### CHAPTER I

1. *Andit.* اندیت The meaning of this word could not be properly made out. It is neither a Persian nor an Arabic word. There is a Hindi word 'Andhurī' which means 'heat-rash.' Probably this is the word meant here. Jahāngīr, in his Tuzuk p. 118, says that Afẓal Khān died of a peculiar kind of boils and sores ( دمل و زخمهاے غریب ).

### CHAPTER II

1. According to Iqbāl Nāma (p. 72) Qāsim Khān was appointed governor of Bengal in the month of Sha'abān 1022 A.H. (middle of September, 1613 A.D.). So 27th, Rabi'u'l-Awwal, the date of Qāsim Khān's arrival at Dacca corresponds to 6th May, 1614 A.D. It took nearly eight months for the governor designate of Bengal to reach the capital city after the death of Islām Khān.

2. Gilahnay i.e. Gilahnaw or new Gilah is the same as Gilah the capital of Rāja Parikshīt. Its original name was Ghila Bejoypur. After the Mughal conquest the name was changed into Jahāngīrābād.

3. Rāja Pātkumār was the title of Raghū Dev, the father of Parikshīt. He was so called because he was the *Pātkumār* or heir presumtive to the throne of Nara Narāyan before the birth of Lakshmī Narāyan. (*Kamrupar Buranji*, 6). The widow mentioned here must be one of the step-mothers of Rāja Parikshīt.

4. Anirāy Singh-dalan was the title of Anup Rāy, a personal attendant of Jahāngīr. He was given this title of Singh-dalan i.e. 'tiger-slayer' in recognition of his bravery shown in killing a tiger and thereby saving the life of the Emperor in a tiger hunt. The Emperor placed great confidence in him and he was raised to the rank of 1,500 personal and 500 horse. (Memoirs, I, 185-87, 263, 373; Iqbāl Nāma, 46-48).

5. Bundasil is in Chapghāt *mauẓa,* Thāna Karimganj, district Sylhat. (Village Directory of Sylhat).

## CHAPTER III

1. There are contraditory versions as to the fate of Rāja Parikshīt after his surrender to Mukarram Khān. Dr. Wade in his History of Assam (p. 216) says, "He was immediately sent under a General to Dili in the month of Magh 1534" (1612 A.D.). *Kāmrupar Buranjī* (pp. 10, 102.), and *Puranī Asam Buranjī* (pp. 73, 80, 200), say that Rāja Parikshīt was taken as a prisoner by Mukarram Khān to Delhi. But the actual fact as mentioned in the Bahāriṣtān is that Parikshīt and Lakshmī Narāyan were detained at the governor's court at Dacca and after sometime they were sent to the Emperor by Qāsim Khān. Jahāngīr mentions in his Memoirs (I. p. 269) about the arrival of two daughters of Rāja Parikshīt with his son and 94 elephants at the imperial Court in the beginning of the ninth year of his accession i.e. in 1614. But he is silent about Parikshīt's arrival. His arrival at the Emperor's Court must have been sometime about this period. With regard to his ultimate end almost all the indegenous Assamese chronicles agree in substance with that of Mīrzā Nathan.

2. Jahāngīr mentions of it in his Tuzuk (vide Rogers and Beveridge, I, 269).

3. Jahāngīr does not mention about the sending of the pearl earrings to the Bengal officers. He simply records the sending of winter dresses of honour to Qāsim Khān and other Āmīrs of Bengal through Ihtimām Khān. This was sometime in November 1615. (Memoirs, Rogers and Beveridge, I, 303).

4. The Garang or Gaurang river rises from the Bhutan hills and falls into the Brahmaputtra. Martin in his Eastern India (Vol. III, 385) says, "It is a beautiful little river, at all times navigable for canoes to the frontier of Bhutan, and in the rainy season would admit boats of a large size."

5. The fort of Rangmāti was situated on the mouth of the river Gadādhar near its confluence with the Brahmaputtra. In Major Rennell's time the place is said to have been a large town. Martin in his Eastern India (III, 471) says, "I met several people, who said, that they remember Mogul chiefs, who occasionally visited the place, which contained 1,500 houses, among which were several inhabited by Portuguese. At present its condition is miserable." The fort was situated at a distance of 14 miles from Gilah.

6. Athiara Kuth or Athara Kutha is the name of a place situated near Gilah on the west side of the Gadādhar. (Martin's Eastern India, III, 416). Dr. Fancis Buchanon says that *Athāro Kotha* or eighteen castles, is another name of Gilajhar. (See *Kāmrūpar Buranjī*, Appendix, C, 145).

## CHAPTER IV

1. Manṣụr Ḥallāj was a great Ṣūfī of Persia who appeared during the reign of the Caliph Al-Muqtadir (A.D. 908-932). His full name was Al-Ḥusayn bin Manṣur al-Hallāj (the Wool-carder). He was persecuted and arrested for preaching heretical doctrines in Baghdād and other places in A.D. 913 and put to death with great cruelty in A.D. 921. The charge against him was that in a state of ecstasy he cried, "*Ana'l-*Haqq" "I am the True one" i.e. God. The Ṣūfīs regard this utterance "as the outcome of a state of exaltation wherein the Seer was so lost in rapture at the contemplation of the Beatific vision of the Deity that he lost all cognisance and consciousness of himself, and indeed of all phenomenal Being." Frequent mention of him is made by the Persian Ṣūfī poets and he is generally regarded as a saint and a martyr. The great Persian poet Ḥāfiẓ says:—

*Kashad naqsh-i-Ana'l Ḥaqq bar zamīn khūn,*
*Chu Manṣūr ar kashī bar dār-am imshab!*

"My blood would write 'I am the True One' on the ground,
If thou wert to hang me, like Manṣūr, on the cross to-night."

Junayd of Baghdad was a great saint and a mystic and was a teacher of Manṣūr Hallāj. He died in A.D. 910. So his presence on the occasion of the death of Manṣūr Hallāj in A.D. 921 is a piece of anachronism. (For details see, 'Aṭṭār's Taẕkiratu'l-Awliyā; Jāmī's Nufhatu'l-uns; Browne's Literary History of Persia, Vol. I, 362, 363, 433.).

2. Kāmrūp Duwār i.e. the gate or pass leading towards Kāmrūp.

3. The pargana of Gūma lies on the western frontier of the modern Goalpara district.

4. Dalgāon is situated in *mauẓa* Gola Alamganj, Thāna Dhubri, district, Goalpara.

5. Jaipur or Jaygarh is probably the same place as Joygong shown in Rennell's Map No. 5, about 25 miles to the north of Byhar or Bihar, new town.

6. Pratapgarh is shown in the Ain (II, 139) as a Mahal in the Sarkar of Sylhat. There is a *mauẓā* of this name in the district of Sylhat situated within the subdivision of Karimganj bordering on Kachar.

7. Khasta is evidently the tribe of Khasia misspelt by the scribe. By interchange of dots the تی of the text may be read as Khasia

## CHAPTER V

1. Kawailagarh or Kailargarh was a strategic position in the district of Tippera. A fort is said to have been built at this place by Ḥusayn Shāh the independent Sultan of Bengal when he conquered Jajnagar or Tippera.

2. Islāmābād was the name of a village near Bhalwa, no vestige of which is found now. It may roughly be identified with modern Lakhipur of Noakhali. It is said that the Mussalmans had an outpost here in about the year 1620.

3. Majwa Khāl may be read as Machwa Khāl. It is the same narrow channel known as Machua Duna about which Mr. Walters says that it was a narrow channel separating the Bami river of Noakhali from the mainland. (Noakhali District Gazetteer, 1911, Ed. 7.).

4. Durmish Carbalu is probably the same person as Antonio Carvalho referred to by Sir Jadunath Sarkar in his article 'Mags and Firingis in Bengal' in the *Prabasī*, 1329 B.S. (1923 A.D.) p. 664.

5. Kinduguri or Kenduguri could not be definitely located. From the text it seems that it was an important station in the pargana of Khuntaghāt. Badantara or Badhantara may be 'Binnasera' about 8 miles south west of Putymari shown in Rennell's Bengal Atlas, sheet No. 5.

6. The author of the Mughal North East Frontier Policy (pp. 173, 174) calls this rebel chief as "*Haman Rāja Tajha*" and "Rāja Nobar." The author has confused the meaning of these words. The former phrase in the ms. is "*Haman Rāja-i-Tāza*" i.e. that very new Rāja, and the latter is "*Rāja-i-naw*" i.e. the new Rāja, referring to the same rebel chief. There is no Rāja of the name of Nobar mentioned either in the Bahāristān or in any of the *Buranjīs*. This Rāja has also been wrongly identified with a subordinate hill-chief of the Ahom king called 'Nadooria Rāja.'

7. Putamari probably is the same place as Putymari shown in Rennell's Map No. 5. It is situated at a distance of seven or eight miles to the south-west of Dhubri.

8. Dhamdhama is in *mauẓā* Khata, Thana Nalbari, district Kāmrup. (Kamrup Village Directory).

9. Barnagar is at present situated within Barpeta subdivision, district Kāmrup.

10. Ibrāhīm *Karorī* has been mentioned in the *Kāmrupar Buranjī* (pp. 27-29, 102, 103), as the first Imperial officer deputed to reform

the revenue administration of Kāmrup. According to this account there was no pargana system in Kāmrup previous to Shaykh Ibrāhīm's appointment. He divided the country into four Sarkars namely, Sarkar Kāmrup, Sarkar Dhakeri, Sarkar Dhakhinkul, and Sarkar Bangālbhum. Each of these Sarkars was divided into a number of parganas. He is called by the Assamese historians as Shek Birāhīm *Karorī*.

11. Mānī is the founder of a religion in Persia known as Manichaenism. He was born at the end of the Parthian period, in the fourth year of King Ardwān's reign (A.D. 215-16). The public announcement of his religion was made on the day of the coronation of King Shāhpūr, March 20, A.D. 242. The King at first accepted his new religion but after ten years at the insistence of the Zoroastrian priests, he renounced that religion and began to persecute Mānī. Mānī fled to India where he lived till the death of King Shāhpūr. Then after some years when Bahrām, the son of Hurmuz reigned in Persia, Mānī returned to his country to propagate his religion. Bahrām imprisoned him and flayed him alive. Mānī was a skilful painter and it is generally believed that he produced a picture-book called the *Arzhang* or *'Artang*, which he appealed as a proof of his supernatural power and divine mission. The Persian poets and other writers often refer to Mānī as a great painter. (For details see, Browne's Literary History of Persia, Vol. I, 154-156).

12. This word is spelt in the Ms. as "kuh-i-kāur" i.e. the hill of Kāur. The word Kāur may be read as Gāur or Gāro. But the Gāro hills are situated on the south of the Brahmaputtra and events described here are of the northern region. This is probably the name of some other hills situated in the Khuntaghāt region.

13. The Khānpūr river emerges from the Bhutan range and falls into the Brahmaputtra flowing through the Khuntaghāt region. (Blochmann, J.A.S.B., 1872, pt. I. 60).

14. Rājkhāt may also be read as Rajghāt. This is probably the name of a ford on the Khānpūr river in the pargana of Khuntaghāt.

15. There is a place called Takua in Habraghat *mauẓā* district, Goalpara. This may be the place mentioned here.

16. Rangalikhata is in Khuntaghāt *mauẓā*, district, Goalpara.

17. Kuhhata has been wrongly identified by the author of Mughal North East Frontier Policy (f.n.p. 180) with the modern village of Kahara situated on the Barnadi. The Pādishāh Nāma (Vol. II, 89) says کوه‌هته که درسمت اوترکل میان سری‌گهات و کلی واقع است و بیشتر شهری بود بغایت معمور و زمینی مرتفع دارد "Kuhhata is situated in the Uttarkul midway between Srighāt and

Kajalī. In former times it was a largely populated city and it is on a high land." There is a village named Kulhati near Chencha hills between Hajo and Kajalī in the district of Kāmrup and close to it there is another village named Manahkuchi which contains many roads properly laid out as if for a town. The situation of Kulhati fairly corresponds to the description of Kuhhata given by the Mughal historians. We also know from Assamese sources that Kulhati was a centre of many a Mughal-Ahom conflict. The town of Kuhhata mentioned here is the same place as Kulhati.

18. Sanatan. The name of this rebel chief is not to be found in any of the available *Buranjis*. Mr. K. L. Barua, however, in his Early History of Kāmrupa makes certain short references to him.

19. Mughal North East Frontier Policy (p. 175) mentions the name of this officer as Bal Bahadur Das but the Ms. clearly shows that it was Balabhadra Das بلبهدرداس and not Bal Bahadur as supposed by the author of the aforesaid book.

20. Kutal has been identified with Kataldi in Chapar *mauẓā* thana Bagribari by the author of "Mughal North East Frontier Policy" (p. 177). But this is not the name of a place. The word *Kutal* means a mountain-pass.

21. From the text it appears that the Kāwarhāda hill is situated in the Khuntaghāt region on the bank of the Brahmaputtra in some place before the confluence of the Manās with the Brahmaputtra. The situation could not be definitely located.

22. This is a quotation from the holy Qur'ān (Chapter III, verse 53). This passage has been misquoted in the Ms. as مکراللہ مکرالماکرین The text of the Qur'ān is ومکروا ومکراللہ واللہ خیرالماکرین This verse refers to the plan of the Jews to put Jesus to death by crucifixion which was frustrated by God. The Muslim commentators say that Jesus was saved by God from being crucified by the Jews and he died a natural death.

23. The grant of title to Makkī has been mentioned by the Emperor in his Tuzuk. The order was issued on 15th, November 1615. (Rogers and Beveridge, Memoirs, I, 303).

24. The pass of Garhī or Talia Garhī is a pass lying between Rājmahal on the south and Ganges on the north. It was a great strategic point on the western frontier of Bengal. The ruins of a large stone fort still exist there. The East Indian Railway passes through this pass. (Hunter's Imperial Gazetteer, XIII, 236; Ain, II, 116).

25. Mukhliṣ Khān was appointed to this office in December 1615. The Emperor records, "As the *diwān* and *bakhshī* of Bengal, Ḥusayn

Beg and Ṭāhir, had not done approved service, Mukhliṣ Khān, who was one of the confidential officers of the Court, was nominated to these duties. I conferred on him a Manṣab of 2,000 personal and 700 horse, and also gave him a standard." (Rogers and Beveridge, Memoirs, I, 306).

26. Jutia may be Gatia Kuchi, a place situated at a distance of about four miles south-east of Nalbari, District, Kamrup.

## CHAPTER VI

1. The name of this Mag Rāja was Meng Khamaung and his title was Ḥusayn. He ruled from 1612-1622 A.D. (Vide Sir Jadunath's article " Mags and Firingis in Bengal ", *Prabasi*, 1329 B.S.|1923 A.D., p. 665.). We do not know why the Mag Rājas of this period adopted Muslim titles. Probably, the Muslim influence was very great in their Court during those days and they felt themselves flattered to adopt the name of some Muslim emperors as their title.

2. Barlia or Borolia river rises from the Bhutan hills and flowing through the district of Kāmrup joins the Brahmaputtra about four miles below Hatimara hill. (Wade's Geographical Sketch of Assam, 22; District map of Kāmrūp.).

3. The Kalong is a branch of the Brahmaputtra. It flows by Kaliābar, Nowgong and Dimarua and rejoins the Brahmaputtra at Kajalī about twenty miles above Gauhati. The confluence of this river with the main channel of the Brahmaputtra is known as Kajalīmukh.

4. These are the names of the high officials of the Ahom kings. Rājkhawa was a commander of 3,000 men. There were twelve Rājkhawas who performed civil as well as military duties. Hāti Barua was the chief of the elephant force. He was also entrusted with other civil functions. The word " Kharghūka ", I think, is a corruption of the word *Khārgharia Phukan,* the Superintendent of the manufacture of gun powder and all instruments of war. He was in charge of all the musketry and ordinance. The title is derived from *Khār*, gunpowder, *Ghar*, a repository or house.

5. The result of this disastrous campaign given in the Ahom chronicles tallies almost with those of Mīrzā Nathan. The *Kāmrupar Buranji* (pp. 14-18, 104, 105) mentions the names of several of the Ahom officers who fell in the first naval battle at the mouth of the Bharali and gives the following account:—A huge army was sent by the Ahom king Pratāp Singh to the aid of his defeated force. This army, with the aid of Akhek Gohāin, a deserter from the camp of the Mughals, surprised

Abā Bakr in a night-attack, both by land and water, and gave a heavy defeat. Saiyid Abā Bakr, Bhagaban Bakhshī, Gakul Chand, Zahir Beg, Mīrzā Makkī, Jamāl Khān, Ilahdād Dakhinī were killed. Rāja Jagdev, Gandharva Rāy, Rāja Rāy, Kālā Rāja, Hara Pratāp Singh, Indramani, Narsingh Rāy, Bhagabān Rāy and Karam Chānd were taken as captives. On the side of the Ahoms, Hāti Barua, Sriphal Bora, Numal Bora, Lecham Handiqoi and some others were killed. Hearing the news of this victory, the Ahom king sent a message to his officers to bring the captives alive to him so that he might see the Āmīrs who came to fight against him. But in the meantime the captives were executed by his officers. The Rāja, enraged at this act of his officers, issued orders to execute his uncle Chawlāi Kunwar and some other officers who were responsible for it, and the three Gohāins were severely censured. Besides a large quantity of arms and ammunition, the Ahoms seized 12 elephants, 900 horses, and 200 *bachāru* boats.

6. Sanghārī or Sangārī is a hilly place in Silā Sindurighopa *mauẓā*, district Kāmrup.

## CHAPTER VII.

1. Katghar or Kathgar has been read by Sir Jadunath as 'Kangkhar' (vide *Prabāsi*, 1329 B.S., p. 668). It seems to be a strategic position of the Rāja of Arracan, situated within the district of Chittagong. There is a village of this name near Sitakunda, two miles off from the railway station of Barakunda. Probably this is the place meant here.

2. Niẓāmpūr is the name of a pargana within the jurisdiction of the Thānas of Mīr Sarāi and Sitakunda, in the district of Chittagong.

3. Baldev or Bali Narāyan, was a brother of Rāja Parikshīt. After the defeat of his brother he went to take shelter with the Ahom king Pratāp Singh in 1615 A.D. Pratāp Singh received him cordially and installed him as a tributary Rāja of Darrang under the name of Dharma Narāyan. (For details see Gait's History of Assam, 67-69, 107, 110, 118; *Kāmrupar Buranjī*, 13-14.).

4. Sahuran Bārī or Sahurabārī, a *mauẓā* in District Darrang. It is situated at a distance of about four miles from the bank of the Barnadi. (Robinson's Map of Assam.).

5. There is a place shown in Robinson's Map of Assam as 'Banksa-Dooar' situated in the northern part of Kāmrūp. But this word may also be read as Bagā Duwār, a corruption of Vagā Duwār a hill tract bordering on Bhutan to the north of Kāmrūp and Darrang. According

to Martin's Eastern India (Vol. III, 620) the chief of Vagā Duwār was a Gāro. I think this is the place referred to in the Bahāristān.

6. *Hizdah-Rāja,* i.e., the eighteen hill-chiefs who ruled over the strip of the level country at the foot of the Himalayas, from Darrang west-wards, in the direction of Bhutan. These countries were called Duwārs or doors through which lay the passes into the hills. There were eighteen of these Duwārs, eleven of which were situated on the border of Bengal and Goalpara and seven in the north of Kāmrūp and Darrang. These hill-chiefs were for a long time vassals of the Ahom kings who were responsible to keep peace in the frontier. Martin mentions of ten hill-chiefs who ruled over the region to the south of the Brahmaputtra, in Kāmrūp, e.g., Bar Duwār, Bhola-grām, Mairapūr, Luki Duwār, Pantam Duwār, Bangrām-Duwār, Vagā Duwār, Beltola, Dumuriya, and Rānī Duwār. Some of these Duwārs are also named as Deshes e.g., Desh Dumuria, Desh Pānbāri, Desh Beltala and Desh Rānī. The Ahom *Buranjīs* mention ten wardens of the frontier, e.g., Hangrabāria Rāja, Jay Rāja, Gukar Rāja, Mankhing, Hāldhibaria Rāja, Barnagaria Rāja, Kantam Rāja, Ruphing, Bāmun Rāja, Barduariā Rāja. Dr. Wade in his History of Assam (p. 259) says, "Between the territories of Narnarain and the prince of Zewointa, eighteen Rajas ruled as many provinces", but he has not given the names of all these Rājas and of their respective territorial limits. They are also called as "*Dātiāl Rāja*" or Rājas of the border. *Kāmrūpar Buranjī* mentions them as "*Athāra Rāja*" or Eighteen Rājas of the frontier. There is no systematic account of these hill-chiefs and all the authorities are incomplete in their list. Mīrzā Nathan's list also does not tally with those given by other writers. (For details see Gait's History of Assam, 229, 298, 311, 334; *Kāmrūpar Buranjī,* 18; Martin's Eastern India, III, 619-22; Robinson's Descriptive accounts of Assam, 283, 289.).

7. Rānī which is also known as Deshrānī is situated at a distance of a few miles on the south-west from Gauhati. According to *Kāmrūpar Buranjī* (p. 113) it was given by Rāja Gadādhar Singh to a Gāro queen who was a descendant of Rāja Arimatta and named it as Desh Rānī.

8. Garal is in *mauẓā* Rānī, Thāna Gauhati. It is about four miles to the south-west of Pāndu.

9. Hātrānī or Rānīhāt may be identified with Rānigāon, about four miles to the south-west of Rānī.

10. Kāmākhya Duwār is the pass leading into the Nilachal hill near Gauhati, where the temple of Kāmākhya, the Goddess of sexual desire is situated. The Nilachal hill is also known as Kāmākhya hill. The temple of Kāmākhya is still held sacred by the followers of Tantrik Hinduism who "base their observances on the *Tantras,* a series of reli-

gious works in which the various ceremonies, prayers and incantations are prescribed in a dialogue between Siva and his wife Parbati. The fundamental idea is the worship of the female principle, the procreative power of nature as manifested by personified desire." The legend concerning it is as follows:—"When Sati died of vexation at the discourtesy shown to her husband Siva by her father Daksha, Siva, overcome by grief, wandered about the world carrying her dead body on his head. In order to put a stop to his penance, Vishnu followed him and lopped away the body piecemeal with his discus. It fell to earth in fifty-one different pieces, and wherever each piece fell, the ground was held to be sacred. Her organs of generation fell on Kāmgiri, i.e., the Nilachal hill near Gauhati, and the place was thenceforth held sacred to Kāmākhya, the Goddess of sexual desire." (For details see, Gait's History of Assam, 11-13, 49, 57, 58, 182, 183.).

11. Kūk Rāja could not be identified with any of the well known hill-chiefs. It may be the name of some Kuki chief.

12. The Dumria Rāja mentioned here, I believe is not the same Dumria, son-in-law of Rāja Parikshīt, reference to whom was made in a previous chapter. This Rāja of Dumria is the Rāja of Dimarua who lived beyond Beltola towards the Gāro hills. Probably he was Rāja Mongal, son of Prabhakar, who had acknowledged Ahom supremacy after the capture of his father by the Jayantia king Dhanmānik about the year 1615 A.D. (For details see Martin's Eastern India, Vol. III, 620; *Kāmrūpar Buranjī*, 18-19.).

13. The orders for Qāsim Khān's dismissal and the appointment of Ibrāhīm Khān were issued by the Emperor Jahāngīr on 8th April, 1617 A.D. (Memoirs, Rogers and Beveridge, I, 373.).

## CHAPTER VIII.

1. Qulīj Khān has been mentioned by Beni Prasad in his 'History of Jahāngīr' (p. 105) as one of the governors of Bengal, appointed in 1026 A.H. (A.D. 1617.). Jahāngīr, in his Memoirs (R. and B., I, 353.), says, "I . . . dignified him with the title of Qulīj Khān, and appointed him to the Ṣūbah of Bengal". He has not mentioned the office to which Qulīj Khān was appointed. The Bahāristān shows that he was appointed as the chief officer in Kuch and he actually took charge of the administration of this territory and he was not a governor of Bengal.

2. The *Trimohānī* mentioned here are the three arms of the Ganges at Jatrapūr. Tavernier mentions in his Travels in India (Phillips, Translation, p. 102.):—"The eleventh (January, 1666), toward evening,

being come to that part where Ganges divides itself into three arms, whereof one runs to Dacca; we lay at a large town, upon the entry of the great channel, which town is called Jatrapur." The three arms of the Ganges at Jatrapūr are also shown in Vandenbroucke's map. In the heading of Chapter I, Book III of the Bahāristān, Mīrzā Nathan also says that Ibrāhīm Khān arrived at "Dhāka after the overthrow of the fort which Qāsim Khān had raised at Jatrapūr". All these facts show that the *Trimohānī* of our text is the Trimohānī at Jatrapūr.

3. The Jamuna or Jabuna mentioned here is the Jamuna of the Rājshāhi district which flows northward from the Bogra district, passes by the town of Naogaon and joins the Atrai at Suktigacha after a total length of 89 miles. The present course of the river seems to have changed a great deal and it is believed to be an old channel of the Tista.

4. The ceremony of *Jawhar* was an awful rite of the Hindus observed particularly by the Rājputs. It is the custom of immolation of every female of their family at the loss of a battle or the capture of the city. "To the fair of the lands the fate of the Rajpootni must appear one of appalling hardship. In each stage of life, death is ready to claim her; by the poppy at its dawn, by the flames in riper years; while the safety of the interval depending on the uncertainty of war, at no period is her existence worth a twelve-months purchase." The molestation of women in the wars of the Rājputs and the capture of the wives of the enemy were the common practice among them. Tod says in his Rajasthan, "I possess numerous inscriptions (on stone and on brass), which record as the first token of victory the captive wives of the foeman." When the society was at such a low ebb of morality and when women were considered nothing more than chattels of use, the Rājputs took recourse to this rite of *Jawhar* in order to preserve the honour and chastity of their women from the brutal clutch of their victors. (For details see Tod's Rajasthan, Vol. I, Chapter XXIV.). But it is a matter of great surprise to find these Mughals observing this Rājput custom which is against the laws and customs of Islām. It seems that the marriage of some Mughal nobles with Rājput women and their presence in the royal harem had brought about a change in their outlook on women's life and had taken recourse to this fatal rite.

## BOOK III

### CHAPTER I.

1. There are a number of streams to the west of the Barlia on the land route to Dhamdhama from Hājo. Jharighāt seems to be the name of a ford on one of these streams. We have not been able to locate this place from the modern district map of Kāmrūp.

2. *Āṣār* is of the same weight as an Indian *seer*.

### CHAPTER II.

1. *Budha Gosāin,* i.e., *Burha Gohāin* is one of the highest military and civil functionaries of the Ahom kings. He occupied a position next to that of the king. This post was ordinarily confined to a particular family or clan and was descended from father to son, although the king had the power to choose any member of the particular clan he liked. There were two other offices of the same rank and conditions known as *Bar Gohāin* and *Barpātra Gohāin.* 10,000 *pāiks* were allotted to each of these officers (Gait's History of Assam, 235-36). The name of the *Burha Gohāin,* who commanded this battle, was according to *Kāmrūpar Buranjī* (p. 20) Thakbak Burha Gohāin. His death has also been recorded in the Buranjī. Mīrzā Nathan mentions that he was killed unrecognised by an unknown soldier.

2. The name of this revel chief has been spelt in various ways, as Shumāruyed, Shumārū and Shumārūd. But the text shows that all these names point to the same person. I believe it is a corruption of Samudra Kāyeth, a Kuch chief whose name is found in local chronicles.

3. Budhādūnagar is probably the place called Bardadhigāon, situated a few miles south-east of Hājo (Village Directory of Kāmrūp).

4. This is a strange custom observed by these Mughals. The practice of taking out a man from his bed before he breathes his last is observed by the Hindus alone. But it is absolutely against Islāmic laws and customs. It seems that these people were very much influenced by Hindu customs.

5. *Khān-jiew* or *Khānjī* is a specimen of Indianised Persian. *Ji* is a term of respect used in India in addressing a superior by an inferior. Nathan has used this suffix in many places after the words Khān and Begum.

6. Mādhava temple is one of the famous temples of Assam. It is also known as Haygriva Mādhava temple. It is situated on a hill called Manikutachal at Ḥājo. It was once destroyed by the famous iconoclast Kalāpahār, a Brahmin convert to Islām. Raghū Dev rebuilt the temple in 1505 Sak (1583 A.D.) and it was consecrated by the sacrifice of many human victims. (*Kāmrūpar Buranjī*, 121; Gait's History of Assam, 63.).

7. Talia is situated at a place about five miles to the north-east from Hājo.

8. Sultan Ghiyāṣu'd-Dīn Awliyā is the name of a saint whose tomb is at Hājo. The detailed account of his life is in obscurity. But local traditions say that he was a great saint and devoted his life in the propagation of Islām in Kāmrūp. He also built a mosque at the top of a hill at Hājo, near which he was buried. This place is held in great esteem by the Muslims as a place of pilgrimage and his shrine is called *Poā Macca*, i.e., one-fourth of Mecca.

9. Temple of Kedār is situated to the east of the Mādhava temple at Hājo. There is a small lake on a stony bed, the water of which is considered to be holy by the Hindus and it is believed as a great act of virtue to bathe in this lake. (*Kāmrūpar Buranji*, 121.).

10. The Rawrowa rises from the Bhutan hills and flowing through Kāmrūp it falls into the Brahmaputtra, a little above Nagarbera. (Wade's Geographical sketch of Assam, 22.).

11. The author of the "Mughal North-East Frontier Policy" (p. 196) is entirely wrong in stating that the first information was given to Qulīj Khān and he 'hastened to meet the enemy'.

## CHAPTER III.

1. Madhūsudan is the son of Brishaketu, one of the eighteen sons of Raghū Dev. (*Kāmrūpar Buranjī*, 7.).

2. Jasīpūr is situated in Mechpāra *mauẓā*, Thāna Lakshipūr, District Goalpara.

3. Bāghwān is situated in the pargana of Mechpāra, district, Goalpara. Chandankuth, Sambhūr and Solmārī were places of strategic importance in the district of Goalpara during the Mughal days. But at present they are no better than ordinary villages.

4. Kantabārī may be identified with Katasbārī, in Mechpāra *mauẓā* District Goalpara.

5. Mechpāra and Mālawpāra are situated on the southern bank of the Brahmaputtra within the district of modern Goalpara.

6. From the text it appears that the *Makrī parbut* named here is situated on the south-eastern portion of modern Goalpara at the foot of the Gāro hills.

## CHAPTER IV.

1. Kaltakari and Tahana were two hill-chiefs of the Rangdān region, the hilly tract lying to the north of the Rangjulī hills. Though they gave great trouble to the Mughal authority, the details of their exploits are not to be found in any of the *Buranjīs* or local chronicles.

2. Bālijāna is in Mechpāra, District Goalpara. Martin (Eastern India, III, 479.) mentions of the remains of small mud forts at Bālijāna erected by the Mughals.

3. The Jijrām river is a tributary of the Brahmaputtra. It comes from the north-western extremity of the Gāro hills and enters the low country in a waste relinquished to elephants; but soon flows into a beautiful valley in which is situated Nivari, one of the chief marts of the Gāro trade. The river at present has considerably changed its old course. (Martin's Eastern India, III, 393, 396, 474.).

4. Tashpūr is a village in the Rangdān region in the district of Goalpara.

5. According to Tuzuk Rāja Lakshmī Narāyan was allowed to return to his kingdom on the 23rd Rabi'u'l-Awwal, 1027 (March 10, 1618). The date of the departure of Rāja Parikshīt has not been mentioned. The account given here of the release of Parikshīt on his promise of paying a ransom of Rs. 700,000 tallies in general with that of *Kāmrūpar Buranjī*. *Kāmrūpar Buranjī* (pp. 10-13) gives the following interesting account of the interview of Lakshmī Narāyan and Parikshīt with the Emperor and their release thereafter:—The Emperor advised Lakshmī Narāyan and Parikshīt to live amicably and to rule in their respective territories and he ordered Parikshīt to kiss the feet of Lakshmī Narāyan who was his uncle. But Parikshīt refused to do so and replied that he would not kiss the feet of Lakshmī Narāyan even at the risk of his own life. The Emperor became displeased at this and directed that Parikshīt should remain at his Court for sometime more. Lakshmī Narāyan was permitted to return to his principality. At the time of his departure, the Emperor desired him to apply for the present of any article which was not available in his own country. Rāja Lakshmī Narāyan represented:—"Everything is obtainable in my dominion except *purud kālī*

sword and 'Irāqī horse." The Emperor presented him with these things and sent him back to his territory. After sometime Parikshīt obtained his release through the intercession of Mukarram Khān. At the time of his departure, the Emperor desired him to apply for any article which was not available in his country. Parikshīt said,—"Everything is to be found in my country. Present me with a portrait of yours. I will make obeisance to it." The Emperor replied thus:—"We do not present it to anybody and everybody. However we present it to you. You shall not be enemical to our dynasty. If you do so you shall ruin yourself." Then Rāja Parikshīt paid the ransom of seven hundred thousand rupees and started for his territory leaving his four sons Dhir Narāyan, Darpa Narāyan, Shur Narāyan and Bhim Narāyan as hostages. Hearing the report of Parikshīt's return to his territory, the principal persons of Kāmrūp sent a representation to the Nawāb of Dhāka saying that it would be impossible for them to remain in Kāmrūp if Parikshīt was allowed to return. The Nawāb forwarded this petition to the Emperor with the following remark:—"Parikshīt has these defects. The tiger of the jungle which had been seized was again let loose. It would be impossible to capture him again when he returns to his jungle." The Emperor then ordered the Nawāb to send Parikshit back to the royal Court. On his way to the imperial capital, he committed suicide at Tribeni. The *Kāmrūpar Buranjī* wrongly mentions Islām Khān as the Nawāb of Dhāka at this time. It is not Islām Khān but Ibrāhīm Khān Fatḥ-jung who was the Ṣūbahdār of Bengal during this period.

According to Bahāristān Parikshit promised to pay his ransom at Dhākạ. But it seems he could not manage to pay it off and hence he was not reinstated to his territory.

6. Māmū Govinda was the ruling chief of a small territory called Beltala, in the Kāmrūp District. In para 585 of the Bahāristān he is called Govind Māmūn, the uncle of Rāja Parikshit.

7. Āmjūnga and Rangjūlī are two adjacent places on the border of the Rangjūlī mountains, offshoots of the Gāro range to the south of the Brahmaputtra in the District of Goalpara.

8. Mānikpūr is in Habraghāt *mauẓā*, Thāna Rangjūlī, District Goalpara.

9. Jakhlī is in Habraghāt *mauẓā*, District Goalpara.

10. Dr. Sudhindra Nath Bhattacharyya in his Mughal North-East Frontier Policy (p. 205) is entirely wrong in stating "Nathan marched to the foot of the Karwan hills." There is no hill of this name in Assam. The Ms. distinctly says that it was the hill of the Garoes,

11. The Rābhas constitute a tribe of Kāmrūp which is chiefly confined to the parts of this district, that lie towards its eastern extremity. They are akin to a branch of the Kuch tribe known as 'Pāṇī Ḳuch who are thinly scattered over all the parts of Assam and the lower parts of Bhutan. (For details see Martin's Eastern India, III, 546.).

12. Jadū Nāyak's name is mentioned by some writers as a chief of the Chutiyas and by others a Kachari. (Gait's History of Assam, 110.). According to *Kāmrūpar Buranjī* (p. 7) Rāja Parikshīt had a brother named Jadū Rāy. This may be the person referred to here.

13. Udaypūr was the capital of Tippera during this period.

14. Bāohānti is probably the place known as the pargana of Baronti situated on the north-east of Luki Duwār in the Kāmrūp district.

15. The hill of Panchagīrī, which is also known as the Pancharatan, is situated on the south of the Brahmaputtra further up from Jogighopa. It was a strategic position during all the Ahom-Mughal conflicts.

16. Bakū is in *mauẓā* Chapāgurī, Thāna Bajālī, District Kāmrūp.

17. Chatsa Rāja is probably the Bhutia chief named Sat Rāja who ruled over the hilly tract on the east of the Bhutan Duwārs of Darrang known as the Koriapāra Duwār. (Gait's History of Assam, 312.).

18. Bar Duwār is the name of a territory adjacent to the passes to the Gāro hills. Martin in his Eastern India, Vol. III, p. 619, says, "The Rāja is a Garo, and lives at Bhagpoor, two days' journey south-west from Gauhati. It is close to the mountains, inhabited by independent Garos; but these consider the Baraduyar Rāja as their chief. It is for his low lands only, that he pays tribute to Assam. In his territory is a market-place, named Kukuriya."

19. Bāmun Rāja and Kanwal Rāja were the hill chiefs of the territories lying adjacent to Bar Duwār. For want of contemporary maps and topography it is difficult to locate the exact geographical positions and the extant of the territories of the Rājas. According to Mīrzā Nathan the territory of Bāmūn Rāja was situated between Bar Duwār and Haldiya Duwār, a stronghold of Kanwal Rāja.

20. *Lāmdānī*, i.e., the lower hill regions on the southern border of Assam. The higher range of this hill region is called '*Upparia*' by our author.

21. Hangrabārī is in *mauẓā* Beltala, Thāna Gauhati, District Kāmrup.

22. These are evidently the titles held by smaller hill-chiefs.

23. This is probably the Kamārgāon of *mauẓā* Bijnī, District Kāmrūp.

24. The Mughal North East Frontier Policy (p. 213) says that this stockade was placed in charge of Rāja Satrajit and Rāja Bhū Singh; but the text shows that it was placed under Satrajit, Rāja of Bhusna, and not Bhū Singh, who had already rebelled and joined the enemy's force.

25. Hāligāon is about six miles south-west of Garal, in *mauẓā* Rānī and Thāna Gauhati.

26. Chumria or Chamoorea is in *mauẓā* Paschim Chumuria, Thāna Singra, District Kāmrūp. It is situated on the bank of the river Singra, about ten miles south-east of Nagarbera.

## CHAPTER V

1. Mālikūti may be identified with Māligāon, situated in *mauẓā* Ramsha, Thāna Gauhati.

2. Suālkuchī is in *mauẓā* Saru Bangsur, Thāna Hājo, District Kāmrup. It is on the right bank of the Brahmaputtra, about six miles west of Pandu.

3. Rāmdiya is an important village situated at a distance of a few miles to the south-west of Hājo, district Kāmrup (vide Kāmrup district map).

4. Jogīghopa is situated near the confluence of the Manās and the Brahmaputtra. The fort of Jogīghopa is situated amidst jungles on a hill on the north of the Brahmaputtra to the east of its confluence with the Manās. It was one of the most strategic forts of the Kāmrup kingdom.

5. Nagarbera is in *mauẓā* Paschim Chumuria, Thāna Singra, district Kāmrup. It stands on the left of the Brahmaputtra to the south of its confluence with the Koolsi river.

6. Jumuria or Jamira is situated to the north of Karaibari, district Goalpara.

7. Dhaknabuyi is at a distance of about twelve miles from Chumuria Thana, district Kāmrup. It is situated on the right bank of the Koolsi river, about ten miles south-west of Palasbārī.

8. Jumna, is about three miles north-west of Dhaknabuyi.

9. Minārī is situated at a distance of about three miles to the south of Hāligāon, district Kāmrup.

10. The district map of Kāmrup shows a place called Khamranga situated on a hilly region on the south of the Brahmaputtra in the Gauhati subdivision. There is also a road leading from Palasbari to Khamranga. This is probably the place mentioned by our author.

11. Phuldubi was a station on the Andal Khān river at present included within the district of Farīdpur. The course of the river changed so much that it is difficult to identify the place at present.

12. Dakhin Shāhbāzpūr is the name of an island at present included within the district of Bakarganj. It is bounded on the north and west by the Ilsha or Titulia river, on the east by the Meghna and on the south by the Bay of Bengal. According to the Ain (Vol. II, 132) it was included within the Sarkār of Fatḥābād.

13. Baliyā or Boaliya is in *mauẓā* Kalumalupara, district Goalpara. It is situated at a short distance from the bank of the Brahmaputtra.

14. Ghalwapara or Goalpara is in *mauẓā* Khuntaghāt, district Goalpara.

15. Bhujmala is in *mauẓā* Habraghāt, district Goalpara.

16. Bhaba Singh was one of the brothers of Rāja Parikshīt. (*Kāmrupar Buranjī*, 7.).

17. Takunia may be identified with Takua of Habraghāt *mauẓā*, district Goalpara.

18. Bagrībārī is in the *mauẓā* of Khuntaghāt, district Goalpara.

19. Khatribhāg is in the *mauẓā* of Chumuria, district Kāmrup. It was included during the Mughal rule as a pargana in the Sarkār of Kāmrup. (*Kāmrupar Buranjī*, 102.)

20. The "Mughal North East Frontier Policy" (p. 234) says that Mīrzā Nathan was "promoted to the *manṣab* of 300 personal and 150 horse." But the text says that it was granted in addition to his former rank.

21. Kānurhāda or Kānurhāta is a village in the pargana of Khuntaghāt, district Goalpara.

22. The account given here of the part played by Ibrāhīm Khān Fatḥ-jang and Aḥmad Beg differs from that of the Tuzuk. According to the Tuzuk the Bengal and Orissa governors were taken by surprise by the rebel army and they could not get sufficient time to make neces-

sary preparations to check the army of Shāhjahān. But Mīrzā Nathan accuses these officers for their inactivity and lukewarmness. We think that the account given by Mīrzā Nathan is more accurate than that of the Tuzuk.

## CHAPTER VI

1. Aḥmad Beg Khān was appointed governor of Orissa in the sixteenth year of Jahāngīr's reign about the beginning of July 1621. He was a nephew of Ibrāhīm Khān Fatḥ-jang. According to Jahāngīr, at the time of Shāhjahān's march to Orissa, Aḥmad Beg Khān was engaged in an expedition against the Zamīndārs of Khurda. On the approach of Shāhjahān he fled from Cuttack to Bardwān in a state of confusion and reported the matter to Ibrāhīm Khān. (Memoirs, Beveridge II, 210, 298). Some writers (Beniprasad, *Jahangir*, 368, 369; Stewart, *History of Bengal*, 252; *Riyāẓu's-Salāṭīn*, 190) assert that Aḥmad Beg was taken unawares by Shāhjahān. But this is in direct contradiction to Nathan's statement. Aḥmad Beg Khān was already informed by Ibrāhīm Khān about the probable advance of the Prince towards Orissa. The authorities in Bengal and Orissa were fully aware of the move of the Prince. But their cowardice and negligence had given an easy triumph to Shāhjahān in Bengal. Aḥmad Beg did not go to Dacca to meet Ibrāhīm Khān as suggested by Beni Prasad and some other writers but he joined Ibrāhīm Khān at Akbarnagar.

2. Bānpūr is the name of a Mahal in the *Sarkar* of Tirhut, Subah of Bihar, (Ain, II, 156). But this word may also be read as Mānpūr. There was a fort of Mānpūr described in the Akbar Nāma (Beveridge, III. 969) which was situated between Telingana and Orissa.

3. The pass here referred to is the Chatar Diwār pass. Mr. Sri Ram Sharma in his article "Prince Shāhjahān in Bengal" (Indian Historical Quarterly. Vol. XI, 92), says, "Here is a pass where 500 marksmen could hold up 3,000 or 4,000 men." But the text says سیصد هزار و چهارصد هزار 300,000 or 400,000. His mistake arose out of a wrong translation of these words.

4. Rāja Pancha is probably the Rāja of Panchera, a territory situated to the west of the Baitarani, about 24 miles west of Bhadrak in Orissa. Nilgīrī is about eleven miles south-west of Balasore.

5. 'Aml-i-Ṣāliḥ (I, 179), mentions that Shahājahān occupied cuttak in the early part of December, 1623.

6. It seems that Mīrzā Nathan has made some confusion regarding the name of the Portuguese officer who visited Shāhjahān at Cuttak.

According to Portuguese and other modern historians the Portuguese governor of Hughli and Pipli was Miguel Rodriques and not Captain Chanika as mentioned by Nathan. Captain Chanika may be an envoy of the Portuguese governor. The European historians (Stewart and Campos) suggest that this meeting took place at Bardwān, while Manrique places it at Dacca. But from the accounts of Nathan it is evident that this interview took place at Cuttak and not in other places mentioned by them.

7. Muḥammad Taqī entitled Shāh Qulī Khān was deputed to lead the imperial expedition against Kangra along with Rāja Surajmal in 1617. Then he was recalled and appointed to the post of the Fawjdār of Malwa and commander of the garrison at Māndū. It seems that he joined the forces of Shāhjahān from Māndū. (Ma'āṣiru'l-Umarā, III, 367).

8. Mīrzā Ṣāliḥ, nephew of Āṣaf Khān Ja'far Beg was sent to Bengal in March, 1618 with the Manṣab of 1,000 personal and 300 horse. He was appointed as the Fawjdār of Bardwān. (Memoirs, II, 3, 298, 299). Pādishāh Nāma (Vol. I, part II, 307) mentions that he held a Manṣab of 1,000. He died in the second year of the reign of Shāhjahān.

9. 'Abdu'llah Khān began his career as an *Aḥadi* and gradually rose to eminence. He was entrusted with several important expeditions in which he served very creditably. In 1611 in recognition of his splendid services rendered in the subjugation of Rānā Amar Singh the ruler of Mewār the Emperor raised him to the rank of 5,000 and conferred on him the title of Firūz-jang. When Shāhjahān rebelled, 'Abdu'llah Khān played the part of a traitor and joined the rebels. Seeing his treacherous conduct he was styled by the Emperor as La'natu'llah i.e. accursed of God, and henceforth he is mentioned in the Tuzuk as La'natu'llah. (For details of his career see Rogers and Beveridge Memoirs I, 27, 72, 140, 155, 200, 219, 310, 331, 335; 420; and II; 94; 239; 251; 255; 257; 262; 266; 289; 299).

10. Rāja Bhim was the son of Rānā Amar Singh of Udaypur. He was given the title of Rāja in the 15th year of Jahangir's reign (Memoirs II, 123, 162).

11. For details of Khwāja Ṣābir's career see Pādishāh Nāma. Vol. I, 266, 267.

12. Dārāb Khān, son of 'Abdu'r Raḥīm Khān Khānān, who held responsible positions under Jahāngīr, joined the rebel prince and was appointed governor of Bhātī (i.e. Eastern Bengal). Beni Prasad in his

History of Jahāngīr (p. 373) presumably on the authority of the Iqbāl Nāma and the Ma'āṣiru'l-Umarā states that Dārāb Khān was kept in confinement till the conquest of Jahāngīrnagar. This is contrary to Bahāristān which says that Dārāb Khān took active parts in all the campaigns of Shāhjahān in Bengal. Later on he rebelled against Shāhjahān and consequently he was executed. (For details see Memoirs, I, 21, 180, 313, 418; II, 40, 49, 88, 156, 176, 254.).

13. For an account of the Sepulchre cf. Ma'āṣiru'l-Umarā, I, 138; Iqbāl Nāma, 219, 'Aml-i-Ṣāliḥ, I, 179.

14. Āṣāf-jāh i.e. Āṣaf Khān IV, brother of Nurjahān. His original name was 'Abu'l Ḥasan. (For details see Memoirs, I, 202, 203, 249, 252, 260, 278, 279, 282, 283, 319, 320, 373, 381, 388; II, 1, 24, 37, 46, 81, 90, 100, 158, 168, 175, 200, 230, 245, 247, 250, 254, 282.).

15. Pantī is the Pointee of Rennell's Bengal Atlas, sheet No. 4, situated at a distance of about thirty miles east of Rājmahal.

## BOOK IV

### CHAPTER I

1. Abu'l-Fazl says in (Ain, 3), "His Majesty established the ranks of Manṣabdars, from the *Dahbāshī* (Commander of ten) to the Dah Hazārī (Commander of ten thousand), limiting, however, all commands above five thousand, to his august sons." These ranks were later on distinguished with the distinction of *yak-aspa* (one-horse), *dū-aspa* (two-horse) and *sih-aspa* (three-horse). The author of the Pādishāh Nāma (I, 113) says that the pay of a Commander of *dū-aspa sih-aspa* troopers was double the pay of a Commander of *yak-aspa*. The former had to maintain double the number of men and horses than the latter. The same authority in (Vol. II, 506) describes the system of these ranks in the following way:—"The following law was made during the present reign (Shāhjahān). If a manṣabdār holds a Jāgīr in the same Ṣūbah, in which he holds his Manṣab, he has to muster *one-third* of the force indicated by his rank (literally, he has to bring his followers to the brand (*dāgh*) according to the third part). Thus, a *Sih hazārī ẕāt and sih hazār suwār* (a Commander of 3,000 personal, 3,000 horse) has to muster (bring to the brand) 1,000 cavalry. But if he holds an appointment in another Ṣūbah, he has only to muster a *fourth* part. Thus, a *Chahār hazārī chahār hazār suwār* (a Commander of 4,000) has only to muster 1,000 cavalry. When the imperial army was ordered to conquer Balkh and Samarqand, His Majesty, on account of the distance of those countries, ordered that as long as the expedition should last, each Manṣabdar should only muster *one fifth.* Thus a *panj hazārī panj hazār suwār* (a Commander of 5,000; 5,000 horse) mustered only 1,000; if the income of his Jāgīr was fixed at twelve months, he mustered 300 *sih-aspa* troopers, 600 *dū-aspa* troopers, 100 *yak-aspa* troopers (i.e. 1,000 men with 2,200 horses); if the income of his Jāgīr was fixed at eleven months, he had to muster 250 *sih-aspa* troopers, 500 *dū-aspa* troopers, and 250 *yak-aspa* troopers (i.e. 1,000 men with 2,000 horses); if the income of his Jāgīr was fixed at ten months, he had to muster 800 *dū-aspa* troopers and 200 *yak-aspa* troopers (i.e. 1,000 men and 18,000 horses), if at nine months, 600 *dū-aspa* troopers, and 400 *yak-aspa;* if at eight months 450 *dū-aspa* and 550 *yak-aspa;* if at seven months, 250 *dū-aspa* and 750 *yak-aspa;* if at six months, 100 *dū-aspa* and 900 *yak-aspa;* if at five months, all (1,000) *yak-aspa.*

But if the troopers to a Manṣab had all been fixed as *sih-aspa, dū-aspa* (i.e. if the Commander was not a *panj hazārī, panj hazār suwār,* but a *panj hazārī, panj hazār suwār-i-dū-aspa sih-aspa*) he musters, as his proportion of *dū-aspa* and *sih-aspa* troopers, double the number which he would have to muster, if his Manṣab had been as in the preceding. For example a *panj hazārī panj hazār tamām dū-aspa sih-aspa* (a Commander of 5,000, all consisting of *dū-aspa* and *sih-aspa*), would muster 600 troopers with three horses, 1200 troopers with two horses, and 200 troopers with one horse each (i.e. 2,000 men with 4400 horses), provided the income of his Jāgīr be fixed at twelve months, and so on." From these lines quoted above it appears that the proportion of *sih-aspa, dū-aspa* and *yak-aspa* troopers was for all Manṣabs as 300: 600: 100 or as 3: 6: 1., and the average strength of the contingents was one-fourth of the number of troops with which the rank of a Manṣabdār was designated. (For details see Blochmann's note, 'Ain I, 238, and Irvine's Indian Mughals, 23).

2. Mīrzā Mulkī is probably the same person mentioned as Khwāja Mulkī in the Tuzuk (p. 322), who was appointed Bakhshī to Bengal in December, 1620. He now joined Shāhjahān and was appointed Dīwān of Bengal after the occupation of Jahāngīrnagar by the Prince.

3. Āqā Taqī has been wrongly named by Mr. Sri Ram Sharma and Bhattacharyya as Aqalqi (Journal of Indian History, Vol. XI, 95).

4. Sarai Pathari or Sarai Patihari was a camping station near about the city of Pandua. The modern maps do not help us in locating the exact position of the place.

5. 'Aml-i-Ṣāliḥ (I, 184) and Iqbāl Nāma (p. 222) say that after the surrender of Jahāngīrnagar, Shāhjahān had seized a large property belonging to Ibrāhīm Khān. He secured about four hundred thousand rupees in cash over and above elephants, horses and other valuable articles.

6. Compare the accounts given in the Iqbāl Nāma (p. 223), and Ma'āṣiru'l-Umarā (Beveridge I, 452).

7. According to Ma'āṣiru'l-Umarā (Vol. III, 933-36) Wazīr Khān was a noted physician. For sometime he was the Qāẓī of Shāhjahān's army and then he was appointed to the post of the *Dīwān-i-Buyutāt* when the Prince was deputed to the expedition against Rānā Amar Singh of Chitor. He was a staunch supporter of Shāhjahān and followed him in all his campaigns in Bengal and the Deccan. When Shāhjahān ascended the throne he was promoted to the rank of 5,000 horse and appointed governor of Agra. From 1632 to 1639 he was the governor of the Punjab, and the founder of the town of Wazirābād. He also built many mosques, madrassahs and other things of public utility in the city of Chiniot which was his birth place.

8. In 1615 Mukhlīṣ Khān was appointed Dīwān and Bakhshī of Bengal. Then he was recalled to the Court in 1619 and was appointed

the deputy of Prince Parvīz in Bihar. He enjoyed a Manṣab of 2,000 with 700 horse. (Memoirs, Rogers and Beveridge, I, 306; II, 104, 107.).

9. Jaunpūr is a well-known city in the United Provinces. According to Ain (II, 159), the city was built by Sultan Fīrūz Tughlaq and named it after his cousin Fakhru'd-Dīn Jauna. It was included within the Ṣūbah of Ilahābās (Allahabad).

10. In the list of the Manṣabdārs of Shāhjahān, Saiyid Mubārak is shown as a Commander of 500, 250 ḥorse. He died in the sixth year of Shāhjahān's reign (Pādishāh Nāma, I, Pt. ii, 323).

11. Kara Mānikpūr are the names of two *Sarkārs* in the Ṣūbah of Allahabad. The town of Karrah or Kara is now a ruined town on the right bank of the Ganges, about 40 miles north-west of Allahabad. Mānikpūr is situated opposite the town of Kara on the left bank of the Ganges (Ain, II, 164, 167.)

12. Saiyid Muẓaffar, son of Saiyid Shajā'at Khān Barha is shown in the list of Shāhjahān's Manṣabdārs as a Commander of 1,000 with 500 horse. (Pādishāh Nāma, II, 735).

13. Munīr or Maner is an important village situated in the north-west of Dinapūr subdivision of the Patna district, ten miles south-west of Dinapūr and six miles north of Bihta station on the East Indian Railway. It contains tombs of two well-known saints known as Shāh Dawlat or Makhdūm Dawlat and Shaykh Yaḥiyā Munīrī. Makhdūm Dawlat died at Munīr in 1608 and Ibrāhīm Khān, the then governor of Bihar, erected a Mausoleum over his tomb in 1616. There is also a mosque inside the compound built by Ibrāhīm Khān in 1619.

Yaḥiyā Munīrī was born at Munīr and died there in 1290-91 A.D. He was the father of Makhdūm Sharfu'd-Dīn of Bihar, son-in-law of Shaykh Shihābu'd-Dīn, whose shrine is at Jethuli, and the brother-in-law of Bibi Kamalo, a female saint of the Gaya district. The tomb of Yaḥiyā Munīrī lies in a mosque to the east of a large tank, with masonry walls and *ghāts*, and a pillared portico jutting out into it, which is connected with the old bed of the Son by a tunnel of 400 feet long. A three domed mosque and some cloisters around the tomb were built by Ibrāhīm Khān in 1605-06. It has been a place of pilgrimage from a very early time and was visited by Bābar and Sikandar Lodī. The pargana of Munīr is sometimes called Munīr-i-Shaykh Yaḥiyā after the name of the saint. According to local tradition, its first settler was Imām Tāj Fatḥ, grand-father of Yaḥiyā, who came here from Arabia. (For the antiquity of the place see History and Antiquities of Maner by Syed Ẓahiru'd-Dīn, Bankipore, 1905; Report Arch. Survey of Bengal, 1901-92; Journal of the Photographic Society of India, June 1902, and the Patna Gazetteer, 1924).

14. Chausa or Chaunsa was the name of a Mahal in the Sarkar of Ghazipur, Ṣūbah, Allahabad. (Ain, II, 162). It is a well-known ford of the Ganges situated about eight miles south-west of Buxar.

15. The Gumtī river of the United Provinces passes through some of the important places like Sultanpūr and Jaunpūr and falls into the Ganges near Sayyidpur to the south-east of Benares.

16. Aryal is situated on the Ganges south-west of Jhusi. The Ain (II, 164) says that it had a brick fort.

17. Barhar or Burhai of Rennell, is situated at a distance of about thirty miles north-west of Allahabad.

18. Allahabad is spelt as Ilahābās in the text. This was a corruption of the word Illahābād. The Persian termination *ābād* (place or residence) has been changed by the common people into the Hindi form of *ābās*. This form continued to be in use to the end of Jahangir's reign. Shāhjahān introduced the original and correct form of the spelling during his reign. Elliot (Glossary, II, 104) is wrong in stating that Shāhjahān changed this termination *ābās* which savoured too much of Hinduism (cf. Jarret, Ain, II, 161, f.n.1).

## CHAPTER II

1. 'Aml-i-Ṣāliḥ (Vol. I, 187) says that Shāhjahān entered the city of Jaunpūr in the month of Ẕu'l-hijja, 1033 A.H. (15th September 1624).

2. Charkhata is situated on the confluence of the Jumna and the Sakaror. It is on the road to Bengal, Bihar and Allahabad. The territory of Hasand mentioned here must be the region around the confluence of these two rivers. But its exact position could not be located.

3. Mr. Sri Ram Sharma is wrong in reading this name as "Mabrian." Dr. Sudhindra Nath Bhattacharyya also calls this place borders of Mathabhanga (vide Indian Historical Quarterly, Vol. XI, No. 4, 715 and Vol. XI, No. 1, 100). But the text reads as نواح باهربن environs of Bāhirbun(d). Both the writers have confused the name with some other place. It was a well-known pargana in Kūch territory. (Vide my note No. 9, Chapter XI, Book I.)

4. Chunadah or Chunār was famous for its stone fort on the summit of a hill. It was an important place in the Ṣūbah of Allahabad. It is situated on the bank of the Ganges. (Ain, II, 169).

5. Bahādurpūr is at a distance of thirty two miles on the south-east of Allahabad.

6. Manmil, I believe, is a corruption of the word Manoel Tavares who had joined the Prince at the time of the battle of Akbarpūr. Durzisuz sometimes spelt as Zarrīsūz may be D'souza, another Portuguese chieftain.

7. The strength of the parties given here seems to be an exaggeration. Iqbāl Nāma (p. 232) says that the army of Shāhjahān had 10,000 horse and Prince Parvīz had 40,000. The *Riyāẓu's-Salātīn* and other authorities also differ regarding the number of the forces employed in this battle.

8. According to 'Aml-i-Ṣāliḥ (I, 186), the Prince was born in the fourth *gharī* of the night of Wednesday, the 25th Ẕu'l-hijja, 1033 A.H. (9th October, 1624).

9. A kind of gold coin, in weight and value equal to two round *muhrs*, having on one side *Allahu Akbar* and on the other *Yā Mu'yin* Its modern value in Indian currency is about Rs. 32 (Ain, I, 29).

10. The battle fought here was at a place on the right bank of the Tons near its confluence with the Ganges. This battle is known as the battle of the Tons.

11. This word may be read either as Hajrahati or Majrahati. The ms. is not very clear. The context shows that it was a small stream situated in the region between Patna and Akbarnagar.

## CHAPTER III.

1. Khiragarh was included in the *Sarkār* of Allahabad. It had a stone fort on a hill (Ain, II, 161). It is situated on the Ganges.

2. Sahsaranum or Sahsaram is spelt in the Ain as Sahsaraun It was included within the *Sarkār* or Rohtas. (Ain, II, 157).

3. Khān Khānān i.e. 'Abdu'r Raḥim Khān Khānān father of Dārāb Khān.

# INDEX

## A

## C

## D

## E

## F



## G

## H

## I

## J

## K

## L

## M

## N

## Q

S

## T

## U

## V



## W

## Y

## Z

## ERRATA AND ADDENDA

| PAGE | LINE | CORRECTIONS |
|---|---|---|
| 24 | 33 | Add (") after the word doing. |
| 24 | 36 | Omit , after Ilahyār. |
| 25 | 14 | Add , after I. |
| 25 | 15 | Add , after excellency. |
| 26 | 15 | Omit , after howmuchsoever. |
| 28 | 32 | Add , after honour. |
| 36 | 15 | Add , after cavalry. |
| 36 | 27 | Add , after people. |
| 36 | 28 | Add , after *Rath.* |
| 36 | 30 | Read 'one another' for each other. |
| 37 | 20 | Add , after therefore. |
| 41 | 1 | Read 'hazardous' for hazarduous. |
| 42 | 30 | Add , after midnight. |
| 42 | 35 | Read 'Respect' for aspect. |
| 47 | 11 | Read 'waters' for water |
| 47 | 18 | Omit , after canal. |
| 66 | 31 | Omit 'with' after shoot. |
| 66 | 34 | Omit , after wagons. |
| 68 | 34 | Read 'liquified' for liquefied. |
| 94 | 15 | Read 'at' instead of a after halted. |
| 107 | 2 | Add , after Raja Rāy. |
| 122 | 5 | Read 'scourged' for scouraged. |
| 152 | 34 | Read '*Pākri*' for *Pāgīrī.* |
| 155 | 5 | Add , after Khān. |
| 157 | 31 | Read 'sacrificed' for sacrified |
| 164 | 33 | Add (") and omit (") before Islām. |
| 186 | 32 | Read 'where' in place of when. |
| 196 | 5 | Add , after Kamāl.. |
| 217 | 36 | Read 'his' for its. |
| 273 | 24 | Read 'prove' for proves. |
| 277 | 22 | Read 'into' for to after converted. |
| 277 | 36 | Omit 'the' before God's. |
| 413 | 13 | Add , after Mīrzā. |
| 414 | 22 | Read 'had' in place of have. |
| 414 | 23 | Omit have. |
| 417 | 22 | Read 'had' in place of has. |

| | | |
|---|---|---|
| 421 | 12 | Read small 'j' in joined. |
| 423 | 13 | Read capital 'U' in upholder. |
| 449 | 27 | Read 'does' in place of do. |
| 458 | 25 | Read 'of' in place of to, after period. |
| 488 | 4 | Read 'an' in place of on. |
| 496 | 7 | Read 'has' in place of had. |
| 496 | 11 | Omit would. |
| 497 | 11 | Omit , after Besides. |
| 653 | 24 | Read 'have' in place of had. |
| 756 | 4 | Read 'morning' for nothing. |
| 766 | 12 | Omit 'to' after elephant. |

# Government of Assam

# Department of Historical and Antiquarian Studies

## D.H.A.S. PUBLICATIONS FOR SALE

The Department has published several old historical masterpieces in English and in Assamese, edited on most up-to-date lines by Rai Bahadur Professor S. K. Bhuyan. Each Assamese chronicle is furnished with Preface and Introduction in English and Assamese, and Marginalia against each paragraph. The *Asamar Padya-Buranji* and the *Kachari Buranji* have elaborate Synopses in English. Publication No. 6, *Tungkhungia Buranji,* is the first systematic English translation of an Assamese chronicle. In the paucity of written and authentic record about Jayantia and Cachar, our publications *Jayantia Buranji* and *Kachari Buranji* will serve as valuable sources of information to all interested in the history of the two kingdoms. The Persian chronicle *Bahāristān-i-Ghaybī,* the only extant manuscript of which is in the Bibliotheque Nationale of Paris, is already well-known to scholars in India. The complete English translation of this chronicle, published for the first time, will be a valuable mine of information to students of Mogul history.

## LIST OF PUBLICATIONS

ASSAM BURANJI.—A history of Ahom rule in Assam, 1228-1826 A.D. An enlarged version of Kasinath Tamuli-Phukan's chronicle by Harakanta Barua. Pp. xii + 152. Cloth, Rs. 2-8 ; Paper cover, Re. 1.

2. KAMRUPAR BURANJI.—A detailed history of the Assam-Mogul conflicts. Pp. xvii+152. Cloth, Rs. 2-8; Paper cover, Re. 1.

3. DEODHAI ASAM BURANJI.—A collection of old chronicles dealing with earlier Ahom history, neighbouring tribes, Ahom customs, etc. Pp. lxx+222. Cloth, Rs. 3.

4. ASAMAR PADYA-BURANJI.—Two metrical chronicles of Assam, 1679-1819 A.D., by Dutiram Hazarika and Bisweswar Vaidyadhipa respectively. Pp. lv + 278; Synopsis in English, Pp. 279-308. Cloth, Rs. 3.

5. TUNGKHUNGIA BURANJI.—A History of Assam from 1681 to 1806 A.D., by Srinath Barbarua of the Duara family. Pp. xlvii + 186. Cloth, Rs. 2-8.

6. TUNGKHUNGIA BURANJI.—A History of Assam from 1681 to 1826 A.D., in English. With Genealogical Tables, Bibliography, Glossary and Index. Published by the Oxford University Press.* Pp. xxxii+262. Cloth, Rs. 10.

7. BULLETIN No. 1.—With an Introduction by His Excellency Sir Laurie Hammond, Governor of Assam, 1927-1932. Pp. viii+48. Re. 1.

8. BULLETIN No. 2.—With an Introduction by His Excellency Sir Michael Keane, Governor of Assam. Pp. xii+76. Re. 1.

9. KACHARI BURANJI.—A History of Cachar from the earliest time to the reign of the Kachari Raja Tamradhwaja Narayan and the Ahom King Swargadeo Rudra Singha. With a frontispiece of King Rudra Singha receiving the homage of the Rajas of Cachar and Jayantia. Pp. xxxiv+124; Synopsis in English, Pp. 125-143; and An Episode in the History of the Kacharis, Pp. 144-149. Re. 1-8.

10. JAYANTIA BURANJI.—A History of Jayantia from the earliest time to the reign of Jayantia Raja Lakshmi Singha and the Ahom King Swargadeo Siva Singha; Ahom-Jayantia relations; Jayantia matriarchal system;

*This book can be had of the publishers,—Oxford University Press, Mercantile Buildings, Lal Bazar Street, Post Box No. 530, CALCUTTA; and Amen House, E.C. 4, LONDON.

History of Khyrim. With a frontispiece of King Rudra Singha receiving the homage of the Rajas of Cachar and Jayantia. About 250 pages. *In the Press.*

11. BAHARISTAN-I-GHAYBI.—A History of the conflicts of the Moguls with Assam, Bengal and Orissa during the first three decades of the Seventeenth Century, by Mirza Nathan, Mogul Fouzdar at Gauhati. Translated from the original Persian by Dr. M. Islam Borah, M.A., B.L. (Dacca), Ph.D. (London.), Head of the Department of Persian and Urdu in the University of Dacca. In two volumes, Pp. xxix + 933. Cloth, Rs. 10 per set.

12. BULLETIN No. 3.—Containing (1) the Speech of His Excellency Sir Michael Keane, Governor of Assam, at the Opening Ceremony of the Narayani Handiqui Historical Institute; (2) Honorary Provincial Director's Speech; (3) Account of the Opening Ceremony; (4) Introductions to Bulletins I and II; (5) Extracts from the D.H.A.S. Publications. With portraits of His Excellency Sir Michael Keane, Rai Bahadur Radhakanta Handiqui, Mrs. Narayani Handiqui, Sir Edward Gait, Narayani Handiqui Historical Institute, etc. Published in August 1936. Pp. iv + 52. Re. 1-8.

13. TRIPURA BURANJI.—Or Tripura Desar Katha. A historical and descriptive account of Tripura, with special reference to the events of 1710-1715 A.D., by two Assamese ambassadors of King Rudra Singha, 1696-1714 A.D. From the original manuscript in the British Museum, London. *In the Press.*

**To be had of:**

**Office of the Department of Historical and Antiquarian Studies,
Narayani Handiqui Historical Institute,
GAUHATI, ASSAM, India.**

***In Europe*—Our publications are stocked for sale by
Mr. Arthur Probsthain,
Oriental Bookseller & Publisher,
41, Great Russell Street, LONDON, W.C. 1.**

www.ingramcontent.com/pod-product-compliance
Lightning Source LLC
Chambersburg PA
CBHW020350100426
42812CB00001B/17

* 9 7 8 1 4 4 3 7 2 8 1 7 1 *